Servant of Power

"I have always advocated the necessity of taking the world as we find it, and following the logic of events." —William M. Stewart

Servant of Power

A Political Biography of Senator William M. Stewart

Russell R. Elliott

University of Nevada Press
Reno
1983

Nevada Studies in History and Political Science No. 18

STUDIES EDITOR
Wilbur S. Shepperson

EDITORIAL COMMITTEE

Don W. Driggs   Joseph A. Fry
Jerome E. Edwards   Andrew C. Tuttle

Library of Congress Cataloging in Publication Data
Elliott, Russell R.
    Servant of power.

    (Nevada studies in history and political science ;
no. 18)
    Bibliography: p.
    Includes index.
    1. Stewart, William M. (William Morris), 1827–1909.
2. Nevada—Politics and government. 3. Legislators—
United States—Biography. 4. United States. Congress.
Senate—Biography. I. Title. II. Series.
E664.S838E44 1983   328.73'092'4 [B]   83–6946
ISBN 0–87417–076–1

University of Nevada Press, Reno, Nevada 89557 USA
© Russell R. Elliott 1983. All rights reserved
Printed in the United States of America

Cover and title page designed by Dale Smith
Cover photo from Special Collections, Getchell
Library, University of Nevada, Reno
Title-page photo from Nevada Historical Society, Reno

*To Brenda
and Michon*

CONTENTS

Preface . . . . *ix*

1. Young Man on the Move: The California Years 1
2. The Comstock's Leading Attorney, 1860–1864 18
3. Driving Nevada's Statehood Bandwagon 34
4. The United States Senate: First Term Achievements 46
5. Second-Term Problems 66
6. Vacation from Politics 83
7. Seeking National Solutions to Nevada Problems 101
8. Matters of Political Survival and Sentiment 124
9. Reelection in 1892 with the New Silver Party 144
10. Engulfed by the Silver Issue 161
11. The Election of 1898 Turns a Friend into an Enemy 195
12. The End of a Nevada Political Era 220
13. A Dream that Failed: The Bullfrog–Rhyolite Years 253
14. Postscript 268
Notes 277
Bibliography 321
Index 329

PREFACE AND ACKNOWLEDGMENTS

AN OBJECTIVE VIEW of William Morris Stewart and his accomplishments, elusive during his lifetime, has proven equally so since his death. The difficulty lies not so much in the scarcity of materials from which to fashion such a judgment as in the contrast between Stewart's achievements and his means of attaining them.

Resources for a biography of Senator Stewart are reasonably plentiful. Court records, various territorial, state, and national records, correspondence, newspapers, and secondary sources provide substantial coverage of his exploits in mining, law, and politics. There are, however, some gaps. Stewart's own papers, the most important single source for analyzing motivation, do not begin until 1886, when he returned to Nevada to try to regain his seat in the United States Senate. His earlier papers evidently were destroyed in fires in Virginia City and Washington, D.C. Materials for the study of Stewart's early years in California, and for the twelve years between 1875 and 1887, while he was out of public office, are not as plentiful as those for the period from 1886 until his death in 1909. Yet the total volume of source material is impressive.

Those records detail Stewart's achievements: his authorship of the National Mining Law of 1866 and of the final draft of the resolution which became the Fifteenth Amendment, his efforts at legislative compromise during the Reconstruction period, his service as chairman of the Senate committees on Mining and Indian Affairs, and his long legislative fight for bimetallism. No one has a better claim than William Morris Stewart to be the "father figure" of Nevada. He was instrumental in guiding Nevada from territorial status to statehood. Court records indicate his importance in the development of the California bar and the founding of the legal profession in Nevada. Stewart also has a place in international legal history as senior counsel in the Pious Fund Case before the Hague Tribunal.

Besides the achievements, however, the records also reveal Stewart's driving ambition, his ruthless desire to win at any cost, and instances of questionable behavior, which led to such incidents as his reprehensible vendetta against Judge John North and his unfortunate involvement in the Emma Mine scandal. Also recorded is Stewart's long association with California financial interests, particularly the Bank of California and the Central and Southern Pacific railroads. Those connections were so well known during his senatorial career that on more than one occasion he was referred to as the third senator from California. Stewart was not the only Nevada senator accused of being controlled by California economic interests, but since he was the most important and the most vocal, he received the greatest attention from unfriendly reporters.

Those who have written about Stewart have made little effort to reconcile the man's achievements with his methods. Consequently, evaluations of Stewart have run the full spectrum from hero to villain. Thus Merlin Stonehouse, in his biography of John Wesley North, focuses on Stewart's harsh methods, with little or no attention to his undeniable achievements. The figure who emerges is a blackguard of the worst sort, with no redeeming features. On the other hand, two biographers of Stewart, Effie Mona Mack and Ruth Hermann, deal favorably with the man, glorying in his accomplishments, but generally ignoring the dark aspects of his political career.

The present study is an attempt to portray in some detail both facets of Stewart's political career: his many notable achievements on one hand, and, on the other, the often unethical methods he used to achieve his ends.

The acknowledgment section of a manuscript is generally approached with mixed emotions — relief that the task is nearing completion and pleasure in acknowledging the many debts incurred in its writing.

The staffs of the various institutions visited were particularly helpful; without exception they were courteous and cooperative, going far beyond the normal call of duty in filling my numerous research requests. I especially wish to thank the staff members at the Nevada Historical Society; the Special Collections Department of Getchell Library at the University of Nevada, Reno; the Henry E. Huntington Library and Art Gallery at San Marino, California; and the Bancroft Library at Berkeley, California.

The manuscript has been improved substantially by the time and expertise given by the following individuals: Mary Ellen Glass, director of the Oral History Project, University of Nevada, Reno, for her careful reading of the entire manuscript; Elizabeth Raymond for her patient and skillful editing; Guy Rocha, director of the Nevada State Archives, for continued interest in my research and for supplying information about Stewart's early career in Nevada; Edward Johnson, for supplying information on the Stewart Indian School; Wilbur S. Shepperson, series editor, and the other members of the Nevada Studies Board, for reading and evaluating the manuscript and making numerous helpful suggestions; Nicholas Cady and Robert Laxalt of the University of Nevada Press, for their help, encouragement, and patience; and my colleagues Jerome Edwards, William Rowley, Michael Brodhead, and James Hulse, for their continued interest and support.

The task of writing this biography was made easier by the earlier publications on Stewart by Effie Mona Mack and Ruth Hermann.

Errors, omissions, inaccuracies, of course, are my responsibility.

Research for the manuscript was aided substantially by financial grants from the Graduate School, University of Nevada, Reno, and from Henry E. Huntington Library and Art Gallery, San Marino, California. The latter grant enabled me to spend an unforgettable summer as a fellow in an atmosphere so conducive to study and thought that it has to be experienced to be believed.

The work would not have been completed without the continued support, encouragement, and patience of my wife, Annie, during the many years this study was in progress.

R.R.E.

Reno, January 11, 1983

CHAPTER 1

YOUNG MAN ON THE MOVE: THE CALIFORNIA YEARS

THE LARGE, unkempt figure sprawled on a bed of leaves near the mountain spring seemed more dead than alive to passersby heading for the Deer Creek Diggings (Nevada City). With thousands of others caught up in the California gold rush, he had taken the Panama route, and, like many of them, he was slowed in his quest for riches by Panama fever. After eight days of rest and copious amounts of water, the fever broke, and the gaunt hulk of a man left the makeshift bed to resume his personal search for gold. His name was William Morris Stewart.

The oldest of seven children, Stewart was proud of his family which could be traced on both sides to the colonial period. His father's Scottish ancestors were among the early settlers of Massachusetts. His mother, Miranda Morris, was of English-Dutch background and included among her forbears a signer of the Declaration of Independence. Stewart's father, Frederick Augustus Stewart, was born near Shoreham, Vermont. He inherited property that he exchanged in turn for land near Lyons, county seat of Wayne County, in western New York. It was on the farm there that William Morris Stewart was born, on August 9, 1825.[1]

The Stewart farm was located but a short distance from the Erie Canal, which, despite an official opening date of October 25, 1825, was in operation at Lyons some two years earlier.[2] The proximity of the canal to the Stewart farm seemed to promise a bright future for the family. Unfortunately, a defective land title stripped Frederick Stewart of the farm. Again the family moved westward, this time to Trumbull County, Ohio, where they settled along the Grand River in the northwest corner of the county.

Except to note that the "lock tender of the Erie Canal taught me to swim about as soon as I could walk," Stewart seldom discussed his early

The scene of Stewart's legal and political activities in Nevada and California. Triangles identify the sites of his law offices and homes.

years in western New York.[3] However, he later wrote in some detail about the years spent on the family farm in Ohio, time that he passed in hunting, fishing, swimming, doing farm chores for his father and neighbors, and, at least occasionally, in attending the district school. This schooling was minimal, just three months, usually in the fall or winter. It was sufficient, however, to stimulate the young Stewart to further his education at nearby West Farmington Academy. Following this decision to continue his education, he left the family farm and struck out on his own. Apparently the leaving was amicable. Stewart later reported that when he asked his father if he could hire out to a neighbor, his father immediately assented, "Why certainly, you can go and stay as long as you have a mind, and you need not come back any more unless you wish to."[4]

At the time, William Stewart was just fourteen years of age; but he was physically well developed and had a self-reliance born of his varied experience working on the family farm and earning small sums of money by helping neighbors clear land and harvest crops or selling skins from raccoons he had hunted. In all his activities Stewart showed a capacity for hard work, a quick intelligence, and a driving ambition to achieve. His efforts to make his own way also demonstrated a resourcefulness that became his most consistent characteristic. That inventiveness was put to a major test during the next three years as he struggled to pay for his education at the West Farmington Academy. To save money he cooked his own meals. After the first term, he paid for his lodgings by working mornings and evenings, and during the summers he labored hard at various jobs to get the money he needed to continue his schooling.[5]

Before completing his studies at the academy, Stewart heard about a new college preparatory school near his birthplace at Lyons, New York, and decided to enter. Stewart's account of his journey from Ohio to Lyons suggests the strength of his will. A self-reliant young man who thought nothing of striking out on his own with minimal funds, he had both definite ideas of what he wanted from life and a belief in his ability to achieve these goals:

> After visiting my home and making some presents to my mother, brothers, and sisters, I had barely enough left to pay my passage on the lake steamer and canal boat to Lyons. I walked to Ashtabula, a distance of about twenty-five or thirty miles, and took a steamer for Buffalo. The boat stopped at Erie, Pennsylvania. I arrived at Lyons on a canal boat about four o'clock in the afternoon with fifty cents in my pocket. It was haying and harvesting time and I apprehended no difficulty in getting immediate employment.[6]

Just as he expected, Stewart had no trouble finding summer work. He entered the Lyons Union School during the fall term and once again tried to support himself while attending classes. In Lyons, however, he was employed as a teacher, first in the district school and later instructing his favorite subject, mathematics, in the high school. He continued both his studying and his teaching until the fall of 1848, when he felt sufficiently prepared to make the next step forward and enter a university. Stewart's lack of money was a potential obstacle to this plan, but James C. Smith, a member of the Lyons Union School board of trustees, generously loaned him the necessary money. Smith was a lawyer who later became a justice of the New York Superior Court. He was impressed with the young Stewart, and allowed him to read some law in his office during the years Stewart spent at Lyons.[7] Stewart was admitted to Yale University by examination.[8]

The cry of "gold in California" interrupted Stewart's college education, for when he returned to Lyons at completion of the school year in 1849, he found the rumors about the new discoveries difficult to resist. Too late to join the mass of humanity trying to reach the gold fields by crossing the plains, he decided to try the Panama route. The latter would take him by ship from New York to Panama, and following a portage across the Isthmus, by coastal steamer from Panama to San Francisco. The first obstacle to such a plan, the matter of money, was solved when a friend from Lyons loaned him the necessary funds; but when Stewart arrived in New York City he found it impossible to book passage until Christmas, so he returned to Yale for the fall semester.[9] At the completion of that school term, in January of 1850, he left New York City on the steamer *Philadelphia*.

Stewart's experiences in reaching California, although romanticized in his *Reminiscences*,[10] were probably little different from those of thousands of others who followed this route to the gold fields.[11] The journey from New York City to the mouth of the Chagres River in Panama, although quite rough, was but the beginning of a long, hard trip that continued in small boats from the mouth of the Chagres, up river to Gorgona. From there, a short hike on foot brought the travelers to Panama City, where they frequently had to wait a few days for one of the coastal vessels to arrive. Stewart managed to get a ticket on the *Carolina*, a rather small ship which, overloaded and old, required over a month to reach San Francisco.

When he arrived in the latter city on April 7, 1850, Stewart found the community still seething with excitement despite more than two years of the "gold rush fever" that had been set off by James Marshall's discovery of gold in January, 1848.[12] Stewart, like many others at the end of a long journey, was in need of funds. He had no trouble finding employment on the wharf, helping to unload incoming vessels, and soon had sufficient money for the 150-mile trip inland to the gold fields.

He traveled by river steamboat to Sacramento, but became quite ill shortly after arriving there. Scorning a local hospital where sanitation was poor, Stewart set off for the mines, going by boat to Marysville and then by wagon to Roger Williams Spring. Near that point the teamsters deposited him on the makeshift bed of leaves, which began this account.[13] The fever eventually subsided in the face of Stewart's youth and strength. As he recovered, he learned he was only one among thousands who shared the same vision of riches and were now trying to make those dreams into reality.[14]

Stewart chose to focus his early mining activities in the northern section of the Mother Lode country, in Nevada City, Grass Valley, and the area immediately north and east. Hours of exhausting physical toil brought little profit, so Stewart expanded his activities. With Charles Marsh and George Pettibone, he formed a company to bring water from the Yuba River by means of a ditch from Bloody Run through Grizzly Canyon to North San Juan, a mining camp some fourteen miles north of Nevada City. The Grizzly Ditch, some forty miles in length, was complemented shortly thereafter by construction of a sawmill on Cherokee Creek. These ventures, according to Stewart, proved more profitable.[15]

Although mining was exhausting work, it did not provide enough scope for the enormous energy, ability, and ambition of William Morris Stewart. Thus, early in 1852, he ended his connection with the Grizzly Ditch and began to study law, a field that had interested him from his high school days in New York.[16] The decision to read law effectively ended Stewart's career as a working miner. Although he was to be associated with mining law and mining promotions through the rest of his life, his principal interests after 1852 were law and politics.

There is some confusion over Stewart's political actions and affiliations during his early California years. Apparently, his earliest venture into California politics came in 1851, when he tried unsuccessfully to become sheriff of Nevada County.[17] His next foray into the political arena was more fruitful. On February 20, 1852, at the Whig State Convention in Sacramento, Stewart was selected as a delegate to the party's national convention, receiving the highest number of votes cast for any of the candidates.[18] Although there is no indication that Stewart played any active part in its development, the Whig platform of June 7 included a plank opposing the sale or lease of mineral lands in California, insisting instead that such areas be left free to the industry and enterprise of American citizens.[19] Stewart later helped to incorporate that idea in the Nevada County mining district rules of 1852, and in the National Mining Law of 1866.

Stewart's association with the Whig Party did not last long. Shortly after the convention he entered the office of John R. McConnell, district attorney of Nevada County, to study law. There he associated with the Southern Democrats who used McConnell's office as their headquarters, and within a short time Stewart listed himself as a Democrat. For the next two years, at least, he remained with that party. He wrote later that his being a Democrat was contrary "to the traditions of my family, who were Federalists. . . . I was a Jackson man, and hence a Democrat."[20]

McConnell's office offered an ideal preparation for both law and politics, for McConnell was considered one of the best mining attorneys in northern California and an excellent teacher. It was no doubt from McConnell, first as a student and then as a partner, that Stewart learned and perfected the skills which later made him one of the most successful attorneys on the Comstock.[21] McConnell, on the other hand, recognized his pupil's ability. When he resigned as district attorney to campaign for the office of California attorney general, he recommended that Stewart replace him. McConnell's resignation and Stewart's appointment coincided with Stewart's admission to the California bar in November, 1852, after a few months of intensive study and the passage of a "rigorous examination."[22] The timing of these three events seems more than mere coincidence.

In taking over McConnell's office and duties, Stewart apparently also temporarily accepted the leadership of the Southern Democrats in Nevada County. He wrote that although he was a Northerner, "the Southern boys refused to recognize me as such, and against my protest continually claimed me as one of their kind."[23] In that capacity he seems to have been the motivating force in starting a Democratic paper—first called *Young America,* and later, *The Nevada Democrat*—to oppose the Whig *Nevada Journal,* edited by Aaron A. Sargent.[24]

While serving as district attorney, Stewart participated in one of the most important miners' meetings ever held in California. The assembly took place at Nevada City on December 20, 1852, to draw up rules and regulations for the conduct of mining in Nevada County. Stewart acted as chairman.[25] It was not the first such gathering in California, but it proved to be one of the most significant.

At the time of Marshall's discovery of gold in January, 1848, there were no well-defined American mining codes and no specific federal regulations governing such activity. Miners from Latin America and Europe who entered the California gold fields in the early years of the rush brought with them a knowledge of the mining codes prevailing in their native countries. Through what came to be known as the ''miners' meeting,'' this body of expertise became the basis of western mining practice. In such meetings, miners adopted their own rules for determining titles to property, the use of water, and the handling of disputes. In 1851, the California legislature adopted a statute which recognized the legality of the locally adopted miners' codes.[26]

The Nevada City meeting is of particular importance because the regulations adopted there in 1852 were copied widely throughout California and the west. They have been looked upon as the backbone of the National Mining Act of 1866, which Stewart is credited with writing.[27] Stewart thus became the means by which these local miners' regulations were firmly embedded in national law.

Miners' district meetings were only some of the many Nevada County activities that brought Stewart into contact with men who became important nationally and whose careers touched and influenced his own in the years after he left California. Along with the criminals and ne'er-do-wells, the California gold rush also attracted many young, aggressive, intelligent, and able people. Among them were: Stephen J. Field, who became an associate justice of the U.S. Supreme Court and remained friendly with Stewart throughout his career; Niles Searles, with whom Stewart formed a law partnership in 1853 or 1854, and who went on to become district judge, state senator, and later justice of the California Supreme Court; Aaron A. Sargent, who became a member of Congress and then senator from California; David Terry, who became a justice of the California Supreme Court and, later, one of Stewart's main legal opponents on the Comstock; J. Neely Johnson, Know-Nothing governor of California, who presided over the 1864 constitutional convention in Nevada, and later became a justice of the Nevada Supreme Court. They and others like them moved in and out of Stewart's life, on the Comstock, in the halls of Congress, in the state and national courts of law, and in a myriad of other connections. Among these talented Nevada County residents Stewart's abilities were recognized early, through his activities as chairman of the Nevada County miners' meeting, and by his appointment and then election as district attorney of Nevada County, in November, 1853. This was the same election that gave John McConnell the office of California attorney general, like Stewart, on the Democratic ticket.

On April 10, 1854, the California legislature granted McConnell a six-month leave of absence from the office of attorney general. Stewart, his political star still on the rise, was appointed acting attorney general by Governor John Bigler, on the recommendation of McConnell. Stewart served from June 7, 1854, until December of that year, while his place as Nevada County district attorney was taken by Niles Searles.[28] As attorney general, Stewart performed his duties satisfactorily, helping to solve the heated controversy which had developed when the state capital was moved to Sacramento from San Jose, February 25, 1854.[29]

After completing his six-month term as attorney general, Stewart moved to San Francisco and formed a law partnership with Henry S. Foote, former U.S. senator and Mississippi governor; Louis Aldrick, former California District Court judge; and Benjamin Watkins Lee of Virginia. Foote, like many others, came to California as much for the political opportunities as for any chance for riches from the gold mines. According to Stewart, the partnership did a good business, but lasted for only about a year. During his stay in San Francisco, he met and married Annie Elizabeth Foote, third daughter of his law partner, on May 31, 1855.[30]

It was at this time, probably due in part to his contacts with Henry Foote, that Stewart switched affiliation from the Democratic to the American or Know-Nothing Party. The latter party had come into existence nationally in the early 1850's, to combat the so-called "alien menace." Because of the large number of immigrants in the California gold fields, the anti-foreign bias of the Know-Nothings met with favor among the native United States citizens gathered there. Although it wasn't until late in May, 1854, that the Know-Nothing Party held its first organizational meeting in San Francisco, the rapid disintegration of the Whig Party, both nationally and in California, made it almost at once one of the two major parties in California.[31]

Ex-Senator Foote was attracted to the new political party because it offered a chance to revive a fading political career and the Know-Nothings would faithfully execute the Compromise of 1850.[32] Stewart's switch to the American Party was more likely due to the fact that the new party offered him a better chance to fulfill his political ambitions. He performed the same sort of party-switching maneuver many times during his career, in efforts generally dictated by an overriding desire to be on the winning side.

At the Know-Nothing nominating convention, held in Sacramento on August 7 and 8, 1855, Stewart was one of many candidates for the post of attorney general. Henry Meredith, a later law partner on the Comstock was also a candidate for the post, but the nomination was won by

W. J. Wallace on the sixth ballot. In November, the entire Know-Nothing slate of officers was elected.[33] Stewart's father-in-law fared no better. Initially he had been the frontrunner for the party's nomination for the United States Senate. However, by the time the convention was held, enough former enemies from Mississippi had moved to California to block Foote's most recent political ambition.

Stewart's association with the Know-Nothing Party was short-lived. In June of 1855, Stewart and his wife moved to Nevada City where he again formed a partnership with John McConnell and returned to the Democratic fold. At Nevada City Stewart at first seemed to find some permanence, and he built a large house, which became a showplace for the area.[34] However, the extremely fluid nature of the California gold rush attracted attention to other camps north of Nevada City, and Stewart soon added a law practice in Downieville, county seat of Sierra County, to the one in Nevada City. Ultimately he chose to cast his lot with Downieville and moved there in the fall of 1856.[35]

In Downieville, Stewart established a partnership with Peter Van Clief, a leader among Sierra County's Chivalry (pro-Southern) Democrats.[36] From 1856, until he left the area for the Comstock, after 1859, Stewart was engaged in law practice in Downieville, first with Van Clief, and when the latter was appointed district judge, with Harry I. Thornton.[37] During these years Stewart was very active politically, always as a Chivalry Democrat. Yet in spite of his obvious ambitions, he was never elected to office by the voters of Sierra County. He was, however, selected as one of fourteen delegates from that county to the 1858 State Democratic Convention. The Southern-sympathizing Democrats in the delegation to which Stewart belonged were supporters of Buchanan and of the Lecompton Constitution.[38]

During these months, when North-South rivalry was strong in Sierra County, the local Lecompton Democrats selected Stewart, probably because of his earlier newspaper contacts in Nevada County, to edit the *Sierra Citizen,* the party organ. At the time there seemed to be some ambivalence in Stewart's party allegiance, for he was accused by opponents of belonging to an organization called "North Star," which opposed the election of Southern men. The *Sierra Democrat* described Stewart as a liar and Van Clief's "chief fugleman and advocate," charging him with passing himself off as "a straight out Alabamian when he actually came from Ohio."[39]

In Downieville, Stewart engaged in important mining and criminal cases, gaining a reputation as an intelligent, aggressive lawyer who could use any technicality, trick, or threat to secure a victory for his client.[40] His court experiences in Sierra County, against exceptionally able opponents and involving complex legal problems, tested again the great resourcefulness he evidenced earlier. Stewart's Sierra County years were the last three of his early stay in California, and they enlarged his personal contacts with many individuals destined to become important in national politics. In one criminal case at Downieville, when David Butler was accused of the murder of Robert Moffat, the three defense lawyers later became United States senators: Edward D. Baker from Oregon, Aaron Sargent from California and Stewart from Nevada. In addition, the prosecuting attorney, Sierra County District Attorney John Musser, later became prominent in the politics of Carson County, Utah Territory, representing the dissident element there as "delegate" to Congress from the so-called "provisional territory" of Nevada.[41]

At Downieville, as in Nevada City, the Stewarts entered into the social life of the community. Although their Sierra County home was much more modest than the one in Nevada City, it became the center of many social events.[42] Yet despite his successful law practice, Stewart had no deep roots in Downieville, and when the Comstock rush to western Utah Territory began, in the late summer of 1859, he again became restless. In the late fall of that year, he made a short visit to the new area.[43]

The original discovery of the Comstock Lode in January, 1859, led to little more than a flurry of excitement at the southern end of that ore body. The effective discovery of the Lode came later, in early June, 1859, when two prospectors, Patrick McLaughlin and Peter O'Riley, found what became the famous Ophir Diggings. Public notice of the event in California came on July 1, 1859, when the *Nevada Journal* of Nevada City published an announcement of the "discovery of a vein of ore of extra-ordinary richness at the head of Six Mile Cañon, about ten miles from the Truckee Meadows."[44]

By the time Stewart had made his first trip to the Comstock in the fall of 1859, the reputation of the mineral finds had been enhanced by rich assays made at Grass Valley and Nevada City. In August, 1859, publicity in San Francisco about the value of a shipment of ore from the Ophir claim brought further attention to the new area.[45] The trickle of prospectors who followed the first Nevada County residents over the Sierra Nevada, after news of the first assays, turned into a surge of thousands as the more tangible evidence of the wealth of the newly found Comstock Lode went on public display in San Francisco.

The urge to move with the flow of events, always strong in Stewart, was too great to resist.[46] His visit to the Comstock turned into more than a mining foray when he was elected to chair a gathering of citizens of Carson City and adjoining areas on December 10.[47] The purpose of the meeting was to witness the farewell of Colonel John J. Musser, upon his departure for Washington, D.C. Musser, formerly an attorney in both Nevada and Sierra counties, was to present a memorial from the "provisional territory" of Nevada, in reality a group of citizens disgruntled with the rule of the area by the Utah territorial government. The dissidents wanted Congress to make Carson County, Utah Territory, into a separate Territory of Nevada.[48] The selection of Stewart to chair the meeting suggests how many of the miners then in Carson City, Genoa, and the surrounding area, were from Nevada and Sierra counties in California. It was perhaps prophetic that the first public notice of Stewart in what was to become his new home, should have associated him with the political movement which ultimately led to territorial status in 1861, and to statehood in 1864. No individual was more important in the final phases of these actions than William Morris Stewart.

Evidently impressed with what he saw in the Comstock area, Stewart returned to Downieville, sold his law office to Peter Van Clief, and arranged with Harry I. Thornton, Jr., to continue his legal practice there. He was back on the Comstock in March, 1860, and almost immediately formed a law partnership with Henry Meredith, a young attorney he had practiced with in Nevada City. The partnership was disrupted shortly afterwards, when Meredith was killed in the Pyramid Lake Indian War of 1860.[49]

Relations with the Indians were volatile at the time Stewart returned to the Comstock in March, 1860. When the whites arrived in the Great Basin, the native tribes depended upon hunting and gathering to survive. The intrusion of trappers, emigrants, and particularly the settlers, disrupted a finely balanced system and threatened the tribes with extinction in their harsh environment. Growing animosity between whites and Indians was heightened by discovery of the Comstock Lode in 1859. A few trappers and emigrants passing through their lands was one thing, but the many thousands who poured into the new discovery area in the fall of 1859, and spring of 1860, was quite another. Warnings soon reached the Comstock that large numbers of Indians were gathering at Pyramid Lake, some forty miles to the north, to determine what action to take in the face of white encroachments. After news reached the Indian conference that whites at Williams Station on the Carson River had kidnapped some Indian women and were holding them against their will, a small party of Indians raided the station, rescued the women, killed the whites, and burned the buildings.

On the Comstock, wild rumors about the event resulted in a demand for immediate retaliation for the killing of the whites. A volunteer force of 105 men gathered, improperly armed and without any real leadership. Stewart, his family still in Downieville, did not become involved in the irrational decision to move against the Indians. However, his partner, Henry Meredith, joined the group, despite Stewart's advice against it. The resulting battle, on May 12, was a disaster for the whites. Some 76 men, including Meredith, were killed in the initial encounter.

As was so often the case in Indian-white conflicts, the initial Indian success proved to be their ultimate undoing. The settlers called upon federal and California officials for help. On May 31, two groups of soldiers, 549 volunteers under the command of Colonel Jack Hays and 207 regular army men under Captain Joseph Stewart, met at the big bend of the Truckee River and proceeded toward the mouth of that river, at Pyramid Lake. Now outnumbered, the Indians were dispersed to the north and to the west. The initial confrontation had been costly for the whites, but it led to the establishment of Fort Churchill on the Carson River, in August of 1860.[50] Stewart did not participate with the second group of volunteers under Colonel Hays, either, writing later that "I did not go out with the soldiers, because it was thought more important for me and two or three others to collect and forward supplies to the army."[51]

The end of the Indian difficulties made it possible for Stewart to return to Downieville for his family. Early in July, 1860, the Stewarts crossed the Sierra Nevada on mules, with "Stewart holding their little girl on a pillow in his arms." With this move they exchanged life in the relatively stable mining community of Downieville for tent living in the rather primitive society of Virginia City.[52] The sight that greeted the Stewarts upon their arrival must have been similar to that described by J. Ross Browne when he first visited the Comstock in 1860:

> On a slope of mountains speckled with snow, sagebushes, and mounds of upturned earth, without any apparent beginning or end, congruity or regard for the eternal fitness of things lay outspread the wondrous city of Virginia. Frame shanties, pitched together as if by accident; tents of canvas, of blankets, or brush, of potato-sacks and old shirts, with empty whisky-barrels for chimneys; smoky hovels of mud and stone; coyote holes in the mountain side forcibly seized and held by men; pits and shafts with smoke issuing from every crevice; piles of goods and rubbish on craggy points, in the hollows, on the rocks, in the mud, in the snow, everywhere, scattered broadcast in pell-mell confusion, as if the clouds had suddenly burst overhead and rained down the dregs of all the flimsy, rickety, filthy little hovels and rubbish of merchandise that had ever undergone the process of evaporation from the earth since the days of Noah.[53]

The political and legal systems operating on the Comstock when the Stewarts arrived were hardly more stable than the society. The discovery was located in the territory which Mexico had ceded to the United States by the Treaty of Guadalupe-Hidalgo in 1848. However, because of the national quarrel over the extension of slavery in the territories, political organization of the area did not come until 1850. Under the Compromise of that year, governmental control of the region was placed under the new Utah Territory, with Brigham Young as the territorial governor.

The area that became the state of Nevada remained for eleven years a part of Utah Territory. It was not a happy relationship. From the beginning, troubles of transportation and communication, of religion, and of economics plagued the association. From 1851 to the middle of 1855, the settlers in western Utah Territory, unwilling to wait for stabilization from the Young government, formed a squatter organization and attempted to rule themselves. Not until the late summer of 1855 was the Utah government strong enough to give its western extremity effective control and thus eliminate the need for squatter meetings.

Stability lasted less than two years. Difficulties between the United States government and the theocratic Young regime reached the point that President Buchanan felt it necessary to remove Young as territorial governor. Buchanan ordered federal troops to enforce the transfer to a new governor, Alfred Cumming. At this point, to defend Salt Lake City, Young called back to the capital all Mormons who had been sent to outlying missions. A political vacuum resulted from this exodus, and Carson County, in western Utah Territory, returned to the earlier squatter control in order to maintain some semblance of order and prevent anarchy. Unrest and instability in government continued from 1857, until Nevada became a separate territory in March, 1861. During that period two attempts to establish local control were made, one in 1857 and a more sophisticated effort in 1859, which established the ''provisional governorship'' of Isaac Roop. Neither of these endeavors did more than demonstrate that the local settlers favored governing themselves.

The four-year period of confusion, 1857–1861, was marked also by the attempt of the new Utah territorial government, under Cumming, to reestablish control over Carson County. Cumming appointed a local resident, John Child, as probate and county judge; but Child had little success in achieving a stable local government, and Utah Territory never regained effective sovereignty.

Two events added to the confusion and to Child's problems: the discovery of the Comstock Lode in 1859, and Federal Judge John Cradlebaugh's attempt in the same year to reestablish the authority of federal law in the county. The former event was particularly disruptive, since it caused a mass exodus from the older settlements of Carson City and Genoa, and brought a new dimension to the chaotic legal and political scene with the introduction of the mining district. The Gold Hill Mining District, organized June 11, 1859, was the first functional mining district on the Comstock. This institution, with its regulations for locating, transferring, selling, and buying claims, as well as rules for maintaining political control and regulating social conduct, added another layer of political and legal organization to the already confused situation.[54] Under these circumstances, Judge Cradlebaugh's attempt to reestablish federal law met with serious obstacles.

Chaos reigned as various groups each sought to establish legal and political dominion over the area. It was a much more volatile and fluid situation than Stewart had encountered on the California frontier in the 1850's. However, those California years of success in mining, law, and politics had prepared him for just such opportunities as the Comstock Lode now offered. With the threat of Indian war quieted, the Comstock boom roared forward, and Stewart helped to lead the way. He was soon engaged in a series of legal cases which, within a few years, brought not only financial fortune, but also a reputation as the Comstock's leading attorney.

Upon his first arrival in Carson County, Utah Territory, in November, 1859, Stewart rented part of the old Reese building in Genoa for a law office.[55] However, when he returned to the Comstock, in the spring of 1860, he decided to work in Virginia City. He formed a partnership there with Henry Meredith and, after the latter's death, with Judge Moses Kirkpatrick and Richard Rising. Alexander W. "Sandy" Baldwin was added to the group when Kirkpatrick left, and when Rising later withdrew the firm became Stewart and Baldwin.

The extent of the legal quarrels brewing over the Comstock Lode were not yet evident as Stewart settled his family in Virginia City in July of 1860. An apocryphal story has often been told that Baldwin was taken into the firm after he and Stewart clashed in a legal argument, during which Stewart said, "You little shrimp, if you don't stop those tactics, I'll eat you." To this threat Baldwin supposedly replied, "If you do you will have more brains in your belly than you have in your head."[56]

During the exciting early days when prospectors were busily engaged in staking thousands of claims, there were no serious legal controversies. Surface indications did not suggest the potential wealth hidden underground. As soon, however, as individual and haphazard locations gave way to corporate development, and the newly organized companies began to exploit the Comstock ore bodies in a more purposeful way, the geological character of the district and the distribution of the underground ore deposits became topics of keen interest. The major question, which had important legal and economic implications, was whether the Comstock ore bodies were in narrow veins separated by well-defined barren rock, or deposited in a single ledge. It was Stewart's good fortune to enter the practice of law on the Comstock just as that question opened legal controversies which continued through most of the history of the lode, leading one author to describe the situation as one of "interminable litigation."[57]

Whether through luck or prior reputation or both, Stewart was fortunate enough to be employed by the Ophir Company in one of its first major legal battles. The Ophir was the first company to organize, on April 28, 1860.[58] It had taken over the main claims of the original locators, Henry P. Comstock, Emanuel Penrod, Peter O'Riley, and Patrick McLaughlin, so the legal question of whether the Comstock Lode was one or many ledges was of primary importance to the Ophir owners. Nothing less than economic control of the Comstock was at stake, and the responsibility of convincing the territorial courts to recognize the single-ledge theory rested mainly on the firm of Stewart and Baldwin.

One of the first cases to deal with that issue was the *Ophir Company* v. *McCall et al*. It arose when a group of miners found a fairly rich body of ore west of the Ophir claims. Almost at once the discovery area was claimed by both the Ophir and Mexican companies. In the trial, held in the fall of 1860, Stewart and Baldwin were counsel for the plaintiff, while former California Supreme Court Justice David S. Terry and James Hardy represented the defendants. According to a witness, the courtroom was crowded "with excited partisans, and an unguarded expression might at any moment bring on a collision which would cover the floor with bleeding bodies."[59] The jury could not reach a verdict.

Later in the year a somewhat similar ledge suit was brought by the Savage Mining Company to recover possession of part of their claim then held by a group called the Bowers Company. The latter, in order to defend their rights, erected a crude stone fort, stored it with provisions and ammunition, and set a guard of thirty armed men to defend it. The court viewed the case not from the standpoint of settling ownership of any ledge or ledges, but from that of simple trespass, and the decision favored the Bowers Company.[60]

The question of whether the Comstock was one ledge or many was not settled by these cases, but they did show the difficulties that were certain to develop from further exploitation of the lode. Disputes involved not only the major issue of ledge determination, but also ignorant or intentional inaccuracy in defining claims, neglect in making proper records, and even failure to record locations in the first place. Litigation was the almost inevitable result of most of these controversies.

This legal confusion was compounded when President Buchanan removed John Cradlebaugh from his post as judge for the Second Judicial District of Utah Territory and appointed Robert P. Flenniken to replace him.[61] The action not only complicated the legal questions before the courts, but also forced the issue into the political arena, since Cradlebaugh, in a letter to the United States attorney general, refused to accept replacement and argued that the President had no right to discharge him. While the issue of judicial authority was under consideration by the Utah Territorial Supreme Court, Cradlebaugh opened court in Carson City in January, 1861, thus allowing attorneys to choose which judge they wished to hear their cases.[62]

A local action soon brought the jurisdictional matter to a climax in Virginia City. The case involved possession of a supposedly rich ore body disputed by the Saint Louis Company, represented by William M. Stewart, and the Rich and Lucy Ella companies, represented by David Terry. Since Stewart decided to practice in Cradlebaugh's court and Terry before Judge Flenniken, the Saint Louis-Rich case obviously was the key to the question of which federal judge held local authority.

Moving aggressively as usual, Stewart took advantage of Terry's temporary absence in San Francisco to obtain, on January 11, an injunction from Cradlebaugh which restrained the Rich and Lucy Ella companies from taking ore from the disputed ground.[63] However, the Rich Company, following what appeared to be a custom in such cases at this time, erected a fort on their claims near Devil's Gate and indicated that they would resist any attempts by the Saint Louis Company to dispossess them.[64] At this point, Judge Cradlebaugh sent John L. Blackburn, sheriff of Carson County, to arrest the Rich Company officials for violating the injunction. Before the sheriff could act, however, word was received from Judge Flenniken, who removed himself from the case and acknowledged Cradlebaugh's authority.[65] Apparently the reason for Flenniken's withdrawal was the receipt of a decision from the Utah Territorial Supreme Court upholding his rival.[66]

Stewart's quick entrance into the legal activities of Carson County paralleled a similar move into politics. Not long after settling in the area, on September 12, 1860, Stewart was named acting prosecuting attorney of Carson County by the Probate Court.[67] That assignment lasted but a few months. Then, on April 13, 1861, he was designated selectman, replacing James J. Coddington, who had resigned.[68] These appointments not only demonstrated the fluid nature of political institutions on the mining frontier, but illustrated as well Stewart's willingness to accept political office in the new region.

He became involved at once in mine and mill ownership, partly because his experiences in the California gold fields led him naturally into such investments, but also because many of his clients paid their legal accounts with mining and mill interests. In his memoirs, Stewart indicates that he participated in the actual operation of two mills in which he held stock until a massive flood ruined the structures.[69] He also may have participated in the actual operation of some of his mine holdings during his first year on the Comstock. However, it is quite clear that after 1861, although he continued to hold interest in various mines in the area, Stewart did not concern himself with the actual operation or management of such properties. By that time, demands for his legal talent and participation in developing political activity took most of his available hours.

CHAPTER 2

THE COMSTOCK'S LEADING ATTORNEY, 1860–1864

WHILE STEWART and other lawyers were taking advantage of the chaotic status of mining law on the Comstock to win substantial legal fees,[1] the North and South were moving toward confrontation. This event had considerable impact on the area that became Nevada.

When the U.S. Congress met in December, 1860, John Musser, unofficial delegate from the "provisional territorial" government of Nevada, persuaded a friend to introduce a bill to make Carson County, Utah Territory, into the separate territory of Nevada.[2] There was nothing novel about this move for separate territorial status by settlers in western Utah Territory. They had been petitioning Congress for just such action since 1851; but all attempts had been blocked, partly because the Southern states did not wish to add any new free territories to the Union. Southern objection was eliminated when the formation of the Confederate States of America, on February 8, 1861, removed seven states (later increased to eleven) from the national union. Following that action, the Nevada Territory Bill, which had been dormant since December, 1860, was quickly rewritten and passed by the Senate on February 26, 1861. A companion bill passed the House on March 2, and the Organic Act for Nevada Territory was signed by President Buchanan on the same day.[3]

After some ten years of effort, Nevada Territory was now a reality, brought into being basically through two events: the discovery of the Comstock Lode, which added population and political and legal pressures to an already incompetent government; and the secession of the Southern states, which eliminated congressional opposition to the addition of new free territories. Two days after Nevada became a territory, a new President was sworn into office, and it became his responsibility to make the necessary political appointments in the new territory.

Once in office, Abraham Lincoln used his patronage power to reward party workers and to help insure Union loyalty in the territory. For governor he chose James Warren Nye, a well-known New York politician who had worked effectively for Lincoln's election. Orion Clemens, from Missouri, was named territorial secretary. Two other territorial appointees played significant roles in the history of Nevada: John M. Kinkead, who served in both the 1863 and 1864 constitutional conventions and became Nevada's third governor in 1878, was appointed territorial treasurer; and John W. North, who was appointed territorial surveyor general, later served as a territorial judge and was chosen president of the 1863 constitutional convention.[4]

Governor Nye arrived in Carson City on July 7, 1861. Four days later he began issuing the proclamations necessary to complete the basic work of territorial organization. Under Nevada's Organic Act, the governor was required to take a new census, preparatory to the election of a territorial delegate to Congress, the Territorial Council, and the Territorial House of Representatives. On August 8 Nye called for an election to fill those positions, to be held August 31. Among those elected to the Territorial Council was William Morris Stewart, representing Ormsby County.[5]

Stewart entered into the activities of the territorial legislature with his usual vigor and played an important role in the proceedings of that body. His name was associated with at least two important measures and a number of lesser ones. One of Stewart's many suggestions during the first session of the territorial legislature was of a practical nature, that sawdust should be spread on the floor rather than a coarse cloth called drugget, because sawdust "would be cheaper and a better absorbent of tobacco juice."[6] Perhaps his most significant contribution was the introduction of Council Bill 1, to adopt the common law. Then, on November 7, 1861, Stewart proposed the location of the territorial capital at Carson City.[7] He won support for his proposal by astute political maneuvering, guaranteeing potential rivals the prestige of being named county seats in return for support of Carson City as the capital.[8] Although Stewart undoubtedly aided Carson City's cause, the community also had certain initial advantages. The Utah Territorial Legislature had moved the county seat of Carson County from Genoa to Carson City on January 18, 1861, and Governor Nye had designated that city as the meeting place for the territorial legislature.[9]

Stewart resigned from the council in 1862, to devote more time to his law practice. His decision to do so followed the stabilization of the court system that came with territorial status. Judge Gordon N. Mott opened court in February, 1863, in the First Judicial District, which covered Storey County. Immediately, dozens of cases that had accumulated since the last entry in Judge Cradlebaugh's Utah territorial court, on February 19, 1861, were brought forward. Within a short time, "Every claim of any value in the district was in litigation: the single-ledge theory was passionately combatted, rights of rival locators were hotly asserted, and the confusion was worse confounded by the vagueness of the notices of location and the lack of trustworthy records."[10] "Fighting claims," so called because they were established by new companies merely to contest rich properties, became common. One of the best, or worst, examples of such claims was that of the Grosche Gold and Silver Mining Company, incorporated in 1863 to maintain that 3,750 feet on the Comstock ledge rightfully belonged to it by virtue of the alleged initial discovery of the lode by the Grosh brothers.[11]

With millions of dollars tied to the outcome of such suits, it is easy to understand the intensity and ruthlessness with which the interested parties pursued their cases, both in and outside the courtroom. It was common knowledge that witnesses, jurors, and even judges were bribed. Because of the blatant corruption, each side thought the other unscrupulous and thus felt justified in using any defense necessary. Since there were no statutes governing the points at issue, the often complex questions were generally determined by the local rules and regulations of the mining district and from application of the common law. It was a situation made to order for the talents and ambition of William M. Stewart.[12]

His decade of California experience in mining and the courtroom gave Stewart an excellent knowledge of mining practices, of mines, and of the men who worked in them. He could talk about mining problems intelligently, with sufficient understanding to impress those who depended on the extractive industry for their livelihood. He added to this basic background of understanding and experience a memory for details that astounded his friends and opponents. Clients knew that when Stewart stood up to represent them in court their cases had not only been carefully researched and prepared, but also that, like "a lion on the prowl," their counsel was ready for any contingency that might arise.[13] Just as important to his success was his "known determination to win at any cost, and the belief that he would match his adversary with any weapons which the latter might employ."[14] Stewart took every legal advantage open to him and then, if necessary, used whatever other action might be necessary to bring his case to a successful conclusion. Such practices, particularly since they were so successful, engendered substantial criticism of his ethics.[15]

Whatever one might think of Stewart's legal ethics, there is no doubt that he was a central figure in the Comstock legal wars, which climaxed with the case of the Chollar Mining Company against the Potosi Mining Company. The case lasted from December, 1861, to April, 1865, cost the opposing parties an estimated $1,300,000 in litigation expenses, and, indirectly at least, brought about the resignation of the entire territorial judiciary. It was the basis, also, of the quarrel between Judge John W. North and Stewart, which began as a difference of legal opinion and ended as a political contest that brought Stewart into the United States Senate and ended North's career in Nevada. The dispute was finally settled when the two companies simply merged, a step that, if taken at the beginning, would have obviated the entire process.[16]

The suit started in December, 1861, when the Chollar Company gave notice to the Potosi Company that it was bringing action to recover possession of a "surface claim" which included the Comstock lead and all its dips, angles, spurs, and variations. The Chollar Company followed with a proceeding, started January 17, 1862, to prevent the Potosi Company from infringing its rights under four titles, the Webb, Kirby, Chandler, and Beach locations. The argument between the two companies was meant to test the question of whether the Comstock was a single ledge or a number of parallel ones. The Chollar and its counsel, which included Stewart and his partner Alexander Baldwin, supported the single-ledge idea, while the Potosi, through its counsel, argued the multi-ledge theory. The first trial ended May 29, 1862, in a hung jury; but a second, which began in October, was decided in favor of Stewart and the Chollar Company on October 20, 1862. Motion for a new trial was overruled on November 11, 1862. The Territorial Supreme Court upheld the finding of the district court in March, 1863.[17]

The issue between the two companies arose again after the Potosi sunk a new shaft outside the boundary surface line of the Chollar Company and reached a deposit of rich ore. The original contention by the Chollar was renewed and cross suits were filed by the companies. At this point the case became complicated by extralegal issues involving the real or imagined machinations of interested parties. Judge Gordon N. Mott, accused of being partisan to the claims of the Chollar Company, resigned, and John W. North was appointed to the position.[18] Later, when efforts were made to force North's resignation as judge, sources on the Comstock insisted that North's position was purchased for him when an official of the Potosi Company paid Judge Mott the sum of $25,000 to resign.[19]

There is little doubt that John Wesley North's entrance into Nevada Territory, on June 22, 1861, was politically motivated from the beginning. Prior to his arrival in Carson County, North had been active in the politics of Minnesota Territory. In 1851, as a member of the territorial legislature, he introduced the bill which resulted in the founding of the University of Minnesota. Later he helped to organize the state Republican Party and led its partisans during Minnesota's constitutional convention in the fight for female and Negro suffrage. North is also credited with founding the town of Northfield, Minnesota. In 1860, he became chairman of the Minnesota delegation to the Republican National Convention in Chicago and campaigned for Lincoln in Illinois. After Lincoln's election, North sought appointment as Superintendent of Indian Affairs, but accepted instead the position as surveyor general of Nevada Territory.[20]

Shortly after his arrival in Carson City, at the suggestion of Governor James W. Nye, North opened a law office there.[21] In the succeeding months, he turned away from the booming Comstock settlements and helped to lay out the town of Washoe City, some twenty miles from the capital, at the north end of Washoe Lake. There he made his home, and, in partnership with James F. Lewis, later to become the first chief justice of the Nevada Supreme Court, opened additional law offices.[22] Although not considered a brilliant attorney, he soon achieved a reputation for honesty. When Gordon Mott resigned as territorial judge, a movement developed to make North a justice of the territorial court.[23] At first not interested because of the annual salary of $3,000, he reconsidered when the legislature increased the sum to $6,000.[24] North had strong support from members of the Washoe bar, including William M. Stewart. However, he did not receive his commission until August 20, 1863, since Mott, although elected to Congress September 3, 1862, did not officially resign from the bench until August 11, 1863.[25]

While awaiting his possible appointment to the territorial judiciary, North became involved in a series of commitments which later led to bribery and corruption charges made against him by William Stewart and others. In the spring of 1863, North decided to build a mill in Washoe City and accepted financial backing from one of the owners of the Potosi Mine.[26] He should not have accepted the loan, since the property was involved in a major legal battle with the Chollar Company and he knew that he might have to adjudicate the issue. At the very least, North's action showed a serious error in judgment.

However, before any involvement by North in the Chollar-Potosi case, a major political event halted most of the legal actions on the Comstock. On December 20, 1862, the territorial legislature authorized a September, 1863, election to determine whether the voters wanted statehood. Besides providing for a preference poll on that issue, the measure also called for the election of delegates to a constitutional convention which was to meet in November, 1863, if the vote for statehood was affirmative.[27] It was, by a margin of over four to one. In answer to the mandate, Territorial Secretary Orion Clemens called the convention to order on November 3, 1863, in Carson City.[28]

The fact that Congress had refused to grant an enabling act to the people of Nevada Territory did not deter the delegates from proceeding with their deliberations. Of the thirty-nine individuals chosen to the convention, thirty-five had come directly to Nevada Territory from California. All but four of the delegates had come to the territory after the discovery of the Comstock Lode in June, 1859. They represented a range of professions, including eight lawyers, four miners, two farmers, five merchants, a banker, doctor, notary public, coach-maker, sign painter, hotel keeper, civil engineer, and lumber dealer. A number had no profession listed. Many of the delegates were outstanding persons: J. Neely Johnson had served a term as governor of California and was to serve later on the Nevada Supreme Court; John W. North, appointed surveyor general of Nevada Territory in 1861, was serving as a territorial judge at the time of the convention; William Morris Stewart was to become one of Nevada's most prominent United States senators; John Kinkead later became Nevada's third governor; C. N. Noteware became the state's first secretary of state; and C. M. Brosnan became a justice of the Nevada Supreme Court. John W. North was chosen as president of the convention, gaining 21 of 30 votes cast among five candidates. In light of their later quarrel, it is ironic that William M. Stewart moved that North's election be declared unanimous.[29]

Both Stewart and North played important roles in drafting the constitution which emerged, and although they disagreed over the mine taxation provision, they agreed on a surprising number of constitutional issues. No major dispute between North and Stewart was in evidence at the time the convention adjourned on December 11, 1863.[30]

The constitutional issue which subsequently became so divisive, taxation of mines, was first discussed in detail on the eighteenth day of the convention. As soon as debate began, Stewart moved an amendment that would exclude from taxation unproductive mining claims. He proposed, in effect, that mines be taxed upon their net proceeds only. James H. Ralston, representing Lander County, another mining constituency, argued that a similar provision then should include "unproductive town property and unproductive farms." Stewart replied that the cases were not parallel, since a farm always had a real value but a mine was worthless unless ore was found there. North left the chair to join the debate against Stewart. Shortly thereafter, the provision to tax mines equally with other property passed by a vote of 21 to 10.

Stewart revived the argument the next day, emphasizing that it was a matter of justice that only productive mines be taxed, since an unproductive mine was really not property. His lengthy speech, over ten printed pages, brought a short reply from North, who again left the chair to enter the debate. L. O. Sterns, delegate from the mining town of Aurora, in Esmeralda County, backed Stewart strongly, noting in a prophetic evaluation, that if the equal tax was imposed, the voters would defeat the constitution by a margin of five to one. Stewart then offered an amendment that unproductive mines not be taxed at all and productive ones only on their net proceeds. It was defeated 25 to 6.[31] While all six of the members supporting the Stewart amendment represented mining areas, twelve other delegates from mining counties voted for the equal taxation of the mines. Stewart made a last effort against the equal taxation clause when the taxation article came up again on the twenty-third day of the convention. At that time he attempted to have the taxation provision recommitted, with the idea of allowing the legislature to classify property to be taxed. The proposal was defeated 18 to 6.[32]

Stewart's influence on other parts of the 1863 constitution was sizable and generally mirrored the basic political and economic ideas to which he adhered later. For example, he strongly opposed individual liability of corporations, arguing for a liberal law to induce businesses to incorporate in Nevada. He forcefully advocated foreign capital to develop the mines, in which he was supported by John North. Stewart's position that incorporators not be individually liable for the debts of their corporations prevailed in the final draft.[33] He joined North in opposing a state appropriation to aid the Pacific railroad, arguing that it would be unwise to saddle the state with such a debt while information about the economy was so scarce. He was not opposed to a state donation to help build a railroad, but did not want the state to become involved in raising money to assist corporations. In spite of Stewart's opposition, a provision was placed in the 1863 constitution permitting the legislature to give $3,000,000 in bonds, not to the Pacific railroad, but to the first railroad to connect Nevada by rail with navigable waters.[34]

Stewart's opinion about the location of the state capital was flexible. At first he adopted a suggestion originally made by James Ralston of Lander County, that after the expiration of five years the problem of location of the capital be voted on by the people. In supporting the five-year plan, Stewart argued that a better determination of the population center of the state could be made in time. Later, he suggested that the legislature not appropriate money for capitol buildings for a period of five years. The most novel idea came from another delegate, who suggested that the capital be located for five years at Virginia City, five years at Aurora, then five years at the most prominent place in the state at that time, and then permanently at Genoa. The idea received little support and the provision in the final draft provided for location of the capital at Carson City, but prohibited appropriations for capitol buildings for a period of six years.[35]

A rather unusual clause, the "paramount allegiance" statement, which carried over nearly intact to the 1864 constitution, is credited to John North. This clause stated that the paramount allegiance "of every citizen is due to the federal government, in the exercise of all its constitutional powers, as the same have been, or may be defined by the supreme court of the United States, and no power exists in the people of this or any other state of the federal union to dissolve their connection therewith, or perform any act tending to impair, subvert, or resist the supreme authority of the government of the United States."[36] When the issue was debated on the eighth day of the convention, Stewart argued that the state should concede to the general government only those powers specified in the U.S. Constitution and should reserve all other powers. The final draft of the section did not reflect Stewart's thinking.[37]

Stewart's moderate states' rights attitude showed up more specifically during the debate on the suffrage article. He opposed preventing persons who had borne arms against the federal government from voting. While affirming his opposition to allowing confirmed traitors to vote, Stewart argued that amnesty by the federal government and an oath of allegiance by secessionists should be sufficient to restore suffrage.[38]

Stewart's strong belief in expansion, a persistent theme in his later political years, was clearly defined during the debates on the proposed boundaries for the new state. He favored adding a degree of longitude to the east, since that territory could be obtained easily as part of the statehood movement but would be difficult to gain later should Utah become a state. His position was made clear when he noted that "Congress was not going to refuse the admission of a loyal State . . . so demand the line at once and divide the territory equally with Utah."[39] Other delegates felt that changing the territory's boundaries might hinder acceptance by Congress; this view prevailed under an agreement that a memorial asking for the additional degree would be sent to Congress after admission as a state. Stewart showed his expansionist tendencies again when he moved that a committee be appointed to memorialize the California legislature to relinquish to Nevada the territory east of the dividing ridge of the Sierra Nevada. Not surprisingly, he was selected as one of the original three members of the committee.[40]

During the debate on the judiciary article, Stewart used his legal training and experience to influence nearly every provision. Among other things, he favored three rather than five members for the supreme court. At first a majority of delegates favored the larger court, but Stewart finally won agreement for a chief justice and two associates, with the legislature having the right to add two additional justices.[41] He successfully opposed a movement to allow the legislature the power to abolish the grand jury system, insisting that the arrangement was a wholesome check upon public officers.[42]

Stewart was proud of his work in the constitutional convention and wanted the document ratified. In the closing days of the meeting he advocated submission of the constitution to the people "untrammeled by other issues." He particularly opposed the idea of electing officers simultaneously with the ratification vote, because disappointed candidates and their friends would oppose the constitution in retaliation for not being nominated. North favored holding both elections at the same time and his view prevailed by a vote of 24 to 5.[43] At the time Stewart disavowed any intention of running for the United States Senate, emphasizing that he would not be a candidate under any circumstances.[44]

The constitutional convention of 1863 came to a close at 10:00 P.M., December 11, 1863.[45] Stewart's opposition to the taxation article did not prevent his announcement, just before adjournment, that he would support the constitution before the people, "notwithstanding the taxation of mines, believing, as he did that the Legislature had power to decide that a mere hole in the ground was not property."[46] The day after the close of the convention, a local newspaper noted that "The members all pledged themselves to work for the adoption of the constitution. Patriotic speeches were made, and three cheers for the State of Nevada were given."[47] However, their cheers for a new state were premature. When the ratification vote took place on January 19, 1864, the 1863 document was decisively defeated. How was it possible to change a four-to-one majority favoring statehood, in September, 1863, into a four-to-one margin against it just a few months later?

The forces favoring adoption of the constitution appeared invincible when the ratification fight began. Among supporters were the San Francisco-dominated monopolies and their spokesman, William Morris Stewart.[48] Important Comstock newspapers also supported the document, as did all but three of the nine papers in the territory.[49] A third major faction advocating statehood consisted of strong Union sympathizers, men like John W. North, who wanted another free state admitted.

The only opposition at first came from certain small mining interests, agriculturists, and the so-called "secession" element, which included states' rightists generally. Without major newspaper support they were ineffective. However, public meetings held throughout the territory stimulated vigorous debates on various constitutional issues and gave the anti-ratification element an opportunity to focus on two major weaknesses of the 1863 document. These were the taxation clause, which did not give mining the preferential "net proceeds" tax, and the election provision, which asked the people to vote for ratification of the constitution and at the same time choose officers to serve under it.

It was clear from the opening of the ratification debates that the taxation issue had become a wedge between the large and the small Comstock mining interests. Although both groups favored a "net proceeds" tax, they differed on how such a provision could be obtained. Representatives of the small mining companies, who generally believed in the multiple-ledge theory of the lode, demanded that such a tax be constitutionally guaranteed and opposed the 1863 document because it lacked such an article.[50] Speaking for the large companies, on the other hand, Stewart insisted that a net proceeds tax could be achieved by legislative means. The Union Party was the result of the split in the ranks of the Democratic Party occasioned by the outbreak of the Civil War. The split was so divisive in some areas, such as Nevada Territory, that the Democrats were unable to present an official slate of candidates until the national election of 1864. In the interim, the Union Party, made up of Republicans and Union Democrats, dominated the political arena. Large companies supported the constitution because their control of the Union Party assured them domination of the state government if that document should be ratified. To the large mining interests, statehood meant economic and political control of the Comstock Lode — first by getting rid of Judge North and the territorial judiciary, who were then opposing the single-ledge theory on which their power depended, and second, by giving them three representatves in Congress to protect their mineral rights. The latter point was particularly important because, since 1861, efforts had been made to secure revenue from mineral lands for the federal government. Bills for just such a purpose were before Congress while statehood was being debated in Nevada Territory.

The second major internal weakness of the 1863 constitution was brought into sharp focus when the county conventions began meeting late in December, 1863, to choose a slate of candidates for the January election. Since there was to be a single official ticket, nomination was tantamount to election. At immediate issue was control of the Union Party, which, under the peculiar circumstances then prevailing, meant control of the state government should the document be ratified. The nomination battle developed into a contest between large and small company interests, represented respectively by William Stewart and John North.

North's popularity was at a high point in the weeks following adjournment of the constitutional convention. It was generally assumed that his leadership was responsible for the equal taxation clause. His name was mentioned prominently for the three top offices available, United States senator, governor, or a justice of the state supreme court.[51] His decision to seek the governorship placed him directly in the path of those seeking to control the state government. Not only was North opposed to the net proceeds tax, but, in November, 1863, he had ruled in favor of the multi-ledge theory in issuing an injunction in favor of the Burning Moscow Company against the Ophir Company, represented by Stewart.[52] It thus became important to Stewart and the interests he represented to eliminate North, not only as a territorial judge, but also as a potential candidate for governor. In order to accomplish those ends before the constitution was voted on, a two-pronged attack against North was initiated.

The first part of the campaign began when Stewart, on the basis of a story told by Judge Hardy to Alexander Baldwin, Stewart's partner, accused North of accepting a bribe from officials of the Burning Moscow Company. Since Hardy had been one of the lawyers for the latter company, the story seemed to have a certain plausibility. North immediately challenged the truth of Stewart's accusation and forced him, on the threat of legal action, to publish a card in the *Territorial Enterprise,* disavowing the bribery charges. The published notice read:

> Virginia, Dec. 22, 1863—Hon. J. W. North—Dear Sir: Proceeding upon facts and statements which appeared to warrant me in so doing, I have recently made public charges reflecting upon your character as Judge and an honest man. With your assistance I have investigated those charges and I pronounce them unsustained, and take great pleasure in so stating. In my judgment there can be no just occasion for the indulgence of any suspicion of your judicial integrity or private character. Yours very truly, William M. Stewart.[53]

With publication of the retraction, North apparently thought the matter closed. Stewart, however, did not, and continued to repeat the allegations during the weeks which followed.

The second part of the move against North began with the nominating conventions of the Union Party. The Storey County meeting, held at Virginia City in the last week of December, became a critical test of strength between supporters of North and Stewart. The Stewart faction dominated the proceedings, not only naming their state convention delegates, including Stewart, but their slate of candidates as well. Miles N. Mitchell, a former speaker of the Territorial House of Representatives, was the choice for the post of governor. Not content with omitting North's name from the Storey County slate of candidates, Stewart pushed through a resolution which pledged the Storey County delegates to the state convention to oppose the nomination of Judge North.[54] At that point, Thomas Fitch and eight others who supported North's candidacy withdrew from the meeting. The "bolters," as they were referred to by the opposition, held a December 29 public meeting at the Storey County Courthouse, where they announced an alternate list of delegates to be presented to the State Union Party Convention.[55]

When that convention met at Carson City, December 31, 1863, the two opposing delegations from Storey County each sought to be seated. By that time, Judge North's opposition to the single-ledge theory had been emphasized by his December 28 ruling against the Ophir Company in its suit to obtain a permanent injunction against the Burning Moscow Company. In his decision North concluded that at the depth where the controversy between the two companies arose, there were several distinct ledges. If conclusive evidence at greater depth later showed these veins to be blended into one, it would then be time to determine which would continue and which would run out.[56] Obviously, the owners of the Ophir Company, and Stewart as their counsel, could not afford to have a governor with a viewpoint which might cost them millions of dollars and control of the Comstock Lode. Under the circumstances, then, it was not surprising that the Credentials Committee seated the regular, or Stewart delegates. The "bolters" were given a hearing before the convention, but to no avail.[57]

North still had the support of a number of smaller counties and was nominated for governor. However, by bargaining and repetition of the earlier bribery charges, Stewart was able to gain sufficient votes to defeat him. On the third day of the convention, on the first ballot for governor, Miles N. Mitchell, the Storey County choice, received 29 votes to 22 for North.[58]

The Union Party conventions were the turning point in the ratification fight.[59] The elimination of North from the Union Party slate of candidates proved to be a costly victory. The naked show of power by the large mining companies was held high for everyone to see, and it was now clear that a favorable vote on the constitution would bring into power those candidates supported by "Stewart and company." At that point, it was a simple matter for the opposition press to rally to the anti-Stewart position and portray the ratification fight as one between the "monopolists" who wanted statehood, on the one hand, and the "people," who opposed statehood under the 1863 document, on the other. This became the main theme of the *Virginia Daily Union,* an earlier supporter of the 1863 constitution, which now, with Thomas Fitch as chief editorial writer, began an unrelenting fight to defeat that instrument by focusing on the figure of William Morris Stewart. As one pro-constitution newspaper reported, Stewart became the great "Bugbear," for it was "Bill Stewart by day and Bill Stewart by night."[60]

The *Union* began its attack on Stewart on January 3, 1864, the day after the state convention chose its candidates, noting that if the constitution was adopted, California speculators would run the state government "through their brokers and tools, Stewart & Co.," and their candidate for governor, Miles Mitchell, would be at the "entire mercy of Bill Stewart."[61] Later the paper charged that Stewart's sole aim was:

> . . . to defeat Judge North and secure a District and County Judge for Storey County, and a Supreme Bench for the new State of Nevada of his own choice. . . . Now it is all fixed up. Stewart and his friends have so far, what they want. It now remains to be seen whether the people approve of the programme and are willing to place themselves in the hands of this man and his chosen friend, by adopting the constitution.

The writer argued that it would be better not to have a state than to allow a man of Stewart's reputation to play such a prominent role in its organization. He insisted that the 1863 document was the "sole work of politicians and speculators to promote their own ends and gain, at the expense of an unsuspecting people. . . . they are aided and abetted by San Francisco speculators who intend to fasten the one-ledge theory on the people of the territory."[62]

In its continuing fight against the "monopolists," the *Union* began reporting anti-adoption meetings as "People's Mass Meetings." In covering one such meeting at Topliffe's Theater, it noted that "The result of this meeting will be disastrous to the Stewart interest, and will go far to convince the people that it is just to reject the Constitution and thus escape all the despicable meshes set to entrap them into aiding heartless coteries of public sharps." The *Union* also published a number of letters extolling its point of view. One of these, signed "Cosmos," noted that Stewart and others wanted a state government "because they have come to the conclusion that our present Judiciary care more for the people and for justice than they do for the influence of improper combinations . . . but the people do not want a State, and they do not intend to adopt one at a great loss merely to accommodate a few parties."[63] Another such letter, from "Carl," was more specific:

> Your paper has never faltered in its advocacy of the people's interests, as against the Stewart clique, and let it not falter now that the danger is greater than ever before. . . . No other reason could induce the Stewart crowd to labor for the Constitution save that by its adoption, they will remove Judge North and have a District and State Judiciary of their own making.[64]

The *Virginia Evening Bulletin,* a supporter of the document, recognized the potential danger of the "Stewart versus people" approach and tried to minimize Stewart's role in the ratification fight. It noted, "Bill Stewart is without doubt, a most unscrupulous, wide-awake lawyer, and the Comstock Company is a body ever on the alert to take all advantages . . . the people are not idiots and a thousand Bill Stewarts or any number of Comstock combinations could not force the people to be defrauded of their rights."[65] The owners of the *Union,* however, were well aware of the value of the Stewart name in their battle and refused to minimize his role. Just a few days before the scheduled vote on ratification, when one of the pro-constitution newspapers argued that conditions would get worse in the territory if the instrument were not approved, the editor of the *Union* replied, "To fall into worse hands [Stewart's] is a moral impossibility and the people know it too well to be hoodwinked into adopting the Constitution next Tuesday."[66]

After the nominating conventions rhetoric and feeling ran high. Stewart's every action was scrutinized and often criticized. His attacks against the integrity of Judge North only called attention to his own unprincipled activities. The opposition press effectively capitalized on this widespread distrust of Stewart to picture North as a hero of the "people." Failing to recognize the extent of North's popularity on the Comstock, Stewart continued his efforts to malign North through the closing days of the contest. The confrontation between the two men came to a climax when Stewart challenged North to face him at public forum to be held at Maguire's Opera House on January 16, 1864. Although Stewart issued his challenge just one day before the proposed meeting, North readily accepted. Privately, however, he noted the irony of Stewart's invitation for him to appear while Stewart "vindicated himself against my charges."[67]

Speaking first before a capacity audience, Stewart repeated his earlier charges of bribery and corruption against North. He alleged that the judge had obtained a loan to build a quartz mill from litigants who appeared before him in court, that the mill was mortgaged for $15,000, and that it was impossible for a district judge to own a quartz mill, owe $15,000 on it and remain honest. Mindful of human fallibility, Stewart suggested that "even the angel Gabriel couldn't do so."[68] He then called upon his law partner, Alexander W. Baldwin, who took the floor and repeated the bribery charges against North.

It is indicative of Stewart's style that he would repeat a complaint which had already been refuted publicly by the man who originally made it, and which had been repudiated by Stewart himself in a published card of retraction. Moreover, reviving the bribery and corruption allegations was only part of Stewart's personal attack against Judge North. Cognizant of the strong regional and racial prejudice on the Comstock, Stewart tried to discredit North further by attacking the latter's position on the slavery issue. He emphasized North's part in the fight for Negro suffrage at the Minnesota Constitutional Convention, alleging that North believed in the "equality of the white and black races." Stewart portrayed North as a radical villain who thought a "nigger" was just as entitled to vote as the "good Irish gentlemen" present in the opera house. He himself, on the other hand, opposed Negro suffrage, for "I am one of those who believe that this country was made for white men. . . ."[69]

In his brief reply, North recited the history of the bribery charges and Stewart's repudiation of them. He made no attempt to answer the antislavery charges. Convinced that he had won the support of the audience, North wrote jubilantly to his father-in-law: "The audience was *immense:* and I had 7/10 of them to start with; and 9/10 at the close. I never experienced so complete a triumph as I had that night in the meeting that he had called. The meeting wound up with three cheers for me and three groans for him."[70]

It was the last major meeting of the campaign, although the contest continued in the newspapers, streets, and saloons until the day of election. A carnival-like mood swept the Comstock as voters went to the polls on January 19, 1864. They recorded a major defeat for Stewart and the 1863 constitution, with only 2,157 votes in favor and 8,851 against.[71]

Stewart's personal attack against North on January 16 had served only to focus further unfavorable attention on his efforts to eliminate North and the territorial judiciary in the interests of the San Francisco monopolies. As North later wrote, the meeting at the opera house helped turn "the people of the Territory against the Ticket nominated at the State Convention; and in order to defeat it they determined to defeat the Constitution."[72]

In the aftermath of the election there was no dearth of explanations for the surprising turn of events. Contemporary observers cited a number of reasons for the defeat of the document. The taxation clause failed to give mining interests the preference they demanded.[73] The dual election procedure was not only a bad technical arrangement, but also ended by linking a favorable vote on the constitution to a vote for the Union Party slate of candidates, who were perceived to be controlled by the Stewart interests.[74] The strong pro-Union provisions alienated states' rightists, particularly the pro-Southern element.[75] Finally, property owners, and particularly agriculturists, opposed statehood because it would bring additional taxes.

These various objections were cleverly used by anti-constitution groups, who succeeded in presenting the adoption fight as a contest between "the people" on one side and "the monopolists" on the other. In that campaign the name of William Morris Stewart became an unholy symbol of "a group of unscrupulous men [who] tried to take possession of the new government."[76] As David Johnson has summarized: "Nevadans rejected statehood because they believed that William Stewart would capture the state government and use it to serve the purpose of San Francisco financiers in control of Nevada's largest mining corporations."[77]

Shortly after the election the *Gold Hill Daily News* lightheartedly acknowledged the wisdom of the "people," noting that "the sovereign and intelligent masses; the grave, the unterrified, have taken the sand from beneath our feet, and we sink gracefully, like the tall pines of the forest."[78] The following day the paper similarly addressed Stewart's part in the battle: "The A No. 1, full-rigged ship 'Constitution,' Bill Stewart, Captain, sailed this morning, as per notice from the Bank Exchange." According to the *News,* the ship was headed for Salt River, the destination of defeated causes. In the aftermath of the vote, Captain Stewart and Judge North "seemed like twin brothers" to the newspaper, a reference to the fact that both had favored adoption throughout the campaign.[79]

The defeat of the 1863 constitution was not the end of the statehood movement in Nevada, for neither federal officials nor territorial residents were opposed to statehood generally. The vote on January 19 was not a rejection of statehood, but simply disapproval of a document unfavorable to the political and economic interest of the voters. It was also a major rejection of William Morris Stewart. Consequently, when national pressures opened the door to another statehood attempt, political leaders in Nevada Territory were quick to seize the opportunity.

CHAPTER 3

DRIVING NEVADA'S STATEHOOD BANDWAGON

THE DEFEAT of the first constitution temporarily thwarted the efforts of the Stewart group to control the Comstock, but it did not stop their attempts to rid themselves of North and the territorial judiciary. Even before the ratification vote, a bill was introduced in the territorial legislature which would have neutralized North by defining the judicial districts in such a way as to exclude him from the First Judicial District, which included the Comstock Lode.[1] It backfired when a law was passed to assign North by name to a new district that included Storey and Washoe counties.[2] A vindicated North exulted to his father-in-law: "This was my triumph before the Territory, and I am once more at rest. My enemy has to come before me to attend to business and he is meek as a whipped cur. He tried for a few days to pursue me through hired newspapers: but he was soon glad to stop them and there is once more a calm."[3] North spoke too soon, however. If Stewart were "meek as a whipped cur," his subsequent actions belie those words, for the "calm" lasted but a few weeks.

The battle heated up in the courts. On February 19, 1864, North granted a preliminary restraining order preventing the Chollar Company from working on the ledge claimed by the Potosi.[4] The action reversed an earlier decision of the Territorial Supreme Court, which had favored Stewart's client, the Chollar Company. After hearing arguments in the case, North granted a permanent injunction to the Potosi Company on April 4, 1864, at the same time refusing a writ sought by the Chollar in its suit against the Potosi.[5] By rescinding judicial protection of the single-ledge theory, this decision reopened the legal contest for control of the Comstock Lode. North realized that the decision in the case was based on insufficient expert opinion. Consequently, when another ledge case, the *Gould and Curry Mining Company* v. *The North Potosi Mining*

Company, came before him, North appointed John Nugent, a respected attorney, as referee, on May 17, 1864. North was convinced that he had acted correctly in the Chollar case. In a letter to his wife he wrote, "I suppose Stewart, Baldwin, and Hillyer and Dibble [attorneys for the Chollar Company] are feeling very bitterly towards me; but that is comforting assurance that I am right."[6]

The April 4 decision was appealed immediately by the Chollar Company. Since Nevada's territorial court system provided that the Territorial Supreme Court was to consist of the three district judges sitting together, the Chollar appeal gave North an opportunity to sit in judgment again on a case which he had tried in the district court. Since Justice Turner had concurred with Justice Mott in August of 1863, when the supreme court first ruled in favor of the Chollar Company, it seemed obvious that the third supreme court justice, Powhatan B. Locke (who had been appointed to the territorial court late in 1863, to replace Justice Horatio Jones), would be the key to the decision. Thus both sides attempted to influence Locke, beginning with the appeal hearings on April 28, 1864, and lasting until the case was finally settled on May 13, 1864.

Initially North seemed to control the new justice. His influence over Locke, gained, according to Chollar supporters, by pressures on the justice from prominent Potosi stockholders, held firm to May 5. At that time North filed an opinion, concurred in by Locke, which summarized the dispute and affirmed North's earlier decision favoring the Potosi Company and the multiple-ledge theory. The Chollar partisans did not give up, but by "persistent representations" convinced Locke to add an addendum on the same day as the decision. Curiously phrased, it read: "It is unnecessary to express any opinion as to the merits of this cause, both parties may be heard upon the trial as to what was adjudicated in a former trial."[7]

The Chollar officials were jubilant, accepting the addendum as a withdrawal of Locke's earlier vote. The Potosi again put pressure on Locke, however, and on May 13, the latter filed an order with the clerk of the supreme court, directing that official "to strike from the files in your office my addendum or qualification to the opinion delivered by North, Judge, and concurred in by me. Said addendum or qualification is hereby revoked by me and rendered null and void and to be of no legal effect."[8]

The judicial wavering in the Chollar-Potosi struggle indicates the sad state of the legal system on the Comstock during these years. Judges and contestants alike behaved unethically. When the supreme court decision disappointed them, however, the Chollar advocates simply switched the battle to the political arena. They blamed the judges for all the legal problems of the Comstock and timed their campaign to remove the judges to coincide with the second statehood movement.[9]

That movement commenced on February 8, 1864, when a bill was introduced in the U.S. Senate by James R. Doolittle of Wisconsin, to enable the people of Nevada Territory to write a constitution and form a state government. The bill was a pragmatic response to the needs of Lincoln for additional Republican states to help maintain the party's control of Congress and the presidency. With active administration support, the Enabling Act passed both houses and was signed by President Lincoln on March 21, 1864. Governor Nye accordingly called for an election to be held in June, 1864, to select delegates to a constitutional convention scheduled at Carson City on July 4, 1864.[10]

The second constitutional convention, which met from July 4 to July 27, produced a document patterned after the 1863 instrument, but with a few important changes. Mining interests succeeded in altering the taxation article so as to tax only net proceeds. That change came only after the merchants and businessmen in the mining counties, who had supported taxation of mines equally as other property in the first convention, finally realized that their own prosperity was tied to the prosperity of the large, California-controlled mining companies and so switched their voting alignment. Although not a delegate in 1864, Stewart's position favoring a net proceeds tax had won the day. The dual election procedure was also changed so that ratification would take place approximately two months before the election of officers. With the vote on state officials then part of the national election, both national parties in the territory would be able to present full slates of candidates.[11]

As the 1864 convention drew to a close, however, it became apparent that Stewart and the mining interests he represented planned to make the issue of a "corrupt judiciary" a major part of their campaign for ratification. The *Gold Hill Daily News* initiated the assault on the court on July 19, when it claimed that nine of every ten citizens believed the court to be corrupt and that the judges accused of corruption were defying the people by refusing to explain their actions.[12] This was an interesting switch from the earlier ratification battle, when the people and the justices were linked together in opposition to Stewart and the monopolists. On July 20, the *News* began a series of editorials on the venality of the territorial courts which, among other things, revived all of the old bribery charges previously lodged against the justices.[13]

The initial attacks in the *News* and the *Territorial Enterprise*, both controlled by the same interests which controlled Stewart, were strong enough to force the pro-North editor of the *Virginia Daily Union* to call upon the territorial judges to defend themselves, since "silence now becomes criminal."[14] Following the request, North published a card in that paper on July 23, challenging those who were making the charges to "let their names be known, so that I can know who is, or who are my accusers. . . . No one is in doubt as to whence these slanders come. Now, let their authors come out like men of honor, if they have honor, and give us their names, and something definite to aim at."[15]

North's card brought an immediate reponse from the *Territorial Enterprise*. In its issue of July 24, the *Enterprise* repeated the three main allegations it had made earlier against the judge: that North's position on the bench had been bought for him by the Potosi Company or some of its principal stockholders; that the same parties had loaned North money for a mill site and furnished him with ore while cases involving their company were before the courts; and that North had received a bribe from the Burning Moscow Company preceding his decision in favor of that company.[16] The *Union* in turn attempted to defend North, pointing out that the majority of the territorial bar approved his decisions and that both Stewart and Hardy had previously published retractions of their original bribery and corruption statements. The paper noted, too, that on May 17, 1864, some days after the Chollar decision, Stewart's law partner, Alexander Baldwin, had published a card stating, *"I regard Judge North as an upright man, and an untainted Judge,"* and that he "deeply regretted having made earlier remarks to the contrary."[17]

Evidently North's opponents took their removal campaign to Washington, D.C., for on July 23, North telegraphed President Lincoln: "I have this moment learned that secret efforts are made at Washington to injure my character & effect my removal. I only ask that no action be had until charges are made & I allowed a hearing."[18] If such efforts were made they failed to bring any action from the President. On the Comstock, however, newspaper attacks against the justices were supplemented by public meetings, where all the old accusations against the justices were brought forward. One of the strongest of these came early in August, when a speaker repeated the familiar charges in a meeting before a group of working men, and added the new and interesting suggestion that the current depression on the Comstock was due to "the deep and universal distrust of our judiciary."[19]

Pressure to force the territorial judiciary out of office climaxed when, for three consecutive days, August 9 through 11, the *Territorial Enterprise* published a petition calling for the judges to resign. According to the article, the document had been signed by between 3,000 and 4,000 persons.[20] The *Union* was not impressed by the lists and suggested that they probably were obtained by someone "standing on the streets and getting every passer-by," and that the author of "all this hullabullo" was as well known "as though W. M. S. was written at the bottom of each article."[21]

Finally the public pressures began to take their toll on Judge North. His wife wrote in a letter to her parents that her husband was so exhausted from his court duties that he fainted at the breakfast table. She indicated, also, that her husband planned to resign at once if the constitution was not adopted, but "if it should be, then there will be no necessity for such a step. I feel very little interest in the State questions but he must be relieved of the arduous duties of that office."[22]

There was evidence, however, that North was contemplating resignation before the September 7 ratification vote. On August 13, thirty-one Comstock lawyers, including Richard S. Mesick, later suggested by Stewart and others as a replacement for North, and Thomas Fitch, wrote North that they had "undiminished confidence in the purity and integrity of your public and private life."[23] More specifically, on August 16 and 19, the *Union* published letters from various attorneys, addressed to North, referring to rumors that he might resign because of ill health, and indicating their confidence in him as a judge and support for his continuance in office.[24]

It was not a complete surprise, therefore, when Judge North resigned at the opening of the August 22 session of the supreme court. In his telegram to President Lincoln he stated:

> I am compelled by severe & protracted Illness to relinquish the office of Associate Justice of the Supreme Court & Judge of the first Judicial District of this Territory. I tender my resignation to take effect upon the appointment & qualification of my successor. I beg leave to assure you that in my opinion the necessity of the people require the immediate appointment of my successor. Very Risky. Your Obd. Servt.[25]

North enlarged upon his reason for resigning in a letter to the thirty-one lawyers who had written him earlier:

> My continued illness wholly unfits me for the severe labor of Judge of this District. A due regard for the public welfare requires that I should make way for my successor before the commencement of the next term of Court. I had hoped to be able to finish the business that is in progress before me; but I have tried my strength sufficiently to satisfy me that this is impracticable. I have given the office what health and strength I possessed, and I am now compelled to give up my time to regaining the health I have lost.[26]

The day after the resignation announcement, Judge North accepted the report of John Nugent, the court-appointed referee in the Gould and Curry case, that the Comstock Lode was a single ledge, as Stewart and others had argued. The referee's report was dated August 21, so North no doubt saw it before making his announcement on the twenty-second. There is no evidence to indicate that the report influenced North's resignation, although it completely reversed the judge's earlier decisions supporting the multiple-ledge theory.[27] Judicial acceptance of the single-ledge theory should be viewed as part of the movement away from individualism and toward monopoly on the Comstock that began with the entrance of the Bank of California in the summer of 1864.[28]

William Stewart had won a double victory. He took an active role in the resignation of Judge North, justifying his activities on the basis of a published notice that the Territorial Supreme Court would disbar him at the August 22 meeting.[29] Thus he put pressure on the judiciary to resign in order to maintain his own standing. It became a matter of personal honor.

North's resignation, which was apparently not communicated in advance to the other two justices, placed them under immediate attacks from Stewart supporters. Chief Justice Turner recessed the scheduled meeting of the supreme court until the evening of August 22. In the interim, according to Stewart, Turner assured him that:

> If I would let up on him he would resign. I sent back word that he must put his resignation in a letter addressed to the President, and also in a telegraphic dispatch; that he must put both in an unsealed envelope and deliver them to me before he went on the bench or I would swear out a warrant before the justice of the peace and have him arrested for bribery. He sent the resignations as demanded. I mailed one and telegraphed the other.[30]

Stewart evidently felt no shame about his conduct. He later boasted about the actions he took to force the resignation of the third supreme court justice, P. B. Locke. In his account, Stewart related how he had invited the Comstock bar to an evening of entertainment, after the resignations of North and Turner. During the festivities he sent two young men to bring Judge Locke before the group, by force if necessary. When he arrived, Stewart ordered him to resign. The resignation "was read aloud, to be sure that it was all right, signed and mailed; after which the whole meeting became hilarious, and Judge Locke imbibed so freely that he became more stupid than usual."[31]

Although Stewart undoubtedly exaggerated his own crucial role in the events leading to the resignation of the territorial justices, it is apparent that strong pressures were brought against them and that Stewart played a leading part in the drama. One anti-Stewart paper said as much in its headline, "Stewart forces resignation of territorial judges."[32] Another stated, without mentioning names, that the territorial judiciary resigned because they had been "badgered all day by certain members of the bar."[33] A similar evaluation came from Hubert Howe Bancroft, who wrote that "the whole judiciary was removed in a day by the bar of Nevada, under Stewart's lead."[34]

Many decried the manner in which the justices had been treated and pointed out that they were only part of the legal problems on the Comstock. Witnesses were "induced to commit perjury" and juries bribed to such an extent that "a general demoralization of the public mind had so far gained ground that it is scarcely to be wondered at that the courts were unable to enforce the authority and respect due to the law, no matter how honorable might be the personal character of the judges."[35] And, although there had been great emphasis on the potential benefits of getting rid of the justices, "nothing was said about the benefit it might be to drive out the lawyers, who took hundreds of feet of the best mines to keep litigation going, and used hundreds of thousands of dollars of their clients' money to corrupt whoever stood in their way. Whatever may be said of the Nevada bench at this time, I know of no more trying position than that of an appointed judge."[36] Stewart had effectively focused public attention on the failings of the judiciary, however, and their resignation was his victory.

Shortly after the announcement of the resignations of the territorial judiciary, forty-nine Comstock attorneys, including Stewart, met at Virginia City and submitted a request to President Lincoln that he appoint one of their members, Richard S. Mesick, to replace Judge North. However, another group of attorneys, presumably including John W. North, had already prevailed on U.S. Senator Conness of California, Supreme Court Justice Stephen Field, and Governor Low of California to nominate John F. Swift, a prominent San Francisco attorney, for the position."[37] When it appeared possible that Swift might be selected, Stewart and his followers met again, not only to oppose that appointment, but to pass resolutions suggesting that there be no further involvement in the Nevada territorial courts until Nevada became a state. In summarizing these events later, Stewart wrote, "We were tired of Territorial judges.[38] They were not tired of territorial judges, however, only weary of those they could not name and control. As one local newspaper noted:

There's the rub—there's where the plot is apparently circumvented. A while ago all that the conspirators wanted was that the late Judges should resign; and now when they have been gratified by that consummation, they still remain unsatisfied, they want more—and they will not be comforted unless they can get the whole control and management of the Judiciary into their hands...we propose that the people of the territory choose the forty-odd lawyers of Virginia, who met to nominate a successor to Judge North, as supreme and absolute council to dictate and rule over our public affairs, as the Council of Ten ruled Venice.[39]

An interesting aftermath of the fight to nominate a replacement for North was the 1878 publication of a novel by the same John F. Swift who had been suggested for North's place on the bench. Swift's book emphasized the condition of the Nevada bar at the time of the North-Stewart feud. William M. Stewart appears in the book as Napoleon B. Spelter, whom Swift characterizes as "the eminent leader of the Washoe Bar." The novel has a great deal to say about the graft and corruption on the Comstock and the habit of buying judges.[40] Stewart wrote later that the Swift novel was "humorous and reasonably good-natured," although he couldn't appreciate the flattery of making "me one of the heroes of his novel."[41]

President Lincoln took no action to replace Judge North, consequently he remained on the bench in Nevada Territory until State Supreme Court judges were sworn in on December 5, 1864.[42] But the temporary defeat of the Stewart forces in failing to get an immediate replacement for Judge North was offset on September 7, 1864, when the constitution was ratified by the voters. The overwhelming support for the 1864 constitution, 10,375 approving and 1,284 against, was a remarkable change from the over three-to-one negative margin on the 1863 document, just a little more than seven months earlier.

This remarkable reversal was due in part to the alteration of the constitution. Correction of the taxation clause brought the mining interests together in support of the new document, and elimination of the dual voting procedure, insuring a two-party campaign for the election of officers, somewhat blunted the threat of a Stewart takeover. With these obstacles removed from the second ratification contest, proponents of the 1864 document were able to focus on two major benefits which statehood would bring to the territory: first, the end of the economic depression on the Comstock, and second, removal of the "corrupt" judiciary.

The depression, which began in the spring and worsened in the summer and fall of 1864, added to political, economic, and social confusion in the territory. Stewart and his cohorts blamed it on the inability of the

territorial judiciary to clear the court dockets of a large amount of litigation, so that the "corrupt" judiciary now also became a "do-nothing"
court, directly responsible for the decline of mining activity.[43] The
Stewart faction then mounted a strong, positive campaign to convince
the voters that statehood would end the economic crisis.[44] This attack
against the territorial judiciary became a major issue in the second constitutional campaign. It distracted public attention from the Stewart faction's continuing attempt to gain control of state government and the
three congressional representatives, in order to insure protection of their
property rights.[45] In addition, the elimination of the territorial judiciary
weakened the political threat posed by John North.

Although this campaign was extremely effective, with a state attorney
general later concluding that "Nevada became a State to escape the
deadfall of her Territorial Courts,[46] it seems clear that the 1864 constitution was also overwhelmingly approved because many objections to the
1863 document had been removed. The favorable September vote
opened the door to political activity by both the Democratic and Union
parties, in the various county and state nominating conventions. By this
time Judge North's political star had waned. After the Washoe County
Union convention, North wrote to his wife, "I am not a delegate to the
State Convention, for which I am thankful."[47] Several days later he
added, "The leading Union men here and some at Virginia have been
urging me to run for the State Senate. But (give me credit for once), I
have declined."[48]

With personal ambition dimmed, North turned his attention to support
of the Union Party ticket. His animosity toward Stewart, although sometimes reflected in letters to his wife, Ann, was generally subordinated to
his intense desire for a Union Party victory in November. In those Civil
War years, North's political priority was a loyal state. He made that clear
in writing of Stewart's partner, Alexander Baldwin, "He and Stewart
are at work for the party with all their might, and though they may do it
from base motives, they may carry enough base fellows with them to
save the State. Perhaps the success of such men may not prove as great a
calamity as the loss of Nevada to the Union cause, would be."[49]

As it turned out, North had little to fear. Although the Democrats
fielded a complete slate for the November 8 election, they were defeated
by the Union Republican Party, by a margin of about three votes to two.
Not only were Republicans elected to every state and national office, but
they also dominated both houses of the Nevada legislature, thus assuring
the selection of Republicans as the state's first two United States senators. One of numerous candidates for those seats, Stewart suggested that

the Comstock Union League be polled on their preference, with the results to be used as an instruction to the legislature. The Union League agreed and, according to Stewart, he received 3,640 of the 3,700 votes cast by League members.[50] Comstock newspapers also supported Stewart, with the exception of the *Union*. That paper admitted that Stewart was a successful lawyer, but attributed the fact to his peculiar talents in controlling judges and juries rather than to his intelligence. The writer charged that Stewart had a way of obtaining judicial decision in advance by keeping a set of standing witnesses and "complete arrangements for packing juries,"[51] and opined that it would be too bad for the people if he were elected.

As the meeting date for Nevada's first legislature approached, it was apparent even to North that Stewart would be selected to represent the state in the U.S. Senate. On December 11, he wrote his wife, "The Legislature meets tomorrow. I do not propose to go to Carson; and there is not the least probability of anything being done for me there. There is some opposition to Stewart and Nye; yet they are likely to go."[52] If there was opposition to Stewart, it vanished before the vote on December 15, when Stewart was selected on the first ballot. The second senatorial seat was more hotly contested, and a number of votes were taken before James W. Nye won victory over Charles DeLong and John Cradlebaugh, on December 16.[53] North could not resist a parting comment on what he considered a miscarriage of justice. He noted that Stewart and Nye were "the two most corrupt men in the State. But I am not in the least disappointed, nor do I fret over it."[54]

With his political ambitions in shambles, his financial difficulties increasing as his quartz mill curtailed operation, his continued bad health, and his wife's desire to leave Nevada all weighing upon him, it is small wonder that North wanted to put his Nevada experiences behind him. His conscience would not allow an escape, however, until he had cleared his name of the corruption and bribery charges which had been leveled against him. On December 6, 1864, the day after the new state judges took office, John North initiated slander suits against William Morris Stewart and the owners of the *Territorial Enterprise*.[55] He was the only one of the three territorial judges to seek such official redress.

North was clearly thinking about such a contingency as early as the middle of August, 1864, and his decision to resign from the bench was probably due in part to his desire to bring such suits.[56] However, when President Lincoln failed to name a replacement for him, North's attorney, Thomas H. Williams, advised him to wait until state judges were sworn in and he was out of office.[57] Thus North was forced to wait for Nevada statehood before bringing his charges.

As the suits dragged on through the spring and summer of 1865, pressure for North to settle out of court increased. In the late summer of 1865, the *Gold Hill Daily News,* one of Stewart's strongest supporters, became increasingly antagonistic. One article noted that Justices Turner and Locke, "like convicted felons retired and kept their heads shut," but North had sued Stewart and the *Territorial Enterprise* for $100,000 each. It concluded that:

> Judge North, if he knows what is best for him, had better drop the whole matter; he is opening an old sore that was very offensive to the public last year, and if it is opened by a judicial spear, and the matter allowed to permeate the air of Washoe, it will stink ten times worse than the public nostril ever smelt. Drop it, Judge; you will save what is left of your character.[58]

Besides the newspaper pressure, North believed that Stewart and Baldwin were preventing the sale of his quartz mill and trying to stop the flow of Comstock ore to the operation. Such tactics ultimately modified North's earlier resolve not to settle "unless Mr. Stewart does me justice," and when it was suggested that the suits be given to referees, he welcomed the opportunity for a shorter, quieter proceeding. He informed his wife, "Stewart and I have agreed to submit our differences to three men in Virginia. . . . I waive the question of damages — as my reputation is the thing I fight for."[59]

Opposition newspapers seized upon this move as a sign of weakness in North's position. In reporting that the case had been withdrawn from court and submitted to referees Tod Robinson, George F. Jones, and William H. Rhodes, the *Gold Hill Daily News* stated, "North evidently could not stand a public investigation in Court—and preferred moving it to some dark closet."[60] The move was at least as advantageous to Stewart, however. The latter, now a United States senator, had much more to lose from a public hearing than did North, who had already expressed his desire to leave Nevada. Stewart's personality was such that under normal circumstances he would have preferred a public forum. However, the possibility that North would win the suits made a trial too risky and probably triggered the offer to submit the case to referees.

The three referees handed down their decision on September 16, 1865, generally upholding North's position. They cleared the former judge of corruption charges, noting, "The evidence fails to show any act of corruption, on the part of the Plaintiff, and we therefore pronounce the character of John North free from each and every imputation cast upon it by the accusations of the Defendant Wm. H. Stewart." They also agreed, for the most part, with North's charges against Stewart:

The pleadings and evidence, are sufficient and we therefore find the Defendant Wm. M. Stewart, guilty of the slanderous charges, averred against him in the First, Second, Third, Sixth, and Seventh counts in the plaintiff's complaint. . . . The motives of John W. North, in the administration of his office of Judge as aforesaid were pure, and his conduct in the trial, argument and decision of cases before him blameless; but his conduct towards the Defendant Stewart, on one occasion; and his conduct in connection with Judge Locke's position, in the Chollar and Potosi litigation, in another, meet with the reprehension of the referees.[61]

In analyzing Stewart's motives, the referees distinguished between the published card of December 22, 1863, charging bribery and corruption, and the repetition of these accusations later that month at the county convention at Carson City, where North was a candidate for the gubernatorial nomination. It was the latter event, they held, which constituted slander against North, since they believed there were extenuating circumstances for Stewart's conduct prior to December 22, 1863. After that date, said the referees, the conduct of William M. Stewart was "wrong and unjustifiable."[62]

Despite this straightforward conclusion, the referee's decision was sufficiently qualified to enable Stewart supporters, by taking the pro-Stewart material out of context and ignoring the findings against Stewart, to make it appear that Stewart had not lost the case.[63] Essentially, the decision came too late to help North's political career in Nevada, or to hurt Stewart's. The latter was comfortably seated at Washington, D.C., as one of Nevada's senators. That fact, coupled with North's departure from the state, practically assured that, although the decision actually vindicated North, it was generally interpreted in Stewart's favor.[64]

Years later, in his autobiography, Stewart neatly sidestepped the issue and indicated that he considered the Union League senatorial ballot "a pretty good refutation of the criticisms of my opponents in the litigations during the four stormy years preceding. In fact I regarded it, and still regard it, as my vindication against all charges and insinuations that I adopted or countenanced any improper action in the great Comstock case."[65] To Stewart, the removal of the territorial judiciary, and with it the elimination of North as a political rival, only proved what his frontier experience had taught him, that what mattered was not philosophical or legal right or wrong, but only who was victorious.

CHAPTER 4

THE UNITED STATES SENATE: FIRST TERM ACHIEVEMENTS

WILLIAM MORRIS STEWART and James Warren Nye, Nevada's first U.S. senators, arrived in Washington, D.C., on February 1, 1865. They were sworn in on the same day, after which they drew lots to assign the two-year and the four-year terms allotted to Nevada. Stewart won the longer term.[1] The following day their two votes helped to pass the resolution to add the Thirteenth Amendment to the U.S. Constitution.[2]

Displaying none of the traditional reticence of a freshman senator, Stewart was soon actively involved in the deliberations. A newspaper reporter described him at the time:

> Perhaps none of the younger members of the Senate attract so much attention as Wm. M. Stewart of Nevada. He is 38 years old, a large and good-looking man, has a light complexion and a very long sandy beard and mustache . . . On the floor he is usually quiet and noticeable from his youthful appearance and heavy beard than otherwise. . . . He is a man of executive force and will and deserves much credit for raising from humble life to great wealth and an honorable fame in national councils.[3]

Stewart soon had an opportunity to join the Senate debate on one of his favorite topics, expansion of Nevada's boundaries. On February 8, a bill was introduced from the Committee on Territories, to add one degree of longitude to Nevada on the east at the expense of Utah Territory. Nevadans had recognized the possibility of such action by Congress and included a provision in the 1864 constitution that "whensoever" Congress should authorize such an addition, "the same shall thereupon be embraced within and become a part of this state."[4] Since some mineral development had occurred in the area in 1864, Stewart seized upon mining as the reason why Nevada, rather than Utah Territory, should have the land included in the bill. In a speech before the Senate, he claimed that Brigham Young was opposed to mining, while it was Nevada's main economic support. Under Utah Territory the area would not be developed and miners would not be protected; but under Nevada, he implied, substantial improvements would take place.[5] The bill was passed in the Senate, but the House failed to act on it during that session of Congress.

Stewart's activities during his first term centered on three major issues: mining legislation, Reconstruction policies, and the Fifteenth Amendment. His fight to aid the western mining industry started during his second week in the Senate, when, on February 10, 1865, he proposed the establishment of a new Committee on Mines and Mining.[6] Although action on his resolution was postponed, a similar measure introduced by Senator Anthony of Rhode Island on March 8, was approved. The first members of the new committee were John Conness of California, chairman, Zachariah Chandler of Michigan, Edwin D. Morgan of New York, William Fessenden of Maine, Charles R. Buckalew of Pennsylvania, James Guthrie of Kentucky, and Stewart.[7]

The arrival of Nevada's senators in Washington coincided with a developing congressional fight over disposal of the mineral lands of the United States. Stewart's seat on the new committee enabled him both to initiate and to influence mining legislation, a subject of considerable interest to his constituents. He now moved aggressively to support the cause of western miners, and his success in helping bring about the passage of the National Mining Law of 1866 marked the high point of his legislative career.

Ownership of mineral rights is a perennial question, and the answer has always affected the type and extent of mining activity in an area. Traditionally, both in Europe and colonial America, mineral rights were retained by the national government. In America this practice of reservation derived from English common law. The original grants to North American colonizing companies retained any gold that might be discovered for the Crown, and most colonies continued the reservation of mineral land when they became states. The Ordinance of 1785 in turn reserved for the federal government one-third of all gold, silver, lead, and copper mines. When the Constitution of 1787 took effect, the policy of reservation was continued; but it did not become a matter for legislation until after the Louisiana Purchase of 1803. That massive territorial addition, plus the discovery of copper in the Lake Superior region, led the national government to experiment with a different practice, although still holding to the basic tenet that minerals on the public lands belonged to the national government.[8]

Stewart during his first term in the United States Senate. *(Nevada Historical Society Photo)*

On March 3, 1807, Congress passed a measure which turned to a system developed in the Germanic states during the Middle Ages, that of leasing. The German properties were surveyed in the form of a square, including the area of the surface and the space below, bounded by vertical planes or surfaces parallel with the dip of the vein. Under the Act of 1807, the Lake Superior copper region was leased, with a royalty to the government of 6 percent of the mineral value extracted. The first leases were granted in 1822, and for the next twelve years the system expanded rapidly. It ultimately failed, however, mainly because of fraud and speculation. The legal end to the leasing system came after President Polk, in his message to Congress, December 2, 1845, recommended that the lands be sold, with the national government reserving a royalty. In answer to the request, Congress passed two acts on July 11, 1846, and March 3, 1847, opening the mineral lands of the Great Lakes region and the Mississippi for sale.

Within just a few years, Congress was forced to reexamine the question, when the Treaty of Guadalupe-Hidalgo, on February 2, 1848, added a sizable amount of territory to the western United States. Political events prevented congressional action in regard to the Mexican cession until the Compromise of 1850 was worked out, in September of that year, so the onrush of hundreds of thousands of gold seekers into the ceded area predictably led to chaos. The instability of the local governments was compounded by the sometimes heated question of legal title to the mines. Commodore Sloat, at Monterey, California, had declared Mexican law to be in effect in July, 1846, and General Kearney reiterated the point later. However, Colonel R. B. Mason, the military governor of California, abolished Mexican law in regard to the location of mines by decree. In effect, Mason's law meant that there was no law regulating the location of claims and no way of acquiring legal title to mining property, although it was quite clear that the United States had acquired ownership of the gold and other minerals on the former Mexican lands. Colonel Mason encouraged indiscriminate location when he stated, ''I am resolved not to interfere with [the miners], but to permit all to work freely.''[9] It was soon apparent, however, that the potential value of the California mineral lands to the national government would force some kind of regulation.

Shortly after President Polk announced the California gold discovery in his December 5, 1848, message to Congress, Senator Sidney Breese of Illinois introduced a bill to ''ascertain land titles in California and New Mexico,'' with the ultimate objective of sale of mineral land in two-acre lots with rectangular survey.[10] Opposition to the idea of sale came almost immediately from expansionist Senator Thomas Hart Benton of Missouri, who offered a substitute bill urging that the mines should be worked as freely as possible. He argued that orderly development, not revenue, should be the goal in controlling western mineral lands. Senator Benton's speech of January 15, 1849, oppposing Breese, probably marks the beginning of the theory of "free mining" in the United States.[11] After the introduction of the Benton measure, Breese's bill was recommitted to committee.

California's admission on September 9, 1850, brought additional pressure to force the national government to set some sort of policy concerning mining titles. Although only three weeks of the session remained when California's Senators Gwin and Frémont took their seats, the latter immediately introduced a number of measures dealing with mines and mining titles. One of these followed the idea of "free mining" enunciated earlier by Frémont's father-in-law, Senator Benton. During the debate over Frémont's bill, discussion centered on whether the land should be sold, leased for revenue, or simply left to the miner to develop as he pleased. Frémont's bill passed the Senate, but Congress adjourned before any action took place in the House.

When Congress failed to act in 1850, thousands of miners in California found themselves without legal means to establish and work mineral claims. In an *ad hoc* solution, they turned to squatter sovereignty, the basic philosophy behind the mining district which then developed.[12] Representing as they did many diverse nationalities, the California miners were able to draw precedents for their rules from numerous sources, particularly from ancient European codes brought in by the Mexicans and from English common law, which came to the gold fields with the Cornishmen and others. Although the exact place and time of the first miners' district meeting in California is unknown, by 1851 there had been enough activity along such lines to warrant adoption of a California law which declared that "in actions respecting 'Mining Claims,' proof shall be admitted of the customs, usages, or regulations established and in force at the bar, or diggings, embracing such claim; and such customs, usages, or regulations, when not in conflict with the Constitution and Laws of the State, shall govern the decision of the action."[13]

The proliferation of gold discoveries in California brought a similar burgeoning of mining districts, which resulted in a plethora of local rules and regulations. An attempt in the early 1850's to call an official state miners' meeting to formulate a statewide system of mining regulations failed. However, the use of the county convention to establish some kind of uniformity was more successful.[14] The most significant of these county meetings was the one held in Nevada County in December, 1852, in which Stewart had participated as chairman of the committee charged with designing rules for quartz claims.[15] The rules adopted at that assembly became a model for later mining district codes. They were spread throughout California and into Nevada as miners moved from one discovery to the next. One of the most important rules adopted at that gathering had a tremendous effect upon western mining,"Each proprietor of a quartz claim shall thereafter be entitled to one hundred feet on the quartz ledge or vein; and the discoverer shall be allowed one hundred feet additional. Each claim shall include all dips, angles and variations of the vein."[16]

By the time the Comstock Lode was discovered in January, 1859, the mining district, with its basic rules and regulations, had become a functional part of every new discovery in the path of the California miners. The Gold Hill Mining District, formed June 11, 1859,[17] was the first successful mining district on the eastern side of the Sierra Nevada. Its rules bore a marked resemblance to the earlier regulations adopted in Nevada County, California.

This lack of national regulation might have continued indefinitely if the increased expenses of the Civil War had not forced the national government to search for additional funds. The fabulous production of the Comstock Lode during the early 1860's naturally attracted congressional attention in that respect, and spawned a number of measures aimed at raising federal revenue from mining. The eastern press and public, stimulated by exaggerated stories of the Comstock's riches, saw congressional action as a means of gaining part of that wealth to help support the government.

On the other hand, mining companies on the Comstock, including the dominant, California-owned companies and their counsel Stewart, favored the "free mining" concept. They supported Senator Benton's argument that the nation would be well repaid "if the gold was put in circulation, without tax or royalty."[18] The threat of action by the Thirty-eighth Congress, which began in December, 1864, brought a resolution from the Nevada legislature. Read in the Senate on January 5, 1865, the resolution asked that body to take no action on any bill to tax mines until Nevada's representatives took their seats.[19] Upon arrival in the Senate, Stewart and Nye joined other western senators in preventing an increase of the tax on mines at that time.

The major attempt at mining regulation during that session was a bill introduced in the House of Representatives on February 2, 1865, by George W. Julian of Indiana, Chairman of the House Committee on

Public Lands. The Julian bill provided for the subdivision and sale of gold and silver lands of the United States. Julian argued that such a measure would have many advantages. Besides providing substantial revenue for the national government, it would bring stability to the mining industry by changing its short-lived, migratory character. Ownership of mining lands would also promote the investment of capital. The Julian Bill did not reach the Senate during the session, but it did promote discussion of the problem, particularly in the west. A number of other bills or resolutions to encourage mining were introduced in Congress during the session, but most were not passed.[20]

The important mining legislation that did come from this Congress was part of a measure to provide federal courts for Nevada. The "Courts Bill" was introduced in the House of Representatives by Henry G. Worthington of Nevada, in January of 1865. When the Senate added amendments, a conference committee was requested. Both Stewart and Worthington were members of the conference committee which approved an amendment offered by Senators Conness of California and Johnson of Maryland, recognizing that individuals had possessory rights in mining property.[21] This stipulation was incorporated in the "Courts Bill" as section nine and passed into law on February 27, 1865.

A few months later the concept of possessory rights in mining property was tested in the U.S. Supreme Court. The case had originated some years earlier, when Erasmus Sparrow brought action in the Territorial District Court of Storey County, Nevada, to recover an interest in a mining claim. Stewart, Kirkpatrick, and Rising were attorneys for the defendant, Charles L. Strong. The district court's decision in favor of Strong was upheld by the Territorial Supreme Court (Justices Mott and Turner) on March 16, 1863. The case was taken from the Nevada Territorial Supreme Court to the United States Supreme Court on a writ of error.

In a December, 1865, opinion written by Chief Justice Salmon P. Chase, the U.S. Supreme Court upheld the defendant, Strong, and generally sustained the points made by Stewart in the original suit. Chase noted that the laws of Nevada Territory recognized the validity and binding force of the rules, regulations and customs of mining districts and pointed out that vast western mining interests had grown up "not only without interference by the National Government, but under its implied sanction."[22] In addition, Chase incorporated in his opinion an open letter from Stewart to Senator Ramsay of Minnesota, explaining the idea of mining rights.

That lengthy letter extolled in glowing terms the development of the mining district meeting and the rules and regulations which emanated from it, and recounted how these had become part of the common law. Stewart wrote, "The miner's law is part of the miner's nature; he made it and he loves it, trusts it, and obeys it. . . . Persons who have not given this subject special attention can hardly realize the wonderful results of this system of free mining." According to Stewart, it had promoted development and transformed the desert into "great gold and silver fields." In the face of such success Stewart thought it absurd to extend the preemption system to the mines and argued instead that the federal government should recognize local rules of mining districts.[23] The inclusion of Stewart's letter to Ramsay as part of a U.S. Supreme Court decision added immeasurably to his reputation as an authority on mining regulations and law.

The Thirty-ninth Congress, which began its first session in December, 1865, was responsible for a number of laws concerning western mines; the most important of these became known as the National Mining Law of 1866.[24] As the session opened, many of the bills that were proposed provided for some kind of lease or sale by the national government. That the law that was enacted did not concern itself with revenue, but turned to "free mining" instead, was a tribute to the fight waged by representatives from the western mining states, particularly those from Nevada and California. In final analysis, the congressional debate became a contest between Representative Julian, supporting the sale of the mineral lands for revenue and for security of title, and Senator Stewart, favoring the concept of "free mining." Thus, a House-Senate confrontation was inevitable.

Activity in the House of Representatives began on December 13, 1865, when Julian reintroduced his bill of the previous session calling for the sale of mineral lands. The proposal was referred to the Committee on Public Lands, which he chaired, since the House Committee on Mines and Mining was not established until December 19. Although no positive action on the Julian bill was taken, it was apparent that any mining plan that did not include the sale of mineral lands for revenue would meet with strong objection from the congressman.[25]

The issue of regulation of mineral lands arose in the Senate somewhat later, when, on April 9, John Sherman introduced a bill written by the Treasury Department, to regulate the occupation of mineral lands. It provided that such areas were to be surveyed into legal subdivisions and sold to the highest bidder. The bill was referred to the Committee on Mines and Mining, where it met a cool reception and Senators Conness and Stewart were appointed to draft a substitute. Although Stewart generally has been credited with authoring the mining measure which emerged from the Senate, Conness may have played a more important role than is usually assigned him.[26] Whatever Stewart's part in the authorship of the document, there is no doubt that the success in passing it was due to his leadership. The legislative history of the bill provides an interesting demonstration of the resourcefulness of the senator from Nevada.

The substitute Conness-Stewart bill was reported from the Mines and Mining committee on May 26, with Conness providing a written argument for the committee's draft. Senate debate began on June 18, with a major speech by Stewart. The committee bill struck out all of the original Sherman version and substituted language which endorsed the idea of "free mining" and the right to follow the vein "with its dips, angles and variations to any depth." It also included a procedure to patent mining claims at a price of $5.00 per acre, while agricultural lands were to be set apart and opened to settlement. The measure was debated extensively in the Senate, with Williams of Oregon offering a number of objections.[27] However, the bill passed the Senate on June 28, 1866, with a new title, "A bill to legalize the occupation of mineral lands and to extend the right of preemption thereto."[28] It was sent to the House on the same day, but instead of being referred to the Committee on Mines and Mining, it went to Julian's Committee on Public Lands. Stewart was unable to convince Julian to release the measure to the mines committee, and it appeared to be hopelessly stalled for that session of Congress.[29]

Only temporarily thwarted, Stewart and others saw an opportunity to defeat Julian by tacking their bill on as an amendment to a measure that had already passed the House. The bill in question was one sponsored by Higby of California, which dealt with the right-of-way for ditches and canals over public lands. The only relationship it bore to the Stewart-Conness measure was the fact that they both concerned public lands, but the brevity of the canal proposition made it relatively easy to add the entire mining bill to it. This procedure was made even easier by the fact that Stewart was a member of the Senate Public Lands Committee to which the measure had been referred. The amended canal bill was returned to the House on July 21, where Julian made strong efforts to have it referred to his Public Lands Committee. Debate as to which committee should get the bill was short, but acrimonious, resulting at one point in Julian's being called to order for "making reflections on the Senate." The Stewart-Conness forces won the argument and the House passed the bill July 26, 1866. Shortly thereafter the President signed the first national mining law, under the somewhat unusual title "Act granting the right of way to ditch and canal owners."[30]

The 1866 law has been called the miners' Magna Carta, "since it legalized what under ordinary circumstances would have been a trespass."[31] The act gave legal status to local mining district regulations that were initially based on squatter sovereignty, and recognized the principle of "free mining," which had been advocated by western mining interests since 1850.[32] The law obviously aided mining companies, for it made public land available without charge.[33] Little wonder, then, that Nevada newspapers hailed Stewart as the great benefactor of western mining. Many Nevadans and others shared the opinion of Charles C. Goodwin, who later wrote of his friend Stewart's part in the 1866 law, "For that service he is entitled to the gratitude of every mining man in the Nation."[34]

Almost simultaneously with the passage of the national mining law, Congress enacted another measure affecting Nevada's mining industry. On July 25, without debate, Congress granted to Adolph Sutro by special legislation the right-of-way and other privileges to aid in the construction of a tunnel to the Comstock Lode.[35] The bill was introduced by Senator Nye of Nevada. Although Stewart was president of the Sutro Tunnel Company, he urged passage of the act, which gave the company the right to buy any mineral lands within two thousand feet on either side of the tunnel at $5.00 an acre. The Comstock Lode and any other mining claims already filed and occupied were excepted from this right, and the measure included a provision that the mines to be served by the tunnel had to pay royalties for its use.

Although this mining legislation was significant, its importance was overshadowed by July, 1866, as Congress engaged in a serious confrontation with President Johnson over Civil War Reconstruction and related problems. Stewart's role in these debates was as active, if not so successful, as his role in helping to bring about national mining legislation. His position on Reconstruction policy flowed with the tide of Republican Party politics, influenced at first by a pro-Southern bias and later by a strong anti-Johnson feeling, which was strengthened by pressure from the Radical Republicans.

Stewart's Southern sympathies, influenced greatly by his marriage to Annie Foote, had been evident in his early political career in California. He continued to support the Southern position during his first year on the Comstock, voting for Breckenridge in the 1860 presidential election. However, he entered the Senate in February, 1865, as a Republican supporter of Lincoln. Lincoln's assassination precluded the development of any political arrangement between the two men, but in his autobiography Stewart gives his relationship with Lincoln a rather prominent part.

According to Stewart, he visited the White House on more than one occasion, being invited by Lincoln to sit on the stand next to General Grant while the latter's army was being reviewed, shortly before Lee's surrender at Appomattox.[36] Stewart also related that on the evening of April 14, 1865, he and an old friend from California, Judge Niles Searles, visited the White House so that Searles could meet the President. Lincoln was unable to see the two men, but sent a card which read: "I am engaged to go to the theater with Mrs. Lincoln. It is the kind of an engagement I never break. Come with your friend to-morrow at ten and I shall be glad to see you. A. Lincoln." According to Stewart:

> Those were the last words Abraham Lincoln ever wrote. I did not preserve the card, not considering it of any importance, for I had received many such from the President at various times. . . . on our way out, I dropped the President's note on the floor. At the front entrance Mr. Lincoln was placing his wife in a carriage. I was intending to pass without interrupting them, but he saw us and extended his hand cordially. I introduced Judge Searles to him. . . . It was the last time I saw him alive.[37]

After taking Searles to the train, Stewart went to Ford's Theatre, but could not get in because of the crowd. He went instead to visit Senator Conness of California, where he was later joined by Senator Sumner of Massachusetts. The three men were interrupted by a servant, who reported that Secretary Seward had been assassinated. They rushed to Seward's lodging place to find that he indeed had been shot, and was not permitted to see visitors. From there they went to the White House, where they heard of Lincoln's assassination, and then to Ford's Theatre and the house where the President had been carried. Sumner was the only one of the three who entered the President's room; Stewart walked the streets until shortly after daylight.

When news of Lincoln's death reached him, he was talking with Senator Foot of Vermont, chairman of the Republican caucus and master of ceremonies in the Senate. Foot suggested that they get the chief justice at once and have him administer the oath of office to the vice-president. They went to the home of Justice Chase and alerted him, and the three men then journeyed to the Kirkwood House, where Johnson was staying. Stewart's account of the episode in his memoirs was highly critical of Johnson, who was in his bare feet when the three men entered: "He was dirty, shabby, and his hair was matted, as though with mud from the gutter, while he blinked at us through squinting eyes, and lurched around unsteadily. He had been on a 'bender' for a month."[38] In his memoirs, Stewart also insisted, "There were only three persons present besides Johnson when he was sworn in—Chief Justice Chase, Senator Foot, and myself. All statements to the contrary are absolutely false."[39]

However, Stewart's reminiscent account, written when he was an old man, varies considerably from reports of others who witnessed the swearing-in ceremony, and even from earlier accounts by Stewart himself. In 1888, writing to his old friend, former Senator Conness, and recapitulating the events following Lincoln's assassination, Stewart mentioned nothing about Johnson's physical appearance or about his being drunk.[40] Accounts by Chief Justice Chase and Hugh McCulloch, Lincoln's secretary of the treasury, differ sharply from Stewart's later version, both as to Johnson's alleged drunkenness and about other people being present.[41] Stewart may have been one of the "two or three senators" mentioned by McCulloch as observers when Johnson took the presidential oath, but evidence indicates that there were more persons present than the four indicated by Stewart and that Johnson, far from being drunk, was sober and restrained.[42]

In spite of Stewart's later, rather bitter denunciation of Johnson, his early relations with the President were quite friendly and his position on Reconstruction was moderate. In a Senate speech on December 21, 1865, Stewart supported Johnson's policy regarding the return of Confederate states to the Union.[43] It is quite clear from that speech and others made shortly thereafter that Stewart was not a Radical Republican, but his position was not unchallenged for long.

During the debate over the Freedmen's Bureau Bill, Senator Wade of Ohio charged that Stewart's sympathies were with the Southern white people. On January 18, 1866, Stewart answered Wade in an interesting speech that did little to assuage the feelings of Wade and other Radicals. He admitted that his sympathies were with Southern white women and children just as he had sympathy for Northern white women and children, "I have sympathy for erring humanity always, on all occasions." He went on to suggest that the repatriation of the Confederate states should take priority over the question of Negro suffrage, a position that was in basic agreement with Johnson's plan, but contrary to the Radical Republican position that the guarantee of black civil rights should precede the settlement of all other questions. Stewart argued that the war gave the Negroes freedom, but did not guarantee immediate suffrage. Black voting rights might come ultimately, but Stewart did not press for them:

> I believe the Anglo-Saxon race can govern this country. I believe it because it has governed it. I believe it because it is the only race that has ever

founded such institutions as ours. . . . I believe the white man can govern it
without the aid of the negro; and I do not believe that it is necessary for the
white man that the negro should vote. I am for the Union without negro
suffrage, but I am not in favor of turning the negro over to oppression in
the South.[44]

Stewart's position in the January debate differed somewhat from an
earlier speech made at Dayton, Nevada. There he told the audience that
he had a prejudice against the Negro race, "but if it were necessary for
loyal men in the South to have the Negro vote to secure the election of
Union men, he was ready and willing to give it to them . . . a loyal Negro
had a better right to vote than a disloyal white man."[45]

Throughout January and February, Stewart continued his support of
Johnson's Reconstruction plan. In a speech on January 26, 1866, he
favored restoring those Confederate states ready to reenter the Union,[46]
and on February 20, 1866, he voted to sustain Johnson's veto of the
Freedmen's Bureau Bill.[47] In Senate speeches on February 28, and
March 1, he opposed a congressional resolution that the rebellious states
could not be readmitted until Congress declared them entitled to representation.[48]

Stewart's support of Johnson was contrary to Radical Republican
policy and to the views of important Nevada constituents. As political
pressure on him increased, Stewart sought some way to extricate himself
from his dilemma. On March 16, 1866, he submitted a proposal of his
own, a series of resolutions based on universal suffrage and amnesty.
The plan covered four points. First, the seceded states could have their
congressional representation immediately restored by amending their
constitutions to do away with racial discrimination in civil rights or suffrage, repudiating the rebel debt, and renouncing all claims to compensation for emancipated slaves. Second, general amnesty would be proclaimed after ratification of these conditions by a popular vote. Third,
the non-Confederate states would also incorporate such provisions in
their constitutions; and finally, these conditions were to be regarded not
as coercion but as an understanding.[49]

There was noticeable excitement in the Senate after Stewart concluded the explanation of his resolutions. For more than a week after the
plan was suggested it received "wide and enthusiastic" support, which
included both senators from Massachusetts, most of the Senate moderates, Southerners such as Alexander Stevens and Henry Foote, editor
Horace Greeley of the *New York Tribune,* and President Johnson.[50]
Stewart's proposals, wrote a historian some years later, "constituted
the most dramatic proposal so far and occasioned considerable stir."[51]

Others have indicated that it "was the best plan offered on the Reconstruction issue,"[52] a proposal capable of "ending the suspense and re-
moving all the difficulties to resumption."[53]

In spite of such widespread acclaim for the plan, it did not survive
Johnson's veto of the Civil Rights Bill on March 27, 1866. After that,
any moderate approach to Reconstruction was doomed. On April 4,
despairing of any legislative action on his proposals, Stewart suggested
a constitutional amendment embodying his ideas. He was brushed rather
rudely aside by Senator Trumbull and others, who could not wait for the
opportunity to overturn the President's veto.[54] On April 16, in one last
effort to save his plan, Stewart appeared before the Joint Committee on
Reconstruction to plead his case, but the committee took no action.[55] As
a later commentator remarked of the failure, "The name of William M.
Stewart—despite the bright promise of an hour—now brings no echoes
down the corridors of history."[56]

Senate Radicals immediately challenged the President's veto by
attempting to win moderates to their side. Pointed speeches by a number
of Radical senators began to influence Stewart. The first indication that
he had joined their ranks came with the successful attempt to unseat
Senator John P. Stockton, Democrat from New Jersey. Certain questions
had arisen about the election of Stockton; and although ordinarily the
Senate would have ignored them and seated him, when the Radicals
were forewarned of Johnson's veto they moved against Stockton.[57]
Stewart earlier had supported the seating of Stockton, but now succumbed to Radical pressure to absent himself from the Senate during
the final vote.[58] Stewart's defection was noted at the time by Secretary
of the Navy Gideon Welles, who wrote on April 5, 1866, "Stewart of
Nevada has persuaded himself that it is best to desert and go with the
majority."[59] When the vote to override the Civil Rights veto came in the
Senate on April 6, both Stewart and Nye voted against the President.[60]
Stewart later justified his vote by arguing that Johnson had promised
him, when he voted to sustain the Freedmen's Act veto, that he would
not veto the Civil Rights Bill. Stewart was quite specific on this point,
"He [Johnson] assured me by all that he held sacred that if his veto of the
Freedmen's Bureau Bill was sustained he would sign the Civil Rights
Bill."[61] Stewart never forgave Johnson for what he maintained was a
breach of faith on the President's part, and besides voting to override the
veto he took many occasions later to ridicule him.

Stewart's vote on the Civil Rights Bill veto was simply a recognition
of political reality, however, and not an immediate change in philosophy. He continued to argue in Senate speeches that Congress should

develop its own plan of reconstruction before it threw out all of the President's, and was chided for his efforts by Senator Howe of Wisconsin, who accused him of trying to play both sides.[62] Near the end of May Stewart acknowledged in a Senate speech that he would support a congressional plan if it were better than the President's, even if it omitted amnesty and suffrage. In a statement that could well have served as his personal creed, Stewart noted, "I have always advocated the necessity of taking the world as we find it, and following the logic of events."[63]

That logic ultimately led him to reverse his position on Negro suffrage. Stewart now insisted that the black man had either to be destroyed or trusted with his own political and civil rights. He contended that "the Negro must have the ballot or have no friends; and being poor and friendless, surrounded as he is by enemies, his fate is extermination." But, said Stewart, if the Negro were given the vote he would have lots of friends, "for the people of the United States love votes and office more than they hate negroes."[64] Such remarks brought more pointed statements by Senate Radicals, and on June 5, 1866, Stewart stated in the Senate that he would vote for the plan agreed upon "among my political friends [Radicals]," since the proposal, although it was not what he wanted, was better than expected and he was certain that both amnesty and Negro suffrage would follow.[65]

On another issue associated with the Reconstruction fight, the impeachment trial of President Johnson, Stewart also supported the Radicals.[66] When the vote was taken in the Senate, May 26, 1868, Stewart supported each of the articles, later justifying his action in his autobiography:

> The world will never know the extent of the misfortune to the people of the United States, particularly to the South, sustained by the substitution of Andrew Johnson for Abraham Lincoln. Lincoln was the wisest, kindest, most impartial, and just man I ever knew; Johnson was the most untruthful, treacherous, and cruel person who ever held place of power in the United States. I voted to impeach him, and I would do it again.[67]

As the 1868 elections approached, Stewart confirmed that he would stand again for the U.S. Senate. He also announced that, due to the crucial nature of his work in Congress on the issue of Reconstruction, his campaign in Nevada would be handled by A. P. K. Safford, a longtime friend and political supporter. After this announcement there were isolated articles in the Nevada newspapers concerning his candidacy, but certainly not the widespread interest that might have been expected in view of Stewart's accomplishments during his first four years in the Senate.[68]

For a time it appeared that Charles DeLong, who had lost close contests with Senator Nye in 1864 and 1867, would announce against Stewart. The *Carson Appeal* thought that DeLong might well beat Stewart.[69] However, just before an August 22 Union Republican meeting in Carson City, DeLong withdrew as a possible senatorial candidate, "in the interest of party harmony."[70] It is unlikely to have been coincidental that DeLong was later named minister to Japan, receiving strong support from Senator Stewart.

Stewart returned to Nevada to take charge of his campaign during the last weeks before the November election. The Republican ticket won the solid support of the voters on November 3, thus assuring the choice of a Republican when the state legislature met in January, 1869, to select a U.S. senator. At a Republican Party senatorial caucus, held before the legislature convened, Stewart was chosen for the United States Senate. It was the first such party caucus held in Nevada, and both the choice and the method of nomination received criticism from the editor of the *Gold Hill Daily News*:

> At present it certainly looks as if Senator Stewart had it all his own way — and we shall not feel aggrieved if he is reelected. We bear him no ill will personally or politically — but he is not our choice for the position, nor is he the choice of a vast number of staunch and true Republicans we know of; nor do we consider him the most worthy and competent man in the ranks of the party. . . . But why hold a caucus when but one candidate is named? Is it to introduce for the first time in this State an arbitrary party custom?[71]

On January 12 the Nevada legislature made its choice for the United States Senate. Meeting separately, as required by law, the Senate gave 15 votes to Stewart and 5 votes to Democrat Thomas H. Williams. The Assembly gave 34 votes to Stewart, 4 to Williams, and 1 to C. B. Whitman. The legislature then met in joint session on January 13 and ratified the choice.[72]

When Congress convened after the election it was ready to deal with the question of a constitutional guarantee for Negro suffrage. The issue had not arisen in the 1868 presidential campaign, due partly to the equivocal action of the Republican Party. In their platform that year the Republicans were willing to endorse Negro suffrage for the South, but suggested that in the North the question should be determined by each state. The Democrats, not surprisingly, insisted that control of suffrage belonged to the several states. The real drive for a protective Negro suffrage amendment came when the Radicals realized that their control of Reconstruction would be lost without such a provision, and that protection of the Negro vote in Northern states was important to continued Republican control of such states.[73]

In the congressional fight for the amendment, those in favor of Negro suffrage were hampered by disagreement as to the form any revision should take. The tortuous progress of the numerous proposals that came forward after the Civil War reveals that many different individuals were involved in the successful passage of the final version.[74] The germ of the Fifteenth Amendment evidently came from a meeting of the Joint Committee on Reconstruction, January 20, 1866. At that time a plan was discussed to amend the Constitution so as to deprive the states of the power to disqualify residents politically on the basis of race or color. The committee had two proposals before it. Senator Fessenden of Maine proposed that "all provisions in the Constitution or laws of any State whereby any distinction is made in political . . . rights or privileges on account of race . . . or color shall be inoperative and void." Representative James G. Blaine suggested instead that states which excluded persons from voting because of race or color should be penalized in determining their total representation in Congress. The Joint Committee initially disregarded the Fessenden suggestion, although it contained the basic idea finally adopted in the Fifteenth Amendment. In March, Senator John B. Henderson of Missouri introduced a measure embodying the Fessenden idea. Aware that the measure would not win support at the time, Henderson remarked before the Senate, "Let them vote it down. It will not be five years from today before this body will vote for it. You cannot get along without it."[75] The wait was not that long. The 1868 elections convinced Northern Republicans that they had to give up their objections to a constitutional guarantee of Negro suffrage.[76]

Evidence of the new interest in affirming black voting rights came when eleven proposals calling for some such protection were introduced in the first session of Congress following the 1868 elections. The majority of these, particularly the ones authored by Boutwell in the House and Henderson in the Senate, insisted that the rights of citizens of the United States to vote and to hold office should not be denied or abridged on account of race, color, or previous condition of servitude.

Stewart entered the action when the Senate Judiciary Committee, on motion of Roscoe Conkling, charged him to review the various Senate and House proposals and to draft a new amendment. Before doing so he asked U. S. Grant and a number of state delegations for advice. His suggestion was basically the original Henderson proposal, with the words "by the United States, or any State" inserted after the phrase "shall not be denied or abridged."[77] The Judiciary Committee approved Stewart's recommendation, with Senator Trumbull in opposition and Senators Hendricks and Freylinghausen absent. Acting for the Judiciary Committee, Stewart reported the modifications to the full Senate on January 15,1869. That body first considered the Boutwell proposal, which had been approved by the House and forwarded. The enormous difficulties of agreeing upon the exact wording of a suffrage amendment were demonstrated by the six days of Senate debate over the House bill, during which there were thirty different propositions advanced, seventeen amendments suggested, and twenty-four roll call votes taken. The House concept finally was rejected, and the Senate returned to the Stewart version, but passage was not immediate.[78]

One of the most serious objections to the Stewart proposal was the obvious loophole that allowed states to prevent suffrage by tests other than race, color, or previous condition of servitude. A number of amendments were offered in each house to correct that deficiency, but none was successful in passing both bodies. The impasse brought a demand for a conference committee, to which were appointed Stewart, Conkling, and Edmunds from the Senate, along with Boutwell, Logan, and Bingham from the House. The conference committee arrived at a compromise version, with the words "to hold office" struck out. This wording was then accepted by the House, 145 to 44, and in the Senate by a vote of 39 to 13, on February 26, 1869.[79] There was some bitterness towards Stewart and Conkling for agreeing to eliminate "to hold office" and Edmunds refused to sign the conference report because of that change.[80] However, the Radicals recognized the necessity of accepting the resolution as better than nothing and easily mustered the two-thirds majority necessary to win the approval of both houses.

In addition to his work in phrasing the proposal, Stewart's participation in the debates and his excellent work as floor manager for the bill in the Senate were key ingredients in the final success of the measure.[81] Throughout the course of the debates on the Fifteenth Amendment he maintained a moderate posture, realizing astutely that only such a measure had an opportunity to pass. He was correct in his judgment of the political winds, as the Radicals eventually accepted the reality of the situation.[82]

Stewart was instrumental, also, in obtaining ratification of the Fifteenth Amendment by Nevada, which was the only far western state to do so. He sent two telegrams to the Nevada legislature, the first alerting that body to passage of the act by Congress and the second emphasizing that President-elect U. S. Grant strongly supported ratification.[83] Apparently, the party pressure exerted by Republicans in the Nevada legislature was also Stewart's work. Curtis Hillyer, an assemblyman from Storey County and a good friend of Stewart's, warned members of the assembly that the national Republican organization would forsake Nevada Republicans, with a possible loss of federal patronage, if Nevada failed to ratify the amendment. When opposition developed because some feared the Chinese would benefit from passage of the amendment, Stewart sent a telegram to another old friend and law partner, Federal Judge Alexander W. Baldwin, explaining that the word "nativity" had been struck from one of the early versions of the Negro suffrage resolution specifically in order to exclude the Chinese.[84] Evidently convinced, the Nevada legislature approved the Fifteenth Amendment on March 1, 1869, by a vote of 23 to 16 in the assembly and 14 to 6 in the senate.[85]

The lame duck congressional session which adjourned on March 4, 1869, marked the end of Stewart's abbreviated first term in the United States Senate. From the standpoint of legislative efficacy, the years had been fruitful ones. Authorship of the National Mining Act of 1866 and of the final draft of the Fifteenth Amendment resolution were accomplishments of some magnitude. Important to Nevada and the mining west was his work in helping to establish the Carson City mint. Stewart was instrumental in gaining a congressional appropriation for this mint, which struck its first coin on January 8, 1870.[86] Mine owners could now ship their bullion directly to Carson City, eliminating the more costly haul to San Francisco.

Not so flattering to his reputation were the connections he had made with officials of the Central Pacific Railroad. Although he had opposed state appropriation for the building of a Pacific railroad during the 1863 constitutional convention, he quickly became tied to the interests of the Central Pacific as a senator. His close relationship with Collis P. Huntington and the railroad was originally cemented when Charles Crocker presented him with two hundred shares of railroad stock in 1866.[87] In that year Stewart worked particularly hard on behalf of the railroad in the Senate, helping to amend the original acts, which limited the Central Pacific to a one-hundred-and-fifty-mile penetration into Nevada. By terms of the 1866 act, the railroad was allowed to proceed eastward across Nevada to meet the Union Pacific at a point to be agreed upon later by officials of the two lines.[88] On May 17, 1869, just one week after the meeting of the two railroads at Promontory, Utah, Huntington wrote Crocker to suggest some means of showing their appreciation:

Stewart leaves here this week for California and you must see him and let him into some good things in and about San Francisco and Oakland. He has always stood by us. He is peculiar, but thoroughly honest, and will bear no dictation, but I know he must live, and we must fix it so that he can make one or two hundred thousand dollars. It is to our interest and I think his right.[89]

That suggestion was acted upon sometime later, when Huntington wrote Leland Stanford, "I have agreed, with your consent, that the Southern Pacific Railroad Company will give William M. Stewart fifty thousand acres of land of the average quality of the lands along the line of the road, say on the first two hundred miles. He will select some person to whom the land is to be conveyed.[90] Stewart also received other favors from the railroad, as evidenced by a letter from Huntington to Mark Hopkins, "I shall telegraph Crocker today to have sleeping car at Ogden for Senator Stewart and Judge Field. They were in the office yesterday and to-day. Stewart did not care much about it, but it will please Field very much. Stewart is a *trump* and *no mistake*."[91] Stewart's "railroad connection," made during his first term in the U.S. Senate, continued to be a major factor throughout his political career.

An interesting sidelight of Stewart's first Senate term was his relationship with Mark Twain. At the time, Stewart was living alone in a Washington rooming house while his family traveled in Europe. According to the senator, Twain showed up one day looking for a place to stay while he completed a book about the Holy Land. Stewart agreed to hire Twain as his clerk and told him there was "a little hall bedroom across the way where you can sleep, and you can write your book in here. Help yourself to the whiskey and cigars, and wade in."[92] For his part, Twain maintained that Stewart had offered him the clerical job sometime earlier, while Twain was traveling in Europe, and that his employment was meant to enhance the prestige of the senator's office.[93] Whatever the facts, the relationship did not last, and after a few months, Stewart asked Twain to leave. According to the senator, Twain usurped his living room and was much too liberal in the use of his whiskey and cigars. He also antagonized the owner of the rooming house, a Miss Virginia Wells, to the point that she decreed they would both have to leave unless Stewart ordered Twain out. When confronted with Stewart's edict to reform or depart, Twain chose the latter, but he retaliated later when he wrote that the senator had cheated him out of mining stock.[94] As one writer subsequently noted, it was a "strange relationship," but the two men did share certain traits: "an intense dislike for practical jokes when the target was themselves and the inability to set down the truth in their autobiographies."[95]

CHAPTER 5

SECOND-TERM PROBLEMS

STEWART'S next Senate term, from 1869 to 1875, was not nearly so productive as his first. Nonetheless, his activities in and out of Congress during these years were central to his later political career, for they involved him in a major mining scandal and in the aftermath of the passage of the Mint Act, the so-called Crime of 1873.

Stewart seldom took a leadership role during these years, but he adroitly managed to protect the interests of himself and his constituents. When a joint resolution to assist the Union Pacific Railroad came before the Senate, Stewart moved against such aid, insisting that the interests of the nation were being jeopardized by the activities of the Credit Mobilier.[1] Although the purity of his motives in speaking against the Union Pacific might be questioned because of his close ties with the Central Pacific, his analysis of the Credit Mobilier was borne out in the later scandal.

The first session also gave Stewart an opportunity to place himself on record against Chinese naturalization, for the benefit of his Nevada constituency. The occasion arose when Charles Sumner of Massachusetts introduced and pushed strongly for the passage of a bill to naturalize the Chinese in the United States. When Stewart opposed the proposition, Sumner pointed out that Stewart's antagonism was inconsistent with the provisions of the Fifteenth Amendment, which Stewart had written. Stewart denied this and argued that his opposition was based on the fundamental religious differences between the Chinese and citizens of the United States, noting that pagans had no concept of a Christian oath.[2]

Except for random speeches on other matters, Stewart's major legislative concern after 1869, as it had been earlier, was mining. The 1866 National Mining Law had exhibited a number of deficiencies in operation which Stewart attempted to correct in a bill he introduced in 1870. Criticism was leveled at the bill almost immediately because it did not give sufficient protection to the Sutro Tunnel right-of-way. When it was suggested that he provide such shielding in his bill, Stewart objected strongly, saying he was unalterably against Sutro and his tunnel and had no intention of sponsoring any more legislation for him: "I am opposed to any more legislation about Sutro: for him or against him, I am opposed to any more of that humbug one way or another. It is a mere advertisement for Sutro. . . . He seems to have been tunneling Congress and not the mines. He never will make his tunnel."[3]

It was a rather remarkable outburst from the first president of the Sutro Tunnel Company, but it indicated a profound change in loyalties. Stewart was now following the lead of the Bank Crowd, who feared that completion of the Sutro Tunnel might deprive them of control of the Comstock Lode. By 1870, the monopoly established by the Bank of California had a firm hold on Comstock mining production. It was now threatened by Sutro's plan to build a new town at the mouth of the tunnel. Sutro boasted that this community, which he proposed to name after himself, would switch control of the Comstock Lode from Virginia City and Gold Hill. The threat was enough to turn the Bank Crowd from its earlier support to intense opposition. As beneficiary of their political influence, Stewart represented their views in Congress. In a later discussion of the issue, Stewart embellished on his earlier condemnation of Sutro and his tunnel:

> I have told the Senate what the Sutro tunnel is and I give notice that it is going to take, with rapid progress, fifteen years; with ordinary progress thirty years; and with Sutro's progress, one hundred and fifty years . . . I have given notice to those who own stock in New York, Boston, or elsewhere in these great mines, that they need not apprehend any danger from Sutro: that his boring is in Congress, and not in the rock. He bores Congress, and there is where he tunnels . . . He has bored me for the last five years.[4]

Stewart's stubborn opposition to Sutro caused the Senate to turn from his proposed legislation to a similar measure which had passed the House of Representatives, introduced by Aaron Sargent of California. With his own bill pushed aside because of his own failure to compromise, Stewart bowed to the political realities of the situation and accepted the task of guiding the Sargent Bill through the Senate, where it was passed with amendments on June 14, 1870.[5]

The most important provision of the 1870 act opened placer claims to the same type of entry that had been granted to lode claims by the 1866 law. In explaining the law in the Senate, Stewart suggested that the bill's aim was to reward the miner who had failed by giving him an opportunity to obtain title in fee simple in order to put his claim to agricultural use. He added that when the lands were exhausted for mineral purposes, the miners on the properties should be allowed to obtain homes and titles.[6] Under the 1870 law, no placer claim could exceed 160 acres total, but it could be taken in 40-acre plots, which in turn could be subdivided into 10-acre tracts, at a price of only $2.50 an acre.[7] Stewart was the first to suggest that the 1870 amendment, far from being a measure to promote placer mining, was in fact a relief bill to aid the miner who had failed at mining.[8]

A more important amendment to the National Mining Law of 1866 was passed in 1872. Like the 1870 measure, it was written by Aaron Sargent of California and managed in the Senate by William Stewart.[9] The 1872 revision sought to erase some of the weaknesses of the 1866 act and to check efforts by federal and state supreme courts to limit the vein provision of the 1866 act. In doing this the 1872 act aimed to bring some uniformity to local mining codes by specifying what information the local records should contain, the annual work necessary to hold a claim, and the method for marking claims. The 1866 law had neglected to require such data, creating thereby a mass of confusion. However, Congress failed to remedy a major flaw of the earlier act and provide proper safeguards aganst loss of or tampering with local records. Although correcting some weaknesses in the original mining law, the 1872 version also took a step in the wrong direction. It "introduced a new speculative element into quartz claiming and proved a prolific cause of litigation."[10] Under the new act, the miner was to locate the surface boundaries of his claim in such a way as to include the top or "apex" of the vein. If successful in doing so, the locator could then follow the vein as it went downward from the surface, through the side limits, but not the end limits, of his rectangular claim. If the miner guessed wrong and failed to include the apex in his boundaries, then he lost the right to follow the ledge downward. As a consequence of this provision, millions of dollars were spent in litigation attempting to prove or disprove the location of the apex within a claim.[11]

The 1872 measure was also criticized for not going further to correct the abuses inherent in accepting local rules as the basis for a national mining law. But pressure to protect the property rights of those who had benefitted from application of the so-called "California Common Law" was just as great in 1872 as in 1866, when Stewart convinced Congress that it would be unwise to erase the legal status of the mining industry which had developed on the public domain. Stewart continued to defend the "customary law" of the miner in 1872 as he had done earlier. His efforts were essential in securing national recognition of local regulation, a concept he had evolved and refined from the Nevada County, California, mining code of 1852, through the national laws of 1866, 1870, and 1872.

More significant to Stewart's later career, as well as to the political history of Nevada, was the act which later became known, particularly in silver mining circles, as the infamous "Crime of '73." The law, which stimulated a national confrontation between advocates of the gold and silver standards, began its history innocuously on April 28, 1870, when Senate Bill 859 was introduced by John Sherman of Ohio, as a measure to revise the laws governing mints, assay offices, and United States coinage. It was read twice by title and referred routinely to the Committee on Finance, of which Sherman was chairman.[12]

The bill's congressional history during the next three years was anything but routine as it went through a bewildering series of recommissions, reintroductions, and amendments.[13] On the surface it seemed to have little to do with the mining industry of the west, and during its passage it elicited little response from western congressional delegations. However, in the process of becoming law, the section (16 in the original draft) which provided for the minting of the silver dollar was deleted, and a larger dollar, to be used only in trade with Asia, was substituted. The elimination of the regular silver dollar and the method by which it was accomplished later led to the belief among silver-standard supporters that legislators and private interests had conspired to demonetize silver and place the United States on a single monetary standard —gold.[14] Recognition sometime later that the Mint Act of 1873 had demonetized silver brought the act into focus as one of the most important mining measures ever passed by Congress.

There is little doubt that the Mint Bill of 1873 was complex and that when the final bill emerged it had been so altered and reworded that "no member outside the committees could possibly know its provisions."[15] Yet the lack of attention on the part of Nevada and other western senators to an important mint and coinage bill is difficult to understand. Since the west, and particularly Nevada at this time, produced most of the minerals used in the coinage system, it might legitimately be expected that western senators would take an active part in any debates on such an issue. They did not do so. Senator Nye of Nevada spoke only two or three times, on unimportant sections dealing with gold. Stewart spoke but once, an unimportant, single sentence remark on bullion. The two California senators, Cole and Casserly, did better, speaking a number of times during the final Senate debates on the measure. However, except for a few questions from Casserly on the silver provisions of the bill, the Californians were more concerned with the gold provisions of the proposed act.

It is quite clear from the debates on the bill that John Sherman was less than candid with his colleagues. He deliberately led the Senate to believe that the bill in its final form provided for both the 384-grain regular dollar and the new 420-grain trade dollar, when in fact it included only the latter.[16] At one point, Senator Casserly asked Sherman if the bill provided a silver coinage up to the standard of other nations. Sherman replied that the bill proposed a silver coinage exactly the same as the French, that is that the "dollar provided for by this bill is the precise equivalent of the five-franc piece."[17] Sherman was well aware of the consequences of his bill for silver coinage, and his later plea of ignorance is not credible.[18] His direction of the measure in the Senate was such that "most senators voted for the amended measure ignorant of the facts needed for an intelligent judgment on the change in monetary standards."[19]

Stewart had not kept abreast of the changing monetary situation which ultimately led to coinage revision, nor had he done his homework on the Mint Bill as it passed into law in 1873. Apparently, when Stewart left the Senate for the first time, in March, 1875, he was still unaware that the Mint Act of 1873 had demonetized silver. Actually, on three occasions in 1874 he endorsed the gold standard in Senate speeches. On February 11 he stated, "Let us do as all the people of the world have been doing from the beginning, measure our values by gold, adopt the standard that all can understand, and get rid of this mystery. . . . I want the standard gold, and no paper money not redeemable in gold." On February 20, in reference to redeeming bonds, he noted, "I do not propose to pay the bond by issuing irredeemable currency; I propose to pay the bond with value; I propose to pay it in gold, from the earning and taxation of the people; and that is, the only way it can be paid. . . . Why, sir, everything you have got is measured by gold. Your greenbacks are measured by gold."[20] Again a few months later, on June 11, Stewart responded to the query, "Suppose we had no paper currency, but only gold":

> I wish that supposition was true . . . I do not care how much you discuss it
> or how many resolutions you pass; they do not make any difference; you

must come to the same conclusion that all other people have—that gold is recognized as the universal standard of value. It is the measure that must be used. . . . It is the greatest sin that can be committed to teach the American people that money can be printed not earned.[21]

Stewart insisted later that he had not favored the gold standard in 1874, alleging that his enemies had taken his words out of context, and that when he spoke of gold, he meant specie and not "gold as distinguished from silver."[22] A careful reading of the three speeches provides some justification for Stewart's position that his main emphasis at the time was against the printing of paper money to redeem bonds. However, they do show that Stewart was, at the time, unalterably opposed to inflation, a position which he later altered dramatically when he began to advocate the free and unlimited coinage of silver at the ratio of 16 to 1.

Stewart's actual voting record on the Mint Bill, as it wound its way from one committee to another and back again, was clouded by the fact that there was no recorded vote in the Senate on the bill itself nor on the conference committee report. When accused later of voting for the Mint Act, Stewart replied, "I never voted for the demonetization of silver. The act of 1873 was passed without a division on the statement of John Sherman that it contained a silver dollar the exact equivalent of the five-franc piece of France, to float all over the world."[23] However, there is no evidence in the Senate debates that Stewart made any objections to the bill during its three-year legislative history. Both he and Senator Nye voted in favor of Sherman's bill in January, 1871, when it already had eliminated the regular silver dollar from coinage. Therefore, it seems that Stewart's denial of support for the 1873 Mint Act may have been a sophistry, indicating that he did not *intentionally* or *knowingly* vote for the demonetization of silver, not that he did not vote for the bill itself.[24]

If Stewart and Nye were unaware of the dangers of the Mint Act, some of their constituents in Nevada were not. Shortly after the Mint Bill appeared for debate in the Senate in December, 1872, one of the Comstock newspaper editors wrote that the Sherman Bill would depreciate the value of silver. He declared that the bill would decrease silver coinage and suggested that it should instead be increased.[25] Much more to the point was a February 4, 1873, letter to the same paper from Conrad Weigand, an assayer in Virginia City. Weigand noted specifically that the trade dollar had been substituted for the regular dollar in the Mint Bill and that the devaluation which would inevitably result would be disastrous to Nevada.[26]

However, these were isolated incidents, for there was little reaction in Nevada to the passage of the Mint Act of 1873. One reason for the lack of interest was the fact that, shortly after passage of the act, the richest ore body ever discovered on the Comstock, the "Big Bonanza," was announced by the owners of the Consolidated-Virginia mine. The resulting prosperity in Nevada lasted for approximately six years and distracted the state from the unknown threat of the new act. Stewart and his elated constituents were not alone in their failure to recognize that the Mint Act demonetized silver. Apparently no one in the United States made any real protest of that demonetization until 1876. Meanwhile, Stewart continued to serve out his second Senate term, blissfully unaware of the act's dire consequences for Nevada's economy.

He continued actively to support the interests of the Central Pacific Railroad, a political alliance that was particularly apparent during Nevada's attempt to have Congress cede the public swamp, or overflowed, land in the state. The Central Pacific had become Nevada's largest private landholder when, between 1862 and 1864, Congress granted it more than 5,000,000 acres along the Humboldt River. Railroad officials immediately began strong lobbying efforts in the Nevada legislature, seeking to insure protection of this resource and the maximum financial gain from it.[27] However, in spite of the strong railroad presence, agricultural interests in the state legislature succeeded in passing the Nevada Swamp Land Act on March 6, 1869. This act asked Congress to cede to the state all overflowed lands. The act also directed that if Congress did make such a cession then each board of county commissioners was to identify and administer such areas within its jurisdiction. Under the Nevada act, contingent upon Congressional approval, entrants could purchase 640 acres of this land at $1.00 per acre, with credit extended over five years. In addition, no survey was necessary, and married women could apply for a separate 640-acre grant. Once $5,000 was collected in any county, the commissioners were to use the funds for dams and canals for irrigation districts. The Central Pacific opposed the Nevada Swamp Land Act because its marsh tracts along the Truckee and Humboldt rivers would revert to state control if any federal grant were made.[28]

Before attempting to obtain congressional surrender of swamp lands, an effort was made to have the United States General Land Office make an immediate grant to the state. When that effort failed, Nye introduced a bill, on June 4, 1870, requesting extension to Nevada of the benefits of the 1850 Swamp Land Act.[29] The bill was referred to the Committee on Public Lands, of which Stewart was a member. Stewart clearly demonstrated his own allegiance to the Central Pacific and the latter's opposition to any land cession by preventing action on Nye's bill during that session. Stewart insisted, at the time and later, that there were no swamp lands in Nevada and thus no need for such a congressional cession.[30]

Nye's bill, asking that the provisions of the Swamp Act of 1850 for Arkansas be extended to Nevada, was reintroduced at the next session of Congress, but was reported unfavorably by the Public Lands Committee on March 3, 1871.[31] At the same time, the Nevada legislature sent two separate resolutions to Congress, urging that body to act. Caught between his loyalty to the railroad and obvious support for a swamp land law among his constituents, Stewart introduced a bill on March 9, 1871, defining swamp and overflowed lands. Stewart's bill further complicated the issue, with the result that Congress took no action at all on the Nevada swamp land cession in 1871.

Stewart's railroad connection became even clearer in the spring of 1872, when Nevada Representative Charles W. Kendall managed to steer through the House a measure similar to that proposed by Nye. It was received in the Senate on May 23, 1872, and referred to the Committee on Public Lands the following day. Stewart opposed even the referral: "Let the bill be read, and then I desire to have it indefinitely postponed. There are no swamp lands in Nevada." His colleague, Nye, wanted it referred, but Stewart insisted, "There are no swamp lands there unless you bring the water and put it on them and water is valuable there. We have no swamp lands that we want to reclaim, and we do not want any of that swindling business in Nevada. I hope, therefore, the bill will be indefinitely postponed." Although Stewart lost the fight to prevent referral, he won the battle for postponement when the Public Lands Committee, on May 27, 1872, requested that the Kendall Bill be put aside indefinitely. Nye then tried to get it on the Senate calendar, but Stewart insisted any such action should carry with it an adverse report from the committee. With that, Nevada's proposed swamp land cession died.[32]

Its demise in Nevada did not come so swiftly, however. The question of a federal cession of swamp lands became a political issue in the campaign of 1872, and although Stewart was not himself a candidate, he was pressured to defend his position on the question. He did so in friendly newspapers, stating that he had acted in Nevada's best interest in protecting the public lands from swindling schemes. He argued that the state school fund would be affected adversely and that land titles of occupiers would also be disturbed by such passage. It was quite clear that the school fund would not have been affected greatly by any swamp land cession, and the only title to be disturbed was the Central Pacific's right to its millions of acres already granted.[33]

Stewart's ties to the Central Pacific were strengthened by the fact that he was a member of the Senate Committee on the Pacific Railroad from 1867 to 1872, and its chairman from 1872 until his retirement from the Senate in 1875. It was a position that did not go unnoticed in Nevada. When Stewart became chairman of the committee, an editorial in a Reno newspaper implied that the Senator had made over $500,000 on an annual salary of $5,000, with the rest contributed by the railroad. To the editor, at least, Stewart's selection as chairman of the Pacific Railroad Committee was an insult, since he represented the railroad and not the people of his state, in the Senate.[34]

During the last year of his second term, Stewart became involved in the investigation of alleged frauds by the so-called "District Ring" in Washington, D.C. On March 17, 1874, Stewart was appointed chairman of a "joint select committee on the part of the Senate to inquire into the affairs of the District of Columbia." The appointment was made by the president *pro tem* of the Senate, but Stewart refused to accept it because he doubted that officer's authority to make him chairman. Stewart was right and the Senate *Journal* was corrected the next day to show simply that he had been made a member of the committee, with the group to name its own chairman.[35] When the committee later chose Senator Allison as chairman, one Nevada newspaper assumed that the selection was the result of strong public reaction against Stewart's appointment, since it was the "general opinion that Stewart has benefitted from the 'Ring'!"[36] Although the record indicates that the change was simply to correct a parliamentary error, the reaction in Nevada reflects the fact that Stewart's reputation suffered from a growing opinion that he was too friendly with the railroads and other industrial corporations.

Stewart's extralegislative activities during these years were varied, interesting, and controversial, beginning with his relationship to President Ulysses S. Grant. According to Stewart, his friendship with the President started while the latter was an army lieutenant stationed on the Pacific Coast and ripened into an even closer relationship when Grant took office. Stewart later wrote:

> One night in nearly every week during Grant's first term I visited the White House, when the President and I would retire to a private room to smoke and talk. He was a slow but accurate conversationalist. He never said a foolish thing in my hearing. On these confidential occasions Grant would inquire of me as to the character and actions of various public men. I gave him my opinion freely, as I could afford to do, for he always kept his own counsel.[37]

The Senator noted many other instances of his close ties with Grant, none more interesting than a purported offer of appointment to the United States Supreme Court: "In 1871 he tendered me an appointment to the Supreme Court of the United States, and was anxious that I should accept, but, after considering the matter for a short time, I declined it. I have always been devoted to the law, but life on the bench seemed too inactive, and the more stirring career in the Senate appealed to me far more strongly."[38]

Vastly more important was Stewart's involvement, during 1871, in a mining venture that ultimately developed into one of the great mining-fraud scandals of the nineteenth century. This incident touched prominent politicians and statesmen in the United States and Great Britain and plagued Stewart well into the 1890's.[39] The scandal involved the Emma Mine, discovered in 1868 by two prospectors, in Little Cottonwood Canyon near the town of Alta, Utah. One of the miners, James E. Lyon, later declared in testimony before a House committee, that after the discovery the claim was "jumped." In order to protect his own interests, in 1870 he brought an injunction suit in Utah's territorial court, to prevent the "claim jumpers" from working the mine. At this point Stewart became involved in the case as one of Lyon's attorneys.[40]

While Lyon was pursuing his suit in Utah, those in possession of the mine organized the Emma Company of Utah and, in the spring of 1871, began efforts to sell the property. During these negotiations, two central figures entered the picture: Trenor W. Park of Vermont, a banker and speculator; and General H. Henry Baxter of New York, a railroad magnate and Wall Street broker. Their contribution of $375,000 bought them a one-half interest in the mine. When a reorganization took place on April 26, 1871, and the Emma Silver Mining Company of New York was formed, the two controlled half the total shares in the new company.[41] The Lyon claim continued unsettled under the reorganization.

In the summer of 1871, the prospect of selling the Emma Company to London investors forced settlement of the Lyon interest, since it would have been difficult to promote the mine in England with such an encumbrance. Consequently, a "Memo of Agreement" was worked out early in August, by Stewart, representing Lyon, and the Park-Baxter group. Lyon was to receive a sum based on the future sale of the mine, but in no case more than $500,000, although he had originally claimed $1,000,000. The agreement was signed by the contracting parties on August 18, 1871. Before it was signed, Stewart wrote Lyon a letter from New York, on August 5, 1871, describing the deal as the best he could make. He was optimistic that the mine would be sold in London for five to eight million dollars, and promised Lyon that he would not give up the lawsuit "under any circumstances unless you get $500,000. You will, without doubt, get that."[42] It was a promise Stewart did not keep, although the words caused him many difficult moments when the Emma Mine speculation was later investigated by the House Foreign Affairs Committee.

Stewart's August 5 letter to Lyon acknowledged that the owners of the Emma Mine were engaged in a publicity campaign in London, preparatory to offering the mine for sale there. This campaign included a policy of notifying the British press whenever rich shipments from the mine arrived in England, knowing that such information would in turn be relayed immediately to the public.[43] The yield of the Emma Mine from May 1, a few days after Park and Baxter entered the picture, to September 1, was greater than it had been before or was ever after to be, for any four-month period.[44]

The production figures and accompanying publicity set the stage for the September, 1871, arrival in London of Trenor W. Park, representing the owners of the Emma Mine, and Stewart, representing Lyon. After some initial difficulties, Park and Stewart worked out a secret agreement with Albert Grant or Gottheimer, an international promoter with perhaps the most notorious and controversial reputation in England at the time.[45] Under terms of the agreement, Grant organized the Emma Silver Mining Company, Ltd., with a capital of 1,000,000 British pounds, divided into 50,000 shares at 20 pounds each. Half of the shares were to go to the vendors, Park and Stewart, or more realistically, to Park. The company was incorporated on November 8, 1871.[46]

Stewart's activities in aiding the sale of the Emma property might justifiably be regarded as part of his charge to represent the interests of his client, James E. Lyon. However, after the incorporation of the London company it became increasingly difficult to separate his actions as counsel for Lyon from those in which he acted on behalf of Park. The prospectus for the sale of stock in the Emma Silver Mining Company, Ltd., was issued by Baron Grant the day after the company was incorporated. Its purpose, to entice investors, was enhanced by the rather unusual list of trustees and directors assembled by Grant. It included three members of Parliament: Edward Brydges-Willyams, Edward Leigh Pemberton, and George Anderson; John C. Stanley, an heir to Lord Stanley of Alderney; the three Americans already involved in the Emma negotiations, Trenor W. Park, General H. H. Baxter, and Senator Stewart. The most important name of all, however, was that of General Robert Cumming Schenck, the United States minister to Great Britain.[47]

Grant did not agree to promote the enterprise until he was certain Schenck would become a director.

Apparently Stewart helped to interest Schenck in the Emma Company. Ostensibly, they met for the first time at a dinner given for Schenck in the fall of 1871, by William Evarts, later United States secretary of state. Also present at the dinner were Trenor W. Park and Stewart's wife.[48] However, in his testimony later, before the House Foreign Affairs Committee, Stewart indicated that he had been well acquainted with Schenck in the United States and had met him a few times in London prior to the Evarts dinner. Stewart testified that the Emma Mine was not discussed in the earlier meetings with Schenck, but that it had been mentioned at the dinner, and that Schenck was the first to bring up the possibility of getting some of the Emma stock. Stewart was not certain, in the testimony, whether Schenck's request for stock had come directly after the dinner or the next day. In any event, Stewart reported that he had told Schenck it was a good proposition and had suggested to Park both that the minister be allowed to have stock and that Park "carry" Schenck, since the latter did not have funds for that purpose.[49] Although Stewart's role as the originator of the suggestion is ambiguous, just such an arrangement was made between Park and Schenck.

In addition to this involvement with Schenck, Stewart recalled in his testimony before the House committee that he played an active part in having Schenck named to the board of directors of the Emma Silver Mining Company, Ltd. Although Stewart could not remember whether the suggestion came from Park or himself, the House committee assumed in the preface to its report that Stewart had made the original proposal.[50]

Stewart's client, James E. Lyon, had been almost ignored in the promotional activities, yet he still held claim to a one-third interest in the original Emma Mine, and that claim had to be settled before Grant's scheme could be consummated. Thus, early in November, Stewart wired Lyon to come to London, since "we had better make a final settlement before I leave here."[51] Lyon arrived in London on November 20, 1871, and shortly thereafter settled his one-third claim in the Emma for a lump sum of $250,000, from which $100,000 was paid in legal fees, $50,000 each for Stewart and for Curtis J. Hillyer, a good friend of Stewart's and a recognized authority in mining law. The sum Lyon received was just half of the $500,000 minimum Stewart earlier had promised.[52]

After completing the arrangements with Lyon in London, Stewart returned to the United States for the opening of Congress and to "take care of" the ten other American stockholders, who held some 21,875 shares in the old New York company and were entitled to a proportionate share in the new one. Stewart was able to obtain these shares for Trenor W. Park at a profit to the latter of over $1,000,000.[53]

The settlement of the Lyon claim became the focal point of a dispute between Lyon and Stewart which lasted from 1873 into the 1890's, long after it was clear that the Emma Silver Mining Company, Ltd., had been a gigantic swindle.[54] The crux of the disagreement between the two men concerned Stewart's position as attorney for Lyon in the settlement of the latter's claim in the original Emma Mine. The story of this relationship unfolded in detail in a hearing conducted in the spring and summer of 1876 by the House Committee on Foreign Affairs, in an effort to ascertain Schenck's part in the promotion of the Emma Silver Mining Company, Ltd.

The gist of the Lyon testimony was that Stewart and Park had cheated him. He insisted that they had misrepresented the Emma property to him and that he had initially agreed to settle his one-third claim for $500,000 only because Park, Stewart, and others described the mine as exhausted.[55] When asked why he had settled finally for $150,000 rather than the original figure, he replied that he needed the money and Stewart and others advised him to do so.[56] Nowhere in his testimony did Lyon deny the fact that he had settled for $150,000, "relinquishing all my right and title," nor that the sum had been paid to him. What he did object to was the fact that in all of the transactions Stewart had effectively acted as Park's attorney when he should have been acting for Lyon.[57]

Stewart's testimony before the committee painted an entirely different picture. He insisted that Lyon "had all the information that I had, everything that I could give him."[58] The Nevada senator stated that he had wanted to litigate the Lyon interest in order to get more money for his client, but that Lyon insisted on a cash settlement. Stewart recalled that when Lyon left England for the United States he stated that he was pleased with Stewart for making the cash settlement.[59] As to his activities as counsel for Lyon, Stewart remarked that "I would have given up everything to satisfy him. At that time I thought a great deal of Lyon, and had seen nothing in Lyon, up to that time, but what was square; he was my client and I had been working for him."[60] Some members of the House investigating committee were not convinced of Stewart's loyalty to Lyon and asked him specifically, "Were you not, at some time, the attorney for both Park and Lyon?" In reply, Stewart drew a fine line, noting, "I was not for both at the same time. As soon as I acted for Park and telegraphed and he accepted, then my relations with Lyon ceased."[61] In spite of Stewart's testimony to the contrary, it seems quite clear from the House report, that his own interests and not those of his first client, Lyon, were given priority in the negotiations leading to the settlement of the Lyon claim. That his work on behalf of Park proved financially rewarding to Stewart became evident from Park's testimony that he gave Stewart a total of $275,000. This sum included payment of $50,000 to Lyon in June, 1872, when the latter threatened a suit against Stewart.[62]

Evidently, in the spring of 1872, Lyon discovered details of the transactions which brought Stewart much of the money Lyon himself should have received for his one-third interest. As a result, Lyon approached Park, threatening suit against Stewart. Park then paid Lyon $50,000, for "I saw at a glance that he had the advantage over Mr. Stewart in that respect. I said, 'I see what it is Lyon; it is blackmail. How much do you want?'" Lyon suggested $50,000, and Park agreed to pay him on behalf of Stewart.[63] Stewart corroborated Park's testimony about the $50,000 payment to Lyon, but emphasized that it was pure blackmail and that he would not "have settled it at all." Park settled because he felt that Stewart, as a United States senator, could not "afford the publicity."[64]

The total amount expended to settle the Lyon claim was approximately the $500,000 which had been promised him originally, but he had to share it with Stewart and others. That fact did not escape the attention of the House committee, and Stewart was asked if this was just a "coincidence." He assured the members of the committee that there was no collusion in the matter.[65] Nonetheless, in the final settlement Stewart received $225,000 more than his client, Lyon, who received but $200,000, including the so-called "blackmail" sum of $50,000.[66] The fact that his attorney received more from the negotiations than he did obviously angered Lyon, and he spent the next two decades in a futile attempt to "get even."[67]

Lyon's main target was Stewart. The $50,000 which he received from Park in May of 1872 silenced him only for a few years. Early in 1875, he began demanding an additional $200,000 in threatening letters to Stewart: "The house you have built and furnished is with my money and you know it. . . . You will find you have injured the wrong man."[68] Lyon's new demands were made despite the fact that when he accepted the $50,000 from Park, he signed a notarized release agreeing to:

> . . . fully and forever release and discharge the said Stewart from all and
> every demand, claim, or right of action of every description that I have or
> may claim to have against him, whether legal or equitable, and especially

from any and all claims, demands, or causes of action of every description,
growing out of his relation as attorney or counsel or agent for me in the
litigation concerning the Emma Mine, so called and the various proceedings, negotiations, contracts, and conveyances concerning or connected
with said Emma Mine.[69]

Lyon renewed his demands for money just as Stewart was leaving the
Senate to return to private law practice. The "harassment" by Lyon,
mainly in the form of letters, followed Stewart into political retirement.
In the late 1880's, after Stewart had returned to the U.S. Senate, Lyon
turned from letter writing to legal action. A suit filed against Stewart in
New York City in 1891, was settled two years later on terms favorable to
Stewart and Lyon's personal attack against him finally came to a close.[70]

Stewart's involvement in the Emma Mine scandal ranks as one of the
lowest points in his career. A lawyer of his training and experience
should never have become entangled in such a situation. However, for
most of his life, after entering the California gold fields in 1850, Stewart
was fascinated with mining promotion. That weakness, along with a
constant need for additional funds to cover his expenses, may well have
led him into arrangements with Trenor Park that he did not contemplate
when he entered the Emma Mine case as attorney for James Lyon.

His expenses were abnormally high during this period, since he had to
maintain a home in Washington for himself, and at the same time provide funds for his wife and two daughters, who had left Washington,
D.C., for an extended European stay shortly after the Senator was sworn
in. Stewart met his family in London in September, 1871, when he went
to represent Lyon in the sale of the Emma Mine. Shortly after their return
to Washington, late in November, 1871, the Stewarts began construction of a magnificent five-story house on land at Dupont Circle.[71] Soon
labeled "Castle Stewart," the imposing structure was described by an
admiring observer as surpassing in "magnificent elegance anything to
be seen in this city. . . .The dining room is furnished in black walnut, the
chairs are covered with the finest Morocco and ornamented with gilt
monogram, and everything in the room is in perfect keeping."[72] Another
viewer noted that visitors neglected "the White House itself in their
desire to see and exclaim over the sharp windows, steeple and columned
porticos of Stewart Castle."[73] The Castle and its owners soon became
an important part of the Washington social scene,[74] but they had hardly
become comfortably settled before Stewart announced, in 1874, that he
would not be a candidate for reelection. In reporting Stewart's statement, the paper editorialized, "Senator Stewart has stated positively
that he is not a candidate for re-election. In that he shows good sense."[75]

The Stewart home in Washington, D.C. Built in 1873 on Dupont Circle and soon labeled Stewart "Castle," the five-story building was later purchased by William A. Clark of Montana. *(Nevada Historical Society Photo)*

The announcement brought immediate speculation as to why an obviously ambitious senator would step down from a position he seemed
to enjoy, particularly since his record of legislative achievement was
one upon which most politicians would have been proud to campaign.

Although in 1874, Stewart was already bothered by what came to be
lifelong financial difficulties, his decision was actually a pragmatic reaction to the ambitions of Comstock millionaire William Sharon.
Sharon's desire to become a senator was well known. He had announced
for the post in 1872, but withdrew in the face of competition from another Comstock magnate, John P. Jones. In 1874, with his ambition as
strong as ever and the possibility of election much greater, he announced
again. Since Sharon was a major official in the Bank of California, his
candidacy meant that one of Stewart's main financial backers in his
earlier campaigns was lost to him. Moreover, his formerly staunch supporters at the Central Pacific Railroad were unenthusiastic about another
term, although it is possible that the attitude of the railroad officials was
the result of pressure from Sharon.[76] In any event, since he had limited
resources of his own, it was absolutely essential for Stewart to have
strong outside financial backing. Without it, he could not hope to counteract the strong newspaper opposition to his candidacy, particularly from
the *Nevada State Journal*.[77] Thus, when Sharon announced that he
would be a candidate for election to the Senate, Stewart's own political
career came to an abrupt halt. It is difficult to believe that Stewart withdrew voluntarily from the 1874 Senate race, although in his autobiography he emphasizes the precarious state of his finances, "I was engaged
in mining operations many of which proved disastrous and I thought it
time to retire from politics and return to the practice of law."[78] Whether
he himself decided not to run, or the decision was made for him, Stewart
found himself, in 1875, once again a private citizen.

CHAPTER 6

VACATION FROM POLITICS

AMONG Stewart's first activities in this new role was, characteristically, a mining promotion, in the Panamint Mountains on the western edge of Death Valley, California.[1] Actually, it began nearly a year earlier. Along with Senator John P. Jones and others, Stewart became interested in developing a series of claims which had been discovered in Surprise Canyon in the Panamint Mountains, probably early in 1873, by Richard C. Jacobs, Robert B. Stewart, and W. L. Kennedy.[2] Although initial reports indicated that a rich ore body had been found, the area's inaccessibility hindered quick development. The first professional notice of the discovery came in August, 1873, when the *Mining and Scientific Press* published an article on the strike, indicating that assays ran as high as $3,000 per ton. According to the article, a recorder's office had been established and had registered some 100 locations, and a townsite had been surveyed.[3]

The transition from individual locations to mining companies, which was necessary in order to attract the capital for development, evidently began with the formation of the Panamint Mining Company on November 24, 1873, with a capitalization of $2,000,000.[4] In order to help promote their stock, that company and others began to issue glowing reports of the area. One of these revealed that every mining expert who had visited the district voiced "wonder and astonishment at the immense amount of silver ore in sight," and that several expressed the opinion that in a few years it would eclipse the famous Comstock Lode.[5] Comparison with that great discovery, already a traditional way to boom new mining camps, was particularly grandiose at the time, since the biggest mineral strike in the Comstock's fabulous history, appropriately labeled the "Big Bonanza," had just been reported in 1873.

In spite of the publicity campaign, however, capital was slow to reach the Panamint district, and it wasn't until after the entrance of Jones and Stewart that the area really began to develop. There is some confusion as to how the two became involved in the Panamint promotion, one source indicating that the initial impetus came from Stewart,[6] and others insisting that Jones suggested the partnership to Stewart after the latter announced his decision not to run for reelection.[7] In any event, the two men purchased the main claims of the Panamint Mining Company for $350,000. In the fall of 1874, they consolidated those claims with a new company, the Surprise Valley Mill, Mining and Water Company, which they had organized to build a mill for their ores. The latter, incorporated on September 2, 1874, was capitalized at $2,000,000. It was to build a projected twenty-stamp mill and to act as the parent company for the group's Panamint holdings.[8]

Stewart was named general manager of the company, at an annual salary of $25,000, with the immediate responsibility of supervising construction of the mill and bringing the mining properties into production.[9] Since he had little money of his own, Stewart contributed his time and expertise to the project. It was also probably due to Stewart that Trenor Park, with whom he was allied in the Emma Mine promotion, became an investor. Park's association with the Panamint promotion was a mixed blessing, however. As soon as his connection became known, San Francisco papers began to question whether the Emma Mine speculators were similarly involved in the Panamint development. The *San Francisco Bulletin* noted in November, 1874, "We shall rejoice if any really valuable discoveries should be made there [Panamint], but the agitation begins in a suspicious way. The shapes of some of the Emma and Mariposa speculators are flitting about in connection with Panamint. . . .The old operators and old apparatus are distinctly visible."[10] The association of Park and Stewart in the Panamint operation discouraged potential investor J. Barr Robertson, who lost interest when he found out that Park was affiliated with Stewart and Jones.[11] Rumors persisted that the Stewart-Jones operation was only speculative. Even later observers could not give an unequivocal answer to the question of whether "Jones and Stewart conscientiously believed they had a bonanza lurking behind those colorful cliffs," pointing out only that "the opportunity for stock-rigging was certainly present."[12]

During the development period, reports of the mineral potential of the Panamint district continued to be good. The 1874 annual review by the United States Geological Survey incorporated a favorable report by prominent western engineer C. A. Stetefeldt, who noted, "There is scarcely a mining district where more continuous and bolder croppings are found than in Panamint.'' He indicated that there was an abundance of wood, water and salt, although the area was difficult to reach.[13]

It was clear, though, that the Panamint district would not become productive without proper milling facilities.[14] A mill was part of the promotion by Stewart and Jones, and although transportation and construction problems were enormous in that inaccessible region, a twenty-stamp mill was completed in the summer of 1875. The ''Big Mill,'' which reportedly cost $385,000, was scheduled to begin production on July 4.[15] Although a formal opening took place as planned, actual milling didn't begin until August 24, 1875. Stewart and Park visited the camp shortly after the July 4 celebration, and Stewart, at least, remained until September.

Although solid production had to await completion of the mill, the boom did not. The appearance of two U.S. senators and a number of eastern investors promising a mill, encouraged a mild rush to the district, centering in the town of Panamint. As in other mining camps, the twelve saloons were out of all proportion to the reported population of between 1,000 and 2,000 persons. In November, 1874, *The Panamint News* began triweekly publication, and about the same time a brewery came into existence.[16] Owner of one of the saloons, the Oriental, was Dave Neagle, a left-handed gunslinger, who had known Stewart earlier on the Comstock. Neagle, according to one report, was the camp's ''Chief cheer-dispenser'' during the period when the mines began to fail.[17] His presence at Panamint, however, no doubt had something to do with the security of the Jones-Stewart interests, since the Surprise Canyon area was reputedly a haven for outlaws.[18]

Unfortunately for the developers, the Panamint boom was over too soon. Although the stamp mill operated successfully for a time, there simply was not enough good ore in the district.[19] Stewart had been quite optimistic about the mines in the beginning, and was genuinely disappointed when exploration indicated that the ore body did not extend in depth: ''Out of these pipes [narrow slivers of silver ore], and the ore on the surface, we extracted about a million of money, and if we could have continued a few months longer we would have received all our investment back without loss. The abrupt termination of the ore involved a large loss to the investors.''[20]

Part of the company's difficulty had been the problem of transportation, not only of goods into the area, but also of bullion out. Stewart later reported that he attempted to get Wells Fargo to haul the bullion, but that the company refused because of the reputation of the Panamints as a hangout for thieves. There had been some effort, mainly by Jones, to arrange for a spur into the mines from the proposed Los Angeles and Independence Railroad, but such plans evaporated with the rapid decline of the camp. According to Stewart, the bullion that did leave Panamint was carried out in a rather unconventional form. Since the threat of robbery was so great, the company did not wish to risk ordinary means of conveyance, and Stewart devised a novel scheme. The ore was smelted into "enormous cannon-balls" weighing 750 pounds each, far beyond the capacity of any outlaw to haul away quickly.[21]

The mill that had opened so proudly closed down permanently in May, 1877.[22] By that time it was clear that Jones and Stewart had experienced a substantial loss. While Jones had invested most of the money, he was not the only financial loser. Stewart lost not only time and effort, but also the potential fortune he was always hoping to find in the mines. His setback in the Panamints forced him to turn more directly and specifically to the task of restoring his law practice, but it did not end Stewart's interest in mining or promotion of mining stocks.

Stewart repeated his Panamint experience again in 1879 and 1880, this time involving the Noonday Mine at Bodie, California. Again, the venture included Stewart's participation in the building of a costly mill. It was at Bodie that Grant Smith, later a successful San Francisco attorney and historian of the Comstock Lode, met Stewart, while employed as a messenger boy for the local telegraph office. Smith described the fifty-five-year-old Stewart's majestic appearance at the time, "His hair and luxuriant beard were white as snow and he walked like a cathedral in motion, always alone."[23]

Months before the Panamint mill closed permanently in 1877, Stewart had formed a law partnership in San Francisco with Clarence Greathouse, described by the former senator as "a young man of attainments and brilliant intellect."[24] William F. Herrin, later Stewart's law partner and legal counsel for the Southern Pacific Company, was law clerk for the firm. The arrangement with Greathouse was dissolved about a year later, and a new partnership was organized which included Stewart, Herrin, and Judge Peter Van Clief, a former partner of Stewart's from Nevada City and Downieville. Van Clief left the firm a short time later, but Herrin continued his association with Stewart until the summer of 1886, when the latter's campaign for the Senate forced a dissolution of the partnership.[25] During these years Stewart maintained law offices and a residence in San Francisco.

Stewart's reputation as a mining lawyer brought him numerous important suits; two of the most significant took him to Tombstone, Arizona Territory, and to Eureka, Nevada. At Tombstone, Stewart represented the Contention Mine in litigation against most of its neighbors. At the time Stewart was employed as counsel, the mine was owned by a San Francisco corporation. While preparing his case, Stewart concluded that there were so many possible title conflicts that the mines would be exhausted before the legal fight could be finished. He therefore suggested a consolidation, and although many of the investors were disappointed with the solution, his plan was accepted by the directors and he received $25,000 for his legal activities. Stewart later recalled that the Contention suits took place during the battle of the Clantons and Earps at the O.K. Corral (Oct. 26, 1881), and that he "witnessed this fight—from a safe distance."[26]

One of the most difficult of Stewart's mining cases involved two prominent mining companies in Eureka, Nevada. That silver-lead camp was discovered in 1864, but the ore was so complex that reduction methods used on the Comstock and elsewhere were not sufficient. Real production from the district had to await certain metallurgical innovations, which came in 1869.[27] As a result of these, Eureka produced millions of dollars during the 1870's and 1880's, making it at the time the most productive mineral district in Nevada, outside the Comstock Lode. With the production boom came the usual litigation.

The case that attracted Stewart and his partner, Herrin, involved the Albion Consolidated Company against the Richmond. The Albion suit developed out of an earlier action, which had started in 1873, to determine the rights to certain ground claimed by both the Richmond Consolidated and the Eureka Consolidated. The Albion claimants sought to recover $608,520 in ore taken out by the Richmond Company from land beyond the line set earlier by the court.[28] Stewart was chief counsel for the Albion, and Thomas Wren, later an important figure in Nevada's free-silver movement, was the main counsel for the Richmond. Stewart complained later that it was a long, hard, and costly suit, but ultimately the Albion won.[29] Perhaps just as important to Stewart as the victory were the contacts he made at Eureka with individuals who later rose to prominence in local and state politics.[30]

In addition to mining litigation, Stewart participated in a number of important legal cases involving agricultural lands and the water rights. The question, which became of prime importance to water users in California, Nevada, and other western states during the 1880's, was whether a private corporation with appropriated water rights could deprive users with riparian rights from use of the water without compensation. In a major 1877 California case involving this issue, Stewart was employed as counsel by James B. Haggin. Haggin was an important landholder who sought to obtain large amounts of property in Kern and Tulare counties by using "dummy" entries and filing under desert land laws. One newspaper noted that even Stewart's recognized ability to manipulate witnesses was not sufficient "to overcome the stubborn fact that the lands are not desert," and believed that Haggin should decide to claim the property as swamp land.[31] Haggin also purchased railroad land in Kern County, with a view to reclamation by irrigation.[32] However, Haggin's plans conflicted with the riparian rights of Henry Miller, one of the great cattle and land barons of the west. The ensuing legal contest between the two landowners ultimately resulted in a landmark decision regarding riparian rights versus appropriated water rights.

Miller was represented by a battery of attorneys, led by the prominent Hall McAllister of San Francisco. Haggin and his partner Lloyd Tevis were represented by the Stewart-Herrin partnership and others. The legal action began when Miller sued for an injunction against the Haggin-controlled Kern River Land and Canal Company, to prevent that company from diverting the waters of the Kern River, which Haggin claimed through right of appropriation. The district court ruled in favor of Haggin and his Kern River Land and Canal Company, thus upholding the concept of appropriated rights. Miller and his partner, Charles Lux, appealed on April 26, 1886, but by that time the partnership of Herrin and Stewart had left the case.[33]

The most controversial case with which Stewart was involved during his twelve-year absence from the Senate was the celebrated legal battle between Sarah Althea Hill and William Sharon.[34] Sarah Hill, the orphaned daughter of a Missouri lawyer, had moved to California in 1871, while still in her teens. A few years later she met Sharon and became his mistress, according to Hill, only after he promised marriage. Although there was never a formal ceremony, Hill later testified that they both signed a written declaration of marriage. Under the California Civil Code, when followed by cohabitation as husband and wife, this procedure constituted a legal marriage. The marriage declaration was dated August 25, 1880, but Hill agreed not to make it public for two years. Sharon paid her $500 per month for her part in the relationship, but insisted that he had not given any promise of marriage, orally or in writing.[35] The arrangement between Sharon and Sarah Hill lasted for about a year. At that point Sharon accused her of revealing his business and private affairs and stealing his papers. Sharon's efforts to work out some kind of agreement failed and the relationship ended. Shortly thereafter, on the advice of her attorney, Hill decided to take legal action against Sharon.

In September, 1883, Hill made public her claim that she was Sharon's wife and, as a result, he was accused of adultery and arrested. His lawyers filed suit in federal court, alleging the certificate of marriage to be a fraud. Her attorneys, George Tyler and David Terry, the latter a former chief justice of the California Supreme Court, followed with a suit in state court, for divorce and a property settlement. The legal proceedings emanating from these two suits lasted for over six years and resulted in twenty published judicial opinions, three from the United States Supreme Court. In the process six attorneys were employed for Hill and ten for Sharon.

The divorce trial in the state court started on March 10, 1884, before Judge Jeremiah Sullivan in San Francisco, without a jury. The lurid court disclosures, reported daily in the newspapers, were followed avidly by the public. Although there were many contradictions in the testimony offered by Hill and her witnesses, Judge Sullivan held in favor of Miss Hill on December 24, granting her a divorce and $2,500 monthly alimony. Sharon's lawyers immediately appealed the state court's decision and at the same time petitioned the federal court to have the declaration of marriage declared a forgery.[36]

At this point, Sharon hired Stewart to handle the case in the United States Circuit Court.[37] Hill's lawyers questioned the federal court's jurisdiction, but their objections were overruled. An official examiner was appointed to take the testimony of witnesses and report back to the circuit court. This hearing before the master of chancery began on August 1, 1885, and immediately turned into a series of legal battles between George Tyler, representing Hill, and Stewart, representing Sharon, interspersed with emotional outbursts by Hill herself. Almost as soon as the hearing opened, Sarah began to abuse Sharon and Stewart while Stewart was questioning a witness. She drew a pistol from her satchel and remarked that it was her intention to kill Stewart and the other Sharon attorneys. Stewart appeared to pay no attention and continued to question the witness.[38] At another point, after reading a deposition about her, she stated, ''When I see this testimony, I feel like taking that man Stewart out and cowhiding him. I will shoot him yet; that very man sitting there.''[39] After she had been quieted and the gun taken from her, the special examiner reported the incident to the U.S. Circuit Court.

As a result, on August 5, 1885, Judges Lorenzo Sawyer and Stephen Field held a contempt hearing for Hill. The judges sternly instructed the U.S. marshall to make certain that Hill thereafter appeared before the examiner without firearms. Several weeks later, 1,723 pages of completed testimony in the equity hearing were turned over to Circuit Judge

Lorenzo Sawyer and District Judge Deady, since Field had returned to
Washington, D.C. On December 26, 1885, the circuit court held that
the declaration of marriage was a forgery. Sarah was ordered to surrender the document for cancellation and was enjoined from alleging its
validity.[40]

The circuit court decision did not end the Sharon-Hill case. Sarah did
not surrender the marriage certificate and was supported in that action
by one of her attorneys, David Terry, who became her husband on
January 7, 1886. Terry maintained that the order was not enforceable,
since William Sharon had died on November 13, 1885, and the order
had died with him. On the basis of that reasoning he did not bother to
appeal the circuit court decision. Meanwhile, attorneys for the Sharon
estate carried on a two-year struggle to overturn the earlier state court
decision, which they finally succeeded in doing.[41]

Stewart's direct legal participation in the Sharon-Hill case ended in
1885, when his place was taken by his partner, William Herrin. According to Stewart, Herrin ''managed the case with skill and ability,''[42] but
Stewart's interest did not end. Indeed, his advice to Herrin, in a letter of
March 11, 1888, initiated the events that ultimately brought success to
the Sharon heirs. Stewart was convinced that the California state courts
would continue to rule in favor of Mrs. Terry, and that the only way to
win the case was in the federal courts. As he suggested to Herrin, ''The
first and most important step, therefore, is for both Mr. Newlands and
Fred Sharon to become *Bona Fide* residents of some other State. The
change in residence must be positive and in good faith, as you know.''[43]
The advice was taken by Sharon's son-in-law, Francis G. Newlands.
After first trying New York State, he finally established residence in
Nevada and began a notable political career, which was capped by a distinguished record in the United States Senate.

Late in the summer of 1888, attorneys for the Sharon estate, following
Stewart's advice, petitioned in federal court for a revival of the order of
December 26, 1885, which had ordered Sarah Althea Hill to surrender
the certificate of marriage. On September 3, 1888, the justices brushed
aside Terry's arguments and unanimously agreed to revive the order
against Mrs. Terry.[44] The proceedings angered the defendant, but Field
ordered her to be seated. When she failed to comply, Field told the marshall, Dave Neagle, to remove her. As Neagle attempted to do so, Terry
sprang to his wife's defense. The couple were finally subdued after a
loaded pistol had been taken from Mrs. Terry and a bowie knife from her
husband. They were immediately adjudged guilty of contempt.[45] The
final act in this strange and interesting case came on August 14, 1889,

when Dave Neagle shot and killed David Terry while defending Justice Field from an alleged attack by Terry.[46]

In 1885, Stewart's interest began to focus once again on Nevada and the possible resumption of his political career. The state had been rather poorly represented by the two men who were elected after Stewart left office in 1875. The first, William P. Sharon, was a near disaster, who had purchased his office. Many Nevadans agreed with the editor of a Reno newspaper, who wrote that Sharon's selection by the state legislature was a good argument for the popular election of senators, for "on merit Sharon would not have succeeded in obtaining 300 disinterested voters."[47] Sharon's absenteeism was so great that the state of Nevada had in effect but one senator from 1875 to 1881. His dismal record tempted Nevada's Democratic Party, which had never been successful in electing a senator. Since Sharon desired reelection and seemed willing to pay for it, the problem for the Democrats was to find a party member who had as much money. They found their candidate in James G. Fair, one of the "Bonanza Kings" of the second Comstock boom, who had millions of dollars to match against Sharon. With Fair's "sackbearers" traveling through each county of the state dispensing funds to buy votes, the Democrats were successful. Fair was chosen to succeed Sharon by the Nevada legislature in January, 1881.[48]

Fair's performance in office was almost as lackluster as that of his predecessor. He attended Senate sessions somewhat more frequently, but offered no constructive legislation. In spite of his weak performance, he wanted a second term and so announced in the spring of 1885.[49] The notice of Fair's candidacy brought immediate adverse reaction from a number of local newspapers, one of which suggested the names of a number of candidates better than Fair. Included in the list were Rollin Daggett, former editor of the *Territorial Enterprise* and a one-term congressman from Nevada; C. C. Stevenson, former governor of Nevada; and John Mackay, another prominent millionaire member of the Bonanza firm.[50] During the latter part of May, 1885, a new name was added when it was reported that William M. Stewart would return to Nevada in time to enter the senatorial fight in 1886.[51]

A possible Stewart candidacy began to attract more attention in Nevada after the former senator launched a speech-making campaign in the middle of September, 1885. Although he did not announce his availability during the opening address in that campaign, at the Carson City Opera House on September 15, 1885, he did indicate in some detail the direction such a candidacy might take. He reviewed the history of the currently raging silver controversy and indicated his proposed solutions to the problem. According to the editor of the *Morning Appeal,* the speech was made before a large audience, "after which there was a call for three cheers which was responded to in the heartiest fashion by the enthusiastic audience."[52]

In addressing the silver issue, Stewart faced the major subject of current political discussion in Nevada. The production of the fabulous Comstock Lode had started to decline rapidly in 1879; by the end of 1884, annual production was but $2,600,000, down from a high of $38,000,000 in 1876. The continued depression in mineral prices sparked a number of political responses in the 1880's. In 1882, both major parties in Nevada placed silver planks in their platforms. Two years later they condemned the "silver crime" (Mint Act of 1873) as they repeated the silver program from the 1882 campaign. When the state legislature met in January, 1885, a resolution was introduced urging Congress to resume the free coinage of silver. A few days later, a group of state senators led a successful movement to hold a silver conference in the senate chambers in Carson City on January 31, 1885.[53] Although no permanent organization grew out of this conference, it did increase the militancy of Nevada's political parties, and served as a warning to prospective office-seekers that the silver issue could not be ignored.

Stewart needed no prompting along those lines. He wrote later that the principal reason he wished to return to the U.S. Senate was the "act of John Sherman smuggling the silver dollar out of the list of coins in the Mint Act of '73 . . . I felt it my duty to return to the Senate and do what I could to rectify the crime which was clandestinely committed without my knowledge or the knowledge of the American people, in the passage of that infamous mint law."[54] Despite this noble purpose, attacks against Stewart increased in the fall of 1885, as his candidacy became more of a possibility. Some wondered how he could cast himself in the role of the great defender of silver after voting for the 1873 act which had demonetized the white metal.[55] They emphasized the fact that Stewart was not a resident of Nevada, having been "lugged into the State just in time to make him available for the Senatorial race."[56] Stewart acted to eliminate the latter complaint when he bought a house in Carson City, in November, 1885. The announcement of the purchase indicated that Stewart planned extensive improvements which would convert the former Willis home to a two-story frame building with a stone foundation. After describing the plans for remodeling, the news article noted, perhaps with tongue in cheek, that the real reason Stewart wanted to acquire Nevada citizenship was because he had been appointed by the Most Sovereign Grand Lodge of E Clampus Vitus to establish a State Grand Encampment of that order in Nevada.[57]

In spite of his purchase of a house in Carson City and establishment of a law office there, accusations of nonresidency against Stewart continued throughout the 1886 campaign. Such charges probably had little effect since, as one writer noted, Stewart had already represented Nevada "with distinction" and consequently could not be "called a carpet-bagger, or an imported candidate."[58] Stewart's campaign was also materially assisted by important financial contributions. One potential source was John W. Mackay, who had become disenchanted with his former partner, Senator Fair, and, according to a San Francisco newspaper, now wanted Stewart returned to the Senate.[59] There were suggestions, too, that Central Pacific officials would support Stewart. The railroad had received little help from Sharon and Fair when national legislation detrimental to its interests was passed by Congress. Stewart's activity on behalf of the Central Pacific during his first ten years in the Senate was well known, and it was clear that he would be more supportive of railroad interests than other potential candidates.[60]

The role of the Central Pacific in Stewart's campaign became clearer during the early months of 1886, when meetings were held in San Francisco and Carson City, to test the political winds and settle the matter of Nevada's senatorial candidate.[61] Representing Stewart at these meetings was Charles C. Wallace, often referred to as "Black" Wallace because of his strong Republicanism. Wallace came to Nevada in 1863, and was county assessor at Eureka for a number of years. From this position he began a career which eventually made him one of the most powerful political figures in the state.[62] Sometime in the early 1880's, he became the Central Pacific's paid agent in Nevada. Thus his position as Stewart's campaign manager in 1886 left no doubt about the railroad's commitment to the reelection of the former senator.

The fact that the first two political meetings to nominate Nevada candidates were held at the Palace Hotel in San Francisco outraged the editor of the *Morning Appeal*. Early in March he suggested that it was time to start a "Nevada party" to fight the "Palace Hotel party."[63] Following the proposal, a March 24 meeting was held in the Ormsby House in Carson City, to form a political group to combat the Californians. In attendance were representatives of a number of potential senatorial candidates, including both Fair and Stewart.[64] Since many of those present had strong ties to California interests, particularly to the Bank of California and the Central Pacific Railroad, it seemed particularly inappropriate that they met to produce a "Nevada Party." Apparently, they effectively squelched the movement, for the proposal soon disappeared from the news.

Although he had representatives at the Ormsby Hotel meeting in

March, Senator Fair had not announced for reelection. His reluctance, no doubt, was due to his record of inaction during his term. Evidently, in a move to gain favorable publicity, he suggested that the Chiricahua Apaches and their chief Geronimo be moved permanently from Arizona territory to Santa Catalina Island, off the coast of California.[65] Fair received much publicity, but hardly the kind to further his reputation as a smart politician. His reelection received little attention during the remainder of the campaign. While many newspapers were having fun with Fair's "Catalina" plan, late in April, a San Francisco newspaper came out strongly in support of Stewart, noting that he was "by long odds the ablest man among the Republican candidates, and the Republican party, not only of Nevada but of the whole Coast, would be advantaged by his presence in the Senate."[66]

Stewart officially opened his campaign for the Senate on June 12, 1886, and gave a housewarming in his newly renovated Carson City home on June 22. Although there were obvious reasons for choosing the state capital to reestablish his Nevada residency, his action placed him in the middle of the anti-Chinese movement which swept that city in the spring and summer of 1886, and forced him into some interesting political maneuvers in order to escape being hurt politically.

Anti-Chinese prejudice was nothing new in Nevada. It had first surfaced when the Central Pacific imported Chinese laborers to assist in the construction of the railroad. In the late 1870's, a number of acts directed against the Chinese were passed by the Nevada legislature, including one which provided for a statewide referendum on Chinese immigration in 1880. The results of the 1880 poll, 183 votes in favor and 17,259 votes in opposition to Chinese immigration, left no doubt where the voters of Nevada stood on the issue.[67] Passage of the federal Chinese Exclusion Act in 1882 somewhat lessened the antagonism shown the Chinese in Nevada, but the growing business depression in the middle 1880's renewed resentment. Removal of the Chinese became a volatile local issue in Carson City in 1886, which placed Stewart in a difficult position because the Central Pacific, one of his chief supporters, still used Chinese labor extensively and successfully in the maintenance of its railroad lines. Stewart knew he had to take a stand on the question, but was careful to keep his name off of the many petitions advocating complete removal of the Chinese from Nevada. In order to clarify his position, he distributed a lengthy pamphlet entitled, "The Chinese Question: The Threatened Invasion, How the East May Be Convinced on the Chinese Question. . . ." In it, Stewart traced the historical invasions of Europe by Asiatics and warned that the Chinese would do the same in the United

States. "The Asiatic," he wrote, "by his presence in a country excludes the Caucasian as the sheep does the ox. *The Chinese will occupy America.* . . . They will exclude us as we excluded aborigines." He went on to note that he did not oppose the Chinese because of their color, but because they were not Christians and were coolies, that is, owned by Asiatic slave masters.[68] The editor of the *Morning Appeal,* who had supported Stewart since the end of 1885, stated that the anti-Chinese pamphlet was an "exhaustive and able document and handles the entire question with a broad and powerful scope. . . . The senator stands square and strong on the anti-Chinese proposition and gives Nevada the benefit of an argument that no pro-Chinese logic can refute."[69] In addition to the pamphlet, Stewart tried to strengthen his position in letters to constituents. To one correspondent he wrote that he would be in Austin shortly, "when I would be glad to see you and your friends and consult in regard to the best way of getting rid of the Chinese evil."[70]

As the campaign moved into the summer of 1886, it became clear that the Republican race would be a battle between C. C. Powning, Thomas Wren, and Stewart. Powning, who had served in the Nevada Senate from 1879 to 1883, now wanted to move up the political ladder to the United States Senate. His candidacy had been given some notoriety at a San Francisco gathering in January, 1886, which Senator John P. Jones also attended. Some reports of that meeting, no doubt encouraged by Powning, gave the appearance that Nevada's senior senator, who was extremely popular, would support him in the race against Stewart. Jones, however, made no public announcement in favor of any candidate, and the battle for his political blessing continued through the summer of 1886. One Carson City paper noted that Rollin Daggett, an early front-runner in the Republican race for the Senate, had spent all day July 30 in Gold Hill, meeting with Sam Jones, the brother of the senator, "arranging a racket to throw the ward against Stewart."[71]

In July, Stewart made a number of moves to win additional support. First, he sent letters to a number of his friends throughout Nevada, urging them to supply him with lists of "Citizens of your county, Republicans and fair-minded Democrats to whom I can send papers and documents during the campaign."[72] Next, he chose a few prominent Republicans to whom he wrote letters emphasizing that Mackay and Walter S. Hobart, a prominent Lake Tahoe lumberman, were actively supporting the Republican Party and urging united action.[73] Then, in a major speech at Carson City on July 17, he summarized the main positions he would support in Congress if elected: a strong irrigation program for Nevada and the west; restoration of silver to its rightful place in the monetary system; opposition to Chinese labor; and proposals to expand Nevada's boundaries, to the north at the expense of Idaho Territory, and to the east at the expense of Utah Territory. In a forceful conclusion, he stated, "I am for the Republican party and not William Stewart. . . . I am no man's enemy. I want to help every man in the state and better his condition." The editor of the *Morning Appeal* predictably thought the speech an excellent outline for building up Nevada.[74]

The following month, Stewart attempted to strengthen his position in Humboldt County, rumored to be a stronghold of one of his opponents, C. C. Powning, by establishing a newspaper in Winnemucca. The project was in difficulty from the beginning and the paper had little influence in the area. Stewart sold the press shortly after the election, in November of 1886.[75] By September, Stewart was in need of additional campaign funds. He wrote to a number of friends in San Francisco asking for help in obtaining financial contributions: "I do not know that I shall have an easy fight but I intend to make a winning fight. Talk to your friends Harmon, Requa, and others, and have them use their influence with their Companies. They may be needed in the primaries, if we shall have primaries, which is uncertain. . . . Have them give orders at once for their Companies [on the Comstock] to stand in for me."[76] The extra money Stewart needed was to help in the county primaries, since he had to have friendly delegations to assure victory in the state convention, and, in turn, in the state legislature in January. Stewart exhorted his supporters to nominate good Republican candidates, promising that "If good men are nominated we can elect them."[77]

Stewart's most significant victory in the county primaries came when C. C. Powning was defeated in Washoe County. The *Morning Appeal* gleefully reported that Powning had lost his own county and that Stewart now was the favorite to win Republican Party support since there was no longer any opposition within the party.[78] The announcement was somewhat premature, for antagonism to Stewart within the party continued, with Powning leading the way. At the Republican State Nominating Convention, which began at Carson City on September 24, 1886, Powning, Rollin M. Daggett, and Thomas Wren tried to take advantage of the carpetbagger designation they had placed on Stewart, by proposing a "home-rule" regulation. A resolution limiting party support to Nevada residents did pass the convention, but had no effect on Stewart's candidacy because he was again a bona fide resident.[79] Although it was obvious at the nominating convention that Stewart was the leading candidate for senator,[80] Powning did not remove himself from the race until October 16, 1886.[81]

Stewart's campaign was given a real boost when Senator Jones returned to Nevada and agreed to participate with Stewart in a speaking tour on behalf the Republican Party.[82] Generally there was little trouble attracting crowds to the speeches, but on at least one occasion Stewart was sufficiently worried about attendance to suggest "special cars from Wadsworth and Verdi at my expense to everybody who will attend [Reno speech]. Make this public at both points."[83]

Stewart recognized, however, that crowds at speeches were largely cosmetic. The senator would be selected by the state legislature, and his own election would depend on obtaining "good" men from each county at the November election. "Good," of course, meant staunch Republicans pledged to Stewart and capable of being elected. The process of electing such individuals, and then keeping them guaranteed for Stewart from the November election until the January meeting of the state legislature, cost money which the candidate personally did not have. Thus, in spite of denials that Stewart had "a railroad sack behind him,"[84] evidence indicates that he did receive substantial contributions from that source. Henry M. Yerington, lobbyist for the "Bank Crowd" generally and the Virginia & Truckee Railroad particularly, doled out considerable sums to see that Republicans were elected to the Nevada legislature. Abner C. Cleveland, Yerington's representative in eastern Nevada, advised the latter, "I think the best way is for you to consult with Stewart and others and place to my credit at the Pacific Bank, San Francisco, $5,000, and do it right away as there are so many places to go to and so little time to do it that I must act promptly."[85]

Throughout the month of October, Stewart continued to address the popular issues of silver, irrigation, and the Chinese. At the same time he was faced with continuing criticism on four points: his part in the Emma Mine scandal, the allegation that he was a carpetbagger, the fact that he had voted for the so-called "Crime of 1873," and his supposed pro-Chinese bias. Attacks against him became strong enough that he hired Piper's Opera House in Virginia City to refute the charges. In his talk, on October 23, he produced a signed receipt from James Lyon showing that the latter had accepted Stewart's arrangements for the sale of the Emma Mine. Stewart implied in his speech that Lyon was the real crook in that affair. As for his support of the 1873 Mint Law, Stewart noted (incorrectly) that he was the first to call attention to the fraud perpetrated by John Sherman and others in passing the act, and reiterated his strong support for the remonetization of silver. Disposing of the carpetbagger label, Stewart reviewed the role he had played in helping Nevada to statehood, insisting that he was a legitimate resident of the state and had been since his return in the fall of 1885. To refute the charge that he favored Chinese immigration, he reminded his listeners that he was the one responsible for defeating the congressional attempt to guarantee Chinese naturalization in 1870. According to newspaper reports, Stewart's speech was well received.[86] Probably just as effective a defense as his own speech, however, was one by Senator John P. Jones, which followed. Jones indicated strong support for his former colleague and characterized him as a real anti-Chinese fighter and a strong supporter of silver.

Stewart's prospects for a Republican victory in the November election were heightened by the fact that the Democrats did not field an effective candidate against him. Fair, the incumbent, had announced earlier that he would seek a second term, but his abysmal record hardly encouraged voter support. The Republican press in Nevada was quick to pick up any report from Washington that might fortify the negative opinion of Fair. For example, an article in a Carson City paper repeated an evaluation from the national capital, that "Fair is the most conspicuous failure of the rich men who have purchased into the Senate. He has absolutely no influence upon public affairs. . . . His absence attracts as little attention as does his presence."[87]

If Fair really wanted to return to the Senate, he would have to buy his way in as he had done in 1880. However, Stewart's aggressive and positive campaign, bolstered by support from the railroad interests, from John Mackay, and from Senator Jones, caused Fair to reconsider his earlier decision. An effective campaign would have cost more than he was willing to gamble, so he did nothing.[88] Fair's indecision forced the Democrats to join "hands with the anti-Chinese, anti-railroad, and anti-everything else men—with the hope of controlling the legislature, County Commissioners and Assessors."[89] It also kept other Democratic hopefuls out of the Senate race. George Cassidy, a former Democratic congressman, and Colonel A. C. Ellis, another prominent western Nevada Democrat, waited until late in October to announce they were in the Senate race.[90] Coming so late, their declarations had little effect on the November 3 election.

On the day of the poll, the *Morning Appeal* trumpeted, "Republicans make the Usual Sweep" and "Stewart the next U.S. Senator." The next day, when results seemed firmer, the paper indicated that Stewart would have 42 votes in the next legislature, substantially more than enough to insure his selection.[91] It was evident that the Republican victory in Nevada pleased railroad and other business interests, both in and out of the state. In a letter to his boss, D. O. Mills, Yerington reported that the Nevada legislature would have 47 Republicans out of a total of 60 members, and that a U.S. senator was certain for the party. He wrote that Stewart would have a rough fight within that group, although, "I guess he will pull through which would be to the interest of the State without a doubt."[92] A San Francisco source noted, "Stewart is a very able man mentally and as a speaker, but his strong point is that when he takes a task in hand he sticks to it, night and day in all weathers and seasons, and uses all means until he carries his point. In point of brains and ability he is worth an acre of Jim Fairs or George Hearsts."[93]

The rough fight in Yerington's letter referred to a plan initiated by C. C. Powning to capture the Republican Party caucus, which was to be held just prior to the opening of the state legislature in January. Powning was charged by a Carson City newspaper with touring Nevada after the November election trying to gain votes to defeat Stewart.[94] At first Stewart appeared unworried, writing to friends that he thought Powning and others would be powerless to defeat him. He was sure Powning would stay out of any Republican meeting, since he had "just four friends—all Democrats—and they will not be likely to go into a Republican caucus."[95] Nevetheless, Stewart was worried enough that he warned John Mackay that Senator Jones thought his selection by the legislature to be in doubt.[96] Leaving nothing to chance, Stewart decided to keep his name before the people and particularly the legislators. A few days before the Republican caucus was scheduled to meet in Carson City, Stewart made a quick tour of Nevada, "to learn people's needs and capabilities" and to help him formulate plans for aiding the state. He emphasized to his listeners that he wanted the U.S. Army to survey land in Nevada for irrigation, and he reiterated his proposals to annex parts of Idaho and Utah territories.[97]

When the caucus was held on January 5, it was obvious that Stewart and his supporters had been unduly concerned; Stewart received 34 votes, while Wren received 9, and Powning just one.[98] A number of California newspapers cheered the results, illustrating as they did the close ties between Stewart and California interests. One reported that Stewart "is a statesman of ripe experience, a lawyer of great ability, and a miner. . . . The new Senator from Nevada will be the peer of any man who now has a seat in the Senate." Another noted the political ties between Nevada and California, "Nevada is simply a child of California; her people are mostly Californians, and Senator Stewart will be as much a representative of California as of Nevada." Still others praised Stewart as the ablest representative in Congress on the silver issue, saying that his selection would give Nevada the strongest senatorial delegation in Congress.[99] Since one of the most persistent campaign charges against

Stewart had been that he was a carpetbagger, it was fortunate that the California newspapers held their remarks until after the caucus had practically assured him of selection by the full Nevada legislature.

When that body met to select a United States senator on January 11, 1887, Stewart was chosen by a vote of 43 to 14 over his Democratic opponent, George Cassidy, with 2 votes for Republican Thomas Wren.[100] Stewart accepted his selection in a speech before the legislature on January 13, in which he vowed to fight for the remonetization of silver, to strive to get help from Congress for irrigation, to support the laboring class, to have the Burlingame Treaty, which guaranteed the Chinese unrestricted immigration to the United States, modified, and to press for the exclusion of all Asiatic laborers from the United States. In addition, he reiterated his advocacy of boundary additions to Nevada from Utah and Idaho, and promised to fight to restore the U.S. Mint at Carson City, closed earlier by President Cleveland.[101]

After his selection by the legislature, the Stewarts held a public reception at their Carson City home, to thank the people for their support during the campaign.[102] However, Stewart would not have been able to thank anyone for his victory had not the California and Nevada railroad and mining interests decided they had had enough of senators like Fair and Sharon and encouraged Stewart to return to politics. The twelve years spent as a private citizen had been a mixture of successful legal cases on one hand and mining promotion failures on the other. The former senator was now eager to return to Washington, D.C., to promote the interests which had brought success to his senatorial campaign.

CHAPTER 7

SEEKING NATIONAL SOLUTIONS
TO NEVADA PROBLEMS

UPON HIS RETURN to Congress, in the six years from 1887 to 1893, Stewart proved true to his campaign promises and pushed forward on the main issues he had earlier identified as the framework for his legislative program. He focused in particular on three: annexation of territory from Utah and Idaho, irrigation of arid land, and remonetization of silver. For each local or regional issue, he sought a remedy that was national in scope.

Stewart had been among the first to recognize the ineffectiveness of Nevada's efforts to relieve economic depression in the state and to suggest turning to the federal government for help. His successful campaign for reelection had demonstrated the strong voter support for this position, but irrigation and remonetization had to await the opening of Congress, in December, 1887, and the delicate political negotiations necessary there. On the other hand, boundary extension at the expense of Utah and Idaho territories offered, in Stewart's view, a more immediate means of expanding Nevada's economic base. It also had the added advantage of profiting Nevada at the expense of her politically weaker neighbors. Consequently, shortly after the November, 1886, election, Stewart began to publicize his position.

In developing his program for annexation of Utah and Idaho lands, Stewart was alert to the advantages of exploiting growing anti-Mormon prejudice in the United States. He reminded Nevadans of the unhappy eleven years they had spent under the control of the Utah territorial government. In a letter to Charles C. Goodwin, an old friend from Comstock days and editor of the *Salt Lake Tribune,* he set the tone for his crusade:

Annie Foote Stewart, first wife of the Nevada Senator. *(Nevada Historical Society Photo)*

The growing rebellion in Utah must be crushed while it can be done without bloodshed. The first and necessary step is to deprive every Mormon and every sympathizer with Mormonism of all political power, and treat them as they have elected to be teated—as alien enemies located in our midst, only entitled to the protection of the law so long as they refrain from violating it, but subject to the severest penalties when they place themselves in oppositon to the Government which tolerates their presence.[1]

Expansion eastward by taking part or all of Utah was only part of Stewart's plan. Two weeks after writing to Goodwin, he sent a letter to California's Senator Abram P. Williams, outlining his plan to add southern Idaho to Nevada and asking Williams for his aid in adopting a Washington statehood bill which would add the Idaho panhandle to the state of Washington. Stewart noted that the northern Idaho counties belonged geographically to Washington, and "the remainder of Idaho belongs legitimately to Nevada." He informed Williams that he thought the people of southern Idaho were willing to be annexed to Nevada if the northern counties were given to Washington. He warned, however, that his letter should be kept private, or the people of Idaho "might become jealous of my actions."[2] In both letters, Stewart emphasized Nevada's need for additional territory, to help overcome the long economic depression and put the state "on a par with the other Western States."

From letter writing Stewart turned to the Nevada legislature. In a speech before a joint session, on January 12, 1887, he outlined his proposals to extend Nevada's boundaries. He suggested that joining southern Idaho with Nevada would double taxable property and reduce the rate of taxation, making Nevada "a state which would take rank, in every respect, with the other new States of the West." He noted that it might also be wise "to include some part of the Territory of Utah in the annexation. But that is more doubtful. We must not under any circumstances place our institutions under the hostile rule of the Mormon Church." Stewart was not concerned about the Mormons in Idaho, for that territory had adopted a test oath against polygamy, "which the Mormons decline to take, and therefore they are excluded from participating in the government of the Territory." It was his hope, he told the legislators, that if Nevada extended its boundaries to include a Mormon population, that a constitutional amendment similar to the test oath of Idaho would be adopted. Expansion, then, would have to be a cooperative effort, for, as Stewart reminded his audience in closing, "The boundaries of Nevada were fixed by Congress, not by the people of our State."[3]

Following the speech, Stewart's supporters in the legislature submitted a series of proposals to carry out his suggestions. These included
both temporary legislative measures and permanent constitutional ones.
The first bill gave Nevada's formal consent to the annexation of additional territory. It was signed into law on February 2, 1887.[4] At the
same time, a resolution was introduced to amend the state constitution
by mandating a test oath that would disenfranchise the members of the
Mormon Church. It required any challenged voter to:

> Solemnly swear (or affirm) that you are not a bigamist or polygamist; that
> you are not a member of any order, organization or association, which
> teaches, advises, counsels or encourages its members or devotees, or any
> other persons, to commit the crime of bigamy or polygamy, or any other
> crime defined by law, or whose members or devotees practice bigamy or
> polygamy, or plural, or celestial marriage with the sanction or approval of
> such order, organization . . . or who instruct members that the U.S. is to
> perish or that the L.D.S. church or any other such organization will destroy
> or supercede the U.S. government.[5]

This resolution passed the senate without difficulty; a few days later, the
assembly ratified an amended version. Stewart was invited to testify on
the proposed constitutional amendment in the Senate. In his speech on
February 9, Stewart repeated his belief that the Mormon church had to
be checked before any portion of Idaho could be joined to Nevada, and
insisted that no one should enjoy the vote who was bound, as were Mormons, by oaths to violate the laws of the United States.[6] Although there
was some opposition to the proposed amendment, its passage by a vote
of 16 to 3 indicated strong support for Stewart's position.[7] Stewart was
worried about the consequences of adding a large Mormon population
to Nevada, as he noted in a letter to Goodwin: "The Mormons must not
obtain control of our State. If by amending the Nevada Constitution and
making a test oath alien enemies can be excluded from the franchise, we
can take in some Mormon territory with safety, otherwise not."[8]

Passage of the resolution was only the first step in the procedure, since
constitutional amendments in Nevada had to pass two successive
legislatures and be approved by the voters at the next general election.
To insure immediate action, Stewart supporters in both houses introduced measures on February 14 and 15 to provide for a legislative test
oath. The assembly bill passed both houses on March 2, 1887.[9] Titled
An Act prescribing the qualifications of electors and modifying the oath
for registration," it was signed by the governor on March 3.[10] The
legislative oath was basically the same as that set forth in the constitu-

tional proposal, specifying that, ''I am not a bigamist or polygamist; that I neither teach or practice bigamy or polygamy; that I am neither a member of nor belong to the Church of Jesus Christ of Latter-Day Saints commonly called the Mormon Church.''[11]

Stewart's efforts to enlarge Nevada's boundaries now shifted to Congress. Early in March, 1888, that body passed a bill to transfer northern Idaho to Washington, and it appeared that Stewart's plan to annex southern Idaho would soon be consummated. The scheme came to a sudden halt a few days later, however. President Cleveland, having been informed of strong opposition to the bill in Idaho Territory, killed it by a pocket veto. Almost at once, support in southern Idaho for annexation to Nevada turned to opposition, and a movement to keep the northern and southern sections of the territory together gained strength.[12]

In spite of the President's veto, Stewart continued to promote the annexation of southern Idaho counties to Nevada, insisting that the best interests of the people of Nevada and Idaho would be served by such action.[13] When it appeared that the main opposition to annexation came from Boise residents, Stewart suggested that Boise and Carson City could be made dual capitals of Nevada, citing as historic examples of such division the cases of Hartford and New Haven in Connecticut and Providence and Newport in Rhode Island.[14] Recognizing that the annexation move was being blocked primarily by statehood advocates in Idaho, Stewart argued that statehood was impracticable. He continued to believe that as soon as Idaho residents understood this, they would ''undoubtedly be willing to join in doing the sensible thing and become part of Nevada.''[15]

In the summer of 1888, Stewart made one last effort on behalf of his annexation proposal. In a Senate speech on July 18, he reiterated his position that Washington Territory should be admitted as a state with the northern Idaho counties included. If that were done, then the southern Idaho counties should be added to Nevada in order to increase the population of the latter state. Rearranging the facts to suit his own purposes, he told his fellow senators that it was not Nevada's fault that she did not have a large population, since ''Nevada was brought in by an Act of Congress without her request.''[16] His pleas fell on deaf ears, however, and statehood movements for both Washington and Idaho territories went forward without Stewart's boundary changes.[17]

Although the annexation of southern Idaho had failed, the ''Mormon Test Oath'' was still Nevada law, and could be used to further Stewart's plan for annexng all or part of Utah Territory. His strategy in this regard was primarily passive. Stewart made no direct effort to have Congress

Senator Stewart after his return to the U.S. Senate in 1887. *(Nevada State Historical Society Photo)*

add Utah to Nevada, but he continuously opposed Utah statehood. Apparently he was convinced that if Utah statehood could be defeated, Congress would turn to the idea of annexing Utah's territory to the non-Mormon state of Nevada.

Thus when Utah Territory petitioned for admission in December, 1887, Stewart spoke against printing the document, stating that he was opposed to any vote that would "give countenance to the idea that the people of Utah are fit to become a state."[18] He repeated and broadened this philosophy in a letter declaring his opposition to the admission of Utah Territory: "Unless American Civilization develops more rapidly in Utah in the future than it has in the past the question of making Utah a State ought not to be discussed in this generation."[19]

Stewart's attitude appeared to undergo subtle changes in the early months of 1888. In February of that year, he suggested an appointive legislative body for Utah, "until a majority of the people are free from control of the Mormon Church."[20] A month later, he introduced a bill in the Senate asking that legislative control be given to a governor and twelve citizens of Utah.[21] Later, in a letter to his friend C. C. Goodwin at Salt Lake City, he leveled another blast at the Mormon hierarchy, assuring Goodwin, "There is no danger of any affirmative action being taken at any time in favor of the Mormons. Utah never will become a State until it is certain that the Territory is free from Mormon rule."[22] In the midst of this fight against the Mormons, in 1888, Stewart was accused of slandering James G. Blaine at the Republican Convention at Chicago. In what must be one of the wildest statements he ever made, he wrote, "I never mix nationality or religion with politics."[23]

Stewart's effort to annex part of Utah Territory ran into major difficulty in the fall of 1888, when George B. Whitney, a Mormon from Panaca, Nevada, tried to register to vote. The registry agent, A. M. Findlay, refused to register Whitney unless he submitted to the test oath required under the 1887 statute. Whitney refused and sought a writ of mandamus from the Nevada Supreme Court to force Findlay to register him under the earlier statute, which did not require such an oath. Before the supreme court hearing on the request, Stewart stated his position to one of Findlay's attorneys, Thomas H. Wells:

> It would be very dangerous to allow the Mormons to vote in our State. The proposition to colonize and take possession of our State Government is seriously considered by the Mormon Church...The suggestion that the Mormon Church is a religious association is not well taken. It is a political oligarchy, and I hope the Supreme Court will not by a strained construction of the Constitution make a decision which will place Nevada at the mercy of the Mormons.[24]

Despite Stewart's hopes, the Nevada Supreme Court held in favor of Whitney in October, 1888. The 1887 test oath was declared to be unconstitutional. The court refused to grant that legislative power was superior to the organic law of the state, stating that "The right of suffrage, as conferred by the Constitution is beyond the reach of any such legislative interference."[25]

By the end of the decade it was apparent that Stewart's attempts to annex Utah had failed. The supreme court decision in the Whitney case was only part of the reason for failure of his expansion plans. By 1887 it was also obvious that Congress was not in favor of boundary extensions for Nevada at the expense of Utah Territory. Instead, Congress acted directly to impede the operation of the Mormon Church in Utah, passing a number of laws, of which the Edmunds-Tucker Act was the most important. This dissolved the corporation of the LDS church and appropriated all of its property, abolished the Perpetual Emigrating Fund Company, took away the right of women to vote, and denied the right of suffrage to all polygamists. In addition, schools were placed under the rule of a new commissioner, the territorial militia law was annulled, and judges of the probate courts were to be appointed by the President of the United States. With the passage of these measures, Stewart's own anti-Mormonism subsided. In the spring of 1890, his opposition to the admission of Utah was beginning to abate:

> The sooner we bring Utah in harmony with the balance of the United States the better. If the people of that Territory could learn that the laws of the United States are paramount and obey them, Utah would be a most desirable country and might then become a State. It seems too bad to have a country located as Utah is with an industrious population, in hostility to the laws of the country, but this evil will be eradicated in time.[26]

As the possibility of statehood for Utah did become firmer, in the spring of 1893 a number of congressmen from the eastern seaboard revived the proposal to annex Utah to Nevada. At first Stewart met such suggestions with caution, indicating that he wasn't prepared to take any action until he heard from his constituents, because he didn't "want to force the people of Nevada to any proposition distasteful to them."[27] Of course he had not considered such input from his constituents necessary earlier, when he had so forcefully advocated annexation of Utah to Nevada. However, in view of his past position, Stewart could not afford to favor annexation to Nevada formally unless some kind of test oath to prevent Mormons from voting was included. Ultimately there was little support in Congress for combining Utah Territory with Nevada, although Stewart continued to suggest that such a move would be of overall economic benefit.

The Nevada senator's position switched dramatically to support of Utah statehood after enabling legislation allowing Utah residents to petition for statehood was introduced in Congress on September 6, 1893. Although the measure was not passed immediately, the obvious support for it in the Senate caused Stewart to reevaluate his position. In an 1894 letter to George Q. Cannon, former editor of the Mormon newspaper, *The Deseret News,* he reversed his earlier stand: "You are right in regarding me as a friend and as in favor of the admission of Utah. I am opposed to annexation of Utah to Nevada and able to assure you that Utah will be admitted at this session of Congress. . . . I shall continue to work for the independent and unconditional admission of Utah."[28] After President Cleveland signed the Utah Enabling Act on July 18, 1894, Stewart's conversion seemed complete:

> The great Territory of the Interior [Utah] will soon be one of the most prosperous States in the Union. In industry, frugality, and economy it will surpass all the other States. In natural resources—mineral and agricultural —Utah has few equals. In climate and scenery, she has no superior. I congratulate the honest law-abiding and self-supporting people of the new state of Utah that they now have an opportunity to liberate themselves from the evils and disadvantages of a territorial government under which they have suffered more than any other Territory of the United States, and that they will enjoy the full privilege of American citizens to govern themselves, subject only to the Constitution and laws of the United States.[29]

And then, no doubt mindful of his own long battle against Utah statehood, he added the hope that the new state would be guided by the motto, "Malice towards none and charity for all."[30]

True to his promise to Cannon, from 1894 until statehood was finally achieved in 1896, Stewart strongly favored the movement. His support later brought him an interesting letter from Cannon, then an official of the Church of Jesus Christ of Latter-day Saints, congratulating Stewart on reelection to the Senate in 1899. Cannon wrote, "You certainly deserve the honor, for you have served your people faithfully and well. I as one of your host of friends am proud of your record, and in expressing my sincere congratulations to you at this time I feel that not less to be congratulated are the state of Nevada, the Great West, and indeed the whole Nation."[31] Thus, through some fancy political footwork, Stewart was ultimately acknowledged by a leading member of the Mormon church as a friend to those whom he had criticized unmercifully for years.

In the interim, while the issue of Utah's political future was being decided, Stewart's attention, like that of most members of Congress, was diverted to the presidential election to be held in 1888. His first concern was the approaching National Republican Nominating Convention, since it was generally assumed that John Sherman would be one of the principal Republican contenders for the presidency. Stewart had convinced himself, and was trying to convince others, that Sherman was the main culprit in the passage of the Mint Act, the "Crime of '73" which demonetized silver. The convention would give Stewart an opportunity to influence the Republican Party to return to the bimetallic standard, as well as a chance to thwart the ambitions of the Ohio senator.

In order to work for Nevada and against Sherman, Stewart first had to become a delegate from his state. This proved more difficult than he had expected, since certain Republicans, particularly C. C. Powning, continued to resent Stewart's return to Nevada and the threat he posed to their own political ambitions. He tried to overcome objections to his candidacy by attaching himself to the popular Senator Jones, writing one Nevadan, "I think that if Jones and myself attended the convention and a Republican President is elected we might make Jones Secretary of the Treasury—a place that he is peculiarly fitted for."[32] To another friend he suggested that if he and Jones went to the convention they might obtain some patronage for Nevadans from a friendly administration, "We can have a foreign minister, and in all probability a Commissioner of the General Land Office and one or two territorial offices, besides local offices in the State."[33] Nobly disclaiming any personal motivation, he wrote, "I have no desire to go to the Convention on my own account, but want to be able to help our Nevada friends. . . . I ask nothing for myself. Influence with any Administration will not add to my reputation. That must be made in the Senate. Still it will add to my power to help my friends at home."[34]

In other letters to prominent Nevada Republicans he argued that he needed to be in Chicago, because the fight for silver would move from Washington to the convention city during the national convention.[35] In his campaign to be named a delegate he sent a suggested set of resolutions for the Republican State Convention to his friend, F. C. Lord, in Virginia City. These covered such obviously popular Nevada topics as free silver; high tariffs for wool, lead, borax and other Nevada products; and exclusion of the Chinese and all other imported contract laborers.[36]

Whether or not his letter-writing campaign was responsible, Nevada Republicans meeting at Winnemucca selected both Jones and Stewart as delegates. They also adopted a number of the planks which Stewart had suggested. At the national convention, which met in Chicago in June, Stewart managed to have himself placed on the platform committee and later, with his usual lack of modesty, took credit for several planks which were adopted. In a letter to Sam Wright, he boasted, "I accomplished all I expected to and think it was fortunate for our people that I went to the Convention. The silver plank is not so radical as I would have liked, but it is all that I could reasonably ask for. It commits our party to bi-metallism."[37]

To another Nevada correspondent he gave additional details of his work at the convention:

> I accomplished what I went to the Convention for. You will see in the plat-form a silver plank, an anti-Chinese plank, an anti-Mormon plank, a plank in favor of the admission of the Territories, and an indication that the Republican party does not approve of the President's plan of loaning Government money to pet banks without interest. Every citizen of Nevada ought to vote the Republican ticket at the next election.[38]

In his autobiography Stewart was more specific about his role in obtaining the silver plank, which pledged the Republican Party to the use of both gold and silver as legal tender, "This plank I drew myself after an all-night session of the Committeee on Resolutions, discussing the question of silver. The Committee on Resolutions and the entire convention were deliberately pledged to the foregoing proposition."[39]

Stewart also took credit for eliminating John Sherman as a presidential candidate by his exposé of Sherman's deception in engineering passage of the Mint Bill of 1873. Stewart's statements were extensively circulated and probably did help turn delegates against Sherman, although "Sherman appeared to be ignorant of the determined fight made against his nomination by delegates who resented his duplicity in demonetizing silver."[40] Stewart's success in the convention was not complete, however, since he failed to gain western support for the nomination of his longtime friend Leland Stanford. He wrote to Stanford that he and Stephen Gage, lobbyist for the Southern Pacific Railroad, had agreed on a plan of operation; but the California delegates were solidly for James G. Blaine and opposed even a complimentary vote for Stanford.[41] The Stanford incident was minor and did not detract from Stewart's importance in writing the silver plank and obtaining its adoption in the convention.

After the political conventions settled the issue of national candidates, Stewart and other western senators turned to a regional issue which had been gaining political support in the arid west—irrigation. On September 13, 1888, Stewart pushed through the Senate a resolution directing

the Secretary of the Interior to make "an examination of that portion of
the United States where agriculture is carried on by means of irrigation,"
with the purpose of determining dam sites, costs of reservoirs, and
related matters. The resolution received strong support from the "Irrigation Clique," a group formed by Henry P. Teller of Colorado, Stewart, and others, to promote irrigation and reclamation. The clique was
unable to obtain a direct appropriation for the work, but did manage to
attach a $100,000 rider to the Sundry Civil Appropriation Bill to com-
mission a survey under the direction of John Wesley Powell. This bill
passed the Senate on October 2, 1888.[42] When Stewart returned to
Nevada in October to participate in the 1888 election campaign, he
naturally found Nevadans receptive to the irrigation issue. At a banquet
at McKissick's Opera House in Reno, he was praised for the Powell
survey legislation. He told his audience that the next step after the
survey would be the donation of public lands to Nevada, in order to
obtain funds for reclamation work.[43]

Agriculture, or more specifically, livestock, had been for years
Nevada's second industry. In the early 1880's, as the decline of mining
on the Comstock continued, Nevada's political and financial leaders
saw agriculture as a means whereby the state's economy could be pulled
out of the continuing depression and given a more stable base. Irrigation
of arid lands loomed as the means to make that transition from a mining
to a pastoral economy. Unfortunately, legislative attempts to encourage
irrigation in Nevada were unsuccessful in 1883 and 1885. Irrigation was
made a major political issue in the 1886 campaign, both by Stewart,
and by Charles C. Stevenson, running for governor. After his election,
Stevenson emphasized his commitment by making irrigation a major
subject of his inaugural address in January, 1887.[44] In spite of the
governor's presentation, legislators accomplished little for irrigation in
the 1887 session, due mainly to a confrontation between the reclama-
tionists and the mining and railroad interests.[45]

Central Pacific Railroad officials opposed state-funded reclamation
projects because they feared that increased property taxes would result.
Even some groups who stood to benefit from irrigation projects—cattlemen, for instance—had the same qualms and resisted state funding because they felt that federal land cessions would be a better way to achieve
the desired results. Ultimately, though, continued depression in the
mining industry, and concurrent pressure by irrigationists in Nevada
and other western states throughout 1888, set the stage for a more successful program in 1889. William Stewart then became the instrument
whereby the interests of the state irrigationists were focused on efforts
of the federal government.

Stewart was not a newcomer to the irrigation issue. During the last eighteen months of his second Senate term, he had been involved in an attempt to get federal support for a study of irrigation in the San Joaquin and Tulare valleys in California. Backing for such an investigation had come from a group of western capitalists led by William C. Ralston, and the original proposal was drafted by Senator Cornelius Cole of California. It was introduced in the Senate on February 13, 1873, by Senator Stewart, who piloted the bill through the Senate and on to the president's signature on March 2.[46] The 1873 act was the first instance of federal aid to support an irrigation survey, and the 1874 report on the San Joaquin, Tulare, and Sacramento valleys, was an important precursor of a national reclamation act.

Stewart's knowledge of water law and water rights was fortified during his twelve-year absence from the U.S. Senate, when he served as counsel for a number of California landholders, including James W. Haggin and Lloyd Tevis. The legal foundation for the division of water rights that he devised in this connection successfully survived the test of the complex California water laws.[47]

After his return to the U.S. Senate in 1887, Stewart renewed his efforts to promote irrigation in the arid west. In December of that year, he introduced a number of bills and resolutions to segregate irrigable lands, to reserve places for reservoirs, and to obtain rights-of-way for ditches and canals. Partly as a result of his continuing efforts, Congress authorized an irrigation survey on October 2, 1888. In December, 1888, Stewart proposed that a special Senate subcommittee on irrigation and reclamation be added to the Public Lands Committee. The irrigation committee was to have permission to sit during recesses of the Senate and was to report back to that body at the beginning of the next session in December, 1889.[48] Stewart's proposal was accepted, and the Select Committee on Irrigation and Reclamation of Arid Lands was organized on February 15, 1889, with Stewart as its chairman and Senators Allison, Plumb, Hiscock, Gorman, Reagan, and Jones of Arkansas as members.[49] The committee received an appropriation of $80,000 to cover expenses for an inspection tour through the far west.

Shortly after the close of the congressional session, Stewart began plans for what turned out to be a rather extensive journey through the arid states. Included in the group making the trip, besides the seven senators on the committee and staff assistants, were Major John W. Powell, who had been appointed earlier to make a survey of irrigation sites in the west, and, for part of the tour, Francis G. Newlands. Stewart chartered a Pullman car from the Northern Pacific Railroad Company for the expedition, and set the itinerary to start from St. Paul, Minnesota, on August 1, 1899. The fact-finding committee then proceeded through the Dakotas, Montana, Wyoming, Colorado, Utah, Idaho, Nevada, California, Arizona, New Mexico and Texas.[50]

Stewart's invitation to Newlands to accompany the committee as a private citizen was unusual. Newlands and Stewart had worked together closely in settling the William Sharon estate, and Newlands had moved to Nevada in 1888, at Stewart's suggestion, in order to facilitate that settlement.[51] It was well known by this time that Newlands had political ambitions, which Stewart apparently tried to assist by inviting Newlands to accompany his committee. The senator's early friendship for Newlands may well have been prompted by a pragmatic desire to keep the wealthy Newlands on his side in any later battles.[52] Certainly Newlands's close ties to the Bank of California, consistent supporters of Stewart, also made it expedient for the latter to woo the younger man. In any event, Stewart wrote cordially to Newlands in the summer of 1889, inviting him to join the committee:

> There will be room for you in our car, as I was compelled to engage an extra one to accommodate the committee . . . I hope you will not fail to accompany me on the trip . . . it will give you an opportunity to meet prominent men at these points and become acquainted, and make such arrangements as you may desire for some active work in the campaign. It will also give us an opportunity to talk over the political issues involved in the campaign [1890] in the new states.[53]

The committee reached Reno on August 21, 1889, and met the following day with the Nevada Board of Reclamation and Internal Improvements, which had been established earlier in the year by the Nevada legislature. Under the act, granting all unappropriated water to the state, the Board of Reclamation was authorized to divide the state of Nevada into reclamation districts, appoint district superintendents, and supervise the survey and construction of reservoirs and canals. To do all of this, the legislature appropriated $100,000 for the board's use.[54] Meeting with Stewart's Senate irrigation committee, board members summarized the water and forest areas, the grazing, mineral, and agricultural lands in Nevada, and noted lakes which might be utilized for storage and irrigation. Board President Evan Williams of Ormsby County then made a plaintive plea for government aid for Nevada, "At a time in its history when its needs are more pressing than at any period since its organization as a state . . . can the General Government refuse to render assistance . . . or will it allow one of its sovereign states to languish?''[55] The report had inadvertently struck at the heart of Nevada's basic financial difficulty. A supposedly "sovereign" state, established through political motivations without respect for economic considerations, admitted that it could not sustain itself without federal aid.[56]

Stewart's ability to facilitate this assistance was curtailed by a bitter dispute with John Wesley Powell. The disagreement between the two jeopardized efforts to involve the federal government in any irrigation program for the arid west, disrupted the progress of legislation in Congress, and ultimately pushed both men into the background of the movement. The animosity began in August of 1889, when the Secretary of the Interior rescinded all western land entries made after passage of the 1888 act, pending completion of Powell's surveys. The General Land Office estimated that the secretary's action involved withdrawal of some 9,000,000 acres of public land. Stewart blamed Powell. Although Powell had denied, early in 1888, the necessity of withdrawing any irrigable land, Stewart suspected that the Interior Secretary's subsequent decree was the result of Powell's influence.[57] Once he had convinced himself that Powell was behind the efforts to prevent open entry of federal land in the west, Stewart did not rest until he had forced Powell from office.

The conflict between the two men went deeper than Powell's alleged deception. The key to their differences was a fundamental distinction in approach. To Powell, irrigation and reclamation were long-range problems. Not bothered by the political pressures bearing on Stewart and other legislators, Powell pursued an ideal of social stability. He envisioned settlements similar to those of the Mormons, with large family homesteads linking irrigable, pastoral, and timber lands. Powell expected that social, economic, and political unity would come automatically from such irrigation developments, overlooking the fact that Mormon cohesion was basically religious.[58]

Powell advocated a ten-year study of the arid zone, to enable the government to select the 100,000,000 best acres from a possible 800,000,000 acres that could be used for irrigation.[59] His plan was to complete this systematic survey before any settlement began; and his supporters argued that a scientific decision should be made without reference to the short-term economic, social, or political problems that might be involved.[60] Powell would thus have stopped settlement of the entire west for six or seven years in order to insure that irrigable lands were kept from ''water and land companies wanting to accumulate a domain.''[61]

Westerners obviously could not tolerate such an extended wait. To them, irrigation and reclamation were the means to end the economic stagnation that gripped their states, and their representatives consequently demanded immediate action. Stewart, perhaps more than any other western legislator, saw the political implications of the issue. He knew that his position on the question had to be political, or he risked losing public favor in Nevada and, with it, his ability to achieve any kind of irrigation program in the long run. The western view was succinctly stated by two supporters of the Stewart philosophy: "We want crops—we do not want pictures—and the major [Powell] is making pictures. We want results. Our people in the West are practical people and we cannot wait until this geological picture and topographical picture is perfected."[62] The westerners' primary objective was recovery from drought and depression; and they wanted the development to be state-oriented, as opposed to the strong national position taken by Powell. From their point of view, federal government participation should be limited to cession of unsold public lands back to the state governments. Once that was done, the program would be a state one.

The gist of Stewart's plan was that the ceded public lands would be sold by the states to obtain revenue, which could then be used for irrigation projects. Stewart opposed federal construction of reclamation projects and preferred traditional laissez faire development. As he envisioned the situation, the federal government would control only the reservoir sites, in order to prevent monopolization by any private developer.

The long-range implications of Powell's plan contrasted sharply with the more expedient views supported by Stewart and other western senators. This has led some to portray Powell as the farsighted champion of reclamation and to blame Stewart for failing to understand the complexities of Powell's plan.[63] There is little doubt Stewart understood Powell's program thoroughly, but his supreme political pragmatism left him no alternative but to oppose it.[64]

Stewart's relations with Powell deteriorated rapidly after the Secretary of Interior rescinded western land entries in August, 1889. By the early part of 1890, Nevada's junior senator was actively seeking ways of blocking Powell. The major had an initial advantage because Congress had given him the power to "dictate, by his location of reservoirs and canals and his selection of the lands to be irrigated, the precise pattern that future settlement would take."[65] Stewart recognized the risks inherent in a fight with Powell, as he confided to one of his constituents: "In the conflict there is great danger that the whole matter of irrigation will be defeated altogether. But I would rather be defeated than have the whole country tied up under Powell."[66]

Once having decided that Powell had to go, Stewart sought the appropriate means. He found it in the fact that Powell had diverted 80 percent of the original $100,000 appropriation, which western senators had intended to use for dams and canals, for a hydrographic map of the nation—the key to his own plan. Stewart could not see how such hydrographic work had any practical relation to irrigation, and lashed out at Powell. In a letter to a friend, Stewart bitterly indicted Powell:

> . . . ambitious, unscrupulous, and incompetent . . . using the idea of irrigation to get funds from Congress and then preventing settlement . . . while he conducts scientific experiments. . . . Nothing can be done with irrigation until the question can be considered independent of the impracticable, selfish and ambitious schemes of Major Powell. His power comes from jobs he has at his disposal.[67]

Stewart reiterated his charges on the floor of the Senate and in letters sent to individuals throughout the country.[68]

Stewart's battle with Powell continued during the summer of 1890. He won his first victory on August 29, when Congress repealed that part of the 1888 Sundry Civil Appropriation Act which had allowed the reservation from entry of certain irrigable lands.[69] In 1892, Powell's opponents won drastic cuts in the appropriation for the Geological Survey, and they finally brought about Powell's resignation in 1894.[70] While this fight was going on, a number of western senators, including Stewart, introduced bills providing for cession of public lands to the states, for irrigation purposes. None of these was successful.[71]

By the end of 1890, the Stewart-Powell quarrel had helped to bring the national irrigation-reclamation program to a stalemate. Stewart was by then beset by stronger political pressures from Nevada mining interests, and noted disgustedly as he moved away from the irrigation question, "I have about come to the conclusion that irrigation must be prosecuted by private enterprise and not otherwise, and that all the Senators and Representatives from the West can accomplish is to secure laws suitable to the development of the country and such as will permit labor and capital to be united in developing these desert lands."[72] In this analysis, Stewart was perhaps correct. The failure to achieve a national irrigation program has been blamed on the Stewart-Powell difficulties, but the demise of the Powell survey was hardly "catastrophic to a national program of reclamation."[73] An education program, more than a scientific survey, was needed to convince Congress of the importance of a nationally supported irrigation program. It was quite apparent that the federal government was not ready to support such a concept in the early 1890's.

As irrigation activity ground to a temporary halt both in Nevada and nationally, Stewart turned his attention to the silver movement, hoping to gain control of that issue. This course was not without some difficulties, however, as Stewart first learned when he returned to Nevada in 1885, to try to regain his seat in the U.S. Senate.

Stewart was forced by constituents and reporters to spend considerable time during the 1886 campaign and the years which followed, explaining his position on the infamous "Crime of '73." The questions were as repetitious as the answers, as Stewart sought to counter the charge that he had voted for the Mint Act. His election, as well as any possible leadership role in the silver movement, depended upon his success in convincing the electorate that he had not voted for demonetization, and that the Mint Bill had passed only because of Sherman's deception. Stewart chose to base his campaign on Sherman's duplicity, dismissing the voting charge, as he had earlier, on the basis that no division to show the yeas and nays had been called for in the Senate.

According to Stewart, John Sherman and the 1873 Mint Act were responsible for Nevada's economic depression. Although no one at the time cast it in such a light, Stewart's fight against Sherman was a good example of the "devil" theory of history, in which Stewart and his followers were cast as "the good guys," while Sherman and the conspirators became "the villains." In Stewart's view, Sherman and others had brought about by deception the demonetization of silver. This in turn had caused an economic depression in Nevada and other western mining areas. Since a federal law had caused the depression, it followed that a federal law would eliminate it. Thus, if silver was remonetized, prosperity would automatically return.[74] It was a simplistic explanation based on emotion, not fact; but it was one which proved to have great voter appeal in Nevada and other western states.

In detailing Sherman's conspiracy, Stewart insisted that there were, in effect, two conspiracies. One involved the "bondholders at London and Paris," who purportedly initiated the plan to press for codification of U.S. mint laws for the sole purpose of omitting the silver dollar from the list of coins.[75] The other action, the one which silverites condemned the most, was the deceptive way that Sherman convinced Congress to demonetize silver.

On numerous occasions after his return to the Senate in 1887, Stewart criticized Sherman for his part in the passage of the Mint Act of 1873, always charging directly that the Ohioan had deceived the Senate. His most detailed accusation came in a speech on March 8, 1888: "I think I am safe in saying that the Senate passed it in ignorance of its contents or effect. . . . if Sherman had told the Senate that the bill contained a proposition to demonetize silver and adopt the gold-standard, there would not have been a single vote in its favor."[76] Later he added that "the concealment had been so good that it had even fooled so 'lynx-eyed' a watchman" as himself.[77] Lynx-eyed he had not been in 1873, nor had other westerners, who should have been more alert to a measure which affected their constituents. Surely they had ample time, in the years from the bill's introduction in 1870, to its passage in 1873, to study its provisions.[78]

The matter of "conspiracy" in regard to passage of the 1873 Mint Act has been approached by a number of historians and economists. These observers generally agree that government officials worked secretly to bring about passage of the measure without including a provision for the minting of the silver dollar, but that they did so in what they considered the public interest.[79] However, in the highly charged political climate of the 1880's and 1890's, Stewart made a rather convincing case that Sherman and others not only maneuvered secretly to pass the Mint Act of 1873, but did so for selfish reasons.

Stewart attempted to gain stature among silverites by claiming to be the first to expose the Mint Act as the "Crime of '73." Apparently that honor actually belonged to one George Melville Weston, who wrote a letter to the *Boston Globe* on March 2, 1876, in which he charged that there had been a conspiracy surrounding the demonetization of silver in 1873.[80] Indeed, Nevada's senior senator, John P. Jones, in a Senate speech on April 24, 1876, acknowledged his debt to Weston for discovering the conspiracy.[81] However, some twelve years later, after the conspiracy charge had been rather widely circulated, Stewart implied in a letter to a supporter that he himself had uncovered the conspiracy:

> You have stated the case [silver issue] well. The only inaccuracy that I observed in your article was the statement that the discovery of the fraudulent work accomplished by the act of 1873 was not made until 1878. It was discovered in 1876, at which time I wrote several articles, which were published in the "New York Herald" and in Washington and numerous western papers denouncing the fraud.[82]

In his efforts to establish himself as a leader of the silver forces, Stewart was careful not to alienate his Nevada colleague, Senator John P. Jones. Called the nation's first bimetallist,[83] Jones had been involved in the congressional silver fight while Stewart was trying to reestablish his private law practice in California. Jones's reputation as a silver leader was enhanced by his appointment as a member of the Silver Commission. In the fall of 1877, this group made a report to Congress, favoring the free coinage of silver and warning of the threat of economic depression if industry continued "chained" to a single standard. Jones's strong support of the Bland-Allison Silver Act in 1878, made him a hero to Nevada voters; but this early acclaim as a leader in the silver movement, combined with a substantial personal fortune, also made it easy for Jones to withdraw from the limelight. After 1878, he felt little need to occupy the public spotlight or justify himself to the voters. Jones's inactivity opened the door to Stewart. Since the latter had neither personal fortune nor an established reputation on the silver issue, he hurried to fill the void left by Jones and thus assure his reelection in 1892.

Stewart's third term in the U.S. Senate, 1887 to 1893, covered years of growing awareness that silver remonetization had become a major political issue.[84] Consequently, Stewart sought every opportunity to identify himself publicly as a leading national advocate of remonetization. He introduced a silver bill at the beginning of the congressional session in December, 1887, and, a few months later, initiated his long fight to convince the public of the existence of a "conspiracy" in the passage of the 1873 Mint Act. Moreover, he lost no time in informing his Nevada constituents about his activities. In a letter to a good friend in Carson City, he boasted, "We are having a lively fight on the silver question. Everybody said the question was dead when I came here last fall, but I have been kindling fires all around and have got the pot boiling again. I will keep it boiling until it is settled right. The gold bugs shall have no peace until they surrender at discretion."[85]

Stewart's efforts to keep the "pot boiling" on the silver question took many forms between 1887 and 1890. In the Senate he introduced numerous measures to restore silver, attached himself to silver bills introduced by others, and made lengthy speeches supporting the remonetization of silver whenever the occasion arose. In some instances he brought the silver issue into discussion of other topics. For example, during discussion of the tariff after the election of 1888, Stewart stated that industry could be strengthened by encouraging trade with the Pacific Islands, Mexico, and South America, all of which were still on the silver standard. In another debate, this time on the revenue laws, Stewart insisted that the fall in prices of farm products during the previous fourteen years had been due to the demonetization of silver. In all of these speeches he reiterated his charge that the demonetization of silver had been accomplished by stealth, implicating always the "foreign bond-holding conspirators." It was during this period also that he began associating the gold standard with rich and powerful commercial and industrial interests, and silver with the masses.[86]

As Stewart began his push for leadership of silver advocates in the Fiftieth Congress, he associated the free-silver movement with the Republican Party. In a September, 1888, speech in the Senate, he acknowledged that the work of remonetizing silver had started in the late 1870's with a coalition of Democrats and some western Republicans. However, Stewart insisted that the Democratic Party had become a gold-standard party and that silver had depreciated in price by 17 percent since Cleveland's election. He reminded his colleagues that Cleveland had also asked for the repeal of the Bland-Allison Act.[87]

The energetic Stewart sent letters to Secretary of the Treasury William Windom, and to President Harrison, trying to win their support for free silver. He urged Windom to authorize the purchase of $4,000,000 of silver per month until the next meeting of Congress, "It would be readily absorbed and would give some relief, besides having an important bearing on the elections in the four new states [Washington, Montana, North Dakota, South Dakota] that will be admitted before Congress again meets."[88] The seventeen-page letter which he sent to the President blamed all the woes of the country on demonetization of silver and urged Harrison to become a silverite and return the country to the money standard of the United States Constitution. He charged Harrison with a change in monetary policy and asked the administration to buy the full $4,000,000 of silver per month that was allowed under the Bland-Allison Act of 1878. Stewart cited the country's need for more money in circulation, a policy he consistently advocated throughout the fight for remonetization.[89] Stewart even found time to write to a silverite in Michigan, supporting the latter's suggestion of forming silver clubs throughout the nation;[90] and he made certain that newspaper editors in Nevada received copies of all of his Senate silver speeches.

By 1890, it was evident that neither the Cleveland nor Harrison administrations were willing to carry out the provisions of the Bland-Allison Act. Consequently, Senate supporters of silver renewed their efforts to obtain a new silver purchase act. Their attempts were not successful until the middle of 1890, when political circumstances made possible the passage of a new silver act. What became known as the

Sherman Silver Act was introduced in the House of Representatives on January 20, 1890, by Edwin H. Conger of Iowa.[91] It was referred to the Senate Committee on Finance on June 10.[92]

While the Conger Bill was working its way through the House of Representatives to the Senate, silver leaders in Nevada took a step toward forming an alliance to fight for the remonetization of silver. Following the suggestion of the National Silver Committee, Thomas Fitch, a former congressman from Nevada, issued a call for county residents to select delegates for a state silver convention, to meet in Carson City on May 29, 1890. This Nevada Silver Convention made no attempt to form a political party, indicating that it was concerned with politics only insofar as politics affected the free coinage of silver. The convention did, however, send instructions to the Nevada congressional delegation not to support any monetary measure which did not call for the remonetization of silver.[93]

Meanwhile, the Conger Bill was reported favorably from the Senate Finance Committee and passed by the Senate, with amendments which effectively made it a free-coinage measure. It was returned to the House on June 17, 1890.[94] The House refused to concur with the Senate amendments, and a conference was called. The house appointees were Conger, Joseph H. Walker of Massachusetts, and Richard P. Bland of Missouri. The Senate sent John Sherman, John P. Jones, and Ishman G. Harris of Tennessee.

Stewart had taken an active part in the debates on the silver bill, stressing the need to retain the provision that forced redemption of a certain amount of silver bullion each month. He pointed out that the failure to include such a feature in the 1878 Bland-Allison Act had robbed that measure of its effectiveness.[95] If he was disappointed at not being named to the conference committee for the Conger Bill, he did not show it. He voted with the Senate majority to approve the bill as reported from conference, and it was signed by President Harrison on July 14, 1890.[96]

Sherman's support of silver on this occasion was a matter of practical politics. The Republicans wanted a higher tariff bill in 1890, and the votes of the silver bloc were necessary to achieve that goal. To obtain those votes a new silver bill had to be passed. For a time during the debate, it appeared that such a measure might provide for the complete remonetization of silver. However, the Republican leadership was able to prevent a silver stampede in the House, and the silver bloc had to settle for a limited purchase plan. Yet it was one that many silver leaders, including William M. Stewart, thought would restore the value of silver.

Shortly after passage of the law, Stewart wrote to a silverite in California, praising its provisions. The senator indicated that it might lead to free silver and the end of the money problems in the United States, but was careful to temper his enthusiasm with some important qualifications. He noted that the Sherman Act would bring the silver price to par "if the law is faithfully executed," and declared, "I have no doubt the administration will execute the law in its true spirit and intent. If it does the silver fight is practically ended."[97] There was reason for Stewart's optimism, for the bill as passed provided for the purchase of 4,500,000 ounces of silver each month at the prevailing market prices. That amount was the estimated total production of the United States at the time. Unfortunately, by the time the act went into effect, the United States was at the beginning of a major depression which prevented proper operation of the plan.

The issues noted above were only some of those that faced Stewart on his return to the Senate. It soon became clear that his responses to these other issues would play a major role in any reelection plans.

CHAPTER 8

MATTERS OF POLITICAL SURVIVAL
AND SENTIMENT

BY 1887, much of the antagonism toward the South, which had been so evident during Reconstruction, had dissipated. Yet two questions which arose in the years immediately following Stewart's return to the Senate made it clear that the "Bloody Shirt" issue could easily be revived.

The first of these, in 1888, concerned President Cleveland's nomination of Lucius Q. C. Lamar to become associate justice of the United States Supreme Court. Although the former Confederate military officer had been "reconstructed" to the extent that he had served after the Civil War in the House of Representatives, the Senate, and as Cleveland's Secretary of the Interior during his first presidential term, Lamar's nomination to the high court was seen by many as too great an honor to bestow on a onetime Confederate soldier. Most Republican newspapers and party leaders took strong stands against the nomination, but Stewart expressed immediate support for Lamar.

Reaction in Nevada was mixed. A number of open letters opposing the nomination appeared in Nevada newspapers;[1] but Stewart also received approval from Nevada and elsewhere. The Carson City *Morning Appeal* noted that the senator's action would win Southern votes for silver and, besides, "The bloody shirt is no longer a factor in politics, and no one knows this any better than Stewart."[2] An editorial in the *Daily Alta California* praised Stewart for his stand on the Lamar case, "The Senator has proved that a man may be a Republican without being a sectionalist, and that there is something greater than personal and provincial politics."[3] An even stronger endorsement of Stewart came from the *New York Times,* which reprinted a long letter from Stewart to a Nevada constituent explaining his support of Lamar, and then commented that Stewart's views were "creditable to his intelligence and patriotism. . . . Opponents of Lamar would find it hard to answer Mr. Stewart's definite and authoritative statements."[4]

The Senate approved Lamar's appointment on January 16, 1888, after a rather bitter battle in which Stewart played a leading role. The appointment had been referred to the Judiciary Committee on December 12, 1887, and reported adversely from that body on January 10, 1888. In spite of the committee report, two Republican senators, Stewart of Nevada and Stanford of California, sided with the Democrats to approve the appointment. The vote of the two Republicans was vital, since the final tally was just 32 for the appointment and 28 against it.[5] After the ballot, Stewart wrote to a longtime Nevada supporter, "I have no fear of him on the Bench, and the full endorsements of Mr. Lamar, as Judge of the Supreme Court, of the war amendments would be exceedingly valuable in putting that question forever at rest." He went on to declare Republican opposition to the nomination a mistake and, unable to resist a blow for silver, suggested, "Wall Street will glory in the 'bloody shirt' if under its shadow it can demonetize silver and rob the people."[6]

In another letter on the same subject, Stewart offered the kind of insight that occasionally took him out of the familiar role of politician and placed him on the higher level of statesmanship:

> The Republican Party must become National or cease to exist. It can only become National by observing in good faith its pledges to the South contained in the various acts of Congress and the Constitutional amendments, wherein the United States granted amnesty and oblivion for the past to all those who would accept the terms of reconstruction. The rejection of Lamar would have been a declaration by the Senate that the Republican Party would not be bound by the obligations of the reconstruction legislation.[7]

In a somewhat similar letter to a correspondent in San Francisco, he noted, "The nomination of Lamar furnished a good and safe opportunity for the Republican Party to treat the war as ended, but I am sorry it failed to embrace it."[8] He followed that same reasoning in a note to a prominent Nevada political leader, "I am glad to know you take a sensible view of the Lamar matter, as you always do of everything. There is no doubt he is thoroughly reconstructed. . . . It was a great mistake for the Republican Party to try and defeat him. It would have been unpardonable in me to have indulged in any such petty spite and destroyed my usefulness to aid my own State."[9] It is clear that Stewart thought rejection of the Lamar appointment meant a permanent ban against all Confederate veterans.[10]

Stewart later took credit for the confirmation vote, pointing out that he had published a letter giving a full history of Lamar's patriotic course after the Civil War: "The facts stated in that letter, together with the report of the Judiciary Committee, removed every objection to the confirmation which the Senate could possibly consider. . . . The contest was a bitter one, and the Senate was very evenly divided. It required two votes from the Republican side to secure the confirmation. I consulted with Senator Stanford of California at his house, with regard to the matter." Stewart stated that Stanford agreed to vote with him to confirm Lamar, "and the Senate of the United States was saved from the disgrace of granting amnesty and then withdrawing it; and of pledging equality of civil and political rights and afterward violating that pledge."[11] Not all analyses of Stewart's role in the Lamar confirmation reached such a lofty plane. The *San Francisco Chronicle* noted that Stewart had filed an able brief in support of Lamar, but that it resembled a lawyer's brief and lacked the ring of sincerity. The paper charged that Stewart and Stanford supported Lamar primarily because the latter was a supporter of large corporations and railroads.[12]

Stewart's Southern sympathies were demonstrated again when the so-called "Force" Bill came before the Senate. His actions in opposing it also displayed his real talents in parliamentary maneuvering. The bill was introduced in the House of Representatives on June 14, 1890, by Henry Cabot Lodge of Massachusetts. It provided for supervision of national elections by the federal government, in order to protect Negro voters in the South against state measures designed to deprive them of the vote.[13] The Select Committee on the Election of the President reported a substitute measure on June 19; and Stewart immediately charged that the substitute changed the original bill so that it would have encompassed nearly all elections, placing them under special officers appointed by the President and backed by the strength of the U.S. Army.[14] The inclusion of areas outside the South reinforced Stewart's original opposition to the bill. From the standpoint of his own political career, Stewart had no desire to see federal inspectors in Nevada.[15] He indicated a clear awareness of the substitute bill's menace when he later wrote, "It seemed to me that its passage would subvert the Government of the United States and substitute military dictation for civil authority in elections in the several states."[16]

The substitute passed the House on July 2, 1890, by a vote of 155 to 149, with Horace Bartine of Nevada supporting it.[17] Stewart was convinced that if the measure was brought up in the Senate immediately, it would pass with a majority of six votes. Delay seemed to be the only hope to defeat the bill, but action on it was imminent when a Republican Party caucus was held to determine the order of business in the Senate. At that point, as he indicated in his memoirs, Stewart made a move for delay by doing all in his "power to assist every Senator who had a favorite measure to advance its consideration, and it so happened that the Force Bill was placed low on the calendar of measures to be considered, and was not reached during the long session."[18]

The Senate resumed debate on the federal elections measure, generally referred to as the Force Bill, on December 3, after the President argued strongly in favor of it. Stewart entered the debate on December 19, 1890, with a rather long speech which emphasized the enforcement of the law by the military. In his remarks he first explained his sympathies:

> I am a friend of the colored man. I deeply sympathize with him for the wrong and injustice which he has suffered and cannot ask him to put his life in jeopardy to fight a political battle for my advantage. I am equally a friend of the white man of the south and desire to refrain from any act which in his own estimation, will justify him in making war upon the defenseless race we have enfranchised.

He then repeated ideas he had enunciated earlier, that "the colored man requires education" and "the colored man needs to acquire property." Given these two things, his rights would no longer be denied him, although Stewart failed to indicate just how blacks could accomplish these ends without political power. He ended his speech by justifying his opposition. "This bill ought not to pass, because it never will be enforced; because it will consolidate the Southern whites; because it will bring further misery upon the Southern blacks, and because it will increase sectional animosities and kindle anew the discords of the past."[19]

When the Senate took up the Force Bill again on January 5, 1891, Stewart used a delaying tactic that infuriated his opponents. With the aid of the newly seated senators from Idaho, who now joined the western silver bloc, and with a friendly presiding officer in the chair, he moved successfully to displace discussion of the Force Bill with debate on a silver coinage measure that was also before the Senate. Senator Spooner of Wisconsin was outraged: "The Confederacy and the western mining camps are in legislative supremacy. Think of it—Nevada, barely a respectable county, furnished two senators to betray the Republican Party and the rights of citizenship for silver. . . . We are punished for making too easy the pathway of rotten boroughs into the Union."[20]

On January 24, Senator Aldrich, who was leading the Republican fight to pass the bill, tried and failed to break Stewart's delaying tactics. Stewart then offered four amendments and presented a strong speech against the Force Bill. He reiterated his belief that the proposal would:

> . . . subvert the liberties of the people by interfering with local elections. . . . I have been a Republican for many years. I have stood by the party; I have never faltered to sustain it; I have never voted for any other. [Here Stewart conveniently forgot his years in California as a member of the Know-Nothing Party and as a Democrat.] I am a Republican and I now want to save the Republican party from this fatal leap. It is putting itself in conflict with the people. . . . Above all I appeal to you to refrain from attempts to deprive the people of a free ballot uncontrolled by Federal power. Leave the election of State offices and Presidential electors to the State according to the guarantees of the Constitution.[21]

Opponents of the Force Bill further delayed the vote by pushing forward the Apportionment Bill, a measure to realign congressional districts based on the 1890 census, of obvious interest to many senators. After considerable parliamentary maneuvering, orchestrated by Stewart, the motion to debate the Apportionment Bill in place of the Force Bill passed by a majority of only one vote.[22] Senator Aldrich had been correct in his earlier prediction "that this vote is to be controlling in this matter; that it is to be the decisive vote."[23] The Force (Elections) Bill was not considered again during the session and the Republicans made no further attempt to revive such a measure.

In his memoirs Stewart gave an interesting account of why the elections measure was never brought again before Congress. During the course of the debate on the motion to table the Force Bill, Senator Stanford was in New York City and could not be reached, because a severe storm had interrupted telegraphic communications. It was clear that any move to revive the Elections Bill would center around Stanford's vote, so when Stewart heard in the Senate cloakroom that Aldrich was going to New York, he acted quickly, "I took for granted that his journey on that night was for the purpose of securing the vote of Senator Stanford to resume the consideration of the Force Bill." Thus, related Stewart, the two senators both set off for New York City; but Stewart was more resourceful than Aldrich and bribed a baggage man to wire ahead for a team to "make the quickest trip ever made from the landing of the ferryboat to the Windsor Hotel." The team was ready, and Stewart paid the driver an extra ten dollars, "with the understanding that he would let the horses run wherever they could." Stewart reached the hotel in record time, only to learn from Mrs. Stanford that her husband had been bruised in an afternoon carriage accident and could not be disturbed. However, Stewart recalled, ''She said she knew what his views were and would make them known.'' She obtained from her husband's secretary a copy of a dispatch, which Stanford:

> . . . had written to send as soon as the wires were again up between New York and Washington. It was directed to me, and read: ''Pair me against the Force bill and all matters connected therewith. Signed, Leland Stanford.'' I asked the secretary to go down stairs with me, and as we reached the office floor we met Senator Aldrich at the elevator on his way to visit Senator Stanford. I told him he was too late, and the clerk showed him the dispatch. He turned away, and there the matter dropped, and thus the Force bill was defeated, never again to be revived. After that it was never endorsed by the Republican party of the nation or of any State.[24]

Responding to various letters congratulating him on his stand on the Elections Bill, Stewart emphasized that his vote was against federal supervision and for states' rights and local government, noting that the latter was the foundation of civil liberty. In one of these communications he repeated a favorite phrase, ''The people must be left free to do wrong or they never will learn how to do right.''[25] In another note, to a supporter in Atlanta, Georgia, he wrote that if the Force Bill were enacted, it would have changed the basic form of government and aimed a blow at the vital principle of free institutions, that of local self-government. In extolling local control, Stewart's racial bias emerged, as he ignored the obvious results of local, white control for black citizens:

> A Republican party in the South composed almost exclusively of colored men can accomplish no good. . . . It is positively certain that the white people of this country must be the controlling force in every State in the Union, and to array the colored population against that force means race war with all its attending calamities. But it does not follow that the colored man will not have some voice in the Government. He has a constitutional right to vote, and in all the Northern States and many portions of the South he exercises that right as freely and effectively, according to his numbers as the white man. . . . He must stay with us. It is for the interest of the white race that he should be protected in all his rights and that his condition should be improved.[26]

Stewart's action on the Force Bill met with more favor in Nevada than had his vote on the Lamar confirmation. This reaction was due to the fact that Stewart had based his opposition on constitutional grounds, and that he advocated a concept most Nevadans supported, states' rights.

Approval came not only from leading Nevada Republicans such as H. M. Yerington, who called his action "dead right, correct and proper,"[27] but also from the Nevada legislature, which endorsed his opposition to the Force Bill in a Senate Concurrent Resolution.[28]

Stewart's activities in regard to the Lamar appointment and the Force Bill suggest a sincere belief in states' rights, particularly in regard to federal supervision of local elections. No such idealism, however, can be attributed to his relations with the Walker Lake and Pyramid Lake Indians after his return to the Senate in 1887. His actions in that regard were stimulated by pressures from railroad and mining interests.

In his first term in the United States Senate, Stewart had shown some sympathy for the Indians when he opposed the Indian treaty system. During debate over appropriation of monies to negotiate treaties with the Indians of the upper Missouri and Platte rivers, he argued, "The whole system is wrong; it corrupts your agents; corrupts the men you send to the frontiers; corrupts the Indians; causes a large number of persons to be murdered every year. . . . You murder them by the whiskey you carry among them and they retaliate by murdering your women and children. That is the system and I do not think any system can be devised which is worse than this."[29] Recognizing the inadequacies of a national policy towards Indians was one thing, but defending them in conflicts with voters in his own state, particularly representatives of special railroad and mining interests, was quite another. The issue in Nevada specifically concerned authority over land on Nevada's two Indian reservations.

The conflict over control of the Walker River Reservation started sometime before Stewart returned to the Senate. It broke into the open in March, 1883, when the *Walker Lake Bulletin* began a campaign to have the reservation abandoned because of reports that there were large mineral deposits there, along with timber and agricultural resources, which the newspaper noted were of no great use to the Indians. An article explained that opening the reservation to whites would bring additional revenues to the state, a particularly appealing suggestion in the middle of a severe economic depression.[30] The same arguments were repeated a few months later, with the additional point that the Indians would be better off among the whites, for they tended to congregate near whites anyway. One report declared, "It is simply absurd to maintain a reservation merely for the shadow of sentiment, when by abandoning it no hardship would be worked upon the Indians, in fact, they would be benefitted."[31]

By 1885, the fight to have the Walker River Reservaton abandoned had spawned a bill in the House of Representatives, introduced by Nevada's George Cassidy, allowing prospectors to enter Indian reservations for mining purposes. This was not enough for the *Bulletin,* which demanded that the entire Walker River Reservation be abandoned.[32] About the same time, Nevada legislators approved two resolutions. One of these called for relinquishment of a large part of the Walker River Indian Reservation; the other for reduction in the size of the Pyramid Lake Reservation. The resolution concerning the Walker River Reservation indicated that it should be decreased in area because it "comprises within its boundaries some of the most valuable mineral lands that can be found in this State, and which said mineral lands are entirely worthless to the Indians residing and being upon said reservation." Since a large number of white settlers were desirous of "prospecting and searching for valuable ores of gold, silver and other precious metals," the resolution continued, the part of the reservation supposedly containing mineral lands (these were specified) should be relinquished.[33] The resolution calling for reduction of the Pyramid Lake Reservation sought to take away the southern part of the reservation, around the town of Wadsworth, where a number of whites had "squatted" on the land and now wanted a chance to confirm their squatters' rights.[34]

After Stewart had been reelected to the Senate, but before the beginning of Congress in December, 1887, he had an opportunity to state his philosophy about the tribal system of Indian government. In a letter to a correspondent in Kansas, he wrote:

> The recognition of the tribal relations of Indians was a mistake in the beginning and is now a sham and a fraud. Indians should be treated as are all other human beings. Lands should be allotted to them in severalty. Each individual should be held responsible for his own acts. Every acre of land not allotted to the Indians should be opened to settlements. The reservation system pauperizes, demoralizes and degrades both Indians and white men. . . . The Indians never will be civil until they are forced to accept the responsibilities of civilized men. No Indians on this continent are so worthless and degraded as those in the United States—all the result of the vicious system of feeding them in idleness.[35]

Stewart's rather generalized statements about eliminating the tribal system of land allotment soon became more specific to Nevada, as pressure from his constituents alerted him to the direction he should take. Early in March, 1888, he wrote a letter to the Secretary of the Interior, suggesting that all of Walker Lake should be thrown open to the public and the reservation abandoned, except for a small part at the north end to be kept for the Indians. In the same letter he also suggested limiting the Pyramid Lake Reservation, as "it is unreasonable and unnecessary to retain the whole of Pyramid Lake in the reservation."[36]

Inevitably, Stewart was drawn to the editor of the *Walker Lake Bulletin,* John M. Campbell, and was soon in correspondence with him. He wrote Campbell for advice as to "exactly how much ought to be left to the Indians," suggesting that the newspaper editor consult with his neighbors and then "write me fully the views of yourself and citizens."[37] In spite of letters and occasional speeches in the Senate, Stewart's fight to obtain abandonment of Nevada's Indian reservations was a desultory one from 1887 to 1890, since he was engaged in those years in the more important battles over remonetization of silver and irrigation. In 1889, he indicated strong support for opening the Walker River Reservation to mining, when he complained to a constituent:

> No prospectors can go upon Indian reservations. There is nothing that our Government protects with so much zeal as places which they call Indian reservations. These reservations are dedicated to barbarism in a most barbarous and unreasonable manner. They are of no use to Indians nor anyone else. I have been trying to get reservations in our State which include mining lands reduced so as to leave the mines open to prospectors, but have been unsuccessful thus far. I hope to succeed in the future.[38]

That "future" came closer in 1891, as agricultural, mining, and railroad interests pressed Stewart for action. The first complaints came from white settlers in the Wadsworth area, who demanded reduction of the Pyramid Lake Reservation to accommodate their claims to the lands they had squatted on. In the spring of 1891, Stewart succeeded in obtaining an appropriation for the Secretary of the Interior to appoint a committee to negotiate with the Pyramid Lake Indians for surrender of the southern end of their reservation. The commission was to convene at Wadsworth.[39]

Evidence that the Indians were not without support came at the same time, when T. J. Morgan, Commissioner of Indian Affairs, wrote to each of the three commissioners pointing out that the Pyramid Lake Reservation dated from 1859. At that time Indian agent Frederick Dodge had suggested the area be set aside as a reservation, and the surveyor general of Utah Territory had been ordered to reserve the land outlined by Dodge. Morgan took a strong stand that the reservation predated the President's Executive Order of March 23, 1874, which officially established the two reservations. He insisted that the earlier date gave the Indians a solid claim to the land, "This office therefore holds that the reservation as originally established in 1859, clearly remains intact except so far as the right-of-way of the Pacific Railroad is concerned."[40]

Before the commissioners visited the Nevada Indian reservations in October, 1891, the owners of the Carson and Colorado Railroad (heirs to the interests of the powerful Bank of California group from the Comstock) complicated the issue. On September 6, they ordered that the Walker Lake Indians should be charged for any freight hauled by the railroad.[41] This was a clear violation of the original contract between the railroad and the Indians, and marked the beginning of an effort by the former to have that agreement redrawn, or to force abandonment of part or all of the Walker River Reservation. The original contract had been signed in 1882. It provided that the railroad would be granted a sixty-foot right-of-way through the reservation, in return for $750 in cash and the privilege of free transportation for the Indians resident thereon, "their fish, game and products to and from all points on the road operated by said company."[42] The Carson and Colorado Railroad was built in 1880, to serve mining developments and other interests south of Virginia City. It did not prosper as expected and the movement to halt free Indian haulage no doubt was associated with its failure to show a profit. In addition, agricultural interests in the valleys serviced by the railroad complained of unfair Indian competition.

Henry M. Yerington, general manager of the Carson and Colorado Railroad, argued that the 1882 contract provided only for the free haulage of goods for the Indians' own consumption and did not include the unlimited haulage of Indian produce to market. Indian Agent Warner disagreed and wrote Yerington that the railroad order was a clear violation of the 1882 contract, "The matter of their [Indians] coming into competition with the Mason Valley ranchers cuts no figure in the case. I must insist upon the fulfillment of your part of the contract and in case you still refuse, must take other and prompt action."[43]

Meanwhile, the commissioners appointed to deal with the Indians about reduction of their reservations arrived in Nevada. They were joined at Carson City by William M. Stewart, Congressman Bartine, and Carson and Colorado Railroad officials D. A. Bender and James A. Yerington. Guided by the latter two men, the party arrived in Hawthorne, at the south end of Walker Lake, on October 17, 1891. As they passed along the east side of the lake, the commissioners were shown supposed mineral ledges, which the local newspaper reported were "plainly visible on both sides."[44] In Hawthorne, the commissioners met with residents and listened to an address from Stewart, who, not surprisingly, pointed out the many advantages that would come from abandonment of the Walker River Reservation.[45] The commissioners also visited the Pyramid Lake Indian Reservation; shortly thereafter, the chairman of the commission, former Governor Ormsbee of Vermont, suggested unofficially that the Walker River Reservation be abandoned.[46]

A month later, Senator Stewart unveiled a plan which would make relinquishment of the Walker River Reservation easier. The idea was as simple as it was unheeding of Indian rights. In a letter to the Commissioner of Indian Affairs, Stewart suggested that since Pyramid Lake was a better area for "civilizing the Indians" than the Walker Lake area, all of the Indians on the latter reservation should be relocated to the Pyramid Lake Reservation. To make this transition more effective, he suggested that part of the latter region be reclaimed by irrigation, and indicated that he would seek funds for a survey of Pyramid Lake lands in order to determine their suitability for irrigation.[47] He repeated this idea to a number of correspondents, noting to one that he would continue to try to get the Indian lands near Wadsworth thrown open to sale to whites. Money from such sales would then be used to irrigate other lands near the southern part of the Pyramid Lake Reservation where all the Indians would be transferred.[48]

By the spring of 1892, Stewart's efforts to bring about abandonment of the Walker River Reservation were explicitly tied to the attempts of the railroad officials to nullify the 1882 Indian agreement. In a letter to H. M. Yerington, early in April, 1892, Stewart supported the railroad's position, assuring Yerington, "There is no sense in having two reservations for Indians that could just as well live on one." Stewart also indicated that he had obtained a promise from the Secretary of Interior to use $1,500 for an irrigation survey to prove the feasibility of irrigating lands near the southern part of Pyramid Lake.[49] In reply, Yerington wrote that he hoped Stewart could do something, for "it's mighty rough on us." He added that a favorable report from the commission to the Interior Department "would help a lot of us out of trouble."[50] In another letter, a few days later, Yerington thanked Stewart for working on behalf of the railroad in reference to the Walker Lake Indians.[51] He was more specific in a later letter, "I am very glad that you have got the Walker Lake Reservation matter in such good shape for us, for which I thank you most heartily and hope you will succeed in fixing the Pyramid Reservation in the manner you suggest."[52] The letter referred to Stewart's effectiveness in quieting the vocal opposition to the railroad emanating from Indian Agent Warner. As a direct result of Stewart's intervention, the Commissioner of Indian Affairs instructed Agent Warner "to take no further action" about the Carson and Colorado Ralroad.[53] Stewart himself instructed Warner, "It was certainly not contemplated by either party that hay and grain for sale should be transported on the railroad, although perhaps, it comes within the letter of the contract."[54] Stewart's work for the railroad seemed near success when the Senate Committee on Indian Affairs reported favorably on his bill to abandon the Walker River Reservation, but the end of the congressional session brought his efforts to a temporary halt.[55]

It is somewhat ironic that during the same years that Stewart was trying to deprive the Walker and Pyramid Lake Indians of their tribal lands, he was also trying to aid the Washoe Indians of western Nevada. His first such effort, in 1888, was to urge Congress to provide an almshouse for aged and infirm Washoe Indians, after noting, "No act of violence against a white man is known to have been perpetrated by a Washoe Indian."[56] The effort was unsuccessful, but he repeated his request in the spring of 1892, when it again failed.[57] Some years later he attempted once more to have something done for the Washoe Indians, indicating that they had never received government aid, but deserved it, being "a small tribe of really good Indians."[58] Stewart's interpretation of "good" and "bad" Indians evidently had something to do with whether they had anything the white man wanted. Apparently the Washoes did not.

Stewart seemed to have an insatiable appetite for work. In addition to his obvious interest in Nevada-oriented issues such as free silver, irrigation, and Nevada Indians, he missed few opportunities to debate the many contemporary questions that arose in the Senate from 1887 to 1893, including women's rights, organized labor, and education.

Stewart had first indicated approval of women's suffrage in 1874, when he voted in favor of an amendment to a territorial bill which supported that issue.[59] Upon his return to the Senate, he supported the twin issues of equal employment opportunity and suffrage for women. Early in 1889, in a letter to constituents in Carson City, the Senator pushed for the employment of women in post offices, "It [post office] is also an office which women can fill as well as men, and generally better. . . . I do not think that women have as good a chance to earn a living as men. . . . Why should not Reno set a good example by putting some worthy women in the post-office?"[60] His broadmindedness on the issue of employment for women had limits, however, as a subsequent letter suggested. In 1889, Stewart answered a request from a lady who wanted to be a secretary to the recently formed subcommittee on irrigation: "I am greatly in favor of employing ladies in every place possible as I think they do not have a fair show in the world; but I fear the duties of stenographer to the committee would be unsuitable for a lady. We shall probably travel in a car by ourselves in which there will be no ladies, and under such circumstances you would find it inconvenient to be attached to such a committee."[61] Stewart showed the same ambivalence in another letter in reference to women's suffrage. After explaining that there was no constitutional provision prohibiting distinction on account of sex, and that no constitutional amendment guaranteed all citizens the right to vote, he concluded, "Do not understand from these suggestions that I am hostile to woman's suffrage. I know that there are many very strong reasons in favor of it and that it is a question which must be considered, discussed, and settled sooner or later."[62] He continued to support the idea of female suffrage throughout the decade of the 1890's, and was considered by some leaders of the movement to be in favor of it. Writing to him on April 17, 1900, Susan B. Anthony thanked Stewart "for all you have done for our good cause in the past, and will do in the future."[63]

The Nevada senator also supported another controversial issue of the time, the demand of organized labor for shorter workdays. In a letter to Samuel Gompers, in the fall of 1889, he wrote: "I voted for and advocated the original eight hour law which was passed by Congress, and have been an advocate of the reduction of the hours of labor for many years."[64] His support for organized labor was tested early in the 1890's, when he introduced a bill to establish a military post at Reno, indicating that it would be an economic boon for Nevada. A number of individuals, particularly members of the Virginia City Miner's Union, saw an army installation at Reno as a direct threat to organized labor, and feared that troops might be used in labor strikes.

In two separate letters to Nevada constituents, Stewart tried to assuage these fears. Writing to F. C. Lord at Virginia City, in the spring of 1892, he insisted that no U.S. soldiers would be used against the miner's union. According to Stewart, army troops would be involved only if there was an insurrection that state authorities could not handle:

> It is ridiculous to suppose that the State authorities will attempt to interfere with the Miners' Union. Any attempt to do such a thing would forever put every man who had anything to do with it out of office and keep him out, and ought to do so. The United States troops will never interfere with the affairs of Nevada, but if they were called upon by the State

authorities it would make no difference whether they were in San Francisco or Reno.[65]

Another letter, to prominent Reno journalist-politician C. C. Powning, reiterated the same points, emphasizing that if troops were called by the governor of Nevada for use in a labor strike, "The Governor will go out of office pretty quick. There is not a public man in Nevada who dares advocate any interference with the miners."[66] Although Stewart thought a post "is pretty certain to go through," it never did.

Stewart also became involved, as did all Nevada politicians of the period, in the anti-Chinese feeling which swept the state in the 1880's. He had been forced to face the issue in Ormsby County during his 1886 election campaign. When the issue of Chinese immigration arose in Congress after 1887, Stewart met it with many of the same arguments he had used during that campaign. He insisted that immigration of Chinese laborers should be prohibited, but he based his opposition on religious, cultural, and economic grounds, not upon color and racial prejudice. One of his Senate speeches against the Chinese, delivered on January 12, 1888, is unusual in that it acknowledged Chinese superiority in certain areas:

> I have no feeling of resentment against the Chinese. . . . But I have long since seen that we can not live with the Chinese. . . . We never can be reduced to the standard of food on which they subsist. It is impossible for our race to labor as incessantly as they do. . . . Their persistence in maintaining existence, their tenacity of life, their industry so far surpass ours that wherever they come we must go. . . . I say that opening our gates to Mongolian immigration means nothing more and nothing less than the occupancy of this country by Chinese . . . competition with them is impossible.[67]

Stewart introduced a variety of bills to enforce restrictions on Chinese immigration, none of which got out of committee. His speeches supporting anti-Chinese measures often brought charges from colleagues that he had altered his stand on the Asiatic question since his earlier Senate term. He always answered such charges with the reminder that he had opposed the Chinese in 1870, "when but for my efforts the Chinaman would have been granted the right of naturalization and in that event he would have been a political power and it would have been difficult to exclude him."[68]

Stewart was in something of a dilemma in regard to the Chinese, since the Central Pacific Railroad, an ally crucial to his continuance in the Senate, generally supported the entrance of Asian laborers. There is little to document the inference that Stewart's public stand on the question masked private efforts to aid Chinese immigration to the United States, but one of his letters to Collis P. Huntington, president of the railroad, does suggest that Stewart may have been playing both sides of the issue, "After receipt of your letter with regard to the transportation of Chinese through the United States I attended to the matter before the committee, and I believe the bill reported is in such shape as will do you no great harm."[69]

On the matter of a protective tariff, a proposal that began to gain strength in the late 1880's, Stewart's stand was dictated by specific pressures from his home state. Thus he supported high rates on wool, hides, borax, soda, lumber, and other items produced in Nevada that needed protection. He was particularly anxious to please the capitalists who comprised the old Bank Crowd, with whom he had associated from the early Comstock days. In the last two decades of the nineteenth century, this group had become interested in huge deposits of borax and soda in southwestern Nevada. To H. M. Yerington, lobbyist for the Bank of California interests, Stewart wrote, "If our protectionist friends of the East do not stand by us in that matter [borax] we will make a lively war on their pet schemes. Protectionists must stand or fall together."[70] Later in the year, when he thought the suggested free list on the pending tariff bill was too long, Stewart made a strong speech supporting a "practically prohibitory" tariff "upon everything that can be produced in this country."[71] Although, in 1890, silverites had found the tariff bill a convenient vehicle to insure passage of a silver purchase act, they reconsidered when the tariff question became more closely associated with the gold standard. Stewart reassessed his priorities and resigned from the Protective Tariff League, noting as he did so that he could endorse protection, but not support a gold standard.[72]

Stewart's return to Nevada politics involved him in promoting one of the major interests of his long career, education. Until his retirement in 1905, he maintained a consistent interest in the welfare of the University of Nevada.[73] His first activity involving the school, after its move to Reno from Elko in 1885, concerned location. Stewart opposed putting the university next to a group of cemeteries in the northern part of Reno, insisting that the graveyards would not only impede the growth of the school but would actually be detrimental to it. He suggested that no additional burials be allowed and that the bodies interred there ultimately be removed and the land sold to the state.[74]

Stewart consistently supported increased state appropriations to the university and wrote a number of letters to state legislators emphasizing the institution's importance to Nevada: "It seems to me that more good can be accomplished by providing for the University than any other expenditure of money. In all other things I advise the strictest economy. . . . The State University is more important to Nevada than any other institution, and will ultimately bring larger returns."[75] In another letter, endorsing a change in the makeup of the University's Board of Regents, Stewart presented his philosophy of public higher education: "It must be the University of all the people or it can not prosper. No State University has ever succeeded that was run by a political party. Our University must be absolutely non-partisan or it will ultimately fall into disrepute and be a failure. . . . I want every citizen of Nevada to feel that he has an equal interest in that institution."[76] Aside from these general lobbying activities, Stewart's major contribution to the welfare of the University of Nevada was his role in the passage of the so-called Second Morrill Act. This measure, which became law on August 30, 1890, granted to each state a sum of $15,000 annually, with a yearly increase of $1,000 until the fund reached an annual total of $25,000.[77]

Stewart's interest in education extended beyond Nevada. In addition to an earlier proposal to establish a national mining college, he introduced a bill in January, 1888, to set up a national university to educate teachers, no doubt influenced by his own teaching experience. In a letter to a friend, Stewart wrote, "The profession of teaching should be elevated and made as respectable as the profession of law."[78] Congress took no action, but Stewart was back with a similar measure in 1889, emphasizing as he introduced it the potential usefulness of such an institution in the education of Negroes and European immigrants. Referring to the latter, he noted we "must educate them or they will destroy us."[79] Two weeks later, in a letter to the editor of a national magazine, he explained his bill, "I regard the profession of teaching as the most important and delicate of all other callings. . . . One great drawback to the progress of education is the poor pay which educators generally receive. They have no patronage, and consequently no power to command reasonable compensation."[80]

About this time, Stewart became interested in establishing an Indian school in Nevada and, in early 1888, introduced a measure in the Senate to appropriate money for such an institution. The bill passed the Senate without a roll call vote, on February 14, 1888.[81] However, the school was not built until after Ormsby County dedicated additional land and money for it. Finally located a few miles southeast of Carson City, the school opened on December 17, 1890, with 37 pupils enrolled. Although referred to variously as the Clear Creek Indian School or the Stewart Indian School, it was called in the initial official reports, the Stewart Institute.[82]

Less public-minded than his education ventures were Stewart's many activities on behalf of his friend, Collis P. Huntington, and the Central Pacific and Southern Pacific railroads. Although Stewart's return to the Senate was too late to participate in the passage of the Interstate Commerce Act, he was soon seated again on the Pacific Railroad Committee. It is quite clear that Stewart listened very attentively to what Huntington and other railroad officials suggested, and acted accordingly. His relations with Stephen F. Gage, political lobbyist for the Pacific railroads, were particularly close. On one occasion he sent a copy of a railroad bill to Gage with the request, "I wish you would look over the enclosed bill and write me whether you think it is desirable to pass it."[83] On another occasion he worked for a railroad tunnel in the Sierra Nevada, to be financed with federal help. The scheme would have avoided the use of snow sheds and lessened the possibility of winter blockades, and, incidentally, saved the Central Pacific a great deal of money.[84]

A short time later Stewart wrote Huntington directly for instructions concerning a dilemma in which he found himself. Two bills in which Huntington was interested reached the Senate about the same time. One of these, the Maricopa Railroad Bill, Huntington opposed because the proposed road would provide competition to his own holdings. The other, concerning certain Huntington businesses in New York State, the railroad magnate supported. Stewart told Huntington that if he opposed the Maricopa Bill, its supporters in the committee might defeat the New York bill. He asked for advice in case he couldn't win both fights, suggesting that the railroad president wire "the West," if the Maricopa measure should be defeated, and "the East," if it was more important to prevent hostile action against the New York bill. Not wishing to leave Huntington with the wrong impression, Stewart closed his letter with the reassurance, "I do not mean by this that I will give up either, but I want to know what to do in the last resort if the matter is pushed beyond my control."[85]

Stewart reported to Huntington regularly. On one occasion he wrote that he had succeeded in keeping the Select Committee on Pacific Railroads from placing the Central Pacific funding bill with the Union Pacific funding bill, noting that if he had not done so "the Committee would have been unanimous against me."[86] Sometime later Stewart confided to his protégé, Francis Newlands, that Huntington might be injured by some pending legislation, and that he, Stewart, therefore, had to watch "these matters closely."[87] When he was unable to help the railroad, Stewart was apologetic, "Your telegram reached me too late to take action. When I received it the roll was being called on the passage of the bill. . . . If I had known your views two or three days earlier, I could have worked up an opposition, or secured the amendment you suggested; but it was too late when the dispatch came."[88]

More often Stewart's letters struck a more positive note, reporting, for example, that the Maricopa Railroad scheme was dead, or that he had been able to have a provision in the Army Appropriation Bill struck from the act because it worked to the disadvantage of the Southern Pacific Railroad.[89] When the lame duck Congress met after the 1892 election, Stewart informed Huntington that he would do all he could to prevent passage of an amendment to the Interstate Commerce Act, because the amendment was "very unfair and injurious [to] both the railroads and the general public."[90] Unconsciously, perhaps, Stewart had in the last sentence reflected his own priorities.

The Stewart-Huntington relationship was not entirely one-sided, as is shown by Stewart's attempt to use Huntington to gain favor with the popular John P. Jones and thereby help his own reelection campaign in 1892. Stewart thought he could accomplish that end by having Huntington help Jones with the latter's plan to develop Santa Monica as a port for Los Angeles. Stewart outlined his ideas in a letter to Huntington in the spring of 1891, "I know nothing about your plans with regard to Santa Monica, or whether you have any plans, nor do I propose to give any advice further than to say that if it is consistent with your interest to accommodate Jones, I am quite certain it would be a good thing to do and that he would fully appreciate it."[91] Stewart also kept in touch with Jones on the subject and intimated that Huntington might be willing to construct a wharf at Santa Monica.[92] No action was taken on the Santa Monica project before the election, however, causing Stewart continued worry about the senior senator's political support.

An additional and not inconsiderable benefit that Stewart received from the railroad was the pass. The use of annual railroad passes by politicians was not unusual during these years, yet it is doubtful that any other United States senator took greater advantage of the complimentary tickets than Stewart. Evidently he had passes on the Central Pacific and Southern Pacific railroads from the time of completion of those lines. Through them he obtained temporary passes on other national roads, particularly the Baltimore and Ohio and the Northern Pacific. In Nevada, in order to get free passage on the Virginia and Truckee Railroad, he suggested to its general manager, H. M. Yerington, that he "might

make me an officer or employee of that company so that I could come
under the exception provided by section 22 of the Interstate Commerce
Act. Why could I not be your attorney? I am a pretty good lawyer and
you couldn't get a cheaper one under these circumstances.''[93]

Not only did Stewart get free passes for his immediate family, but he
also obtained them for grandchildren and friends. At times he was quite
willing to use a little pressure to gain results. When he requested a pass
from the Southern Pacific for Thomas J. Stevens, a friend of former
Senator Cannon of Utah, Stewart wrote, ''Senator Cannon was particularly anxious that this favor should be extended to Mr. Stevens if possible, because he said it would in the future redound to the benefit of the
Company, and from what he privately told me I believe it would.''[94]
The pass was issued. On at least one occasion a Nevada constituent used
Stewart's own tactics in order to get a free railroad ticket from Washington to Reno. Attorney Sam Platt suggested to the senator that a pass be
obtained for him ''through your influential friend in New York'' (Huntington). Platt did not promise anything specific, but noted suggestively,
''It is not unlikely that a compliance with this request will not go un-
rewarded. My limited experience in politics and my wide acquaintance
in Nevada assure me that ability to win is only a corollary to the power
to influence and the knowledge to convince.''[95]

Perhaps the climax to Stewart's use of free railroad tickets came several years later, as he was leaving the U.S. Senate. Not only did he get
passes from Washington to Carson City for himself, his second wife,
and her ten-year-old daughter, but also for his brother-in-law, H. S.
Foote, his wife, and their luggage, and Stewart's secretary, James D.
Finch. In addition, Stewart obtained an entire baggage car to transport
his law library, two carriages, and his household furniture. This operation involved coordination among four different railroads, the Pennsylvania, the Chicago and Northwestern, the Union Pacific, and the Southern Pacific.[96]

Stewart's close ties with the railroads were also manifested in the area
of political patronage. The senator kept in close touch with officials of
the Central and Southern Pacific railroads on matters relating to patronage, particularly for federal positions in Nevada and California. His
patronage contacts came mainly through two men, Stephen F. Gage, the
Southern Pacific's lobbyist, and C. C. Wallace, the railroad's political
agent in Nevada. His relation with the latter was particularly close, since
Wallace also acted as Stewart's political campaign manager, beginning
in 1886.

One of the keys to federal patronage in Nevada during these years was the Carson City Mint. Stewart and the railroads found the mint a useful source of federal jobs. Through its superintendent, Sam C. Wright, who obtained his position mainly through Stewart's efforts, the railroad was able to maintain a strong center of political support in the state's capital, particularly in the years from 1889 to 1892. When Wright died in the latter year, Stewart was on the way to Carson City from Washington, D.C. Before his own supporters in Nevada could get organized, those of Senator John P. Jones, well aware of the political importance of the Carson Mint, took advantage of the situation and wired Jones to arrange for the appointment of Theodore Hofer. Stephen Gage and the railroad had wanted the appointment of J. W. Haines; but, as Stewart later informed the railroad lobbyist, by the time he arrived in Carson City, Governor Roswell Colcord and other leading citizens had recommended Hofer, and the matter had gone too far to make a change. Stewart insisted, no doubt with his eyes on the 1892 election campaign then in progress, that he couldn't have supported Haines at that point without injuring himself.[97] As he wrote to another advocate of Haines, the deal for the Hofer appointment had been made before he reached Carson City, "After my arrival I concurred in the arrangements which had been made."[98] Stewart was far too able a politician to have done otherwise.

CHAPTER 9

REELECTION IN 1892 WITH
THE NEW SILVER PARTY

IN AND OUT of Congress from 1889 to 1892, Stewart acted in every respect as a candidate for reelection in 1892. However, before becoming directly involved in that campaign he saw an opportunity to strengthen his political position by helping his friend Francis G. Newlands win the 1890 contest for Nevada's seat in Congress. Stewart's first associations with Newlands concerned legal matters. The first hint that the relationship might have political overtones came in a letter from Stewart to Newlands in the spring of 1889, when he wrote, "There is much speculation here in regard to your residence in Nevada, but the people have generally come to the conclusion that your business interests called you there, and that is nothing very strange at all. That is the best view of the question at present."[1] Later that year, Stewart encouraged Newlands to learn about the silver problem in Nevada and to attend the National Silver Convention, which was to be held in St. Louis in 1889. When Newlands returned to Nevada from that convention, Stewart urged him to circulate statewide the materials he had obtained there.[2]

It was not until the spring of 1890, however, that it became clear that the Stewart-Newlands association was political. In a letter to former Nevada Representative Thomas Fitch, a potential congressional candidate in 1890, Stewart wrote that Newlands had no "present intention of becoming a candidate for office. . . . He is not inclined to say anything which would indicate whether he will or will not be a candidate."[3] Yet, just four days later, Stewart wrote to one of his closest Nevada political advisers, Sam Wright, suggesting that the current representative from Nevada, Horace F. Bartine, might be given a judgeship and, "In the event that Bartine would absolutely fill the bill, our friend Newlands might like to come to Congress. . . . I would like to have your views about the expediency of running Newlands for the congressional nomination in case Bartine should be appointed to the judgeship."[4]

In July, Stewart reported to Newlands that he had told the President and the attorney general about the plan to seek a judgeship for Bartine, and although the President was reluctant to weaken his majority in the House, he had finally agreed to find a judgeship for the congressman. Stewart added, "We are waiting for some little expression from Nevada to avoid the appearance of making a candidate in Washington. I will inform you if there is any change in the situation."[5] The idea of a judicial appointment for Bartine was also the subject of two meetings which took place at Senator Jones's residence at Gold Hill. A group of individuals including Newlands, Will Sharon (nephew of the Bank of California's William), Sam Jones (the senator's brother), and Henry M. Yerington, met to discuss the matter. A similar meeting was held in August at the same place with the same participants,[6] but the "expression" from Nevada never came.

However, shortly after the August meeting, adverse reaction to Stewart's suggestion of a judgeship for Bartine came from Senator John P. Jones and his supporters. At first Stewart could not understand the opposition from his Senate colleague. He wrote Newlands that he didn't know why the Jones people "should be antagonistic to you. They need you and your influence to carry the state. . . . Nor do I see why they should be unfriendly to me. I have never injured them and it seems to me that it is for their interests to be friendly to both you and me."[7] But, at the time Stewart wrote Newlands in September, there was good reason why the Jones people were unfriendly to Newlands. Beginning August 6, 1890, a series of editorials strongly criticizing Jones appeared in the *Reno Evening Gazette*. Since that newspaper was owned by Newlands, it was logical to assume that he had either authorized the editorials or outlined the points to be covered.

The first and longest criticized Jones for being a single issue (mining) senator and for being unaware that "Nevada has possibilities beyond those of a mining camp." The editorial suggested a new deal for Nevada, which would take energetic and progressive men, "who are in full sympathy with the new development." The "new development" turned out to be a philosophy that there were other interests in Nevada besides mining, such as irrigation and agriculture, which should be given consideration. It was pointed out that while Jones was out of step with the new ideas, someone (Newlands) who supported irrigation and agriculture along with mining would not be. The article also criticized Jones for living less than twelve months out of eighteen years in Nevada, for spending his money in Santa Monica and San Francisco, and for failing to keep in touch with his constituents.[8] The August 6 editorial was so obviously slanted in favor of Newlands that the editor of the paper found it necessary a few days later to answer a number of queries about Newlands's political ambitions. He wrote, "Mr. Newlands is not a candidate for Senator Jones' place or any other, or if he is, the *Gazette* knows nothing about it."[9] Nevertheless, *Gazette* editorials continued to criticize Jones.

When the Republican Party convened at Virginia City on September 4, 1890, it was immediately apparent that Stewart and Newlands had been outmaneuvered. Although Stewart had indicated earlier that a federal judgeship would be available for Bartine, the latter indicated that he preferred to stay in Congress. Rather than face a convention showdown with Jones and Bartine, Newlands announced that he would not be a candidate in the congressional race. In reporting this development, the editor of the *Gazette* wrote that it was too bad Newlands refused to stay in the race, since Bartine would have been better suited to the bench, Newlands would have been better in Congress, and the party would have been strengthened by the exchange.[10]

Newlands attempted to mend his political fences at the state convention by seconding the nomination of Bartine on September 5. He took occasion during his speech to offer an explanation of his supposed candidacy. According to a Reno newspaper, his speech was well received,[11] but it was not so accepted by Jones supporters. Without mentioning Jones by name, Newlands practically accused him of betrayal when he stated that opposition to him had come from "a source and were urged by a power from which I had a right to expect better faith."[12] Later, in a letter to Frederick W. Sharon (son of the Bank of California magnate), Newlands wrote, "The Jones people acted, as usual, with gross treachery and bad faith, and they made the situation such that, coupled with my previous declarations, my candidacy was rendered impossible without subjecting myself to charges of bad faith."[13] The *Gazette* accused Southern Pacific officials, working through C. C. Wallace, of cooperating with the "Jones element" to defeat Newlands;[14] but if Wallace was manipulating as the newspaper indicated, Stewart either did not know about it or pretended ignorance.[15]

It was soon apparent that Newlands had not bowed completely out of the 1890 campaign and was threatening either to stand against Jones for the Senate or to bolt the Republican Party. Stewart tried to calm his younger friend and advised against either course of action. He suggested to Newlands that it would be best to support the ticket in 1890, and wait:

"Your energy, enterprise, and ability, if you pursue the course you have hitherto pursued, will secure for you anything that Nevada has to give without combination with or dependence upon any other human being. . . . Above all, do not let the people think that you are lukewarm in the cause for the reason that you were not properly treated in the Convention."[16]

The 1890 State Republican Convention caused Stewart concern about the effect it might have on his own chances for reelection in 1892. He worried that the convention might have caused some friction among Republicans, warning one of his political advisers, "It will not do to have factions in the party."[17] In an effort to prevent that, Stewart followed his own advice to Newlands and returned to Nevada late in October to participate in the Republican campaign. While in Reno he was a guest in the new home Newlands had built and the two participated in a special Republican campaign train, which held an important rally at Wadsworth, about thirty miles east of Reno.[18] The Republicans won all of the state offices in the November election and the Republican majority in the state legislature insured for Jones a fourth term in the Senate.

When Stewart returned to Washington after the November election, he voiced concern about the national outcome of the 1890 campaign. The Democrats had gained control of the House of Representatives, and the new members would take their seats in December, 1891. After that, warned Stewart, the Republicans would lose the opportunity to be associated with the passage of a silver coinage bill. He was convinced that the Republicans would never have another chance to pass a silver bill, for a Democratic Congress "will pass a free coinage bill without qualification."[19] What Stewart really feared was that there would be no salvation for the Republican Party in Nevada without passage of a national silver bill to its credit. The national Republican Party had to take a strong silver stance in order for the Republicans to survive in Nevada. Stewart also saw the possibility that a third national party might form if the Republicans did not address the silver issue. As he wrote to Thomas Wren, "No gold man can be elected President of the United States in 1892. The plan of the gold men however, is to nominate a gold man on each ticket and tell the silver men to take their choice. If this is done there surely will be a third party in the field which may result in the election of a Democrat by the House of Representatives."[20]

Stewart's personal attempts to pass a free coinage measure in the lame duck congressional session of 1890–91 met with failure, but he continued to dispense advice, mostly through letters, on how to solve the money problem. In one such letter, to Olney Newell, an official of the Trans-Mississippi Commercial Congress, he explained the money situation in the United States:

> One of two things must happen: less business or more money. No more gold can be obtained for use as money. . . . The country which exports its money to buy foreign commodities will bankrupt its people; while the country which maintains a constant and sufficient supply of money for domestic commerce will have abundant surplus products to exchange for foreign commodities.[21]

A month later, in an eighteen-page letter to Andrew Carnegie, he berated the industrialist for speaking out so strongly for the gold standard: "I have examined the logic of your Alpha and Omega of the gold trust, and find it even more defective, if possible, than your moral sense. . . . Moderate your tone. Cease to insult the people by telling them to buy gold, which the gold ring has cornered, when you know that every effort to break the corner means disaster."[22]

However, in trying to show the moral justice of his own position, Stewart was led to some outright misstatements. For example, in reply to a letter accusing him of selfish motives in pursuing the silver question, Stewart insisted that he then had no silver interests and had not for ten years.[23] This claim was misleading, to say the least. At the very time Stewart wrote this letter and others on the same subject, he was actively involved in mining silver in Mexico. His interests there dated to the years shortly after he left the Senate in 1875, when he became engaged in promoting the International Mining Company, which had mines at San Miguel del Mesquital in the state of Zacatecas. His letters indicate a continuing major involvement with the company in the early 1890's. There is evidence, also, that within the ten-year period noted, he controlled mines in Amador County, California, which were under the superintendency of his brother, Samuel D. R. Stewart. It is equally clear that he made little, if any, profit from any of these mining ventures.[24]

Stewart's reluctance to reveal his silver interests was a matter of political expediency, since he could not afford to have his motives challenged during the 1892 senate campaign which now faced him. Yet he entered the campaign with a great deal of confidence, writing to a constituent that:

> I am inclined to think that there will not be much opposition to my re-election in Nevada. If re-elected I shall continue the fight for the people. My only object in staying in the Senate is to exert all my energy to resist

the aggressions of the representatives of accumulated capital. You who are not at the center of the Government can hardly realize the power of money over leading men and how little the manipulators of politics think of the real necessities of the masses.[25]

Stewart's major fear as he approached the 1892 election was that Jones's supporters in Nevada would again oppose Francis Newlands's ambition to become Nevada's congressman. This would place Stewart in the middle of the fight and might jeopardize support from Senator Jones, which he thought necessary for his own election.

When it became apparent that continued friendship with Newlands might bring Republican opposition to Stewart's own candidacy, he backed away and began efforts to disassociate himself from Newlands and the congressional race. He wrote to Wallace and cautioned him not to involve Stewart in the congressional campaign, because it might produce combinations against him.[26] In a letter to Stephen F. Gage, Stewart admitted that the congressional election might hurt him, but indicated that it would be his policy to keep out of it and remain friendly with all parties. In contrast to his earlier active campaigning on behalf of Newlands, Stewart now remained distant, "I do not know what kind of a fight Mr. Newlands will make, or whether he will be there in time to enter the contest at all."[27]

Remaining friendly with all parties proved difficult. Early in 1892, two prominent Nevada Republicans, A. C. Cleveland and William Woodburn, publicly accused Stewart of aiding Newlands for the House seat. Cleveland's opposition particularly worried Stewart, for the two had been friends for some time. To an old Comstock acquaintance, Stewart wrote that he could not understand why Cleveland opposed him, but "I shall continue to treat him kindly and let him do what he might." The senator thought he knew why Woodburn was antagonistic, however, since he had recommended Sam Davis rather than the former congressman for the post of minister to the Sandwich Islands. He wrote that Davis was better qualified and a "sober man . . . I do not know how much harm Woodburn can do me, but whatever he can I suppose he will."[28] To his political lieutenant, Sam Wright, Stewart suggested an indirect way to thwart possible Woodburn activities against him:

> Inasmuch as Woodburn threatens to take the stump against me I am anxious that he should not have an organ for that purpose. I know of no paper which he would be likely to get except the *Carson Tribune*, and if you could manage to silence that paper by patronage in the Mint, I should be very much obliged. I do not like to trouble you with this matter, but I should dislike to have the *Tribune* loose under the circumstances.[29]

The possibility of a Republican Party fight over Newlands was not the only matter worrying Stewart in the 1892 campaign. The debate over silver was still raging, and two statewide silver conferences, in 1885 and 1890, suggested that the state would support a separate silver party in 1892. At first Stewart was opposed to such a party, but warned Wallace, ''I do not see how Nevada can in any event support an anti-silver party.'' He was fearful that his own Republican Party might be that ''anti-silver party.''[30] He was prophetic on both counts. As events in Nevada moved rapidly to a political showdown, it became clear that Nevadans would not support an anti-silver party and that Republicans in Nevada would be forced into the role which Stewart hoped could be avoided.

By the spring of 1892, silver leaders in Nevada became convinced that a more direct political approach was necessary. The previous silver meetings had not formed a third party, although it had been suggested from time to time in the years from 1885 to 1892. In the beginning most silver supporters preferred to work within the framework of the traditional two-party system. Thus both parties had been pressed to adopt free-silver planks and had sent resolutions to Congress asking for national legislation to remonetize silver. Nevada's Silver Convention of 1890, which met May 29 in Carson City, and was attended by delegates from all but two of the state's counties, disclaimed any connection with politics except for support of free coinage of silver.[31]

The passage of the national Sherman Silver Act in the summer of 1890, and adoption of silver planks by both Nevada political parties, seemed further evidence that pressure on the two major parties was sufficient to achieve the goals of the silver supporters. However, national events in late 1891 and the spring of 1892, as the two national parties sought platforms and leaders for the 1892 election, forced a re-evaluation of the Nevada political situation. It was apparent that Grover Cleveland, an avowed gold-standard supporter, would become the Democratic presidential nominee. It was clear that the Republicans in Congress were satisfied with the rather innocuous Sherman Silver Act and not interested in further efforts on behalf of the free- silver movement, which sought unlimited coinage of silver, at the ratio of sixteen ounces of silver to one ounce of gold. The only hopeful sign for free silverites was thus the continuing attempt by national farm groups to join hands in a national political party, since these groups favored a free-silver monetary plank.

In Nevada, the movement to form a separate silver party received encouragement when George Nixon, editor of the Winnemucca *Silver State* and one of the state's strongest free-silver supporters, organized the first Nevada Silver Club, April 10, 1892, at Winnemucca. He was elected chairman.[32] Stewart was reluctant to move too quickly in support of the silver club movement in Nevada. When asked by Nixon to participate, he replied, "I do not think it becoming in me to tender advice to the people. It might seem like an attempt to dictate. I am their servant to do their bidding. . . . If they unite to make a bold and aggressive fight for silver, I shall be gratified. If they think it is best to divide while our enemies are united, I shall submit to the superior wisdom of the people of my state."[33] He reiterated this position in a letter to C. C. Wallace. After noting that he had been asked by many for advice about the formation of silver clubs in Nevada, he wrote, "I do not wish to dictate to the people of Nevada whether they should form silver clubs or not. That is their business; but I know that they cannot go far wrong when they follow as cool and conservative a Republican as Wren."[34]

Stewart's reluctance probably was due to two factors. In the first place, he was convinced as late as the first part of April, 1892, that he would have little opposition in his campaign for reelection.[35] Secondly, Stewart did not wish to offend some of his strongest supporters within the Republican Party, who opposed the free-silver movement. The most outspoken of this group, H. M. Yerington, warned Stewart explicitly, "The Democrats are working up this Silver plank, third party moves, etc., and I fear our Repub. friends are blindly tumbling into the trap. . . . I think the whole thing will fall flat for our people will soon see that it means a weakening of the Repub. party and strength for the Democrats." In the same letter, Yerington delivered a thinly veiled threat to Stewart when he noted, "The men controlling the leading interests of Nevada are very anxious that you should continue one of its Senators and I may add that *our* people will do all in our power for your successful re-election next fall."[36] Thus the Senator hesitated before acting, lest he cut off one of his strongest potential financial sources before the campaign.

While careful not to antagonize H. M. Yerington and the Bank of California capitalists, Stewart advised other Nevada Republicans that it would be dangerous for the Republican Party to oppose the silver club movement, "For in case the Democrats should get something more favorable to silver in the national platform than the Republicans, which they undoubtedly will, the whole thing might swing into the Democratic party. If Harrison is nominated on a gold platform, it will be almost impossible to carry any one of the silver States for the Republican Party."[37] To another Nevada friend he wrote that, if the Republicans opposed silver, "the party will be in the minority. . . . I should hate very much to be compelled to vote for any person who is in favor of a single gold standard. I do not think such a person patriotic or fit to hold office."[38]

Although Stewart tried to avoid overt commitment on the silver issue, he was adamant that his name not be connected with the gold standard. Thus he advised Wallace that he did not want to attend the 1892 Republican National Convention, since he was convinced it would adopt a gold plank and a gold candidate.[39] In a letter to a political ally in Virginia City, Stewart stated that he could not become "tainted with gold men," because "Nevada would certainly be for silver."[40] He suggested later to the same correspondent that if the Republican National Convention adopted a gold standard, then Nevada Republicans should leave the national parties alone until after the election.[41]

While he was walking a tightrope on the silver issue, Stewart continued to keep his name from being connected with the Newlands bid for Congress. As he wrote to Yerington, "I am certain it would do more harm than good to Mr. Newlands to have me discussed in connection with his nomination. The charge of combination would be made at once and used to the disadvantage of both."[42] In a similar vein he confided to Sam Wright, superintendent of the Carson Mint, and Stewart's close personal friend:

> I have received a letter from Mr. Yerington in which he tells me that it looks as if the Carson Mint was not favorably disposed towards Mr. New-lands. He did not ask me to take any action in the matter, and I am glad that he did not, because I cannot be mixed up with it. My friends through-out the State will take sides in different ways in this Congressional fight, and I must not be held responsible for their acts, and I must not be mixed up with the fight. . . . But above all things, destroy this letter, so that there will be no evidence that I ever wrote anything about the matter.[43]

The political situation, both in Nevada and nationally, warmed substantially as state and national conventions were held. Nevada's state conventions met in April of 1892, to work out platforms and select national delegates. Although each of the two major parties endorsed the silver cause, the Democrats passed a significant resolution to the effect that, if the Democratic National Convention failed to nominate candidates who were "unequivocally in favor of free coinage of silver," the nominees of the state conventions would be absolved from all obligation to support the party's national nominees.[44]

However, it was the national arena which ultimately forced a decision on the silver issue in Nevada. Most important was the formation of the People's Party of the United States of America (Populists), which adopted a platform that included a free-silver plank. Adding substance to the silver argument nationally was the organization of the American

Bimetallic League in May, 1892, in Washington, D.C. League officials issued a straightforward declaration, "We will not support for a legislative or executive office any candidate who is not thoroughly committed by platform and declaration to the full restoration of that monetary system violently disturbed by the legislation demonetizing silver in 1873."[45] Stewart saw in these developments an opportunity to pressure the national parties to adopt silver planks, and so proposed that a silver convention be held in Washington, D.C., on May 26, 1892, prior to the June meetings of the national parties.[46] No such convention was held in 1892. However, the idea was acted upon in 1896.

When the two major parties held their conventions, it became clear that neither had succumbed to the free-silver argument. The Republicans, meeting at Minneapolis, nominated Benjamin Harrison for the presidency. Their platform was evasive on the money issue, but Harrison had turned a deaf ear to the pleas of the silverites during his presidency. The Democrats, at Chicago, denounced the Sherman Silver Act as a "cowardly makeshift," but refused a silver plank in their platform, preferring to follow the equivocal procedure of the Republicans. Their nomination of Grover Cleveland, an avowed gold-standard advocate, was an indication of the money program the party would pursue if successful in the November election. Congressional action gave silverites no more hope than the major party conventions. A measure introduced by Stewart in July, calling for the free coinage of silver, did pass the Senate by the close vote of 29 to 25, but was killed in the House.[47]

Anticipating the ambivalence of the national parties, the Nevada Silver League, under the guidance of George Nixon and Thomas Wren, called for a meeting to be held in Reno on June 24. Delegates from the various silver clubs throughout the state would nominate three free-coinage electors; discuss the possibility of sending a delegation to the People's Party Convention in Omaha, Nebraska, in July; and do whatever was necessary to perfect a state silver organization. The Silver League convened in Reno in an atmosphere of fervent optimism. Leading the movement to effect a state organization were Thomas Wren, Charles C. "Black" Wallace, George S. Nixon, and George W. Cassidy.

The most important member of the group from Stewart's standpoint was Wallace. The latter's participation in the silver movement at first appeared anomalous, since he received his nickname, "Black," because of his strong ties to the Republican Party. However, joining the silver movement, and attempting to control it in the interests of the Central Pacific Railroad, were due simply to recognition of the fact that the silver issue had become the dominant issue in Nevada politics. If the

railroad was to maintain its power in Nevada, and particularly if its officials wanted to keep Stewart in the U.S. Senate, the only viable option
was to move with the tide of political sentiment. Political pragmatism
dictated the railroad's participation in the formation of a Nevada Silver
Party. It took no great political acumen to recognize the signs strewn
along the political road in Nevada, from the meeting at Carson City on
May 29, 1890, to the call for a silver convention in Reno, June 24,
1892.[48]

Technically, the June 24 meeting did not bring about the organization
of a political party, although the Silver League formed there was occasionally referred to as a Silver Party. What the gathering did was to elect
delegates to the national Populist convention and select presidential
electors pledged to vote for Populist candidates.[49] Most Nevada politicians recognized the fact that the Reno meeting had not established a
bona fide political party. Francis G. Newlands emphasized the point
when he announced that he would be a Republican candidate for Congress, since he could not be a Silver League candidate because it was
not a real party.[50]

Stewart, however, was not interested at the moment in whether the
league was a legitimate party. The action of its leaders and events on
the national political scene gave him the guidance he had been seeking.
No longer hesitant in supporting Newlands, he wrote the latter that he
was anxious to get back to Nevada to "harmonize matters and secure
success." He advised his friend not to be discouraged about the turmoil
in Nevada politics, since he was confident that the various forces could
be reconciled.[51] Stewart encouraged his supporters to work for the
Newlands nomination and election, until he could arrive and "take
action which will be satisfactory to all concerned."[52]

Meanwhile, silver partisans were given a boost when the People's
Party met in Omaha in July, 1892, and nominated General James B.
Weaver for the presidency. At the same time, the delegates strongly
endorsed a platform plank calling for unlimited coinage of silver at the
ratio of 16 to 1. In June, a resident of Illinois had suggested Stewart for
president on the People's Party national ticket. Stewart thanked his
correspondent, but declined, stating that he could do more good for
silver in the U.S. Senate.[53] In a later letter to Newlands, Stewart enlarged the suggestion from his Illinois admirer into "a strong effort" to
encourage him to run for president under the People's Party banner.[54]

In August, 1892, General Weaver and his campaign entourage, which
included Mary Lease, the Kansas Populist who reportedly recommended
that a farming audience "raise less corn and more Hell,"[55] arrived in

Nevada. They were greeted warmly at every stop. Senator Stewart, who had returned to his home state early in August, to evaluate the political situation, joined the Weaver group and participated in political rallies held for them in western Nevada. On August 7, in Virginia City, according to a local news report, General Weaver and Senator Stewart were drawn through the streets in a four-horse coach. The paper also reported that "the Senator will be the Secretary of State when Weaver is elected President."[56] The reception given the Weaver party, and his own evaluation of the political situation in Nevada, convinced Stewart of the necessity for an immediate decision on the silver issue. On August 8, both he and Newlands joined the Silver League in Reno.[57] Evidently each man had decided that the league would soon be a political party, and that their chances for election would be enhanced by association with it. Stewart later wrote that he left the Republican Party in 1892 over Benjamin Harrison's nomination,[58] but his withdrawal was also obviously dictated by events in Nevada.

The two major parties in Nevada, meanwhile, acted as though they would like to avoid the November elections. When their nominating conventions met, in the fall of 1892, first the Republicans and then the Democrats split into factions, testimony to the fact that the silver issue transcended political affiliations in Nevada. The Republicans, meeting in Reno, broke into Harrison and anti-Harrison groups, with the latter adopting a platform condemning the administration and nominating Francis G. Newlands for Congress. Newlands, in accepting the nomination, promised to work to remonetize silver. The "straight-out" Republicans, after failing in an attempt to nominate Newlands, chose William Woodburn as their congressional candidate.

The Democrats showed even greater signs of division. The nomination of Grover Cleveland, who favored the gold standard, forced Nevada Democrats into a real dilemma. Their nominating convention refused to name electors pledged to either Cleveland or the People's Party candidate. However, when the Democratic Central Committee ("old guard" Democrats) met later, they chose Cleveland electors. The strong prosilver wing of the party then tried to name silver delegates, but their efforts were blocked when the Nevada Secretary of State certified the Cleveland electors.

That action, plus the secretary's warning to Silver League officials that Nevada election laws required ballot candidates to be nominees of a legal party, forced the silverites to take immediate political measures. A second silver convention was called to meet at Winnemucca on September 15, 1892. At that time the Nevada Silver Party was formally organized. The delegates approved a platform condemning both Cleveland and Harrison, and endorsing People's Party candidates Weaver, and James G. Field for vice-president. They also praised Senator Stewart's part in the remonetization battle. The new party nominated Francis G. Newlands for Congress. Both Stewart and Newlands spoke at the Winnemucca convention, and Stewart closed his remarks with a stirring promise: "If I go back to the Senate at all it will be by the Silver Party of Nevada and no other party. . . . I shall have no party in any county but the Silver Party. With that party I stand or fall. I am with you, friends, and I rely on you to stand by me as I have stood by you."[59]

From the end of the Winnemucca convention until the November election, Stewart campaigned in Nevada for the Silver Party. He was so buoyed by his efforts that he wrote one supporter, "The silver movement has become irresistible."[60] He warned another to encourage good silver men to run, but, "Do not put up any man for me to assist to elect unless he will be true after election."[61]

During the latter part of the 1892 campaign, Stewart was again worried whether Nevada's senior senator, John P. Jones, would support him. Early in September, Stewart received a warning from a friend in Virginia City that Senator Jones was "in a combination to defeat him in the primaries." Stewart repeated these charges in a letter to Jones, assuring Jones that he was certain the accusations were incorrect, and that if Jones should decide to oppose him he would be the first to tell Stewart.[62] His fears about Jones brought a long letter to C. P. Huntington, asking the latter to try to find out if Jones was involved in action against him.[63] In a letter to a colleague in the Senate, Stewart suggested that Jones might be supporting Horace P. Bartine as a candidate.[64] In spite of his concern about Jones's role, Stewart continued to be optimistic about his reelection, and voiced that confidence to Huntington: "The prospect now is that I will sweep the State. . . . You need not fear that this movement will die out before election."[65]

The continuing equivocal position of Senator Jones made Stewart campaign all the harder.[66] He wrote to Southern Pacific lobbyist Stephen Gage, asking him to visit Nevada, and then requested that Huntington have Gage come over from California to help with his campaign.[67] To a friend in Utah he noted, "My canvass looks well, and I believe I have a sure thing of election. It will not do, however, to trust to chances. I must leave no stone unturned in such a contest."[68] Stewart also enlisted others in his behalf. In a speech before the Stewart and Newlands Club, which had been formed in Reno on October 29, 1892, Stewart's secretary, Charles Kappler, tallied some fifteen items that Stewart had accomplished for Nevada since his return to the Senate in 1887. Kappler ended his talk by emphasizing the fact that Stewart always took care of his Nevada constituents:

> He [Stewart] never takes a vacation, preferring activity to any kind of idleness or recreation, no matter how attractive the pleasure may be. . . . The Senator's correspondence is always promptly attended to. . . . The Senator is approachable to all. . . . Not one of his constituents can say he visited Washington and was unable to see Senator Stewart.[69]

Attacks against Stewart's senatorial record during the campaign were surprisingly few. In one instance he was condemned for supporting the appointment of Justice Lamar, and in another for voting against the Elections (Force) Bill, but these were minor matters. The silver issue dominated the 1892 election in Nevada, and the only important evaluation of a candidate centered on his devotion to the silver cause. Stewart reminded C. P. Huntington of these facts when he wrote, "I fully appreciate your desire for the election of Harrison and [Whitelaw] Reid, but their position on the Silver question made it impossible for any power to carry this State for the Republican Party. The people of Nevada are for the Silver Party and nothing can change them. . . . The paramount interest of Nevada is silver."[70]

Stewart's analysis was correct. Silver Party candidates swept the November 8 election in Nevada. Newlands was elected to Congress by a substantial vote and silver candidates won a majority of the legislative posts, insuring Stewart another Senate term. The latter happily reported the results to Huntington: "The combination to beat me was utterly crushed. Every Senator and Assemblyman elected this year was publicly and privately pledged to me. A majority of the hold-over Senators since the election have declared their purpose to vote for me. There is practically no opposition." In the same letter, Stewart showed that he was watching out for the welfare of Huntington and the railroad in California as well as Nevada. One of the major California candidates for the U.S. Senate was Henry Foote, Jr., Stewart's brother-in-law. As Stewart related to Huntington, Foote:

> . . . told me without reserve that he would cooperate with me in every way to secure a settlement between the railroads and the Government, and whatever I said was right in the matter he would do. . . . He is regarded in California as anti-railroad and would receive the strength of the anti-railroad element in the State. But I thought you ought to know his real position as to the relation between the Government and the roads and what he would do in case he was elected.[71]

Unfortunately, Foote was defeated.

Another evaluation of the election came from H. M. Yerington, who wrote candidly to his boss, Darius O. Mills:

> Am satisfied that we are all ok—Stewart and Newlands are our friends in Congress and the Democrats and Silver men *here* are the same *in and out* of the Legislature, which I believe to be a good one and which I am sure we can control with ease, our good friends Woodburn, Strother, Bliss and Cleveland were knocked higher than a kite, *so local matters* have all gone our way most beautifully and we are on the top *as usual* which delights me exceedingly.[72]

Yerington then wrote Stewart, "Your election *is assured* and you can rely on it that we are with you first, last and all the time." To insure that Stewart would remember his friends, the railroad official added, "I enclose annual passes—have also sent one to Miss Bessie Fox [Stewart's granddaughter]."[73]

Stewart returned to Washington for the opening of Congress in December, but worried about being out of Nevada during the important selection procedure by the state legislature. He asked a friend to "think about the matter and let me know if it is entirely safe for me to stay away."[74] Nevada could not have been "safer" for Senator Stewart. When the legislature met in January to select a United States senator, Stewart's name was the only one submitted in each house. On January 25, 1893, at the joint meeting of the state senate and assembly, Stewart was declared duly elected.[75]

Stewart's sources for financing his 1892 campaign are unknown. The Huntington interests certainly subsidized the race in part, but one analyst asserted, many years later, that the Southern Pacific didn't spend any money on the election, since Wallace "squeezed the money out of a tenderfoot politician, Francis G. Newlands. . . . It cost Newlands about $150,000 to elect himself and Stewart."[76] There appeared to be no direct involvement of Newlands money in the Stewart campaign. However, at the time of the election, the two men were involved in a Washington, D.C., real estate venture known as the Chevy Chase Land Development Company, and it is possible that the financial arrangements for that project prompted the stories.

According to Stewart, in 1890 he purchased 200 acres of land in Washington, for a little less than $100,000. This money was loaned to Stewart by Newlands.[77] The advance from Newlands, plus $70,000 that Stewart was to furnish in cash, would give the senator a one-third interest in the enterprise. However, Stewart raised only $7,000 in cash and had to borrow an additional $63,000 from Newlands. He was able to do this by convincing C. P. Huntington to loan the Chevy Chase Company $150,000, with the stipulation that Newlands would extend the notes to Stewart, now totaling $163,000, for another four years. The arrangement was complex, and it is possible that some of the money raised for the Chevy Chase promotion found its way into Stewart's 1892 election campaign.[78]

Besides the Chevy Chase real estate development, Stewart continued his various mining and mining promotional activities during these years, both in the United States and Mexico.[79] At one point he tried to involve Huntington in his International Mining Company in Mexico. Stewart suggested that Huntington bring the proposed Mexican International Railroad close enough to his mines that railroad spurs could be provided, thus reducing heavy transportation costs.[80] Throughout this period, although they absorbed much of his time and interest, Stewart's mining and promotional efforts continued to be financial failures.

Another financial drain on his limited resources were the many obligations he assumed on behalf of his family. The Senator felt responsible for each member of an extended family, particularly on his wife's side. This solicitude created a constant drain on his time and money and was a major contributor to his constant need for more money. Stewart's sense of family duty was illustrated clearly in 1889, when he became involved with the children of his daughter Annie. She had married Andrew W. Fox, who divorced his wife for desertion in 1884, and was awarded custody of the four minor children. Stewart somehow gained possession of his grandchildren and took them out of California, keeping their whereabouts secret from the father. When Stewart returned to California in October, 1889, Fox asked the court to hold Stewart in contempt of court. When Stewart appeared in court in San Francisco on October 18, 1889, it seemed possible that the judge might rule in favor of Fox. Not only had the senator kept the whereabouts of the children from their father, but he had also failed to tell Fox of one son's death. When the contempt hearing was renewed the following week, Fox reversed his earlier stand and requested that charges against Stewart be dismissed. The court awarded custody of the three remaining children to Stewart, declaring itself convinced that Stewart had taken good care of the children while they were under his protection.[81]

After gaining custody of the three Fox children, Stewart placed the two boys in a private school in Reno operated by Hannah K. Clapp and Elizabeth C. Babcock. The senator kept in frequent touch with Clapp about the progress of the Fox children, at one point writing, "I am glad to hear that the little boys are doing well and are contented, and that you are becoming attached to them. I have great hopes of making good men of them. Your influence and that of Miss Babcock will be of great value to them through life."[82] The other Fox child, Bessie, came under the direct supervision of Stewart's wife, Annie, who directed her education and travel in much the same manner as she had done for her own daughters.

Not only did Stewart take over the financial and other obligations involved in bringing up the Fox family, but he also gave money to educate two other grandsons, the children of his daughter, Bessie Hooker, in Heidelberg, Germany.[83] Stewart corresponded with all of these children throughout his life, with the exchange often initiated by the grandchildren requesting financial help.

Another drain on Stewart's resources came from a two-year world tour by his wife and youngest daughter, Maybelle.[84] The costs of the trip were augmented by Mrs. Stewart's purchases of household items. Stewart indicated their extent in a letter to the Secretary of the Treasury. He informed that official that his wife had been traveling in the Far East and was returning with thirteen cases of household goods, which he requested to have let through customs without his wife "taking another oath."[85] The world tour was part of the education program Mrs. Stewart had mapped out for their daughter, who, after attending private schools in Canada, France, and England, was given the two-year grand tour to complete her education.[86] Understandably, during these years Stewart was constantly in need of additional funds.

CHAPTER 10

ENGULFED BY THE SILVER ISSUE

BY THE TIME Stewart returned to Washington in December, 1892, it had been amply demonstrated that the silver issue could not only dominate the political machinery of one state, but could also become the focus of a national debate on the monetary system. The adoption of a silver plank by the People's Party and the surprising electoral strength of that party in 1892 insured a national spotlight for the question of remonetizing silver. Although the silverites were not so successful on the national level as they were in Nevada, gold-standard advocates were forced to marshal all of their considerable resources in order to retain control of the monetary system.

The first volleys in the monetary clash were fired when it became apparent that the Cleveland administration would attempt to force repeal of the 1890 Sherman Silver Act. In December, 1892, Stewart had warned his friend, C. C. Wallace, that such an effort would be made by the new administration.[1] A few months later, he wrote George Nixon that a successful repeal fight would split the Democratic Party.[2] In the eyes of the silverites, the villain was the newly elected President, Grover Cleveland, an avowed gold-standard advocate. On taking office in March, 1893, the Cleveland administration faced a severe financial depression. Although the roots of the depression went deep into the American economic system, Cleveland chose to blame the situation on the 1890 silver purchase act. The movement for repeal came on June 30, 1893. Cleveland called a special session of Congress for August 7, 1893, to meet the economic crisis, and specifically to repeal the 1890 silver act.[3]

For three years prior to the repeal session, Stewart had been preparing himself for the role of congressional spokesman for the silver issue. In

TRYING HARD TO PUT DEMOCRACY IN A HOLE.

Cartoon from *Puck* magazine (March 2, 1892), typical of many shown in various issues of that publication, ridiculing the fight for free silver. In most of these, Stewart was shown as the senatorial leader in the fight for free silver. *(Nevada Historical Society Photo)*

June of 1891, he participated in a series of written arguments which were carried in the pages of the *New York Telegram*. Editor Nicholas Biddle had opened the paper to a debate on silver as a monetary standard, and Stewart immediately challenged all comers. Beginning with the issue of June 20, and running into the winter of 1891–92, a number of prominent individuals, including Andrew Carnegie, Henry Clews, John Jay Knox, and Theodore W. Meyers, accepted Stewart's invitation. When the debates were over, Biddle thought the victory should go to Stewart, although he insisted that Stewart's views on the money question were all wrong.[4]

Some months later, in a series of articles beginning February 22, 1893, Stewart debated the silver issue in the pages of the *New York Weekly Tribune*. Letters between Managing Editor R. G. Horr and Stewart brought out the classic arguments on both sides of the monetary question. Stewart's last contribution, consisting of thirty-one typed pages, covered his interpretation of the history of money from ancient to modern times, and reiterated the "conspiracy" view of the passage of the 1873 Mint Act. He insisted that the only answer for restoring prosperity to the United States was a return to the bimetallic standard. Horr, on the other hand, maintained the need for a single standard and claimed it would be disastrous to use silver at a 16 to 1 ratio, as the silverites demanded. The two did agree that there wasn't enough gold in circulation at the time. In a letter to Horr after the debates Stewart wrote, "My only regret is that I have not been able to present the question with as much force and clearness as I desired. I can truthfully say that you have presented your side of the question more forcibly than I find in the production of any other author. I am glad that we have been able to conduct the discussion in good temper and decorum."[5]

Stewart welcomed opportunities to engage opponents of silver. He liked such contests and prepared thoroughly for them. Given the chance, he was quick to pick out weaknesses in opponents' arguments and to exploit them aggressively, at times even ruthlessly. He emphasized and constantly repeated the strengths of his own position, for he had great confidence in his ability and a fierce drive to win. The written debates gave Stewart an opportunity to define his thoughts and to prepare for the congressional contest on the money issue. When the special session began on Monday, August 7, 1893, Stewart was ready. Although he lost the battle to prevent revocation of the 1890 act, his ability in debating and in parliamentary maneuvering made the battle more equal than it would otherwise have been.

Shortly after the special session opened, Senator John Sherman whetted the appetite of the silverites for battle by admitting, in a speech on August 8, that the 1890 Sherman Silver Purchase Act was passed "to prevent enactment of a free coinage bill."[6] In his memoirs, Sherman later added, "Some action had to be taken to prevent a return to free silver coinage, and the measure evolved was the best obtainable. I voted for it, but the day it became a law I was ready to repeal it, if repeal could be had without substituting in its place absolute free coinage."[7] Sherman's admission in the Senate, confirming what Stewart and others had been saying and writing for years, simply strengthened the resolve of the silverites to prevent repeal of the Sherman Act.

Cleveland's immediate problem was the necessity to blunt somehow the silver partisans' strength in the upper house, where the bimetallists had often been in the majority from the beginning of the remonetization fight in 1876. Administration forces fought to prevent an immediate vote, while Cleveland sought to weaken silver support in the Senate by liberal use of patronage. While the two opposing camps were organizing, Stewart introduced two silver bills, which were sent to the Committee on Finance and promptly forgotten. At the same time he was again forced to defend himself against charges that he was not a true silverite and was using the remonetization battle for selfish, personal reasons. In answer to charges that he demanded gold to settle mortgages on real estate he owned in Alameda, Stewart explained that California law required payment of all contracts in gold, and that his broker in making a sale simply used the required forms specifying gold. He blamed this attack on individuals who were trying to discredit him prior to the debates on repeal of the silver act.[8]

To refute these accusations, however, Stewart made a number of false statements. When charged with ownership of silver mines, he reported that his wife had invested in a Mexican mine without his knowledge, but that her interest was small and he had ignored it for years.[9] Yet, at that very time he was president of the International Mining Company, which owned a silver mine in Mexico, and actively promoted its stock. Not only that, but he had actually gone to Mexico in July, 1893, noting in a letter to the mining company's board of directors that the mine was in full operation when he arrived, but that he had to shut it down because of the depression, and if the Sherman Act was repealed, the property would be worthless.[10] Stewart's attempts to justify his activities were interrupted by the opening of the repeal debate.

Stewart entered this discussion with a speech on August 18. He insisted that the Panic of 1893 was due not to the Sherman Silver Act, as Cleveland maintained, but to the failure of the administration to execute the act.[11] He warned those who wanted repeal of the statute, "The demonetization of silver and the adoption of the gold standard is a revolutionary movement. Its conception was bold and unscrupulous. . . . No socialist or anarchist has ever advocated a more radical destructive and revolutionary scheme.''[12] A week later Stewart made another major speech, this time emphasizing his belief that the congressional battle over repeal was really a battle between the exporters of gold and the people of the United States. He insisted that the movement for repeal was directed by London bondholders, who used the Wall Street ''group'' for their purposes, ''to sustain the powerful aristocratic organization of wealth.''[13] The idea that gold was the money of wealth and silver the money of the people and the Constitution became a constant Stewart theme during the long fight.

On September 5, Stewart began what became his major oration against repeal. It occupied forty-seven pages in the *Congressional Record*.[14] As usual, he began by tracing U.S. coinage laws from April 2, 1792, up to the 1893 special session. As one might have predicted, a large segment of his speech dealt with the background of the Mint Act of 1873. Stewart read into the *Record* the entire history of the Senate debate that had taken place some twenty years earlier, on the bill which became the 1873 law. This was part of the silverites' filibuster, to try to counteract Cleveland's use of patronage. They set out to prove there had been a conspiracy in the passage of the act which demonetized silver, and that its leader had been John Sherman.

Sherman ridiculed the idea of conspiracy, pointing out that the bill had been publicly and openly presented and debated, and that it was printed thirteen times. He later wrote, ''I know of no bill which was freer from any immoral or wrong influence than this act of 1873.''[15] The very points that Sherman chose to demonstrate that the bill had been thoroughly reviewed and discussed were the same ones that Stewart and others used to charge that there had been a conspiracy. Thus, Stewart emphasized that the constant printings of the bill, and its movement back and forth from one house to the other, were done not to give publicity to the bill, but to confuse and hide what the gold partisans were doing. He pointed out that it wasn't until the Latin Union suspended the coinage of silver in the latter part of 1875 that anyone became aware of demonetization. Stewart noted that no senators except some of the committee members had the slightest idea at the time that the bill had demonetized silver. He listed a number of prominent members of both houses of Congress who had admitted publicly that they did not realize until sometime after its passage that the Mint Act of 1873 demonetized silver. Stewart also maintained that President Grant was ignorant of that fact when he signed the bill.[16] He noted that no political party, in national or state conventions, had ever declared itself in favor of the single gold standard, and that in the 1892 campaign all parties supported the bimetallism that the American public wanted.[17]

Stewart's long speech drew the ire of the editor of the *New York Times*, who wrote on September 7:

> Mr. Stewart has already had the floor for two days, his speech is not yet concluded, and, with super-human endurance, he could talk as he has today, forever and forever. . . . He is not at all averse to filibustering, and would like nothing better than to have the morning hour taken up in this way day after day. He is prepared to talk indefinitely. . . . Mr. Stewart's speech, which is apparently interminable, brought out no new points.[18]

Nevertheless, in the course of many speeches during the repeal debate, Stewart was often called on to explain the conspiracy idea, sometimes by gold-standard supporters and sometimes by silver advocates. This he did happily, over and over again. Senator Aldrich challenged Stewart's assertion that he didn't know what he was doing when he voted for the 1873 act, and insisted that the whole idea of conspiracy was ridiculous. Stewart replied that the bill was presented as a codification of the mint laws and none of its sponsors suggested at any time that a major change was intended. He admitted that the failure to note what was actually happening "may show inattention, but the debate shows that it [demonetization] was not known. The testimony of men living and dead, the most eminent of the time, proves that they did not know it."[19] Furthermore, he averred, the newspapers were similarly ignorant, as were the American people.

From the middle of August through September, Stewart was the most active of the silverites in the repeal debate. His colleague from Nevada, John P. Jones, took little part in the proceedings during the first two months. However, on October 14, Jones began a speech which lasted over two weeks, filled some ninety pages of the *Congressional Record*, and has since been cited as the classic statement of the bimetallists' position. He reiterated many of the points that others had made before him: that it was the contraction of money which had brought on the Panic of 1893, for "a volume of money that does not keep pace with population and demand always ends in a panic"; that gold was the money of the rich and silver the money of the poor; that British bond-holders were behind the movement to demonetize silver in the United States.

Jones maintained that silver was the "national metal" of the United States and that Americans should not let the money systems of other countries influence national policy. He emphasized his view that restoration of silver was needed to supply enough money to balance the economy by providing higher wages for labor and higher prices for agriculture. When a number of senators pointed out the dangers of inflation, Jones replied that runaway inflation could be prevented by government regulation of the quantity of money in circulation, that "in a civilization such as that of the present day, a proper volume of money is as necessary to the freedom of the people as is the ballot . . . a perfect system of money would be one in which the quantity of money, the number of monetary units, should always and unfailingly keep pace with demand."[20]

The long oration by Jones was the last major statement by the silverites. Cleveland's stubborn refusal to compromise and his use of patronage to keep Democrats in line ultimately weakened the filibuster. At the end of the Jones speech, but before the scheduled vote, Stewart took the floor to fling a last bitter remark at the gold-standard supporters:

> Mr. President, the die is cast. The surreptitious and fraudulent act of 1873 demonetizing silver is ratified and confirmed. The gold kings are victorious. . . . The betrayal and capture of the White House and the two Houses of Congress is not the end of the war. . . . The next campaign will be fought in the open field, with no traitors in the army that will do battle for justice and equal rights. . . . Let the vote be taken; let the deed be done; let the object lesson be given. We will abide the result.[21]

Applause from the galleries followed Stewart's final speech, but such support unfortunately had nothing to do with the results of the vote in the Senate. On October 30, the Sherman Silver Act was repealed by a vote of 43 to 32, with 10 not voting. On November 1, the House also voted for repeal, with 194 yeas, 94 nays, and 65 not voting. The repeal bill was signed by Cleveland on November 1, 1893.[22] Although the Sherman Act had been repealed, the editor of the *New York Times* couldn't resist a parting verbal shot at Stewart:

> Of all the tiresome men who have occupied the time during the last two months in the vain effort to prevent the repeal of the silver purchase clause, Stewart of Nevada will be remembered as the one most dreaded, not because of the force of his arguments, which no one will ever examine to find out whether they were forcible or pointless, but because he was always arguing. . . . He always abuses the cause he is against, and he has always been a man of strong methods to enforce his own opinions.[23]

In the midst of this heated fight over repeal, Stewart joined the Populist Party, explaining to a correspondent, "There is no other party in which a true friend of the people can be useful. The Democratic and Republican parties have both been betrayed by their leaders." He added that the presidential nominees of the two traditional parties had been chosen by the power of money, that he could not support either, and also could not deceive the people of Nevada by asking reelection as a Republican.[24] Stewart, as usual, had foreseen the political trends in his home state, which warned him that it would be disastrous to remain in the Republican Party.

During the repeal debate Stewart was placed in something of a dilemma when his good friend and benefactor, Collis P. Huntington, informed him that he wanted the purchasing clause of the Sherman Act revoked. Stewart stood his ground, for he could not afford to support the repeal effort if he wanted to retain any kind of political base in Nevada. In a long letter to Huntington, he explained why it was impossible for him to vote to eliminate the Sherman Silver Purchase Act. At the same time he lectured the railroad magnate on the facts of political life in Nevada:

> Your letter gives me great pain. I cannot understand why you should want the purchasing clause of the so-called Sherman act repealed. I have given the subject more study and reflection than I ever devoted to any other question. The unconditional repeal of the Sherman act would place the United States on the single gold standard, and leave no law for the conversion of silver bullion into legal tender money. It would destroy silver and silver mining in this country and Mexico for all time, unless by a political revolution a new party could come into power and reverse the legislation of Congress which demonetized silver.

Stewart pointed out that the real issue was the lack of sufficient gold in circulation when compared with the population and business of the country, and that if "we take this fatal step the civilization of the 19th century will be on the down-grade from that time forward." Then in an attempt to remain in Huntington's good graces while standing fast for silver, he concluded:

> How can an honorable man, believing, as I do, fail to use all legitimate means in his power to persuade the Senate not to pass a law which he believes to be pregnant with terrible disaster? You know my love and esteem for you, and your great kindness would make me go to almost any length to do you a service. But I feel that your generosity would not allow you to censure me for performing a duty the failure to perform will deprive me of

my own self-respect, and degrade me in my own estimation so as wholly to destroy my usefulness in the future.[25]

Stewart's position apparently did not weaken his friendship with the railroad official. Sometime after the repeal Stewart received a gift from Huntington, to which he responded gratefully, "I have no words which can express my obligation to you for your great kindness. I hope I may be able to show you how I appreciate what you have done for me."[26] Huntington could afford to be conciliatory since his position triumphed.

Stewart was extremely pessimistic about the future of the silver issue immediately after the repeal debate, but his usual optimism soon reasserted itself. Within a few days he was writing to friends in Nevada that repeal was a good thing for the silverites; just the beginning of the war that would ultimately end in victory.[27] Despite Cleveland's opposition, Stewart kept the silver question alive in Congress. Throughout 1894, until election activities intervened, he missed no opening to involve the silver issue in every measure pushed by the administration, regardless of its relevance. He also took an active role in the debate over a bill introduced in the House by Richard Bland, which sought to have the U.S. Treasury issue silver certificates in the amount of $55,000,000, the exact sum of the silver bullion then in its possession. Bland's proposal was an obvious attempt to get more money in circulation and thus cushion the effect of the Sherman Act repeal. The bill passed both houses of Congress, but was vetoed by President Cleveland on March 29, 1894.[28]

Stewart's persistence in linking the remonetization of silver with other measures was demonstrated again when a bill to repeal the Federal Election Law was introduced late in 1893. Although he began his remarks by speaking in favor of state regulation of voting laws, he led his listeners almost immediately to the silver issue, blaming federal power and usurpation for thwarting the will of the people and preventing the restoration of silver. During debate on the measure a number of his colleagues tried to keep Stewart focused on the election law, but he consistently returned to the silver question. Before he was finished speaking, he had filled five pages of the *Congressional Record* and repeated most of his pet theories as to why silver should be remonetized. At the end of his speech he justified his lengthy remarks on silver by noting that the election law was said to be connected with the business decline in the United States, and that he merely wanted to show that the financial depression was caused by the demonetization of silver.[29]

When the Wilson Tariff Bill came before the Senate in the spring of 1894, Stewart sought to link it, too, with the remonetization of silver.

He insisted that the gold standard and protection could not stand together, that either the gold standard had to yield to bimetallism or protection to free trade.[30] Stewart emphasized the silver issue so often during the tariff debates that at one point, when he requested the floor from Senator George of Mississippi, the latter agreed, but stated, "Before you start so that we can go along together, let us agree that all the distress in the country now comes from the demonetization of silver." Stewart replied, "Yes, all the distress comes from that cause; but this is a question by itself."[31]

Stewart's acknowledgement that the tariff was "a question by itself," was no doubt influenced by protectionist interests in Nevada, who didn't want their problems submerged in the fight to restore silver. The Nevada borax interests, particularly, were not interested in the silver question, but were insistent that domestic borax be protected from the cheaper foreign imports. Stewart reacted to the pressure by speaking strongly in favor of a higher borax tariff.[32] Similarly, he spoke a number of times in an attempt to keep wool from the free list, insisting that this would discriminate against the mountain states where most of the sheep were raised. He couldn't resist tying the wool issue to the money question, alleging that all foreign competitors in the wool market were on the silver standard and thus had an advantage of about 50 percent in wages, for, "The property of the world is measured by the gold standard and there is not gold enough."[33] When the Wilson Bill was in the last stages of debate, Stewart again linked it with the silver question, insisting that no matter what was passed in the proposal, it would be of little importance, since the real key to the depression was the money situation, "The tariff does not reach the evil; it does not mitigate the evil."[34] Stewart was convinced that the old-guard Republicans tried to chastise silver Republicans by placing lumber and wool on the free list. Both he and Jones voted against the Wilson Tariff as it passed the Senate on July 5, 1894.[35]

In addition to his defense of silver in the Senate, Stewart also carried on a letter-writing campaign throughout the United States, emphasizing that demonetization was responsible not only for financial problems in Nevada, but for the national depression as well.[36] He also completed a small monograph, "Silver and the Science of Money," which included extracts from his Senate speeches, material from his debates in the two New York papers, and other silver arguments he had used in his political campaign in Nevada. To one supporter, who had contributed $100 to help finance the book, he reported on its progress, "My book will be out in a few days. I will send you a copy as soon as I receive them and ascertain the cost per thousand. They can be franked so that the postage can be saved. If Coin [apparently "Coin" Harvey or his publishing company] would distribute them it can have the book at cost, which will be very cheap."[37] By the time the pamphlet was released Stewart had perfected his basic silver argument. It usually started with a history of money and emphasized the quantitative theory of money rather than that of intrinsic value. By 1894, Stewart could engage in lengthy letters or long-winded debates on the silver question at a moment's notice.

The alignment of Nevada's congressional delegation against the gold-standard administration naturally caused some problems with patronage. Stewart sought a solution by trying to arrange for patronage through the Silver-Democrats in Nevada, particularly William E. Sharon. He suggested to Sharon that General Robert P. Keating, a prominent Nevada Democrat, should go to Washington. If he did, "I believe he could form combinations here which would enable him to control most of the patronage. But it would not do to have it known that he was cooperating with the Nevada delegation; on the contrary, it would probably be best for us to withdraw our recommendations."[38] Evidently Keating did function in this capacity, since Stewart referred prospective applicants to him. On one occasion he wrote that he had little to say in the matter of appointments and the man to contact was Robert Keating.[39] Stewart advised another office seeker, "Mr. Keating seems to control the appointments in the State, and he has a great deal of influence with the Post-Office Department. I would advise you to write to him on the subject."[40] Stewart appeared well-satisfied with the Keating arrangement, which succeeded in obtaining federal positions for Nevadans.

The exigencies of politics also made necessary other adjustments. When Stewart became involved in the march of "General" Coxey's army on Washington, D.C., he was in the strange position of trying to disassociate the silver issue from Coxey's popular cause. Jacob S. Coxey, an Ohio Greenbacker and Populist, suggested that the unemployment problem could be solved by means of federal work relief, with a payment to anyone out of work of $1.50 per eight-hour day. The expenditure would be covered by legal tender notes issued by Congress at the rate of $20,000,000 a month, for a total sum of $500,000,000, with the money to be used for the building of roads. When Congress did not act on his suggestion, Coxey called on the "ragamuffin army" of unemployed to gather from all parts of the United States and march on the national capital. Coxey's call for troops of unemployed caused concern in Nevada because of the imagined consequences of thousands of Californians passing through the state on their way east.[41]

Stewart addressed the problem in a long and rather strong letter to Coxey, pleading with him to give up the idea of a march and noting that the only legitimate way to change the national situation was by the ballot, which should be aimed against the two old parties. He warned that Coxey's march would be used as an excuse by local and national governments to put down anarchy and insurrection. Stewart suggested that Coxey, "Abandon the folly of marching an unarmed multitude of starving laborers against the modern appliances of war under the control of a soul-less money trust. . . . Disorder is all that is required to insure the supremacy of the armed forces of the money powers at the polls. . . . Trust no man who has once deceived you."[42] Since Coxey had earlier declared strongly for remonetization, Stewart worried about the effect his plan might have on the silver issue.

Coxey was not impressed with the Stewart argument, considering it an attempt by the senator to straddle the issue. In an open letter published in a Reno newspaper, he replied that there was no neutral ground in the fight with the administration, one had to be either for the movement or against it. He warned Stewart and the silverites that if they didn't back his march, they then would be in the unenviable position of being allied with the common enemy—gold.[43] However, the Coxey march ended ingloriously on May 1 when Coxey and some of his principal followers were arrested in Washington, D.C., for trespassing on the Capitol lawn; so the crusade had little effect on the silver movement other than to spawn the letter from Stewart.

Shortly after the Coxey incident Stewart immersed himself in the 1894 congressional campaign. Although not a candidate for reelection, he was well aware of the campaign's potential importance both to his own political future and that of the Silver Party as well. The disturbing possibility arose that a state unit of the People's Party would be formed and would then compete directly with the Silver Party for the silver vote. Stewart was in a predicament, since he had joined the national People's Party in the latter part of 1893, and had urged his friends to do the same.[44] Trying to prevent the formation of another state party, Stewart urged his friend, Thomas Wren, one of the most important silver leaders in Nevada, to have the Populists represented in Nevada's Silver Convention.[45]

Unfortunately, the Nevada Silver Party could not please everyone. At the Silver Convention, held at Carson City in September, James Doughty from Elko County and Benjamin F. Curler from Reno, not receiving nominations for governor and supreme court justice, respectively, walked out of the hall. A few days later they helped to form the Nevada People's Party. This event disturbed Stewart, who continued to insist that there was no room for another party.[46] But those who thought, with Stewart, that a local Populist Party would hurt the Silver Party, had nothing to fear. Although the People's Party of Nevada nominated a full slate of candidates, it did not attract enough votes to prevent the Silver Party from gaining every office. The election of 1894 had a more adverse impact on the state's Democratic Party, which came in fourth in the four-way contest. The near demise of the Democratic Party at this time demonstrated the dilemma faced by a local group that espoused a bimetallic standard while its national counterpart stayed with gold.

Stewart was pleased with the silver victory in Nevada, but worried about the issue in other western states such as Colorado, Wyoming, Montana and Idaho, where Republicans had won. He and other western silver leaders felt that mining states must jointly condemn the Republican gold advocates or risk jeopardizing the future of the silver issue.

Back in Congress after the November election, Stewart plunged once more into the game of linking the silver issue to every bill and resolution before the Senate. On January 12, 1895, during discussion of deficiency appropriation bills and the raising of revenue to fund them, he joined Senator Teller in demanding that additional money needed for government expenses should come from remonetization of silver, not from more taxes.[47] The following month, Stewart tied remonetization to the issuance of government bonds. He insisted that the U.S. could not pay its debts with bonds payable only in gold, simply because there was not enough gold in the country to do so. He reminded the senators that contracts already read that the government would pay in coin (that is, either in gold or silver), and that agencies should start abiding by the law.[48]

During these discussions, an issue arose that temporarily broke the silver ranks. An international monetary conference on bimetallism was suggested, and the silverites split into two camps almost at once. Stewart saw such a conference as a plan of the "gold bugs" to ease congressional pressure to remonetize silver, and insisted that the issue first be resolved in the U.S.[49] A number of bimetallists, however, favored the international approach. Their pressures finally brought reluctant agreement from Stewart,[50] although no international conference materialized at this time.

Stewart temporarily turned his attention from the silver issue in the spring of 1895, in order to oblige Collis P. Huntington and the Central Pacific Railroad. He was stimulated to such action by a joint and concurrent resolution from the Nevada legislature, passed by that body on February 5, 1895, requesting Nevada's congressional delegation to secure passage of a bill aimed at adjusting or refunding the indebtedness of the Central Pacific to the federal government. The legislative resolution expressed fear that if the Central Pacific could not pay its obligations it might be taken over by the national government, and thus removed from state and local tax rolls,[51] an event which would severely reduce Nevada's tax base. Stewart submitted the resolution in the Senate on March 2, 1895, but notified Huntington a few days later that he had been unable to pass the Deficiency Bill, which contained appropriations to pay the judgments. He blamed the conference committee for making a unanimous report just eleven hours before adjournment, which did not leave enough time for response.[52] Huntington wrote Stewart, "I regret very much that we did not get the money, for several reasons, one of which is, that the United States government should have done such a dastardly thing as not to pay an honest debt like this. The other is that the Southern Pacific needs the money very much, as we have had very bad years. I suppose, however, we shall get it sometime."[53] As Huntington predicted, the issue of indebtedness of the Central and Southern Pacific railroads reappeared a number of times before the turn of the century.

Also in the spring of 1895, Stewart turned specifically to the possibility of forming a National Silver Party. He converted to this idea after failing to convince Populist leaders to "drop for the time being all other issues but the financial question."[54] When officials of the People's Party refused to give priority to the silver issue, Stewart tried to recruit a number of its leaders for the proposed Silver or Bimetallic Party, but with little success. Most voiced objections to joining a single issue party.

Stewart then turned to a number of Nevada constituents, encouraging them to take the lead in forming a National Silver Party and explaining the benefits that would come from such a national organization. He suggested that the party's presidential candidate be Joseph C. Sibley, a prominent Pennsylvania Populist, "whose heart is in the cause not for Sibley, but for the oppressed people. I have studied the public men of the United States with all the care and diligence possible, and I say to the people of Nevada, without reservation, I prefer Sibley for President of the United States to any other living man."[55] Following these initial contacts, Stewart and others circulated petitions throughout the country calling for Sibley's nomination by the proposed Bimetallic Party. They attempted to demonstrate that the people, and not the "packed conventions," would nominate the candidate. Stewart urged Nevadans to be the first to sign the petitions so as not to lose the leadership of the silver fight,[56] telling his Nevada friends that Senator Jones and Representative Newlands, "are in the movement heart and soul."[57] To Senator Marion Butler, Stewart reported that the Nevada legislature had endorsed the platform of the Bimetallic Party and the candidacy of Sibley for President.[58] Stewart's efforts were not successful, but he continued to support the idea during the next year.

Stewart's efforts to form a new third party early in 1895 shared the spotlight with his other measures to publicize the silver issue. In an effort to widen the conflict, he launched a direct attack on Cleveland's monetary policies, in a series of letters addressed to the President. It is clear from the tone of the missives that Stewart had his eyes on Nevada and the effect his words would have on the silver issue in his home state and, therefore, upon his future political career. In his first letter, April 15, 1895, Stewart challenged the President to point to any benefit that had come from his policy of gold monometallism: "If your gold combination is to be successful you must find some way of satisfying the people that it is right for them to be poor and miserable, if thereby they can secure the smiles of the manipulators of an alien gold trust."[59] Two weeks later he posted a second note to the President, this time linking Cleveland's foreign policy to his financial aims. In sarcastic terms, Stewart accused the President of accepting British rule over Nicaragua at the same time that he was cooperating with England on money policy. Thus both U.S. foreign policy and monetary goals were dictated by Britain.[60]

The third and last letter to Cleveland was sent on May 7, 1895, and was aimed mainly at the administration's farm policy:

> The descendants of Shylock are safe in your hands. Your decree of low prices and less wages for those who produce, and more gain and less sacrifice for those who absorb, will be executed by the power you command, while the Trimmers and Dodgers of the Republican fold are confounded and paralyzed by your boldness and dash.[61]

Although his messages to Cleveland ceased, Stewart's attacks on the President did not. However, after August 15, 1895, Stewart was able to vent his anger against Cleveland and all gold-standard supporters more publicly, through the pages of the *Silver Knight* newspaper, which he acquired on that date.

Stewart's entrance into newspaper publishing was part of a movement that he began on July 18, to establish "Silver Knights of America" clubs throughout the United States. The senator launched the first such organization in the nation's capital, and began publishing the paper shortly thereafter.[62] Stewart promised to show that the principal cause of the country's financial woes was the demonetization of silver. His salutatory essay, on August 15, 1895, informed readers that the newspaper would fill a void by printing real and unbiased information "on the subject of finance, and will discuss with fairness and impartiality, the doings of public men at the Nation's Capital. . . . Unfortunately, the money powers control the commercial press."[63]

The news coverage was hardly fair and impartial as Stewart promised; it did, however, furnish its readers with dozens of articles on the need to remonetize silver. Its circulation was increased to approximately 25,000 subscribers after Stewart purchased the *National Watchman* in December, 1895. The paper was a constant drain on Stewart's finances, particularly after the gold-standard victory in the 1896 election. Although Stewart tried to widen the news coverage to include comtemporary issues such as the Cuban Insurrection, the Spanish-American War, and many of the other items being discussed in Congress, his paper was unable to overcome the burden of the defeated silver issue.

Stewart's unflagging devotion to silver led him into some unusual areas of government policy in the fall and winter of 1895. One of these was the threat of war with England over Venezuela. This event gave the senator an opportunity to renew his attack on President Cleveland, insisting that the President had started the diplomatic war with England in order to divert attention from the domestic silver question.[64] Stewart came to see the possibility of war as a good thing, for even if the United States lost, "it would rid the country of the English bank rule."[65] He enlarged upon this theme in the pages of his newspaper, writing that he favored war against the British, "if that is the only means of relief from financial slavery which Cleveland and Rothschild are fastening on the people of the United States."[66] Early in January, 1896, Stewart charged that Cleveland was using the Venezuela boundary dispute as a ruse to conceal his efforts to make another bond deal,[67] a reference to Cleveland's earlier arrangements with the Morgan banking interests to ease the Panic of 1893.

The Venezuelan affair disappeared from the international scene almost as quickly as it had risen, but Stewart continued the silver battle. The most pressing problem was how to form the various national silver groups into a single organization in time to contend seriously for the presidency in 1896. The monetary issue seemed particularly important in the spring of 1896. More and more observers, both in and out of Congress, were adopting the Stewart viewpoint that the silver question would dominate the national election of that year.

While silver leaders discussed ways to centralize their efforts, Stewart kept the silver question continually before Congress. Once when he proposed a free-silver amendment to a bill under debate, Senator Chandler of New Hampshire interrupted in disgust, "In other words—I will put the question in another form—is the Senator from Nevada in favor of putting a free-coinage amendment upon every bill that is proposed in the Senate?" To this sarcasm Stewart replied in typically spirited fashion, "I am certainly in favor of putting such an amendment on every buncombe bill that you propose. . . .We know we cannot secure the enactment of a free-coinage law; that the President will veto such a measure. So to let you play buncombe while I keep quiet, it seems to me, is turkey on your side all the time."[68]

The effort to join the various national silver groups gained its first success with a proposed meeting of 75 silver men, 25 delegates from each of three important silver organizations, the Bimetallic League, the Bimetallic Union, and the Committee from the Memphis Silver Convention of 1895. The meeting was planned for January 22, 1896, in Washington, D.C. Stewart, still seeking union with the Populists, suggested the gathering be made more representative of the silver issue by inviting the People's Party to meet at the same time to discuss unity with the other three groups.[69] In pursuing this idea Stewart wrote letters to a number of prominent Populists, stressing to each the need for an association of all silver organizations so that they could fuse into one party with one convention. He suggested that such a silver assembly should be held after the major party meetings, since he was certain the two major parties would support gold platforms: "In fact, I think a late Convention is the one essential, if we expect success in 1896."[70]

Although the January 22 gathering did not elicit cooperation from the People's Party, it did form a new national Silver Party. Stewart assured the Populists that although the new party wanted to join forces with them, it had no intention of asking the People's Party to give up its organization and principles.[71] More important to Stewart than such a merger was the fact that the Populists had invited the new Silver Party to hold its national convention with theirs, July 22, in St. Louis. When Stewart relayed that message to friends he predicted that both of the old parties would support the gold standard in the 1896 election.[72]

Meanwhile, Stewart continued to show his versatility in reducing every issue to silver. Late in March, Arthur Brisbane, editor of the *New York Sunday World,* asked him to name the greatest evil of the time, excluding the silver issue and the single tax. If Brisbane meant to bait the senator he succeeded. Stewart wrote in reply:

Your request embarrasses me very much. You want me to state what I consider the greatest evil of the times, and to exclude from that statement the silver question. You might as well ask me to discuss the source of light and heat, excluding from such discussion, the sun. . . . I would be glad to accommodate you if your request did not involve an impossibility for any intelligent man. It would take either a fool or a knave to attempt to answer such a request.[73]

By that time it was clear the Republicans would nominate William McKinley as their presidential candidate. His position on the free-silver issue was unclear. He had supported the Bland Silver Act of 1878 and the Sherman Silver Act of 1890, but, in April, 1896, in a speech before the Young Men's Republican Club of Brooklyn, Senator John Sherman stated that McKinley would support the gold standard. Stewart thought he ought to find out where the prospective candidate stood on the money question, so, on April 3, he addressed an explicit request to McKinley: "Are you for the gold standard, with silver as subsidiary coin, as defined by Senator Sherman, or are you for the restoration of the bimetallic laws as they existed in this country previous to 1873? An answer, yes or no, is requested. Neither silence nor an evasive answer will exonerate you from an attempt to deceive somebody." The question, to which he received no reply, was repeated in another letter of April 28, with Stewart adding that McKinley should confirm or deny Senator Sherman's interpretation of his policy and "throw off all subterfuge and define your position so that they [millions of people] can vote intelligently for or against you."[74] Again there was no answer.

While the Republicans moved steadily toward endorsement of the gold standard, the Democrats, contrary to Stewart's earlier prediction, gradually turned to silver. In May and June, the Nevada senator received a number of letters warning him that the Democrats would support bimetallism in their 1896 platform. The idea was upsetting to many Populists, and at least one of them suggested that Stewart try to thwart the movement in the Democratic Party.[75] Stewart, however, was convinced that the silver movement would be enhanced if one of the major parties adopted a plank favoring bimetallism and he consequently made no effort to interfere.

The prospect of a victory for the silver forces in 1896 seemed enhanced when the Republicans, meeting in June, adopted a gold standard and nominated McKinley. Their action precipitated a bolt from the convention of Senator Henry Teller of Colorado and twenty-two other silver delegates. Stewart saw the defection of Teller as the key to the 1896 behind the Colorado senator. Consequently, he started a campaign to make Teller the Democratic nominee. Early in July, he wrote to a friend that he planned to attend the Democratic convention in Chicago in order to further the nomination of Teller for President. Stewart was certain that the Coloradan's nomination would combine the Populists and Democrats on the national level, for Teller was the one man, "above all others who could unite the friends of silver under one standard."[76]

The move to support Henry Teller drew Stewart away from his original Silver Party presidential candidate, Joseph Sibley. Stewart conveniently forgot his proclamation of just one year earlier, "I prefer Sibley for President of the United States to any other living man."[77] Others had not forgotten and were not pleased with the switch from Sibley nor the attempt to join the Populists with the Democrats. One correspondent warned that joining the Democrats with the Populists would be the end of a separate silver party, and suggested that Stewart work against any attempt to have Teller join the Democrats.[78] A Populist wrote Stewart, "If you are a Democrat go to your own; but don't curse your country by a false pretense." The writer blamed Stewart for attempting to ruin the Populist Party by leading it into the Democrats.[79]

When the Democrats met in Chicago early in July, 1896, Stewart attended, but not as a delegate. There were rumors that Stewart had joined the Democratic Party, but there is no specific evidence that he became a member of that group, then or later.[80] Obviously, he was still trying to effect some kind of consolidation between the Populists and the Democrats, but such efforts proved futile. The Democrats nominated William J. Bryan for the presidency and adopted a silver plank, thus stealing the Populists' main platform. Senator Teller had shown little desire to leave the Republican Party on a permanent basis, and it was doubtful that he could have been nominated even if he had chosen to cast his lot with the Democrats. Ever the practical politician, Stewart accepted the new turn of events and began at once to promote the idea that the Populists should nominate Bryan. He detailed his position in a letter to his friend Marion Butler, warning that any attempt by the Populists to run someone else would not only fail, but would destroy the party, "We must join with it [Democratic Party] or be destroyed."[81]

An interesting result of the Democratic actions was a movement to have Stewart lead Nevada Populists into the local Democratic Party. Charles A. Norcross, a staunch Stewart supporter, suggested that the latter come to Nevada after the Populist and Silver Party conventions in July, and join with Senator Jones and Representative Newlands "to catch the people in the state of mind they are now in, arouse their enthu-

siasm and take the credit of leading them where they are bound to go—
into the Democratic party.'' Norcross indicated that he and others had
organized a non-partisan Bryan Club to keep the ''straight-out'' Democrats from adopting the same idea and forcing others to follow their
leadership. Norcross wanted Stewart to have credit for such a movement, ''The political harvest is very ripe here now for you.''[82]

Many silverites, including Stewart, hoped that the Populist and Silver
parties would select common candidates for the presidency and vice-
presidency, but this was not to be. Shortly after the two groups convened
in St. Louis, on July 22, it became clear that they were unable to agree
on a ticket. The national Silver Party, meeting for the first and only
time, under the temporary chairmanship of Francis G. Newlands, chose
to follow the lead of the Democrats. They nominated Bryan for President
and Arthur Sewall of Maine for vice-president. The Populists, however, would not support the wealthy Sewall for the vice-presidency and
nominated Thomas Watson of Georgia to run with Bryan. Stewart
attended both conventions. According to his own newspaper, at the
Silver convention there were ''loud calls for Senator Stewart, of Nevada,'' who made a rather long speech on the silver issue. The reporter
seemed more interested in Stewart's appearance than in the speech,
noting that the Nevada senator was dressed in glossy black, which contrasted ''strongly with his patriarchal beard and fringe of snow-white
hair, and he presented rather an imposing figure during the progress of
his speech.'' At the Populist convention, Stewart seconded the nomination of Bryan.[83]

It is impossible to tell how much the failure to unify under one banner
hurt the silver movement in 1896. Some states prohibited the same name
from appearing on more than one party ticket. In those states, where the
Democrats and Populists were unable to fuse into a single party, it seems
reasonable to infer that some votes were lost. In states that had no such
rule, the existence of two sets of electors, both running on a silver ticket
but pledged to different vice-presidential candidates, may also have
created confusion.[84] In any event, Stewart's hopes of a single, unified
silver ticket were dashed.

A few days after the end of the St. Louis conventions, Stewart replied
to Norcross. The senator indicated that he couldn't come to Nevada until
sometime later, but hoped Nevadans would stand by Bryan. Meanwhile,
Stewart wrote that he would remain in Washington to push Bryan's
campaign in the pages of the *Silver Knight-Watchman,* returning to
Nevada in the fall to stump the state for him.[85] Stewart's reluctance to
return to Nevada immediately was no doubt caused by his recognition of

the risks inherent in leading a political fusion movement. Others were not so hesitant, however. The national political conventions in June and July, 1896, emphasized the opportunity open to supporters of free silver in Nevada. Adoption of a silver plank by the national Democratic Party revived the local party in Nevada. Approval of a gold plank by the national Republicans, on the other hand, practically eliminated local Republicans from political offices in Nevada.

Taking advantage of this volatile situation, a number of leaders of Nevada's Silver Party invited supporters of bimetallism to join in a united political effort. The task seemed simple enough. All that appeared necessary was to fuse three local silver organizations whose national parties had all accepted free-silver planks. However, important leaders of the Silver Party were former Republicans, and the thought of fusing with Democrats was not appealing. Practical considerations ultimately won out and the several factions met late in August to work out some sort of compromise. Representatives of both Newlands and Stewart were present when the Silver Party, the Democrats, and the Populists decided to present a united front in Nevada. When they did not receive what they wanted, the Populists withdrew their support of a unity movement.[86] The Silver and Democratic parties held their state convention in September at Elko. All of the jointly selected candidates were listed on the ballot as Silver-Democrats.[87]

Before he finally did return to Nevada for the 1896 campagin, Stewart was again besieged by letters criticizing his part in the passage of the 1873 Mint Act and questioning his commitment to the cause of free silver. One of the most virulent of these was a note from Bishop John P. Newman of the Methodist Episcopal Church of Philadelphia. Newman responded to an open letter from Stewart, on August 5, 1896, which criticized the bishop for attacking the National Democratic ticket and its platform, particularly the silver plank. Stewart had written that Newman had taken the side of the "money changers," and that "there is no excuse for a man of your intelligence to advocate the gold standard."[88] Bishop Newman replied some ten days later, "I am a disciple of the Single Gold Standard through your teachings. We were in the Senate together, you as Senator and I as Chaplain. In those happier days you were a magnificent Senator, an eloquent advocate of honest money."[89] Stewart did not want the honor of being Newman's teacher on the money question and reminded the bishop that the demonetization of silver had not come up when they were together in the Senate.[90]

Perhaps the most ridiculous of the many charges leveled at Stewart at this time was the accusation that he was worth forty million dollars and guilty of "inserting in all your papers—the *gold clause* and making both principal and interest payable in gold."[91] Not only did Stewart not have forty million dollars, at this time or any other, but in fact his financial situation was critical at that moment. Just four days after the charge was made, four insurance policies on Stewart's Virginia farm—three for $1500 each and one for $1750—were canceled for nonpayment.[92] In spite of these tribulations, however, Stewart was considered a strong supporter and able advocate of the remonetization of silver. He was in demand as a speaker throughout the months of September and October, 1896, being asked to give talks in Minnesota, North and South Dakota, New Jersey, and a number of cities elsewhere. He was also asked to place his speech-making services at the disposal of the national Populist Party.[93]

Stewart finally returned to Nevada a few weeks before the election, to aid the Bryan campaign and to elect Silver-Democrats to the state senate. Stewart's support for local candidates was well considered, as H. M. Yerington pointed out to his boss, D. O. Mills, "You understand that the hold-over Senators, just elected—will vote for or against him [Stewart] two years hence and I intend to have a square talk with him and believe it will result in his agreeing to stand by us."[94] Stewart was particularly sensitive to such suggestions, because he needed all the outside help, financial and otherwise, that he could get. From 1873 until his retirement in 1905, he was the only Nevada senator who didn't have adequate personal funds to support a Senate race. All the others, John P. Jones, William P. Sharon, James G. Fair, and Francis G. Newlands, were multi-millionaires when they ran for that office.

The election on November 3, 1896, demonstrated that the fusion of the Silverites with the Democrats in Nevada was devastating to the Republicans. It decimated the local Republican ranks and marked the revitalization of the local Democratic Party. Silver-Democratic presidential electors polled 7,802 votes, while the closest opponent received but 1,938. Francis G. Newlands was reelected to Congress with more than a three-to-one majority, and it appeared that state legislators pledged to John P. Jones would be in a substantial majority when the lawmakers met in January, 1897.

Senator Jones, standing for his fifth term, had no real opposition during the campaign and appeared to have none immediately following the election. However, just a short time before the scheduled meeting of the legislature, George S. Nixon, one of the founders of Nevada's Silver Party, startled both opponents and friends when he announced that he would be a candidate against Jones. Jones thought Francis G. Newlands was behind the Nixon move, but considered it a personal matter.[95] C. C. Wallace, while agreeing that Nixon "was prompted behind the scenes by Newlands," had a different evaluation. He was convinced that the Nixon announcement was meant as a test of strength between the Nixon-Newlands forces and the supporters of Senators Jones and Stewart.[96] Under the circumstances, Stewart and Wallace had no choice but to support Jones, since any threat to him in 1896–97 was a threat to Stewart in the 1898–99 election.

Nixon's attempt to challenge Jones ended abruptly. Shortly after his announcement, Nixon had opened campaign headquarters in the Ormsby House, in rooms made famous by the earlier campaign of Stewart and others. He told reporters that he had entered the race to give the people of Nevada a vote on the question of "Nevada for Nevadans." He intimated that he would not have opposed Jones except for the fact that, after the November campaign, Jones had hurried to his home and family at Santa Monica, California. Nixon hammered at the nonresidency of Senator Jones and the fact that Jones paid no taxes in Nevada: "I do not dispute his loyalty to the cause of silver, but I dispute his loyalty to the State."[97] He also criticized the senator's absenteeism, charging that Jones was absent from his post more than two-thirds of the time. In addition, said Nixon, Jones had given Nevada patronage to people from other states.[98]

Nixon's defeat could be predicted when the caucus of the Silver-Democrats met, giving Jones thirty-seven votes and Nixon only the three votes of the Humboldt County delegation.[99] Jones's selection was ratified by the Nevada legislature on January 27, 1897.[100] Although he lost, Nixon predicted that future U.S. Senate races in Nevada would be waged on the issue of Nevada for Nevadans.[101]

The day following the vote, C. C. Wallace wrote Stewart a long letter summarizing the events of the 1896 campaign and emphasizing the need to remind Senator Jones that his reelection had been due to Stewart's "Right hand friends," in other words, to Wallace and others. Wallace thought that the abortive attempt by Nixon in 1897 would help Stewart to be reelected in 1899. However, Wallace warned his friend that certain patronage had to be provided, particularly the confirmation of Sardis Summerfield as U.S. District Attorney for Nevada. He informed Stewart that Newlands was working behind the scenes for another candidate, "You must not lose that fight. It is all important to you. If you can call Newlands down do so. . . . You win that fight and it carries the proper nutriment with it. We care nothing about the other places. On my account as well as your own win the fight." He also warned Stewart that

H. M. Yerington was allied with the Newlands forces.[102]

The 1896 victory of the silver forces in Nevada was not duplicated on the national level. In the showdown, commonly referred to nationally as "the Battle of the Standards," McKinley and gold triumphed over Bryan and silver. The failure of the Populists and Democrats to fuse completely on the national level was often cited as a major reason for Bryan's defeat. However, the Democratic Party's support of a silver plank not only hurt the chances of the Populist Party, but weakened the overall force of the silver issue. The two parties had polled a combined total of 6,595,285 votes in 1892, but could only gather a total of 6,511,073 in 1896, even with silver as the paramount issue.[103] It appears that factors other than the money question, particularly returning prosperity, brought about the McKinley victory.

With the 1896 election over, Stewart returned to his customary activity in the Senate, addressing a wide range of familiar subjects, including silver, the tariff, Nevada Indian reservations, the Carson Mint, and the railroads. There were also many new issues, mostly centering around U.S. foreign policy, including the Nicaraguan Canal, the Cuban insurrection, the possibility of war with Spain, and the related annexation of the Hawaiian and Philippine Islands.

Throughout 1897 and the early part of 1898, Stewart again sought every legislative chance to push for the remonetization of silver. One of the first silver measures to draw extensive debate was a resolution calling for United States participation in an International Bimetallic Conference. The proposal, introduced by Senator Chandler of New Hampshire on February 2, 1897, stimulated strong reaction when Chandler accused those silver supporters opposing bimetallism by international agreement of being monometallists, a designation meant particularly to include Stewart. The latter vehemently denied the charge, indicating that he and his followers were opposed to monometallism, but felt that bimetallism should be adopted nationally before any attempt was made to obtain an international bimetallic agreement.[104] Stewart fought hard against the Chandler measure, both in the Senate and in his newspaper, insisting that the Republicans were using the idea of an international conference for political purposes, knowing that such a meeting would fail, but hoping to gain the support of silverites in Congress.[105] As in past debates on the silver issue, Stewart was accused of voting for the demonetization of silver in 1873. Again he denied the claims, stating with some force during one exchange, "Do not charge me with ever having been for the demonetization of silver or having voted for it. There was no yea and nay vote taken. It was passed viva voce, and nobody knew anything about it [the demonetization of silver]."[106] When the proposal passed the Senate, John P. Jones voted for it; Stewart was listed as not voting. The resolution was signed by the President on March 2, 1897.[107]

Stewart's commitment to silver received a different challenge in the fall of 1897, when an Associated Press dispatch reported that Stewart believed prosperity had arrived. The article quoted Stewart as saying that he was a bull on everything but silver, which he expected would decline to twenty-five cents an ounce, while wheat would advance to one dollar a bushel. He supposedly remarked, "It is time to drop the silver issue for the present and take the good things as they come."[108] Stewart denied the story and claimed that he had never held a conversation with a reporter from the *New York Times,* that he was still strong on silver and had not changed his view on remonetization.[109] Alex C. Lassen, publisher of the *Daily Financial News,* where the article first appeared, wrote Stewart that he had nothing to do with the piece and would brand as false the statement that the senator had changed his position on silver.[110] In spite of similar rebuttals, the editor of the *Times* refused to back down from the original account of the interview, noting in a later article, "Senator Stewart has not denied that he said what *The Times* reported him as saying. Our report was authentic and correct. Senator Stewart expressed the views attributed to him in the report. He has not repudiated them. . . .The Nevada Senator was only the pioneer in the movement to get out from under dropping the silver dollar."[111]

A much more serious matter came to a head in the fall of 1897, when Stewart became convinced that he had to sell his newspaper, the *Silver Knight-Watchman.* Despite Stewart's best efforts, the paper had never made money and its perilous financial position weakened further with the election of McKinley. Yet, because it provided an excellent forum for the silver cause, Stewart made one more attempt to strengthen it. Charles Kappler, Stewart's chief secretary, took over management of the paper while the senator took a trip west to seek additional funds. He made specific requests of a number of millionaires who had made some of their fortunes from mining, particularly Marcus Daly of Montana and David H. Moffat and Winfield Stratton of Colorado.

When these efforts failed, Stewart initiated attempts to sell the *Silver Knight-Watchman.* He turned first to his old friend, Joseph C. Sibley, suggesting that a company be formed with 50,000 shares selling at $1.00 per share. Such a sum would enable Stewart to cover the $30,000 to $40,000 he had expended and allow a little profit. Stewart suggested that only silver men be allowed to hold shares in such a venture.[112] When

Sibley and other Populists showed no interest, he reluctantly sought the aid of Senator James K. Jones of Arkansas, Chairman of the Democratic National Committee. Stewart told Jones that the paper was $8,000 to $10,000 in debt and that he had spent in addition about $30,000, which he would like to recover. Adroitly raising potential interest in the sale, Stewart wrote that he hoped the *Silver Knight-Watchman* would not fall into Republican hands.[113] Jones was not convinced, and sale of the paper had to await a more propitious occasion.[114]

Although free silver dominated Stewart's congressional activities following the 1896 election, other Nevada-related problems also demanded his attention. In supporting the wishes of his Nevada constituents, Stewart sometimes found it hard to be consistent, since the silver question often conflicted with other interests advanced by important Nevada groups. One example was the tariff. In order to further the silver cause, Stewart joined the People's Party in 1892; but that party favored a low tariff, as did the Democrats. Such a program was anathema to the powerful Bank Crowd and its lobbyist, H. M. Yerington. When McKinley called a special session to revise the tariff upward, Stewart and Jones were forced to repudiate the low-tariff plank of the People's Party in order to support their important Nevada friends who sought higher tariffs for borax, soda ash and wool.[115]

An interesting exception to Stewart's expedient advocacy of higher tariffs for Nevada-oriented products came when he fought to lower or remove the proposed tariff on potassium cyanide. The cyanide process of reducing gold and silver ores had replaced older methods of reduction and stimulated a demand in Nevada and other western states for this product, which came mostly from sources outside the United States. Responding to requests from mining constituents, Stewart and others were successful in having the proposed tariff on potassium cyanide reduced by half.[116] Such responsiveness on the tariff reveals again Stewart's conscientious attempts to further the interests of powerful constituents. Unfortunately, similar effort was not devoted to those such as Nevada Indians, with less political clout.

During the term that began in March, 1893, Stewart returned to his earlier campaign to extinguish Indian title to a portion of the Pyramid Lake Reservation and all of the Walker Lake Reservation. He introduced a measure to that end on August 8, 1893, but no action was taken at that time. Shortly after Congress convened in December of that year, he proposed a similar measure, at about the same time he wrote H. M. Yerington, ''I regret that the Commissioner of Indian Affairs is again annoying you. I will see him in regard to the matter at once and have it stopped. If we can get the abandonment of the Walker River Reservation as recommended by the Department, it will be the end of our troubles. I will however, prevent any annoying suits against you in the mean time.'' In the same letter, again ignoring Indian humanity, he wrote, ''It is my highest ambition to serve them [Nevada people] and to serve them as efficiently as possible.''[117] No action was taken on the bills introduced in 1893, but Stewart returned to the attempt in December, 1895, when he offered a proposal to remove the Indians from their reservations. That measure also died in committee.[118] On March 18, 1897, Stewart again submitted the bill, which met the same fate as the previous ones.[119] Obviously, other means were necessary to achieve the objectives of Indian removal.

The proposal to restrict the boundaries of the Pyramid Lake Reservation centered on a group of claims in the Indian territory, the so-called ''white lands,'' in the town of Wadsworth. In a classic assertion of squatters' rights, settlers there maintained that they had improved the land and should therefore be given title to their tracts. On December 17, 1897, Stewart introduced a bill authorizing the citizens of Wadsworth to acquire title to the areas in question.[120] Although the proposal died in the Committee on Indian Affairs, Stewart wrote confidently about the situation to a resident of Wadsworth, ''I do not believe the Indians are really in possession of any town lots, or that they are in possession of 110 acres, or any considerable quantity of land for school purposes. In fact there ought not to be, if there is any Indian school in the town of Wadsworth. The Indians should be kept away from the town.''[121] Apparently discouraged by yet another failure, Stewart made no further efforts to reorganize the Pyramid Lake and Walker River reservations after 1897.[122]

During these same years, Stewart continued his efforts on behalf of C. P. Huntington and the Central and Southern Pacific railroads. His most active work in their interest centered on the railroads' continuing bids to have the federal government extend the time for payment of their debt and lower the interest rate. In a move to curry political favor with Jones, Stewart also tried to interest Huntington and the Southern Pacific Railroad in his colleague's project to develop Santa Monica as the port for Los Angeles.

Stewart's continued ties with the railroad while supporting the People's Party did not go unnoticed. The *Missouri World,* in December, 1896, pointed out that while Stewart was trying to convince the Populists to adopt free silver as their single major political issue, he favored the railroad funding bill, which the Populist platform denounced. Furthermore, as a member of the Committee on Pacific Railroads, Stewart was in a powerful position to support the railroads. The writer noted that he had been warned to "watch old Bill Stewart. He is the attorney of the Pacific railroad . . . he is more of a Pacific railroad man than he is a representative of the people."[123] In spite of speaking strongly in favor of the various funding acts, Stewart and other railroad supporters were unable to achieve any real victory along those lines.

No more successful was Stewart's effort to have Santa Monica designated as the port of Los Angeles. Earlier, as part of his attempt to gain Senator Jones's help in his own 1892 election campaign, Stewart had convinced C. P. Huntington to build a wharf at Santa Monica to join the railroad with ocean-going vessels. If federal aid could be obtained for Santa Monica, rather than for its rival San Pedro, Stewart was certain the Huntington-Jones arrangement would benefit both the railroad and his own political interests. His speeches in the Senate, when the issue arose in 1896, had little impact.[124] And when he continued the fight into the summer of 1897, he was rewarded for his efforts by having both California senators accuse him, not without some justification, of being interested solely because of the Southern Pacific Railroad Company.[125]

Stewart's close personal ties with the managers of the Pacific railroads continued. From time to time he requested recommendations for federal appointments, clearly indicating that he would support the confirmation of such individuals.[126] At other times, railroad officials suggested directly to Stewart that he perform certain favors for them. One such request, from William Mills, asking that prominent San Franciscan Michel Harry DeYoung be appointed U.S. Commissioner at the World's Fair in Paris, illustrates the railroad's assessment of Stewart's role: "There are reasons personal to yourself why an effort should be made by you, and as your friend I request that you make an effort to secure to DeYoung this position. It would greatly promote our wishes concerning yourself, and it is suggested in your interest as well as in the full belief that there is no man in the U.S. so well qualified as De-Young."[127] On another occasion, Collis P. Huntington wrote Stewart about a bill the senator had introduced, allowing foreign ships to register under the United States flag. Huntington admonished him, "Now, I really hope you will not let that Bill become a law," since encouraging the registry of foreign ships would discourage construction of U.S. ships and hurt American laborers. Incidentally, Huntington admitted in the letter that he was building some ships for the U.S. government and would make about 5 percent profit on each vessel.[128] In spite of such political machinations, or perhaps because of them, Huntington and

Stewart shared, at least publicly, a mutual respect. Stewart thought Huntington the superior of any other railroad builder and so indicated in speeches in the Senate and in his writings.[129] Huntington in turn respected Stewart's legal ability and considered him a friend.[130]

In the spring of 1897, Stewart took time from his political activities to report to a number of Nevada constituents eastern reaction to the Corbett-Fitzsimmons heavyweight championship fight, which had been held in Carson City on March 17. The fight may have been Nevada's first attempt to attract the "tourist dollar" as part of a program to aid the state's economy. In order to legalize the proceedings, the Nevada legislature, conveniently in session, passed the so-called "Glove Bill," which made it possible to hold a contest that the state of California had refused to authorize.[131] Stewart was not concerned with the economics involved, but he did comment on the moral issues and the reaction in eastern states:

> The prize fight in Nevada has made our state rather notorious during the last few months. I am glad it was a square fight and that no disorder occurred. Some of the good religious people in the East who worship gold and hate humanity have made it an occasion for some assaults on me. . . . Whether it was a good thing to have a prize fight or not, of one thing I am sure, that the Eastern people have no right to criticize us for most anything we could do because it would be impossible for the people of Nevada to become as rotten as the great cities of the East.[132]

Stewart used the pages of his newspaper to defend one attack on Nevada by a Philadelphia paper, writing that the Philadelphians were hypocrites, since that paper and others in the east had carried advertisements of the Corbett-Fitzsimmons fight. "Hypocrisy," he noted, "is the tribute which vice pays virtue." He also accused the Pennsylvanians of having weaker moral standards than Nevadans, citing ballot-box stuffing, stealing from the poor to pay the rich, and general corruption. He concluded his remarks with a Bible quotation, "Thou hypocrite, first cast out the beam out of thine own eye; and then shalt thou see clearly to cast out the moat [sic] out of thy brother's eye."[133]

More important to Nevada's economy was the issue with which Stewart became involved in the spring of 1898, the quarantining of Nevada cattle. This problem found its way almost at once into the political arena, where it became part of a developing fight for control of the Nevada Silver Party, with the Stewart-Wallace faction lined up on one side against the Newlands-Sharon group on the other.

The affair began when cattle disease raging in California brought a quarantine to parts of that state and a threat that the blockade might be extended to Nevada. Almost immediately, Stewart began to receive letters and telegrams from Nevada cattlemen concerning his position. Unfortunately, the various letters shared no consensus. While all his correspondents agreed that Nevada should not be quarantined and that Nevada cattlemen should be allowed to ship their cattle to eastern markets, some stockmen with both Nevada and California interests wanted the suspension order amended so that they could move cattle from northern California to western Nevada. This group was supported by officials of the Southern Pacific Railroad. The Nevada agent of that company, C. C. Wallace, wrote to Stewart early in March, 1898, pointing out that many prominent cattle interests wanted to move cattle from California to Nevada and consequently wanted the federal government's order amended. He noted in his letter that such a change "will make considerable traffic for the SP. R. Co. and save the stock men great cost."[134]

Stewart moved cautiously in the matter. In a telegram to Governor Sadler, he inquired, "Cattlemen of California want quarantine removed so that they can drive cattle to Nevada and save them from starvation. What do the cattlemen of Nevada say about it. Answer as soon as possible."[135] The senator didn't have to wait long to find out. Telegrams came from E. D. Kelley, Governor Sadler's secretary, from John Sparks, an important Nevada cattleman, and from George Nixon. All indicated strong opposition to any lifting of the California quarantine.[136] The letters were more detailed, but just as adamant in their opposition to allowing California cattle into Nevada. Members of the Elko County Cattle Association sent a long communication pointing out that there was no disease in Nevada animals and that, consequently, they should be protected from possible infection.[137] Just as clear was the opposition of the Nevada livestockmen to placing Nevada in the infected district, since this would stop movement of cattle from Nevada to eastern markets.[138]

Stewart weighed his political priorities, and, despite heavy pressure from Wallace and the Southern Pacific interests and from California livestock corporations such as Miller and Lux, he decided to stay with the Nevadans. To Webster H. Patterson, a Republican stalwart and prominent Elko cattleman, he wrote that herds from California would enter Nevada only if the people of Nevada wanted them, "The cattle men of Nevada will be allowed to have absolute control over the movement of cattle into our State."[139]

As he had done in the impeachment proceedings against Johnson, the formation of the Silver Party in Nevada, and the congressional fight for free silver, Stewart jumped again onto a bandwagon driven by another. Actually, the battle against bringing California beef into Nevada was fought and won by Nevada's governor, Reinhold Sadler. Since Sadler could have allowed California cattle to enter by proclamation, he had to withstand strong pressures from that state. However, in contrast to Stewart, he did not hesitate. Sadler supported the Nevada ranchers from the beginning, clearly and unequivocally.[140] During the pressured campaign, the governor received a letter from a constituent who obviously perceived this difference in approach. He supported Sadler's stand, advising him, "We expect you to stand by Nevada. We can not help being represented at Washington by Californians, but for God Sake let us have a Nevadan for Governor."[141]

Before the 1898 election turned Stewart's focus more directly to Nevada, international events began forcing the country into a changing role in world affairs, soon involving the McKinley administration in the canal controversy, the Cuban insurrection, the war with Spain, and the problem of the Hawaiian and Philippine islands. Stewart moved prominently into the debates on these matters, partly because they gave him an opportunity to raise the silver question on yet another plane of government and partly, it seemed, to give his newspaper broader coverage of both domestic and international news. The latter was obviously an attempt to salvage the paper after McKinley's victory demonstrated the weakness of following only a single issue.

When Stewart entered the debate on the Cuban insurrection in 1896, his remarks were neither imperialistic nor economically oriented. From the beginning, the Nevada senator castigated the rule of the Spanish. He insisted that Spain had lost title to Cuba because of her inability to maintain law and order. The United States should interfere in Cuba in behalf of humanity, he said, for the country should not tolerate a "human slaughterhouse at our doors."[142] He argued that, "The United States is responsible for every outrage against the laws of humanity that occurs in Cuba, because we have assumed that nobody else will act."[143] From then on Stewart advocated recognition of Cuban belligerency as the way to end Spanish rule. The following year he strongly condemned Spanish atrocities and demanded the release of American citizens held in Cuba.

As war drew closer in the spring of 1898, Stewart continued to insist on recognition of Cuban belligerency. He maintained that the President should have given belligerent rights to Cuba in 1896, when Congress passed a resolution to that effect,[144] and blamed the drift into war with Spain on the failure to do so. In a letter to his friend, Stephen Gage, he noted, "There is great excitement here and almost universal apprehension that we will drift into war with Spain.'' According to the senator, this situation could have been avoided, ''by acknowledging the belligerent rights of Cuba and occupying a position of strict neutrality.'' He pointed out that although the Spanish believed the U.S. had assisted Cuba, the contrary was true, ''We have policed the seas with revenue cutters to blockade Cuba and hunted down on land Cuban patriots and others seeking to send supplies to the struggling Cubans. I hope it is not too late to avert war.''[145]

Stewart's letters and speeches were generally couched in rather lofty tones of morality. However, by March, 1898, he had seized the Cuban insurrection and the threat of war as a political weapon to be used against ''the Republican party . . . the agent of an alien gold trust.'' As he wrote in his paper, ''War with Spain depends entirely upon the interest of the bondholders.''[146] In later issues he enlarged upon this idea, maintaining that McKinley and the Republicans were moving slowly on the Cuban situation because of the Spanish bondholders, ''If there had been no bond deal the United States would not have prolonged the war by policing the seas with our revenue cutters to prevent the landing of supplies in Cuba. . . . It was manifestly necessary to prolong the war to give time for bond negotiations.'' The island of Cuba, wrote Stewart, ''must be retained by Spain as security for Spanish bondholders.''[147] In centering his attack on the bondholders he noted that creditors would be paid if either Spain or the United States held Cuba, but if Cuba became independent, the debts would likely be repudiated.[148]

When it became evident to Stewart that the U.S. was going to war with Spain over Cuba, his emphasis turned to a demand that the U.S. recognize the island's independence. McKinley's message of April 11, asking Congress for authority to send troops to Cuba, was looked upon by Stewart as authorizing a war of conquest. In a Senate speech, he stated firmly that intervention without invitation by either party, or before U.S. recognition of Cuban belligerency, would be looked upon by outsiders as imperialist aggression. He noted that a war against Spain based on the destruction of the *Maine* would be a legitimate war and would not bind the U.S. to the question of what to do with Cuba. But, he pointed out, the President had not asked for war on that basis.[149] Stewart reiterated these points in an editorial in his newspaper, adding that independence for Cuba was the only way of insuring that the Cubans would be free of debt.[150] When he addressed the Senate on April 15, again asking for recognition of Cuban independence, the speech drew applause from the gallery.[151]

On April 18, just before the vote on the war resolutions, Stewart asked that the Senate conferees be instructed ''to consent to no report which does not recognize the republican government of Cuba.''[152] However, the House conferees would not agree to this, so Stewart and Jones voted against the conference report. The war resolution carried in the Senate by only 42 yeas to 35 nays. Opposition came mainly from Democrats, Populists, and Independents, and centered on the fact that the resolution did not recognize Cuban independence.[153]

During the weeks Stewart had been pressing for the recognition of Cuban belligerency and then independence, he kept up a barrage of anti-Spanish verbiage in the congressional debates and in the pages of his newspaper. Thus on March 10, he wrote in an editorial in the *Silver Knight-Watchman:*

> If war comes we will make an awful example of the decaying barbarous race which has excelled in cowardice and fiendish brutality on the Island of Cuba the atrocities of any age, ancient or modern. There is no danger of defeat or great physical injury from a war with Spain, and if we assert our independence of Lombard Street, while we defend the honor of the flag and the cause of humanity at the mouth of the cannon, we will come out of the conflict a greater, richer, and better people.[154]

Again on March 24, he editorialized that Spanish cruelty in Cuba ''surpasses in fiendish cruelty and heartless barbarity the horrors of the Inquisition of Spain, which was the most revolting, loathsome and disgusting page in history previous to the exhibition of the utter depravity of the decaying monarchy of Spain now exhibited to the world in the island of Cuba.''[155] Stewart's anti-Spanish sentiment followed a consistent pattern found among silver-oriented newspapers in Nevada during that period.[156]

After the U.S. entered the war against Spain, Stewart focused his attention on the possibility of using war activities as a means of helping the restoration of silver. His first priority was the $50,000,000 of silver bullion then in the U.S. Treasury, which he thought should be used to back the issuance of $100,000,000 in silver certificates, which ratio he thought safe. An alternate plan, which he also supported, was to print $200,000,000 to $300,000,000 in greenbacks, which would be redeemable in either gold or silver.[157]

Later, when the War Revenue Bill was discussed in the Senate, Stewart proposed the issuance of $150,000,000 in paper money to help defray the costs of the war. Again the greenbacks would be redeemed in silver.[158] He spoke in support of the proposal on June 3, quoting extensively from his own pamphlet on the ''Analysis of the Functions of Money,'' which, he modestly stated, ''I regard . . . as about the highest authority.''[159] His efforts to tie free silver to the Revenue Bill failed, although he received a number of letters asking him to oppose the administration's bond issue and not to be afraid to "do so on the charge of being unpatriotic."[160] It was particularly irritating to Stewart that the gold-standard supporters succeeded in accomplishing for gold what he and others failed to do with silver, that is, to tie it to the Revenue Bill.

In contrast to his position on Cuba, Stewart moved with the tide of patriotism and imperialism on the question of annexing Hawaii and the Philippine Islands. Early in May, he suggested in his newspaper that the United States capture and keep the Philippine Islands as indemnity for the war. He maintained that, as a naval power, America needed the Philippines and Hawaii for coaling stations.[161] When Nevada's Representative Francis G. Newlands introduced a resolution to annex Hawaii, Stewart approved in the *Silver Knight-Watchman,* "The Newlands' resolution is right, patriotic and progressive. The Sandwich Islands must and will be annexed. Why waste time in fruitless and annoying opposition to right and manifest destiny?"[162]

Stewart took a somewhat unusual position concerning the legality of acquiring the Hawaiian Islands. He insisted that the United States had a right to take the islands regardless of whether statehood was the ultimate disposition. Although many senators argued that appropriating territory was an executive act which required a treaty, Stewart maintained that a treaty was not necessary, that annexation was a sovereign power of Congress which could be accomplished by legislation.[163] That view was generally sustained and the Hawaiian Islands were annexed by a Joint Resolution of Congress, the same one introduced by Nevada's Newlands.[164]

At first Stewart's position on the Cuban situation was less imperialistic than that evidenced in most Nevada newspapers. However, after Spanish troops surrendered in Cuba in the early part of July, 1898, Stewart recommended that the victors claim all the spoils: "The terms of peace should be the withdrawal of all Spanish troops from Cuba, Porto Rico, the Philippines and all other Spanish islands in the Pacific and the absolute relinquishment by Spain of all right or claim of sovereignty in such islands." He thought the United States should dictate, not negotiate the peace terms.[165]

In spite of his ability to raise the issue of free silver in congressional debate, Stewart was unable to achieve any concrete results in his campaign for the remonetization of silver. The return to prosperity after the gold-standard victory in 1896, and the beginning of the Spanish-American War, virtually eliminated the free-silver issue from national politics, although it continued to play an important role in Nevada until 1908.

CHAPTER 11

THE ELECTION OF 1898 TURNS A FRIEND INTO AN ENEMY

ALTHOUGH Stewart devoted considerable attention to the Cuban insurrection and events leading to war with Spain, his major political focus was on the 1898 election, and what he hoped would be his fifth term in the United States Senate. Actually, his reelection campaign began in 1896, when he supported Senator Jones's legislative ticket in hopes of reciprocity in 1898. George Nixon's abortive attempt, in January, 1897, to withhold support from Jones and advance his own candidacy, gave Stewart and Wallace additional opportunity to place Nevada's senior senator in their debt. Wallace, particularly, worked hard to make certain that Nixon did not defeat Jones in the 1897 legislature, and Stewart, for his part, made certain that his colleague was aware of these efforts.

The possibility that the Nixon challenge was part of a Newlands-Nixon plan to unseat both incumbent senators was not lost on Stewart. Throughout most of 1897 and 1898, Stewart supporters kept alert for signs that Newlands would announce his candidacy for the Senate. One of the first indications of such a threat came early in January, 1897, from a Stewart supporter in Carson City, who wrote that he thought the congressman was "making an underhanded fight," and would "attempt to defeat the Resolution in the State Convention endorsing you for U.S. Senator. Mr. Newlands undoubtedly is anxious for you to commit an error, then he would perhaps see the opportunity he is waiting for. I do not believe he has the courage to make an open fight against you."[1] A few months later, Stewart's secretary, Charles Kappler, confided to his predecessor in that position, "The only conceivable party who would try to make any fight against the Senator would be Mr. Newlands." He added that if the congressman did choose to oppose Stewart, he would be driven out of political life.[2] Despite Kappler's certainty, rumors of a

Newlands challenge to Stewart would not die. Late in 1897, Wallace wrote from San Francisco, indicating that he had talked with William E. Sharon, who denied that Newlands would enter the Senate fight. According to Wallace, that opinion was shared by another Newlands supporter, George Nixon.[3] Clearly, however, the question continued to plague Stewart.

Causing additional worry to the Stewart forces were two newspaper articles that appeared in several eastern and midwestern papers in the fall of 1897, obviously intended to embarrass the senator. The first concerned an alleged switch by Stewart from silver to gold. The story, printed first in New York City, was picked up by a number of midwestern papers, including the *Chicago Journal,* which added its own diatribe against Stewart, "We can wish him nothing better in this era of his new birth than that he may go to sleep and get rich. It seems indeed, a great pity that he did not go to sleep years ago and stay put. . . . the country would have escaped those earth-girdling, endless-chain speeches, from the effects of which, it can never fully recover."[4] The other article was a *New York Times* interview, which reported that Stewart was returning to the Republican Party because the silver issue was dead.[5]

These stories no doubt stimulated Stewart to tour Nevada in the fall of 1897, reiterating his support for silver.[6] His visit was not an unqualified success. One Nevadan noted in a letter to C. C. Wallace that Stewart's advancing years had impaired his ability and that a younger man should replace him.[7] Another was displeased with Stewart for not visiting Nye County during his six-week tour of the state, and blamed the omission on "scheming Silver-Democrats," who wanted to control the Silver Party state convention and deny Silver-Republicans places on the ticket.[8] This complaint spotlighted one of the major dilemmas confronting Nevada's Silver Party—how to keep both former Republicans and Democrats happy under the single silver banner.

Continuing speculation about a Newlands candidacy in 1898 convinced C. C. Wallace that William E. Sharon was, in fact, promoting such a possibility. He suggested that Stewart solicit support from State Senator George Ernst of Nye County, a powerful figure in Nevada politics.[9] This the senator did, writing Ernst that he was a candidate for re-election and, "without being egotistical, I think my services are absolutely necessary in the Senate until the fight [silver] is over and I believe that is the opinion of all my associates." Stewart sagely asked Ernst "to look after my affairs in your section of the State and advise me what to do."[10]

While he was trying to keep his local supporters in line, Stewart was also seeking help once again from the Southern Pacific. In a long letter to William Herrin, his former law partner and now chief legal counsel for the railroad company, Stewart tried to enlist support in thwarting a Newlands candidacy:

> I saw Mr. Huntington yesterday. He will write you with regard to some Nevada matters in which I am . . . interested. Mr. Wallace will explain to you what our friend, the enemy [Newlands], is doing and what a mean advantage he proposed to take. I trust to your level head in conjunction with Wallace to checkmate the contemptible plan suggested by the gentleman while in San Francisco and which is to be executed at the proper time by the use of the local press of Nevada.[11]

Although there is little doubt that some Newlands supporters were considering a contest against Stewart, the congressman's close friend, George Nixon, was not then a party to any plan to oppose the senator. Nixon cautioned Newlands against any attempt to retire Stewart, and suggested instead that he wait and challenge Senator Jones in 1902, "I can unquestionably take Wallace into camp on such a situation as he would promise almost anything to prevent a break between you and Stewart." In any event, Nixon continued, Newlands should declare one way or another at once, "You really owe this to many of your friends who do not desire to break with Stewart unless you should be a candidate for the senatorship."[12]

The mounting conflict between the Stewart and Newlands forces in early 1898 soon involved the issue of patronage. On the basis of his record in the 1896 campaign, and his continuing policy disagreements, Stewart had little reason to expect patronage from the McKinley administration. However, Stewart's political adviser in Nevada, "Black" Wallace, was certain that the state's senators did have political patronage at their disposal and that it could be used judiciously by Stewart. Wallace insisted that Silver-Republicans were the key to Stewart's future, and warned, "We must hold the Republican party together."[13] To accomplish that end, Wallace recommended that Stewart make strong efforts to gain three patronage positions for deserving Nevada Republicans: the superintendency of the Carson City Mint for former governor Roswell K. Colcord, the post of U.S. District Attorney for Carson City resident Sardis Summerfield, and the United States Marshall's position for George Emmett, a former sheriff to whom the party was indebted. Wallace was convinced that control of these three offices would insure domination of federal patronage in Nevada and, with it, leadership of the Silver-Republicans.[14] With the aid of Senator Jones, Stewart was able to win approval for all three of these appointments.[15]

That Wallace was correct in his assessment of the importance of carefully bestowed patronage was demonstrated clearly in an exchange of letters between Stewart and one of his supporters, Charles M. Sain of Lovelock. On June 19, Sain wrote Stewart that he was certain the Nevada Republicans would not support him in 1898:

> In a talk with Colonel Maxson a day or two ago I learned from him that it was the intention of the Republicans in this state not to run a ticket this fall, neither in the state or the counties, but to throw their strength in such a way that it would insure your defeat for reelection. . . . We know that the Republican national committee desires your defeat. They would rather see any new silver man elected than to have you returned.[16]

Yet just two days later, after he had heard about Emmett's appointment as U.S. Marshall, Colonel Maxson reported to Sain, and the latter to Stewart, that he was so happy about the Emmett appointment that he was certain Stewart would be reelected.[17]

Wallace knew, however, that Stewart's reelection would depend on something more substantial than a few patronage bones thrown to Nevada Republicans. In June, he emphasized the need for Stewart to return to Nevada and "take the helm" for the campaign: "Make your financial arrangements East so we will not be caught with our breeches down. See that Senator Jones comes out. Newlands has played the fool so much it is bound to make your fight expensive. Cleve [Abner C. Cleveland] is anxious to have Newlands in the fight so as to split up matters. I will explain the situation in full when I see you." Wallace listed a number of persons for Stewart to contact, emphasizing particularly the need to get a promise of support from Comstock millionaire John Mackay, since "Cleveland is boasting that Mackay is for him."[18]

It had taken Wallace a long time to evaluate Cleveland's position in the 1898 campaign. In November, 1897, he had written Stewart that Cleveland wanted Newlands out of politics. A month later he admitted that Cleveland was supporting Newlands, but as late as March, 1898, he was still convinced that he could take Cleveland from the Newlands camp by suggesting him for governor. Now in June, Wallace had finally decided what just about everyone else knew, that Cleveland was opposed to Stewart and wanted Newlands to run against him. Cleveland had supported Stewart in the election of 1886, but turned against the senator when the latter failed to get him a federal appointment.

The Newlands camp was divided on the issue of whether to challenge Stewart in 1898. George Nixon, perhaps Newlands's most important Nevada ally, continued to caution the congressman about such a race, "With a little missionary work done last fall he could have been downed but to do so now would make a hard dirty fight."[19] Will Sharon, Newlands's political manager in Nevada, took a more neutral stand, reporting to Newlands that A. C. Cleveland was so anxious to have Stewart defeated that he considered running himself, if Newlands didn't. However, Sharon noted, "I am not so sure. You know best whether or not you can afford to tackle Stewart."[20] Others, including H. M. Yerington, were more supportive, the latter even affirming that he would support Newlands in any election endeavor.[21]

Late in June, Newlands wrote Sharon, setting forth his plans for the 1898 election and a possible contest with Stewart. He told Sharon that he thought Stewart's usefulness was at an end, and that "leading men both in the Senate and in the House" concurred. The congressman averred that Stewart had talked himself to death, and that his intolerance and abuse of people who differed with him had intensified enmities and alienated friends. Carefully weighing the question, Newlands continued:

> I recognize the fact that Stewart is weak in Nevada and doubly so because the Silver question will not be the intense question it has been hitherto, but I have never been convinced that there was such a warmth of feeling toward myself as would make me a successful candidate against him in a possible triangular contest which would divide the opposition to him, unless I should resort to the methods which have so disgraced the many Senatorial contests in Nevada and have robbed the office of its honor. At the same time I have not concluded not to be a candidate nor do I think delay in announcement will necessarily strengthen Stewart.

Newlands indicated that he would return to Nevada and "make a trek through the entire state and on my return will be better able to judge of the strength of my candidacy and what is the wisest course to pursue." He warned Sharon that control of the Silver and Democratic conventions was essential, because Stewart's future would be settled there.[22]

Put on the defensive by this possible Newlands challenge, Stewart used his pen and the pages of his newspaper to convince the public that he was still a strong supporter of bimetallism. In the spring of 1898, he wrote and published a small pamphlet on the silver question, "Analysis of the Functions of Money," and summarized its main points in his newspaper. In one of these articles, Stewart enumerated ten principles of money, which included the basic points that he and other silverites had been emphasizing for years: that money was the creation of law; that bondholders secured the demonetization of silver without the knowledge of the people at large; that the coinage of silver was the only practicable way of preventing falling prices; and that money was national, not international.[23]

Stewart's distribution of his pamphlet, using his franking privileges, brought some interesting comment from eastern newspapers. The editor of the *New York Times* observed:

> Mr. William M. Stewart of Nevada, an author of extreme copiousness and a certain kind of originality, is a lucky man. His work called ''An Analysis of the Functions of Money,'' which we had the pleasure of noticing in these columns, has found a second publisher, to wit, the Government of the United States. It appears as Senate Document, No. 336, Fifty-fifth Congress, second session, and was ''ordered to be printed'' July 6 on motion of Mr. Pettigrew. It can now be distributed through the mails under the frank of the author or that of any of his sympathizing friends in the Senate or the House. In this way it will obtain a circulation quite independent of any demand from those who might be willing to pay for it. To Mr. Stewart's reputation as a writer on political economy will now be added a reputation as an economical politician.[24]

A small Massachusetts paper, in commenting on Stewart's use of the frank, was brief, but pointed: ''If you do not care to spend money for Senator Stewart's new book on the functions of money, you can get it free, by sending for the congressional record [sic], in which it is printed on leave. This silver-graybeard has probably cost the government more for printer's ink than any other man in Congress.''[25]

Stewart used the *Silver Knight-Watchman,* sometimes shamelessly, to spotlight his own achievements. In reporting the death of the British statesman, William Gladstone, the newspaper took the occasion to compare Stewart and Gladstone, generally to Stewart's advantage:

> There is only one statesman in public life to-day who may be said to resemble Mr. Gladstone in his hatred of oppression, his eternal industry, his indignant denunciations of wrong and his compassionate nature, and he is the dauntless Senator of the Sierra. . . . Stewart is a gladiator in the arena. He battles for the rights of the people, and is the grand old man of this country.[26]

Stewart returned to Nevada late in July, 1898, after warnings from Nevada friends that Newlands was gaining strength.[27] To discourage

Newlands from opposing him, Stewart began asking senatorial colleagues and other national leaders of the free-silver movement to come to Nevada to support his reelection. Typical was his request to Senator Teller of Colorado, to visit Nevada "now before the contest opens and while there is no other candidate in the field but myself."[28] Stewart also requested letters of support from Senator J. K. Jones of Arkansas, chairman of the Democratic National Committee; from Senator Marion Butler of North Carolina, a prominent Populist leader; and from many others.[29] Locally, Stewart was particularly anxious to gain the endorsement of John Mackay, preferably in written form so that it could be publicized. Although Mackay had liquidated most of his Nevada interests and was deeply involved with his cable company at the time, his name was still magic in Nevada. However, he did not become entangled in the 1898 Nevada senatorial race.[30] Stewart did receive a pledge of support from a former secretary, Isaac Frohman, who informed the senator that he was now attorney for the Miller and Lux interests and would convince those men to aid in his reelection.[31]

The threat of a political battle between Stewart and Newlands placed William F. Herrin, Stewart's former law partner, in a delicate position. Stewart was a former associate, but Newlands, as an interested party in the William Sharon estate, was one of his present employers. Attempting to please both, he suggested a compromise whereby Cleveland would run for governor and Newlands once again for Congress. Herrin wrote Stewart that Newlands favored Cleveland for governor, "I suppose because he thinks that if there is a vacancy in the Senate, Cleveland would appoint him to fill it."[32]

As the state conventions drew near, however, it was apparent that Newlands had decided to contest Stewart by seeking the endorsement of the Silver Party. The Stewart faction within the party, led by C. C. Wallace, was strong enough to force a compromise, and the Newlands camp agreed to back the party ticket to the day of election, but without any obligation beyond that date if Stewart's legislative ticket was defeated. The Silver Party platform called on all Silver Party legislative candidates to work for the reelection of Senator Stewart;[33] but Stewart's victory in gaining this endorsement was neutralized when the Silver Party and the Democratic Party failed to "fuse" as they had in 1896. The Democrats would not agree to the ticket suggested by the Silver Party and the merger failed in 1898.[34] Stewart blamed Newlands and Sharon for preventing fusion of the two parties, and the fact that Newlands received the nomination of both of these parties and ran as a Silver-Democrat, lends credence to the Stewart charge.[35]

Amidst this confusion, the Republican Party met September 15, in Reno. The convention was confronted with numerous difficulties, the most immediate being the lack of suitable candidates.[36] The problem arose because the national Republican administration was pledged to the gold standard, and trying to survive in a state dedicated to the silver issue. The Newlands forces, guided by H. M. Yerington, blocked the convention from nominating any candidate for congressional representative.[37] Thus Newlands was insured reelection to Congress, since the only other candidate, Thomas Wren of the People's Party, was not expected to provide a real challenge.

County conventions held after the state conventions placed the Stewart-Newlands contest on yet another plane.[38] The strategy of the Newlands-Sharon forces in these conventions became clear when they supported a Republican, rather than a Silver Party legislative list, in Storey County. Ultimately, Storey County chose Republican legislators, thus depriving Stewart of support from a normally strong Silver Party region. Stewart supporters claimed that programs similar to that in Storey County were promoted by Sharon and Newlands in other counties in the state.

Whatever may have been going on behind the scenes, there was no apparent animosity between the two factions when the Silver Party opened its campaign at Carson City during the first week in October. Stewart and Newlands spoke from the same platform, and each promised loyalty to the principles of the party.[39] It must be assumed that such a commitment included the party platform statement, that ''We earnestly recommend the reelection of William M. Stewart to the Senate of the United States and pledge the Silver Party of Nevada and the members of this convention to his support for that office.''[40] Certainly Newlands continued to endorse Stewart publicly throughout the campaign. As late as November 2, speaking at Virginia City, Newlands strongly defended Stewart's work in the silver cause, saying that he was ''amazed at the charges of insincerity against Senator Stewart—one of the foremost champions of the silver cause.'' Newlands challenged anyone to point to a single instance when Stewart's ''whole energies were not devoted to the silver cause.''[41]

In spite of this public unity, however, political observers were convinced that the Newlands-Sharon camp secretly worked against Stewart's election. Stewart supporter Charles Norcross wrote to Stewart's secretary, Charles Kappler, that the enemy in 1898 was surely Francis Newlands.[42] Another follower charged that Newlands had encouraged A. C. Cleveland to enter the race against Stewart and that at an opportune moment, Newlands would emerge as the real candidate.[43]

The possibility of a Stewart-Newlands contest forced H. M. Yerington to choose between an old friend and one of his employers, but there was little doubt as to the direction he would take. As general manager of the Virginia and Truckee Railroad and lobbyist for the interests of the Bank of California, he could not afford to oppose Newlands. Yet, there was no easy way for Yerington to turn against Stewart, since he had supported the senator in 1886 and 1892, and had written Stewart a number of congratulatory letters about the excellent work he had done in Congress.[44] Publicly, Yerington justified his position by emphasizing his own devotion to the Republican Party and his support of the gold standard, although these same positions had not prevented him from supporting Stewart as a silverite in 1892. The *Morning Appeal,* one of the few papers in western Nevada that supported Stewart, charged that Yerington was using the Newlands-controlled *Territorial Enterprise* as a "sewer through which all its filth of attack on Senator Stewart is passed."[45] Yerington denied any connection with these articles, insisting that the newspaper had been leased and was at the time a Republican paper, "beyond our control and Stewart very well knows it."[46] It is worth noting, however, that the "Republican paper" attacked only Stewart out of all the Silver Party candidates, and actively supported the candidacy of Newlands, a Silver-Democrat.

The use of Abner C. Cleveland as a "stalking-horse" for Newlands had a distinct advantage, since Cleveland had remained in the Republican Party and Republican papers could thus easily attack Stewart through him. However, Cleveland was a particularly inept candidate. After his October 17 speech in Reno, a Carson City paper gloated, "The Republicans are somewhat rattled over Cleveland's grand fiasco here last night. . . . If he does as well in other towns as he did here, the Silver Party will not need any campaigners. His work will be sufficient to elect the whole silver ticket."[47] The article continued, "We submit that a man who would stand before a cultured audience and read such puerile, silly and disgusting doggerel as Hon. A. C. Cleveland read last night under the guise of poetry written by himself, is a far more fit candidate for the Asylum for Mental Diseases than for the United States Senate."[48] Political rhetoric aside, anyone reading the speech, then or later, would probably agree.

There were few issues in the 1898 senatorial campaign in Nevada. Stewart's opponents repeated charges that he had supported the "Crime of '73" and had made speeches in favor of gold in 1874. Stewart continued to deny the first accusation and insisted that his words were taken out of context in the so-called "gold" speeches. Although there were significant international developments taking place, there was little mention of them in Nevada. The election was fought along local and personal lines. The two sides of the campaign could be followed easily and completely in the pages of two Carson City newspapers. The *Morning Appeal,* edited and published by Sam Davis, supported Stewart, gloried in his past achievements, and castigated his opponents unmercifully. The Republican *Carson News,* on the other hand, criticized nearly every action taken by Stewart in his long political career, accused him of being a gold-standard advocate in disguise, and insisted that he was a tool of the railroads and other industrialists, an enemy of the people. On the day before the election, the *News* listed seven reasons "why good citizens should vote against Stewart." The list included the charge that he had "never cast an honest vote for free and unlimited coinage of silver," that he had "knowingly voted to demonetize silver in 1873," that he had "lied to constituents," that he was a "corrupt tool of the Southern Pacific and Central Pacific Railroads," that he always voted for "corporation interests," that he was not a "bona fide resident of the state," and that he owned "no property in Nevada and was seldom in Nevada."[49]

Both sides claimed victory in the November 8 election. The *Carson News* and the *Territorial Enterprise,* both supposedly Republican papers, but obviously pledged to Newlands, began predicting two days after the election that Stewart's legislative ticket had been beaten. The *News* counted just 16 possible votes for Stewart, 28 against him, and 1 doubtful.[50] The *Enterprise,* on November 27, stated that Stewart had been defeated, claiming that the only way he could win would be if the Southern Pacific bought his return to the Senate. The report ended with what appeared to be an insider's look at coming events, "Be patient, gentlemen. We will be on hand with a candidate when the time comes. It will be someone who will be acceptable to the people of Nevada; someone in whom the people will trust."[51] Since A. C. Cleveland was already an announced Republican candidate, it was not difficult to guess that the mystery candidate would be Newlands.[52]

Newspapers friendly to Stewart predicted an easy victory for the senator. The *Nevada State Journal,* without noting a specific count, thought Stewart would be the winner, while the *Carson Morning Appeal* asserted that Stewart had been elected by a "safe majority" of at least 30 of the 45 Senate votes.[53] An interesting evaluation came from the Winnemucca *Silver State,* normally friendly to Newlands, suggesting that Stewart would be reelected with a total of 30 votes.[54] Apparently George Nixon, owner and editor of the paper, was not then directly involved in any attempt to undermine Stewart.[55]

The only declared opposition candidate, Republican A. C. Cleveland, was reported in a New York newspaper to believe that Stewart could not be reelected. His tabulation showed 14 Republicans, 6 Democrats, and 5 Silver Party men pledged against the senator, despite the fact that all Silver Party candidates had pledged to support Stewart's reelection.[56] A Chicago paper published an embellished report from anti-Stewart forces in Nevada: "An anti-Stewart legislature is believed to have been chosen, and the long-winded silver orator who has imitated Cato of old and tacked on a plea and warning in behalf of silver to any speech on any subject he has ever had to treat in the senate may be relegated to privacy and to other forums than the national senate."[57] A political column in the *Carson News* assumed that Stewart had enough votes, but suggested that legislators pledged to the senator should break their commitments, since there was no moral obligation to back a candidate whose promises were fraudulent.[58]

Edward D. Boyle, Silver Party legislative candidate from Storey County, charged in a letter to Stewart that he had been defeated by irregularities, but would not contest the election because the senator had a safe majority. He wrote, "I hope to live long enough to repay the perfidy of Newlands, Sharon and Co. to the Silver Party. . . the infamy of which they can never shake off."[59] A few days later, the *Morning Appeal* explained the Silver Party's defeat in Storey County by alleging that Republicans there had been aided by Newlands supporters. The paper accused the Storey County Republican legislative ticket of being pledged to a Silver Party candidate other than Stewart.[60]

Some Stewart backers were convinced that the increase in anti-Stewart propaganda following the November election heralded a Newlands announcement against Stewart. To block such a move, the *Morning Appeal* reminded its readers that Newlands was nominated for Congress only after vowing to support Senator Stewart, and that the contract of the Silver Party to vote for Stewart "was submitted to Mr. Newlands before it was presented to the Convention and received his approval. . . . Nobody believes that Mr. Newlands would publicly break a pledge so publicly made."[61]

Stewart's out-of-state supporters also worried about the election results, and at least one made a direct offer of assistance to the senator. A few days after the election, William H. Mills, head of the Land Department of the Central Pacific Railroad, wrote Stewart, "If in the situation of things there is a place where I may be of service to you at any time, do not fail to apprize me of it. I am more than willing to perform any service I may be able to render in your interest."[62]

The continuing rumors of a Newlands candidacy for the Senate gained credibility when William E. Sharon announced from Virginia City, on November 28, that the congressman would contest Stewart for the nomination. Sharon emphasized that Stewart had no more than 18 votes in the state legislature, far short of the necessary majority.[63] This announcement preceded a December 3 public statement by Newlands, that he would seek election to the U.S. Senate when the Nevada legislature met in January, 1899. This notice was given in Winnemucca and carried in detail in the *Silver State* of that town.

Newlands repeated substantially what supporters had been saying since the November election, particularly that "the Stewart forces were beaten and Stewart has lost the Legislature." The congressman addressed the question of whether he could honorably be a candidate under the circumstances: "My opinion is that I can and I have concluded to announce myself as a candidate." He then explained the circumstances which gave him the right to declare himself a nominee: "About the time I announced myself as a candidate for Congress, W. E. Sharon told Stewart's manager, Wallace, that Stewart was to have the field free from any opposition on my part, but that if Stewart failed to carry his legislative ticket the field would be open and that I would be at liberty to pursue such course as my judgment approved." Newlands accused Stewart and Wallace of conspiring to defeat him for Congress in 1898, by supporting Thomas Wren for the post, and concluded, "I have stood four times the test of a popular vote and I have no doubt I can stand the test of a legislative [one]."[64]

Stewart's adherents should not have been surprised by the Newlands announcement, since the path to that statement had been plain from a few days after the November 8 election. Nevertheless, they were bitter and angry; as one supporter pointed out, it now forced Stewart to win the election twice.[65] Another wrote to Stewart, "the very dogs" have turned on Newlands, whose former friends in Washoe "can find no terms strong enough for his condemnation." Yet, he warned the senator, the Newlands group was prepared to buy the necessary votes and would pay three dollars to each one spent by Stewart.[66]

The Newlands candidacy gained strength when George Nixon announced that the *Silver State* would change its endorsement from Stewart to Newlands, since the paper now had a choice, which it didn't have before. Nixon, who had given Stewart strong support throughout the election campaign, took a moderate position as his paper switched sides, "Both Stewart and Newlands have national reputations as silver men, both are statesmen of the first rank, and in case Mr. Newlands should defeat Senator Stewart Nevada will lose no prestige in the United States Senate by the change."[67]

"Black" Wallace, Stewart's manager, wasted no time after the Newlands announcement in recriminations. He knew the remedy and suggested that Stewart ask Senator Jones of Arkansas, chairman of the Democratic National Committee, to write to prominent Nevada Democrats and solicit their support for Stewart. He also implored Stewart to "dig up $40,000 if you can get it."[68] Two days later he wrote a long letter with additional advice:

> The election is over and it is votes that we want and not newspapers. I leave tonight for Nevada and expect to go over the whole field and investigate. I have waited so as to let the Enemy go over the field first and then follow at their heels—if we can't win the fight we must not let Newlands win it. It will be simply a monied fight; if there was no money in the fight you would win by a two thirds vote—but with money in the fight it simply makes mercenaries of nearly all of them [legislators].[69]

Stewart was furious about the Newlands announcement, and his anger showed in one of many letters to supporters: "The efforts of the friends of Mr. Newlands to destroy me have been most outrageous. My life has been an open book. . . . If he can be elected to the U.S. Senate in violation of his solemn pledge to support me . . . the people of Nevada are different than what they were before."[70] In another letter he wrote:

> Mr. Newlands is giving out interviews declaring that I am defeated, and that he will be elected. If his treachery does not disgust the people of Nevada I shall be very much disappointed. . . . Is it possible that Mr. Newlands when he pledged himself to support me, declaring to the Silver Convention that it would be a national calamity to defeat me, intended to harass me with blackmailing suits?[71]

Blackmailing suits referred to an action initiated against Stewart by William Webster, owner of the *Nevada State Journal,* for the collection of $522.80, which Stewart allegedly owed the newspaper. Whether by intention or not, news of the suit coincided with the Newlands announcement that he would oppose Stewart for the U.S. Senate. The issue lost some of its effectiveness through the efforts of Stewart's friend, Sardis Summerfield, the United States Attorney for Nevada, who determined "that inasmuch as the Webster suit was brought for 'campaign purposes' it will be good policy to delay it as long as possible."[72]

Stewart also insisted that he had been "tricked" into keeping C. C. Wallace neutral in the Republican convention, when H. M. Yerington told him that Newlands was his friend and was working for his reelection.[73] That the Newlands forces had deceived him to gain his help in the congressional battle, while secretly working against his election to the Senate, infuriated Stewart. He was angered, too, by the accusation that he and Wallace had conspired to defeat the congressman's bid for reelection, although there was some evidence to support the Newlands complaint.[74]

Charges and countercharges continued throughout December, with the Sharon-Newlands coterie emphasizing their belief that the Stewart legislative ticket had been beaten and the door opened for a Newlands candidacy. The Stewart forces insisted otherwise and continued to denounce the Newlands camp for publicly supporting the senator during the campaign while privately trying to defeat his legislative slate. Following the Newlands announcement on December 3, many Nevadans' sympathies turned to Stewart, as they remembered, or were reminded, that the senator had helped Newlands get his start in Nevada politics. Clever emphasis of this fact made the action of the congressman appear selfish and ungrateful.

Whatever public favor Stewart enjoyed directly after the Newlands declaration was quickly dissipated during the month preceding the convening of the state legislature. Provoking this reaction against Stewart was a "gang of professional gun and knife fighters," who gathered in the Stewart headquarters to combat, by pressure and scare tactics, the abundant Newlands money. Prominent in the Stewart faction, besides "Black" Wallace, was "Colonel" Jack Chinn. He was said by the Stewart followers to be an official observer from the Democratic National Committee, but that was denied by Senator Jones of Arkansas, the chairman of that committee. It was asserted also that Chinn had been employed as one of two bodyguards for Stewart because his friends had become "so fearful of his life."[75] More to the point, Chinn was an employee of the Central Pacific, and was prepared to "give the fractious legislator anything he wants from an argument to a fist or gun fight."[76] Stewart's other bodyguard was David Neagle, a left-handed "gun for hire," whose path had crossed Stewart's many times in the past, on the Comstock, in the Panamints, and during the Sharon-Hill divorce case in the 1880's. It was in the aftermath of the latter case that Neagle won his greatest fame, as the killer of Judge David Terry.[77]

The other members of the Stewart group, Stephen A. Gage and Will Virgin, were not so controversial. Gage, a close friend of Stewart, was a former Nevada lobbyist for the Central Pacific Railroad, now an official for that line. Will Virgin was a member of a Carson Valley family and reputedly Gage's protégé. It was quite clear from the composition of the group, however, that the Central Pacific Railroad had replaced its earlier behind-the-scenes activities with a naked show of force. The people now surrounding Stewart as advisers shouted out the influence of that railroad on the Stewart campaign. Using men like Neagle and Chinn in a state election, to pressure party delegates and legislators, not only seemed to be blatant interference, but also signaled that the Stewart forces were prepared to do anything to win. Neagle's reputation was so unsavory that one editor suggested that a "Citizen's Vigilance Committee" be organized to tar and feather him and ship him out of town.[78]

In December's closing days, the Stewart organizers stimulated a newspaper campaign against Newlands after persuading the owner of the Carson City *Morning Appeal* to employ Stewart's private secretary, Charles Kappler, for editorial and writing chores. Kappler's work centered on the daily publication of a "Supplement," which featured a number of interesting cartoons portraying Newlands in the worst possible light. Some pointed to him as a hypochondriac and an absentee congressman. Others lampooned his voting record and his "turnabout" in regard to Stewart. In addition to the cartoons, daily articles in the supplement emphasized Newlands's activities or inactivity as a member of Congress. He was variously labeled as physically and mentally weak, as a vain and ambitious man who vacillated on important matters, and as unwilling or unable to make a courageous fight for anything. The most consistent word of condemnation against him was "traitor."

In spite of the *Morning Appeal* campaign against Newlands, the newspaper contest was not one-sided. The other important papers of western Nevada and a number of smaller newspapers throughout the state favored the Newlands candidacy. The most outspoken of these was the *Carson News,* and its most consistent emphasis was Stewart's obvious ties to the Central Pacific Railroad and the "hired gunmen." In the anti-Stewart papers, the senator was portrayed as a loud-mouthed, wretched old man, who had to employ gun and knife fighters to intimidate legislators. He was consistently pictured as having lost the November election and now trying to change that defeat into victory by the use of pressure tactics.[79]

Although the newspaper battle was interesting, if repetitious, the real contest was conducted elsewhere. On December 28, just four weeks before the vote in the state legislature, Stewart arrived in Carson City and established himself at the Ormsby House, in rooms made famous as senatorial headquarters from the time Nevada was admitted as a state.[80] The challenger, Newlands, arrived two days later and set up a campaign

center in the nearby Arlington Hotel.[81] The two sides gathered early in
order to marshal their respective forces for the January meetings of the
Silver Party's central committee and legislative caucus. Those two meetings would probably determine the person to be chosen for the United
States Senate.

On January 12, 1899, when the Silver Party Central Committee convened in Carson City, it was apparent that "Black" Wallace had done
his homework better than his opponents. While others had been waging
a newspaper campaign, Wallace had traveled the state gathering proxies
from Silver Party committee members who would not be at the Carson
City meeting. Obviously in control when the assembly began, the Stewart group struck first at Will Sharon, chairman of the Silver Party Central Committee, because his support of Newlands violated the pledge in
the party platform to support Stewart for reelection. When a resolution
to force his immediate resignation as chairman ran into unexpected
opposition, Wallace postponed action for a week, rather than risk a
showdown. The resolution was tabled, as was a similar one condemning
Newlands for breaking the platform promise.[82] However, one of Stewart's friends on the committee wrote optimistically to the senator on the
day following the meeting, "It was very annoying to me the way things
went at the meeting; but what could be done after Sadler, Kelley and
Jones begged for a continuance; however, next week will probably go
different."[83]

In fact, before the next meeting of the central committee, the Stewart
forces showed their legislative strength by controlling the Silver Party
caucus, which met on January 15. Dominance of the legislature was
practically insured after that preliminary show of voting muscle.[84]
Referring to Stewart's activities in the caucus, a Reno newspaper reported, "He has lieutenants worthy of the 'cause' in the shape of sundry
thugs and gun fighters, but his trump card is Jack Chinn of Kentucky who
he keeps shut up in a room directing matters from behind the scenes."[85]

With the cards stacked against them in the central committee, the
Newlands people decided to take their case to the voters two days before
the scheduled second meeting. In a speech in Carson City, which lasted
over two hours and was, according to one listener, "the best effort of his
life," Newlands attempted to refute charges made against him in the
committee.[86] He emphasized that the Wallace-Stewart combination had
packed the central committee against him. He denounced Stewart's
relationship with the Central and Southern Pacific railroads in the
strongest terms and accused the corporations of directing Nevada and
California politics for corrupt purposes. He asked his listeners for help

in ridding Nevada of this control and restoring "integrity to the law-making and elective process."[87]

No amount of oratory could stop the Wallace steam roller, though, and when the Silver Party Central Committee held its second meeting on January 19, the hopelessness of the Newlands position was evident. A resolution condemning Stewart and commending Newlands, introduced by H. A. Comins of White Pine County, lost by a vote of 31 to 13. A second motion by the Newlands faction, attempting to declare the meeting of the central committee illegal, lost by the same vote. A show of power from the Stewart-Wallace combination followed, when a resolution denouncing Newlands passed by a vote of 29 to 15. A similar statement criticizing Will Sharon won by a vote of 26 to 14. The *Morning Appeal,* in reporting the committee's action, stated that Newlands was "ousted from the Silver Party," and "his political career ended."[88] Before being expelled from the party, Sharon made a spirited defense of his actions, again insisting that Stewart and Wallace had acted illegally and that they had betrayed the Silver Party by bringing in railroad support. He stated that Stewart's "only warm supporter" was Wallace and the latter was the slave of the "arch gold-bug of them all [Collis P. Huntington]."[89]

The most fascinating part of the drama, however, was yet to be played. A few days before the scheduled legislative vote to choose a U.S. Senator, a San Francisco newspaper reported that four members of the Nevada legislature, accompanied by Southern Pacific agent Harry Flannery, had arrived in San Francisco and were staying at the Golden West Hotel. One of the legislators, George W. Leidy, an independent from Esmeralda County, was accused in the article of accepting a fifty-dollar bribe from Wallace. In reprinting the San Francisco story, the *Morning Appeal* tried to neutralize the original accusation by adding a quote from Leidy, who denied that he had accepted a bribe and maintained that being on the same train with Flannery was a "coincidence."[90] The Leidy incident was the beginning of the final act in the Newlands-Stewart contest.

On January 23, 1899, just one day before the scheduled vote for U.S. Senator, a test ballot on another matter revealed that the Nevada State Assembly stood "equal Stewart and anti-Stewart—15 to 15."[91] The following day, Stewart was nominated in the state senate, along with Abner C. Cleveland of White Pine County, Warren Williams of Churchill County, and Patrick L. Flanigan of Washoe County. Stewart received 9 votes, to 6 for his opponents (3 for Cleveland, 2 for Williams, and 1 for Flanigan).[92] The meeting in the assembly the same afternoon presented an entirely different situation, for the test vote indicated the possibility of a tie. When the roll was taken, Assemblyman Willard Gillespie of Storey County was not in his seat. He had been seen in the legislative corridors in the morning and presumably was present when the morning session began, since he was not listed as absent. Gillespie's failure to answer the roll call for the afternoon session brought a search by the sergeant-at-arms, but without results. Since Gillespie was considered a Newlands supporter, his absence was charged to the Stewart camp. Attempts by the Newlands forces to delay the vote failed, and nominations proceeded. Stewart, Cleveland, and Williams were again nominated, as well as William Woodburn of Washoe County and N. H. A. Mason of Lyon County.

When the vote was tallied, Stewart had won, with 15 votes to 14 for his opponents. Newlands was never nominated, since the hoped-for tie never occurred. Also, his supporters could still maintain, technically at least, that he had not been beaten by Stewart. Stewart's formal election by joint session of the two houses followed immediately, and the senator began another six-year term.[93] The Stewarts held a public celebration on January 28, at their home in Carson City, thus closing the campaign. The race may have ended with this reception, but the bitterness it engendered lingered on.

Reaction to Stewart's election from the Newlands-controlled press was, understandably, harsh. An editorial in the *Nevada State Journal* summarized the response: "The worst has happened and Nevada's degradation is complete. William M. Stewart has been reelected to misrepresent Nevada in the United States Senate for the next six years. The verdict of the people has been reversed and corporation gold has changed a popular vote of less than one-fourth to a legislative majority of two votes."[94] More important than the newspaper opposition, however, was the demand for an official investigation of the conduct of two assemblymen, George Leidy of Esmeralda County and Willard Gillespie of Storey County.

The *Nevada State Journal* suspected that other legislators were involved in illegal activities. The paper reported that Assemblyman A. J. McGowan of Ormsby County, who had stated publicly that he would "never under any circumstances vote for W. M. Stewart," just three days later nominated the senator, and then voted for him. The *Journal* writer concluded, "There is but little room; or rather none at all, for speculation as to the motive power which brought about this sudden change." It was reported that McGowan would leave for Montana after the legislative session, and the *Journal* added a parting wish, that "the devil speed his departure from the State which he has disgraced."[95]

Official action by the assembly, however, was taken only against Leidy and Gillespie. On January 23, 1899, one day before the vote for senator, E. W. Tremont of Eureka asked that the January 20 statement from the *Carson News,* which accused Leidy of accepting a bribe from Wallace to vote for Stewart, be read into the assembly *Journal.* A committee to investigate the charge was appointed, with Tremont as chairman. The next day, January 24, four of the five committee members voted for Stewart.[96] On January 26, 1899, the Tremont committee exonerated Leidy.[97]

The Gillespie investigation was initiated on January 25, when M. C. McMillan of Storey County introduced a resolution to appoint a committee to investigate the assemblyman's absence. Besides McMillan, who was appointed chairman, the committee consisted of R. T. Wilkerson of Douglas County, a supporter of N. H. A. Mason; W. J. Dooley of Lincoln County, a supporter of Cleveland; and H. H. Coryell of Elko and I. A. Strosnider of Lyon County, both of whom supported Stewart. Coryell later moved that four additional members be added to the investigating committee, but they were never appointed, and the committee never submitted a report.[98]

Gillespie returned to the assembly on January 26, answering the roll call for the afternoon session. Almost at once, I. A. Strosnider, a member of the Gillespie investigating committee and a strong Stewart supporter, moved that further proceedings in connection with the inquiry be discontinued and the committee discharged. The motion carried by 17 to 12. The *Nevada State Journal* reported, ''Through all of the proceedings the accused man sat apparently unconcerned as to the action. He offered no excuse for his absence and in fact took no part in the proceedings.''[99] The *Carson News* added that, after dismissal of the committee, ''Assemblyman Gedney remarked that a ten-gallon bottle of cologne should be broken at the Speaker's desk to remove the stench of the day's proceedings.''[100]

At least one of the anti-Stewart men was still not satisfied. The day after the Gillespie committee was discharged, Assemblyman Frank Paul, who had submitted a minority report as a member of the Leidy investigating committee, offered the following resolution:

> Whereas, We have all been shocked and grieved at the absence of Mr. Gillespie without leave at a very important time and under very suspicious circumstances; therefore be it

> RESOLVED, that before said Mr. Gillespie be allowed to further partici-

pate in the deliberations and proceedings of this body that he be requested and required to furnish a satisfactory explanation of his absence.[101]

Stewart supporters controlled the assembly, however, and the Paul resolution was tabled.[102] Thus Gillespie was allowed to take his seat without an explanation and without any official investigation.

He did offer a statement to the pro-Stewart newspaper, the *Morning Appeal:* "I was not elected to support Mr. Stewart, and therefore, I did not feel justified in voting to carry out Newlands' program or to vote for Senator Stewart; and if I had been present I should have declined to vote. I went home as I had a right to do." He denied the charge that he had received $5,000 to stay away from the assembly.[103] The editor of the *Appeal* agreed that Gillespie had a right to absent himself, and pronounced the investigation of Leidy and Gillespie, "one of the silliest farces ever enacted in a legislative body. . . . Never in the history of that honorable body was a member investigated for absenting himself at will."[104]

Other western Nevada newsmen were not so friendly. Alf Doten, editor of the *Gold Hill Daily News,* recorded in his diary that both Gillespie and Leidy had been bought by Stewart, yet both had been exonerated by the assembly. Doten declared the proceedings to be "wicked as usual."[105] The editor of the *Territorial Enterprise* voiced similar sentiments when he suggested, "The very school children here should be taught to avoid the man Gillespie, who sold us into six more years of bondage." He noted, also, that Leidy's picture in a San Francisco daily, which had been labeled "sell-out Assemblyman from Nevada," should be placed in the "rogue's gallery with honor, and be excellent for future reference."[106]

Sam P. Davis, who was editor of the *Morning Appeal* at the time, later indicated that Gillespie had been offered a ride to the legislative building, but was taken instead to the home of State Senator Williams at Empire, where he remained for two days. Davis reported that Gillespie "was willingly abducted and got $1,800 for his absences from his seat."[107] According to Gillespie's 1907 obituary in a Tonopah newspaper, the incident was engineered the night before the legislative election, when Colonel Chinn proposed that some member of the Newlands forces be kept from the senatorial vote. Gillespie's absence followed and Stewart gained the needed majority.[108]

The chicanery and corruption of the 1898 election campaign in Nevada climaxed in the circumstances surrounding Gillespie's disappearance. There is little doubt that the Stewart-Wallace forces were responsible for his absence during the vital assembly vote for senator. Yet, in spite of the evidence to the contrary, Stewart later stated, "With all his [Newlands's] money he failed to receive one vote in the Legislature. This speaks very highly for the honesty of Nevada Legislatures."[109]

The 1898 campaign was certainly the most corrupt senatorial election in Nevada's history to date. The November results appeared to favor Stewart, but the earlier agreement allowed each side to interpret the election for its own ends. Thus, when Newlands declared for the Senate on December 3, the announcement initiated an entirely new contest between himself and Stewart. In the events which followed, the Stewart-Wallace camp outmaneuvered and out-corrupted the Newlands forces. Since it was essential to the Stewart-Wallace combine that votes once "bought" should stay that way, it was necessary that men like Dave Neagle and Colonel Chinn remain in Carson City until after the legislative selection, in order to maintain pressure on anyone contemplating switching sides. Perhaps the best summary of the campaign came in a few short words in a letter to Stewart from a friend: "Wallace still rules."[110]

Nevada's difficulty with the election procedure for United States senators seemed to be symptomatic of a larger problem. At least nine other states, California, Delaware, Montana, North Dakota, Utah, Pennsylvania, Washington, Wisconsin and West Virginia, had deadlocks in their legislatures in 1899. The lawmakers in four of these states, California, Delaware, Pennsylvania and Utah, adjourned without making a senatorial selection.[111]

When Stewart returned to the Senate following his reelection, campaign issues receded as he found the Senate engaged in a long and bitter argument concerning the disposition of the Philippine Islands. Although the question was far removed from the Nevada political arena, he entered the debate on U.S. imperialism as though he represented one of the more powerful states.

The controversy over the Philippines had been stimulated by McKinley's action in forcing the Spanish government to cede the islands, along with Puerto Rico and Guam, as part of the peace terms ultimately drawn in the Treaty of Paris, December 10, 1898. The treaty ran into immediate opposition; and the outbreak of hostilities between U.S. troops and those of Philippine insurgent Aguinaldo, on February 4, 1899, further complicated the Senate debate. Stewart almost immediately aligned himself with the imperialists, a comfortable position since it united him once again with industrial and commercial interests and with the Republican Party. Democrats and Populists were generally opposed to the treaty, and Stewart's support of expansion was one of the first clear indications that he would rejoin the Republican Party, which he had left in 1892.

The Treaty of Paris was accepted in the U.S. Senate on February 6, 1899, by a vote of 57 to 27, just over the necessary two-thirds majority. Debate then began on the ultimate disposition of the islands by the United States, with Stewart arguing that "the Senate should have a wide-ranging discussion of expansion" before dealing specifically with the Philippines. He saw certain commercial advantages in retaining the Philippines, because the U.S. could furnish them with manufactured goods, since "manufacturing is always done in the temperate zone, always has been, and always will be; and it will not be done elsewhere." Stewart's prejudices showed even more strongly when he discussed government for the islands. He saw no reason why the Philippines should not remain perpetual territories, noting that "republican principles can not be expressed in any language but the English language; and we know that freedom is expressed in the English language and in no other language." He also foresaw no labor problem resulting from annexation, since "people have never immigrated from a tropical to a temperate zone."[112]

A few days later Stewart took the floor to speak out against a resolution which would guarantee ultimate independence to the Philippines. Again he noted that there was no need for immediate action and that the U.S. should retain the islands until proper discussion could be held. He insisted that a decision about their disposal should await the end of hostilities between the U.S. and the insurrectionists, so that the American people could have time to reflect and make their wishes known. He argued that ratification of the Treaty of Paris did not automatically incorporate the inhabitants of the Philippines in the United States, nor permanently annex them. He suggested that America should prepare the islands for local government and dispose of them later, so as to best promote the interests of both the United States and the Filipinos. Naturally, Stewart voted against the guarantee of ultimate independence to the Philippine Islands.[113]

In addition to his many speeches on expansion, Stewart was called on by divergent segments of his Nevada constituency to carry out a variety of tasks. One such request came from Captain J. R. DeLamar, owner of the main mines in the then prosperous gold-mining camp of Delamar, in southern Nevada. DeLamar wanted Stewart to have William Herrin, of the Southern Pacific Railroad's legal division, wire "Black" Wallace to use his influence to defeat two bills in the Nevada legislature. The first called for an eight-hour workday, and the other for a bullion tax. Evidently Stewart carried out DeLamar's wishes, for the captain wrote Stewart the following month thanking him for helping to defeat both bills.[114]

Stewart was also called upon to present a petition from the Nevada legislature for election of United States senators by direct vote of the people.[115] An obvious result of the hard-fought 1898 Nevada senatorial campaign, the resolution was the work of the Newlands faction in the legislature, and was introduced by Henry A. Comins of White Pine County.[116] Two weeks after he presented the petition, Stewart made a speech opposing the direct election of U.S. senators. He continued to oppose the idea in Congress, characterizing it in 1902 as "a fatal movement to the equality of the States." Stewart argued that direct election would not eliminate scandal, but would end any justification for small states having equal representation in the Senate,[117] boldly maintaining that "I do not believe that there is any general corruption in the election of United States Senators." A short time later, in a letter to the editor of the *Carson News,* Stewart emphasized the point made in his Senate speech, that if direct election prevailed, there would be a move to base representation in the U.S. Senate on population, and Nevada would lose.[118]

In the waning days of the session, the senator also spoke out against an earlier congressional act, the Civil Service Law, pleading, in effect, for the return of patronage:

> I am opposed to the civil-service law. I believe it has done more harm than good, and will continue to injure the Government, injure the service, so long as it remains on the statute books, building up an aristocracy of incompetents in the Departments, furnishing a cloak for keeping them in and furnishing machinery whereby suspicion is thrown upon the Departments all the while.

Stewart argued that members of Congress, not the executive, were the best judges of the qualifications of officers in their own districts.[119] Stewart found little support for this viewpoint in either Congress or Nevada.

Stewart's personal affairs during his fourth Senate term were as varied as his political ones. His main investments during these years centered in three areas: his real estate holdings in Washington, D.C., including the "Castle" and Ashburn farms; the properties he held in his wife's name, most of which had come from C. P. Huntington and Leland

Stanford, and were located in Alameda County, California, and Duluth and St. Paul, Minnesota; and his Mexican mining interests. Stewart's involvement in these and other investments brought no material gains. On the contrary, his proclivity for unwise investments kept pushing him further into debt.

In the early 1890's, Stewart had looked upon the mining venture in Mexico as the key to his financial future; but the continuing decline in the price of silver and McKinley's victory in the 1896 election turned the prospect at San Miguel del Mesquital into another broken dream. The annual report for 1899 showed a debt of some $70,000, and efforts in late 1899, to sell the claims to the Guggenheims for $300,000, failed.[120] After 1899, the mine and equipment simply deteriorated. Despite the senator's early optimism, there is no evidence that Stewart and the other investors received any returns from the Mexican venture.

Adding to Stewart's financial difficulties was his inability to dispose of the "Castle," which, with its 19,000 square feet of space, was simply too expensive to maintain. The building had been rented to the Chinese Embassy until 1894, when the Stewarts moved back in. Stewart placed the house on the market in 1897, when he tried to convince Captain J. R. DeLamar to buy it for $200,000, as a "special favor."[121] That prospective sale and all others through the year 1898 were unsuccessful, including an attempt to market the land for an apartment house, in order to avoid a forced sale at auction.[122] Before foreclosure occurred, Stewart was able to get his note extended until the property was finally sold, in August, 1899, to Montana millionaire W. A. Clark, for $144,000.[123]

Early in March, 1893, Stewart wrote, "I have more property than money and unable to entertain any new propositions for investment until something that I have can be converted into money."[124] Yet, late in 1895, before he was able to sell the "Castle," he purchased some farmland, about twenty-five miles west of Washington, in Loudoun County, Virginia. At first Stewart used the place, which became known as Ashburn Farm, for raising thoroughbred horses. A "Catalogue of Trotting Stock owned by Hon. Wm. M. Stewart of Nevada Stock Farm at Ashburn, Loudoun County, Virginia, 1896," shows a stable of twenty-three animals in addition to the most famous of the group, "Bion," which had been bred for Stewart from the stables of Leland Stanford.[125] According to Stewart's secretary, Charles Kappler, Ashburn Farm was not only beautiful, but also a release for Stewart, since "it is always necessary for the Senator to have something on hand which eats up a great deal of money."[126] The Ashburn property certainly satisfied that need, particularly after Stewart sold the debt-ridden *Silver Knight-Watchman*.

His losses in Mexican mining and in the newspaper field did not stop Stewart from becoming involved in a number of other schemes that also proved financially disastrous. One of the most interesting of these was an attempt to provide an electric railway system for the Chevy Chase area, a scheme which, in 1895, brought Stewart into contact with George Westinghouse and the Electro-Magnetic Traction Company.[127] Stewart's association with Westinghouse and the company proved to be brief and, as was so often the case in these years, unrewarding financially. About the same time Stewart invested in a sulphur mine in South Carolina, a Tahoe Medical Company, and the Maryland Standard Telephone Company. It is quite clear from the Stewart correspondence that the senator entered into these schemes without proper checking. In the case of the telephone company he wrote one of the officers requesting that his arrangements to buy stock be cancelled, since he doubted that such a company existed.[128]

From a financial standpoint, the last five years of the nineteenth century were particularly trying for Stewart. By 1899, it was clear that the senator's almost compulsive drive to invest in real estate, newspapers, farms, mines, and various other schemes, coupled with his family's elaborate standard of living, had combined to burden him with ever-increasing debts to individuals and banks alike.[129] In order to pay his obligations, Stewart borrowed from many sources. He owed substantial sums to many old friends, among them John Mackay, William Herrin, W. J. Robinson, and Sam Wright.[130] He was constantly reminded of his debts to banks and trust companies by their requests for immediate payment.[131] Stewart's notable lack of success as an investor seemed to confirm an earlier statement that he could not serve the public and Mammon at the same time, for he tended to neglect the latter.

Stewart's secretary, Charles Kappler, was one of the few people who really appreciated Stewart's financial obligations and difficulties. In a letter to his predecessor, Isaac Frohman, he wrote that he hoped the senator would come again into considerable money, for "if any man ever deserved an easy time in his old age it is the Senator. You know what trials he has undergone and no doubt agree with me that no other man, or at least few men indeed, would have outlived them."[132] Unfortunately, circumstances never brought Stewart any large sum of money, although he continued for the rest of his life to seek the proverbial pot of gold.

CHAPTER 12

THE END OF A NEVADA POLITICAL ERA

STEWART began his duties in the short session of Congress which started in December, 1899, amidst claims by opponents that he had returned to the Republican Party. Although he did not do so officially until nearly a year later, it is quite clear that he was tending in that direction. A Nevada newspaper charged that Stewart had joined the Republican caucus at the beginning of the congressional session, and had received choice committee assignments from the Republicans as a reward.[1] A letter to Stewart from Portland, Oregon, made the same observation, and noted that the Nevada senator had "returned to the fold."[2] The printed list of Republican assignments verified Stewart's realignment with that party.

Changing party affiliation had little immediate effect on Stewart's legislative priorities, however. That became abundantly clear when a House measure, to give official recognition to the U.S. gold standard, reached the Senate. Stewart's first speech against the bill came on January 11, 1900, when he insisted that the country should retain both gold and silver as monetary standards, since the supply of gold would give out if there was not an alternative. In February, Stewart spoke a number of times against the proposal, but his task was hopeless. The bill passed the Senate on February 15, by a vote of 46 to 29, with both Jones and Stewart in opposition. It became law on March 14, 1900.[3] By then, passage of the gold-standard act was anticlimactic, since the basic question had been settled with McKinley's election in 1896. Besides, the nation's interests had shifted by this time from the domestic issues of tariff and silver to the pressing colonial problems which developed from the war with Spain. The President's message in December, 1899, set the course for debate on the question of annexing the newly conquered areas, and Stewart once again jumped on the expansion bandwagon.

In his first major speech on the subject, on February 16, 1900, he invoked the customary justification, "No amount of fault-finding, protesting, or remonstrating will prevent the fulfillment of the manifest destiny of the United States." Stewart then reviewed the history of territorial expansion by the United States, insisting that what it planned to do in the Philippines was not imperialistic, since America would be assisting the people of the islands to establish local self-government. "Thus it will be seen," he affirmed, "that the American people carry with them their institutions wherever they go. The same will be true of the Philippines. . . . The country has a right to know that no imperialism or militarism is intended, that the people of the islands will be treated in the same manner that the people of Louisiana, Florida, and California were treated." That Stewart saw imperialism in economic terms became clear when he added, "The islands we have secured are essential to our financial independence."[4]

Stewart and other senators made some interesting comparisons between the rights of American Indians and those of Filipinos. Stewart stated that the American Indians were "equally entitled to consideration with the savages in . . . the Philippines. It never occurred to Mr. Jefferson that it was necessary for him to consult [the Indians]." He maintained that every acquisition of territory contained aborigines "that will require military force to keep in subjection."[5] His statement was quite revealing, since Stewart was chairman of the Committee on Indian Affairs at the time. Among his western colleagues, only Teller of Colorado failed to give strong support to imperialism.[6]

Three days after his speech on the Philippines, in a discussion about government for Hawaii, Stewart disagreed with those who would limit freedom and rights there. He argued that there was an unwritten constitution for the territories, which had grown up by custom, and that America "must give the Territories all the rights and privileges that we enjoy; that they must have republican government; that they must be governed according to the laws of the most enlightened, being republican, as we are. That we have to do unless we violate every principle that governs us at all anywhere."[7]

A month later he made another lengthy speech in favor of keeping Puerto Rico, Cuba, and the Philippines. He reiterated the ideas he had stated previously and noted that there was no constitutional objection to adding non-contiguous territory, because American territorial rule was adapted to such island holdings.[8] In June, Stewart again insisted that United States policy in the Philippines was not imperialism, but simply an attempt to bring the islands under American control so that local self-government, "capable of protecting life and property" could be established. He took occasion during the speech to strike out strongly against those senators who looked upon the Philippine revolutionary Aguinaldo as another George Washington. Rather, said Stewart, he should be compared to "Tecumseh, Sitting Bull, Old Cochise, or some other celebrated Indian warrior." Again he placed acquisition of the Philippines in the same category of expansion as the settling of the American west, noting that no one doubted the "validity or propriety" of taking over that territory. He affirmed that Americans of that era generally accepted dominion over Indians in the west, even though "irregular warfare was carried on there by Indian tribes."[9] Stewart's interest in the Philippines may have been stimulated by the fact that his daughter, Mary Isabelle (Maybelle), and her husband, Lt. Col. Francis L. Payson, were stationed there at this time.

In addition to Stewart's strong support of U.S. expansion during this period, he also turned his attention, in the spring of 1900, to two projects closer to his normal causes. One concerned a national park at Lake Tahoe, the other dealt with mining interests in Alaska. The park issue came to Stewart's attention as the result of a petition circulated at Carson City in the fall of 1899, which proposed to set aside Lake Tahoe as a public reservation in order to preserve its beauty for future generations. Stewart was informed of the issue by Sam Davis, state controller of Nevada. Davis wrote the senator on November 26, 1899, that he and other state officers had signed the petition, but afterwards found out that it was an attempt on the part of the Virginia and Truckee Railroad to obtain "good timbered lands in lieu of those despoiled lands they are giving up so generously to the public." He asked Stewart to "nip it in the bud."[10] Before taking any action, Stewart contacted William Mills, the Central Pacific's land agent in California, for information concerning ownership of land in the Tahoe basin. Then, early in January, 1900, Stewart introduced a bill "to set apart certain lands in the States of California and Nevada as a public park and forest reservation to be known as Lake Tahoe National Park, and for other purposes."[11] The proposal included all of the Tahoe basin and extensive forestlands on the western slope of the Sierra, the latter suggested by Mills. The bill also provided that surplus waters from Tahoe were to be used for irrigation.[12]

Enthusiastic support for the bill gave way to strong opposition when it became clear that special interests were involved in the movement to make Lake Tahoe a national park. Apparently these groups wanted to exchange privately owned lands, which would become part of the new park, for land transferred from the public domain. The prospect of allowing a gift of thousands of acres of choice public lands to large property owners such as the Carson and Tahoe Lumber and Fluming Company or the Sierra Lumber Company, who had already "denuded Tahoe's forests," was sufficiently appalling to block passage of the Tahoe National Park Bill.[13]

When Stewart recognized the opposition to establishing a national park at Lake Tahoe, he asked that the bill be held in abeyance, but suggested that the Interior Department immediately proclaim the enlarged forest reservation included among the bill's provisions. In order to allay suspicions of the program of in-lieu land selection, Stewart outlined plans to insure that no one benefited at public expense. Unfortunately, his past association with the Central Pacific, and his close contacts during this period with Duane L. Bliss, general manager of the Carson and Tahoe Lumber and Fluming Company, made it difficult to convince others that such land exchanges could be made fairly.[14] Despite his failure to achieve the desired results, Stewart continued to press for enlarged forest reserves in the Tahoe basin. Extension of the Tahoe Forest Reserve in 1904 and 1905 was due, at least in part, to the Nevada senator's actions in support of such protection.

Stewart's interest in Alaskan mining at the turn of the century was also stimulated by pressure from old friends, this time John Mackay and Charles D. Lane. They sought his help in connection with the Alaskan Government Bill, which carried a provision allowing aliens to acquire property. Although foreigners had been granted that privilege by an earlier law of May 17, 1884, a change was proposed in the spring of 1900, to give American citizens exclusive rights in Alaska. The amendment, if passed, would have deprived Lane and Mackay of important mining claims near Nome, which they held through purchase from the original locators, a group of Scandinavians.

Stewart entered the fight over the amendment with enthusiasm, fortified by a background in mining rules and regulations which was, perhaps, superior to that of any of his colleagues. Never niggardly with advice, he now took occasion to pass on some of his knowledge of mining law to those less well educated on the subject. He traced the history of mineral law in the United States, with liberal references to his own part in its development, insisting that the National Mining Law of 1866 should apply to Alaska as it did elsewhere in the United States. Stewart maintained that the proposed amendment would guarantee the property for a group of "claim-jumpers," and take it from the rightful owners. His speechmaking climaxed in a long exposition on April 16, 1900, summarizing much of what he had stated earlier. This time his tenacious fight against the proposal, with important assistance from other western senators, was successful; the Alaskan Government Bill became law without the amendment.[15]

Stewart's attempt to help another old friend was too much for a Virginia City reporter to bear. He lashed out against the senator for supporting William A. Clark, the Montana copper baron, in the latter's unsuccessful attempt to gain a seat in the U.S. Senate. The newsman noted that Stewart's action in backing Clark was in keeping with everything else he had done during the session of Congress, "There was not a proposition in the cause of truth or justice that came before the present session of the United States Senate but what William Morris Stewart was found in opposition." He suggested that nine-tenths of those who supported Stewart in 1898, "are willing to admit they never bought a bigger or more bogus gold-brick in their lives."[16]

Long before the Clark case came before the Senate, in the spring of 1900, Stewart's thoughts had turned to the 1900 election. Not only did he always find a particular excitement in political campaigns, but the 1900 election took on special significance as the possible means of eliminating Congressman Newlands from Nevada politics for all time. The defeat of Newlands in the 1899 state legislature appeared to deal a deathblow to his political future. Yet Stewart and Wallace knew that the Sharon-Newlands-Nixon combine still held a strong position among Nevada newspapers and the rank and file of the Silver Party membership. Consequently, it became important to the Stewart-Wallace faction to stop any Newlands resurgence as quickly as possible. To accomplish this, Newlands would have to be defeated in his bid for reelection to Congress in 1900, and fusion of the Democrats with the Silverites also had to be blocked.

In the spring of 1900, mining capitalist Joseph DeLamar appeared to be a candidate who could defeat Newlands. DeLamar was the owner and developer of a rich gold mine in Lincoln County, Nevada, which had started substantial production in 1894 and continued into the early twentieth century. The mine was the only bright spot on the Nevada mining picture in these years, and its owner had thus been the recipient of much publicity. Although Stewart was enthusiastic about a DeLamar candidacy, Wallace was opposed and warned the senator, "Don't try to get Delamar [sic] to run for Congress. We can use better judgment than that. Put Delamar into the fight for Senator when the time comes."[17] Ultimately, Wallace settled upon Edward S. Farrington, an attorney in Elko County, as the Republican nominee for Congress. He wrote Stewart that he was certain Farrington could beat Newlands.[18]

The question of fusion was more complex. By 1900, it appeared that the Silver Party was splitting in two parts, with the Stewart-Wallace group returning to the Republican Party and the Sharon-Newlands faction moving to the Democrats. Wallace was convinced that the Silver Party was nearing its end as an effective political instrument, and informed Stewart, "You, Cassidy and myself organized the Silver Party. We may be able to continue it for one campaign more. Then we must quit. . . . We must prepare to organize the Republican Party or be left out in the cold. We can go into that Party and take command and win with it."[19] It was also essential to Wallace that the Democrats be prevented from merging with the Silver Party. On the other hand, the Newlands-Sharon camp felt it necessary to accomplish such a fusion, if they were to win in 1900.

The first test of strength between the two groups came with the meeting of the Silver Party State Central Committee at Reno on April 12. Wallace was convinced that he had controlled the meeting. He wrote Stewart that Sharon and Newlands had intended to fuse both state and national silver groups with the straight-out Democrats, but "so far I have held the Fort. At the meeting of the State Central Committee I controlled it and elected my chairman by a vote of 31 to 15." However, he suggested to Stewart that Senator Jones be brought to Nevada to help control the primaries, since Newlands commanded most of the western Nevada newspapers and Sharon was busy traveling all over the state on behalf of the congressman. He added, "If you folks don't show up in season I will throw up the sponge and attend to my Railroad matters. I am not going to make a losing fight. It won't take much money to down them if the matter is taken hold of in season."[20]

Wallace's optimistic view of the April 12 meeting was not shared by another Stewart supporter, who wrote the senator that the Wallace forces had lost control of the committee meeting, "It makes fusion on Newlands almost certain. The fact is that it is mainly Newlands people who are staying in the silver party and they will carry the silver party primaries."[21] If fusion was not made certain by the meeting itself, the activity of Democrats and the inactivity of certain prominent Republicans made such a merger more probable. By June of 1900, Wallace had become worried about the obvious inroads of the Newlands-Sharon group into his own area of influence in the Silver Party. He sent a short but clear message to Stewart, warning that he needed the help of both Nevada senators if Newlands was to be stopped.[22]

Jones was strangely silent during these months. His reluctance to become involved in the 1900 campaign probably stemmed from a desire to leave politics and no doubt reflected a decision not to run for the Senate in 1902. Stewart's inaction was not so simple to understand, although a possible explanation might be drawn from a letter to Wallace. Stewart wrote that he had consulted Herrin, legal counsel for the Southern Pacific, who had told him that "our friends in New York," obviously Huntington and other Southern Pacific officers, were cautious about interfering in Nevada at the time.[23] Such reluctance was understandable. Newlands was tied directly to the Sharon estate and the old Bank of California capitalists, and his immediate threat was aimed at Senator Jones, not at Stewart.

Wallace implored Stewart to return to Nevada, and to do so quickly if fusion was to be prevented and Newlands defeated. In a pointed and critical letter, early in July, Wallace warned Stewart of political realities:

> The course pursued by you and Jones in sustaining the administration has caused the men of Democratic proclivities to abandon you. . . . Neither you nor Jones have any standing with the Democrats and if you don't come at once and lend a quiet hand you won't have any with the Republicans. . . . While we can't carry the state for McKinley if the fight is made with judgement we can elect Farrington over Newlands.[24]

Wallace's analysis was corroborated by another Stewart supporter, Frank Norcross, who wrote that Newlands had complete dominance over the Democrats and would probably be able to fuse them with the Silverites and the Populists. In addition, he warned Stewart, "There seems to be a Newlands wing of the Republican party, led by Fulton, Bragg, McMillan and others who, while active Republicans, are more or less tied to Newlands." Norcross reiterated the plea that Stewart and Jones must return to Nevada, "to get Silver men back to the Republicans."[25]

Conceding the inevitability of fusion in 1900, Stewart remained in Washington and used his position to support the Republican candidate, Edward S. Farrington, against Newlands. He supported Farrington with information such as Newlands's voting record, which could be used against the congressman, and obtained a position in the United States Land Office for a prominent Republican, William McMillan, who threatened to contest Farrington for the Republican congressional nomination.[26]

Stewart further weakened his position within the Nevada Silver Party when he announced, on August 20, that he would vote for McKinley. The move made it virtually impossible for Wallace to prevent fusion of the Nevada Democrats with the Silverites. At the time, Stewart justified his endorsement of McKinley because the latter was an expansionist. Years later he explained his decision differently: "The silver question was disposed of by a sudden and unexpected output of gold. . . . After the silver question was eliminated from politics, having been a Republican from the organization of that party I returned to my natural allegiance, and entered upon the campaign with the Republican party in 1900. . . . They restored to me positions on committees which were reserved for the dominant party."[27] Since the assignments had been made at the beginning of the congressional session, in December, 1899, Stewart in effect admitted what his opponents had claimed all along, that he had become a Republican at that time. In his explanation of the party switch, Stewart again conveniently forgot that he had once been a Democrat, in California in the late 1850's.

Stewart may have felt he had adequate reason for rejoining the Republicans, but it was a feeling not shared by many of his Nevada constituents. Criticisms of the move poured in from all parts of the State and were so consistently violent that it appeared the opposition had been waiting for just such an opportunity to vent their wrath on Nevada's junior senator.

Nixon's Winnemucca newspaper greeted Stewart's return to the Republicans with the headline, "Nevada's Grand Old Fraud Repudiates Bryan."[28] An editorial the next day described Stewart's treachery, "in direct line with other actions of a political career which had been criminal from the beginning, every act being stamped with a rascality and treachery which long ago placed him outside the pale of decency. . . . Four years more of Stewart will give the people of Nevada ample time to reflect upon what fools they have been."[29] A Reno paper added that Stewart's action was not surprising, since "he came to the Silver Party like a thief in the night, and went away leaving the doors of the party open when he had received the swag he entered its portals to secure."[30] Stewart was hanged in effigy at Tuscarora, in northeastern Nevada, and a cartoon depicting the event was reprinted in newspapers throughout the state.[31] Some expressed regret "at being compelled to use an effigy instead of the original."[32]

The intensity of the verbal assault against Stewart reflected the perception that he was still a powerful political figure in Nevada and might be a candidate for U.S. senator in 1904. One writer suggested that Stewart thought he would be better off campaigning for reelection in the Republican Party. Yet the writer was skeptical: "How either Democrats or Republicans can place further faith in this man surpassed belief. Expansion is the old man's hobby this trip and we hope it proves to be the hobby horse that will ride him fast and furious out of the senatorial chair."[33] The editor of the anti-Stewart *Reno Evening Gazette* was one of few individuals with a kind word for Stewart's party switch: "While the *Gazette* has no admiration for Senator Stewart, it will acknowledge that he gives good reasons why he will not support Bryan in this campaign."[34]

Stewart enlarged upon the rationale for changing from Bryan when he charged in a New York interview that it was Bryan who had abandoned the cause of silver, by discarding financial reform to make "the cause of Aguinaldo the paramount issue. On that issue I am for my country and against Aguinaldo and his friend Mr. Bryan."[35] Another writer thought otherwise and insisted that Stewart switched parties because officials of the Southern Pacific told him to give up the silver issue and return to the Republicans.[36]

The Silver Party and the Democratic Party met at Virginia City early in September, 1900. After a few initial setbacks, the two groups were able to unite, and Newlands was nominated by acclamation in each party convention. His victory was a remarkable comeback from the bitter legislative defeat of January, 1899. It was made even sweeter when the Silver Party State Convention passed a resolution expunging from the record the action of the State Central Committee, which had removed Sharon and Newlands from the Silver Party in 1899.[37]

In spite of this successful fusion, Stewart did not halt his campaign to defeat Newlands. He now turned to his Southern Pacific friends for help. Collis P. Huntington had died on August 14, 1900, to be replaced as president of the company by Charles H. Tweed. Stewart cautioned Tweed, "It would be disastrous to turn Wallace down in this campaign. Newlands' gang will blackmail the company in every possible way if they get into power. They can not be trusted."[38] When he did not receive the requested aid, Stewart returned to Nevada, where he made several October speeches supporting McKinley for President and E. S. Farrington for congressman.[39] His efforts, coming so late, were wasted. Newlands easily defeated Farrington, and the Bryan electors won handily over those pledged to McKinley.[40]

Immediately after the 1900 election, Stewart started a campaign to block Newlands from the Senate in 1902. His first concern was recruiting a viable candidate to oppose the congressman. Again he turned to his friend, Captain J. R. DeLamar, assuring the latter that Jones would not be a candidate for reelection, "If you desire the place and are willing to spend some money on newspapers and in organizing Republican clubs, I will assist you to get it."[41] When DeLamar showed no interest in such a candidacy Stewart continued during the next two years to seek some-one to oppose Newlands for the Senate seat.

In this search Stewart did not have the assistance of his loyal political manager, C. C. Wallace. The 1900 election was Wallace's last. He did not attend the Nevada legislative session which opened in January, 1901, noting to Stewart that the legislature was busy with the question of eliminating the constitutional prohibition against a lottery in the state and that, consequently, he had stayed away from Carson City.[42] Obvi-ously worried about his position with the railroad after the death of Huntington, Wallace asked Stewart "to put him in good with Mr. Tweed and Mr. Hayes."[43] Before Stewart could do this favor, Wallace died, on January 31, 1901, at Mariposa, California, where he had gone to inspect some mining property.[44]

His death initiated a contest between the Stewart and Newlands fac-tions over the position of Southern Pacific agent for Nevada, which under Wallace had been the key to control of Nevada politics. Stewart wrote a long letter to William Herrin, opposing potential nominees from the Newlands camp and suggesting instead Charles A. Norcross. The senator wrote that Norcross "would have no difficulty in my opinion, in attending to the legitimate business of the Company without involving large expense."[45] Herrin turned down his onetime partner, informing him that the company's Nevada land agent would now look after political matters. According to Herrin, the railroad's attitude was, "to meddle there as little as possible in politics."[46] Since the current Southern Pacific land agent was Robert Fulton, a close friend of Newlands, it is apparent that the company had switched its support; but this did not mean that it had moved completely out of Nevada politics,[47] nor that it had no more use for Stewart.

Indeed, he continued to support the interests of the Central Pacific in Congress. On March 2, 1901, the Senate agreed to Stewart's amend-ment to the Deficiency Act, giving the Central Pacific $1,496,090.41 in interest.[48] Shortly, thereafter, the company's new president, Charles H. Tweed, reminded Stewart of his proper relationship to the railroad. In asking the senator to help Judge W. D. Cornish obtain a right-of-way across Nevada to Southern California for the Union Pacific, Tweed wrote:

I am inclined to think that you will find some way of being of service to Judge Cornish in connection with this matter. You understand perfectly well the relations now existing between the Southern Pacific and the Union Pacific and I feel sure that it will give you pleasure to cooperate earnestly with Judge Cornish in doing all that can be done in securing this right-of-way and grade for the Union Pacific interests, or I may say, for our interests.[49]

The right-of-way problem ultimately was settled in favor of the Union Pacific.

While continuing to "work for the railroad," in the spring of 1901, Stewart reentered the debate on the Philippine insurrection and the question of final disposition of the islands. In a lengthy speech in the Senate on January 4, Stewart again compared Aguinaldo's rebellion to the "rebellion of Chief Sitting Bull or any other rebellion against the authority of the United States within the limits of our territory." He answered those who tried to justify Aguinaldo's action under the U.S. Declaration of Independence by stating that the right of revolution must give way to the practical situation, "The Filipino rebellion is going to be put down, and the people of the Philippine Islands are going to taste, under our free institutions and under the authority of the United States, the blessings of liberty. These blessings are going to be taken to them and no man can prevent it." Stewart majestically proclaimed, "It is the voice of the American people that the rebellion shall be put down." Although the Filipinos were ignorant of the true meaning of liberty, it was the mission of the U.S. to teach them, "The onward march of free institutions will continue. . . . To call it a colonial system is a misnomer. To presume that the United States when it extends its authority as a territory extends imperialism is absurd."[50] Stewart continued to regard the Philippines in much the same light as earlier western territories, and thus assumed a sequence to statehood.

In spite of his rhetorical emphasis on spreading liberty and justice, Stewart was not blind to other aspects of U.S. territorial expansion. During discussion of the bill to provide a civil government for the Philippines, he stated that among the reasons he supported it was that the bill would open the mints to the coinage of silver. Stewart insisted again that he had never changed his mind about the money question, that the increase in the U.S. gold supply obviated the silver issue until the gold mines gave out. However, this was not the case for the Philippine Islands, where silver coinage for Asian trade was necessary.[51]

Stewart also did not abandon the subject of the Philippines until he had struck a blow in support of railroads. In January, 1903, he introduced an amendment to the Army Appropriation Bill that would authorize the Secretary of War to construct, equip, and operate railroads in the islands, at a rate of development of not less than three hundred miles per year for the following ten years. His speech in support of the amendment emphasized the importance of railroads, not only in trade, but in maintaining law and order, and in civilizing the people of the islands.[52] In his last session in Congress, Stewart again attempted to further such construction, emphasizing that "the building of railroads is the cheapest way to extend civilization into any savage or semicivilized country." In his last speech on the subject he repeated the customary themes, "To talk about civilizing the Filipinos without railroads is idle. It never has been done in any country in the world. . . . Railroads will be the instrumentality of civilization from this time on."[53]

Aiding railroad interests in the United States Senate had become a major commitment for Stewart; his support of the oleomargarine interests in 1901 and 1902, however, was something of a departure from his normal legislative program. His speeches in defense of that industry represented an unusual alliance for a senator from Nevada, especially one who had a major dairy operation at his Ashburn Farm in Virginia at the time his comments were made. While debating a bill to prohibit coloring in oleomargarine, Stewart pointed out that butter was also colored. He pronounced himself unconvinced that coloring in butter was not meant to deceive, and if deception was permitted for butter it ought also to be allowed for oleo.[54] A year later, in March of 1902, when a bill was introduced to make oleo subject to the specific laws of any state or territory into which it was transported, Stewart insisted on numerous occasions that the proposal seemed designed to destroy one legitimate industry for the benefit of another, without just cause.[55] Despite his fervor in the cause, his efforts on behalf of oleomargarine were no more successful than those supporting silver remonetization.

Stewart encountered additional opposition from dairy farmers when he supported measures calling for strong regulation of such facilities. The senator maintained that the examination had to start with the dairies themselves, since "the inspection of dairy products that would look only to the finished product would be a mockery.[56] Stewart practiced what he preached by having his own dairy farm "spic and span," in order "to show that everything is done to make the milk pure and clean."[57]

After Stewart returned to the Republican Party in 1900, he was without a major western or Nevada political issue to promote. The two important causes that had helped to return him to the Senate in 1887, remonetization of silver and irrigation, were lost to other champions by 1900. Although on occasion he continued to promote the idea of bimetallism, his role as chief spokesman of Nevada's silver interests practically ceased after he assisted McKinley in the 1900 election. The silver issue was dead nationally by that time, and if Stewart's recognition of that fact had been handled more adroitly he might not have lost so much Nevada support.

Irrigation was another matter, and remained a major political problem for Nevada and the west into the twentieth century. Stewart's interest in the movement, however, waned after the First Irrigation Congress, held in September, 1891, in Salt Lake City, Utah.[58] No doubt Stewart's perception that the silver question was more important to Nevada and the nation in the 1890's allowed his protégé, Francis Newlands, to assume the leadership role in the western irrigation campaign.[59] Unwilling to pursue the idea of a national program like that promoted by John W. Powell, Stewart may also have concluded that the state-oriented reclamation projects which he preferred could not be funded by state or private means. In any event, his role in the irrigation-reclamation crusade during the 1890's was purely passive.

However, when Congressman Newlands and Senators Warren of Wyoming and Hansbrough of South Dakota began a strong effort late in the decade to obtain federal legislation on behalf of reclamation and irrigation, Stewart quickly joined the movement. Later, when the Hansbrough Bill came before the Senate on March 1, 1902, Stewart spoke extensively in favor of the bill and answered a number of questions by other senators. His replies indicated that he had been studying the irrigation problem even though he relinquished leadership to others. While he was quick to support the bill in the Senate, he belittled the role of Newlands in passing the act, which was signed by President Roosevelt on June 17, 1902.[60] On a number of later occasions after Newlands had been lauded as the father of reclamation, Stewart insisted that the statute was really the Hansbrough Bill, and that passage came not because of Newlands, but because Theodore Roosevelt lent his support to the measure.[61]

Only one other question attracted consistent attention from Stewart during his last term in the Senate, the problem of national policy towards the Indians. His return to the Republican Party brought him the chairmanship of the Committee on Indian Affairs in 1901, and he remained its head until he left the Senate in 1905. In his capacity as chairman he spent a great deal of time defending Indian appropriation bills. His speeches on these occasions indicated a continued ambivalence toward Indians, on the one hand professing sympathy for their needs, while on the other bowing quickly to the white demands when they conflicted with Indian rights. For example, he maintained support of Nevada railroads in their attempts to limit or erase Indian rights, and he made another bid to open the Walker Lake Indian Reservation to certain white intruders, this time miners. When charged by Tonopah newspapers with obstructing the opening of the reservation to mining, Stewart wrote one editor that the facts would show that he had worked for fifteen years to open the area, but government agencies had resisted. He noted, "Nobody from Nevada or elsewhere, outside of myself participated in securing that legislation [opening the reservation]."[62] Clearly, in advocating opening the Walker River Reservation to mining, Stewart was influenced by newspaper stories claiming that the Indian lands held great mineral resources which were being denied development, to the detriment of Indians as well as whites. While no action was taken at this time, it was partly due to Stewart's earlier actions that the reservation was finally opened to mining on October 29, 1906.[63]

On the other hand, Stewart also supported a number of measures which he thought protected Indian rights, generally contending that Indians would be better off, and conflicts with whites eliminated, if the Indians were integrated into white society. He maintained that it was impossible ever again to have traditional hunting grounds for the Indians, and that they must now live as the white man lived:

> They must supply their wants by labor, as other men do. . . . There will be no conflict whatever if you will give the Indians a chance and protect them in their right, let them sell land to white men and be given full consideration, so as not to cheat them; let them live on their homestead that they cannot sell; give them that opportunity and they will become good citizens.[64]

Unfortunately, such sentiments were too often submerged by the desire to promote private interests at Indian expense.

Stewart's activity in the Senate slackened perceptibly during his final term, with no solid legislative accomplishment to match his earlier performance. By far his greatest achievement during these years came in efforts outside the U. S. Senate, in a rather unusual legal endeavor which climaxed in the fall of 1902. On August 16, 1902, accompanied by his secretary, Charles Kappler, and the latter's wife, Stewart left for The Hague to argue the Pious Fund case. This was the first action to be heard by the Permanent Court of International Arbitration, which had been established by the first Hague Conference of 1899.

The Pious Fund case had a long and complex history before it finally reached international arbitration in 1902. The fund itself originated in February, 1697. It was the idea of Fathers Kino Salvatierra and Juan de Ugarte, whereby money could be collected outside the Spanish Royal

Treasury for use in mission work with the California Indians. It became known as the Pious Fund of the Californias and it was understood by the parties concerned that all donations accepted in trust were to be applied to the propagation of the Catholic faith in California. On February 8, 1842, a Mexican law transferred management of the Pious Fund from the hands of the Bishop of California to the Mexican national government.[65]

The chain of circumstances that ultimately brought the case to arbitration began in 1848, the year of the Mexican cession to the United States, when the Mexican government stopped payment of the annual interest to the missions. Approximately six months after California became a state, State Senator Jonathan T. Warner authored a report which concluded that management of the Pious Fund had been usurped by the Mexican government and should be returned to the Bishop of California for completion of the design and will of the donor. Warner proposed a resolution that the President of the United States be authorized to take steps to solve the problem with Mexico.[66]

Following the Warner report, Bishop Alemany of California, who had tried for years to get Mexico to pay the interest on the fund, employed John Thomas Doyle, an expert in Hispanic colonial history and a San Francisco lawyer, to represent him in pursuing a claim against the Mexican government. In the middle of 1868, the two countries agreed on a Mixed Claims Commission to settle such claims, and on March 30, 1870, the Pious Fund claim was filed with that body.[67] After years of delay, the California bishops were awarded $904,070.79, on November 11, 1875.[68] That amount represented accrued interest from February, 1848, to February, 1869, and was paid in installments by the Mexican government to January 21, 1890, at which time that government viewed the settlement as completed.[69]

The California bishops saw the matter differently. They thought the Mexican government was obligated to pay 6 percent annual interest on the fund from May 30, 1869, the date of the last payment covered in the earlier award, forward. Direct diplomatic intervention by the United States government appeared to be the best means of recovering these disputed funds, and William M. Stewart was employed in the early part of 1890, to facilitate such action. On March 1, 1890, on behalf of the California bishops, he filed a request with the State Department for U.S. intrusion to gain additional financial benefits for the Catholic Church.[70] The Mexican government objected to diplomatic intervention, because it regarded the Pious Fund claim as illegal.[71] Stewart visited Mexico City in 1893, but his attempt to break the impasse also failed.[72]

For the next few years Stewart was so involved in the silver issue and his own political activities that he neglected the Pious Fund case. As a result, in September, 1897, Doyle asked Bishop Riordan to obtain Stewart's withdrawal as counsel. Riordan visited Stewart in Washington, D.C., but instead of asking the senator to leave, the Bishop decided to modify the original contracts regarding legal counsel. Under the new arrangements, Riordan had the right to select associate counsel and pay additional attorneys from the 25 percent of any money recovered that was originally to have gone to Doyle and Stewart. The action put Bishop Riordan in charge of the case in place of Doyle.[73]

As soon as the Spanish-American War was over, Bishop Riordan prodded Stewart back into action on the case. The latter hired Jackson Harvey Ralston, a young Washington expert in international law, fortuitously a relative of Secretary of State Hay. Stewart and Ralston obtained Secretary Hay's favorable commitment to the case, and on December 4, 1899, he instructed the American minister to Mexico, Powell Clayton, to reopen negotiations for an adjustment of the Pious Fund claims. Since the 1875 award had decided the matter legally, once and for all time, the new action by Stewart was based upon *res adjudicata,* a principle which mandated that a case settled by a competent court could not be litigated again between the same parties. If this principle were accepted, it would mean that the bishops of California were entitled to receive annually the amount of interest fixed earlier by the Mixed Claims Commission. Mexico held that the failure of the claimants to collect the interest consistently over the years invalidated their rights, by virtue of the Mexican statute of limitations, and thus there was no issue of *res adjudicata*. Moreover, the Mexicans had contended earlier that the principle of *res adjudicata* applied only to decisions by courts, and not to those by arbitrators.[74]

In spite of Hay's active intervention, the Mexican government procrastinated throughout 1900. Then, William Lawrence Penfield, solicitor of the State Department, suggested that the case be submitted to the newly established Hague Tribunal.[75] The California bishops and Mexico agreed to submit the case, and a protocol to that effect was signed by Secretary Hay and Manuel Aspirez, the Mexican Ambassador, on May 22, 1902.[76] At first Stewart did not plan to attend the sessions of the International Court, which were to be held in September, 1902, owing both to the illness of his wife and to the fact that the sessions would interfere with his activity in the Nevada primary elections. However, Bishop Riordan insisted that Stewart be at The Hague, since Doyle could not attend because of his age.[77] Stewart himself was 77 years old, but still vigorous, and he agreed in July to attend the court sessions. As part of his travel arrangements for himself, his secretary, Charles Kappler, and Mrs. Kappler, Stewart requested and received free ship passage, courtesy of the president of the International Navigation Company.[78]

Mrs. Stewart was suffering from diabetes, and the state of her health caused Stewart to believe that she would fare better with friends and relatives in California than on the long ocean voyage to The Hague. Thus it was a party of three that left New York for The Hague on August 16, 1902. Stewart planned to return about October 1, to participate in the final weeks of the 1902 election campaign in Nevada.[79]

The Hague Tribunal was empowered to decide whether the claim of the California bishops for interest from 1869 forward, as a consequence of the earlier decision from the Mixed Claims Commission in 1875, fell within the governing principle of *res adjudicata* and, if not, whether the same claim was just.[80] The Hague Court held its first meeting to adjudicate the Pious Fund case on September 15, 1902. The importance of the proceedings attracted so many diplomats, reporters, and spectators that the courtroom would not hold all of them.[81] After the opening ceremonies, Stewart and his colleague, Charles J. Kappler, filed a statement on behalf of the United States. Stewart, as senior counsel, then began the oral proceedings and made an excellent presentation. He reviewed the history of the case, pointing out that neither the existence of the Pious Fund nor the purposes of its founders were questioned until the beneficiaries became citizens of the United States, after the Mexican cession of 1848. Stewart and the other U.S. representatives made a strong effort to prove that the Mixed Claims Commission was a properly constituted court, one before which such traditional and accepted legal principles as *res adjudicata* were understood and fully accepted.[82]

The hearings extended for ten days. At their conclusion, a party was arranged by Senator Stewart and attended by counsel from both sides.[83] The arbiters withdrew on October 1, and announced their decision on October 14, accepting the United States position that the principle of *res adjudicata* did apply to the awards of international tribunals and that the California bishops were entitled to interest payments from 1869 forward.[84]

Stewart left for the United States before the arbiters' decision was announced, his departure speeded by the sad news, which he received just three days before the opening session, that his wife, Annie, had been killed in an automobile accident in Oakland, California. According to San Francisco newspapers, Mrs. Stewart, accompanied by two nephews, was riding in a big Winton auto on the afternoon of September 12. It swerved to avoid a delivery wagon and hit an electric pole, throwing Mrs. Stewart out onto the sidewalk. She was taken to a nearby house, but died before professional help could arrive.[85] It was the first fatal automobile accident in the San Francisco Bay area and, as a result, received an unusual amount of attention in the newspapers. When Stewart was apprised by wire of his wife's death he cabled his nephew, William W. Foote, to hold the body until his return to the United States, but suggested that a memorial service be held at once.

After his return to the United States, Stewart stopped briefly in Washington, D.C., leaving for San Francisco on October 11, 1902.[86] The funeral was held the day after his arrival there, at Laurel Cemetery. Almost immediately afterward, Stewart left for Nevada to participate in the last stages of the election of 1902, in an attempt to block Francis Newlands in his bid for the Senate seat being vacated by John P. Jones.

Stewart had initiated efforts to thwart Newlands some months before his trip to The Hague, turning again to J. R. DeLamar as a possible candidate against the congressman. Once more, DeLamar was reluctant to enter political life, leaving Stewart without a viable challenger.[87] Further complicating Stewart's efforts to eliminate Newlands was a change in attitude by the Southern Pacific officials. Not only had the railroad officers decided to withdraw from their previously active role in Nevada politics, but they had also turned away from Stewart to support Newlands and Sharon. Their new role was defined in a letter by Henry M. Yerington to D. O. Mills, "You will be surprised to know that W. E. Sharon has taken his [Wallace's] place to a considerable extent—therefore the S. P. Co. will doubtless aid Mr. Newlands in his election to the Senate."[88] Stewart was late in recognizing the shift and never fully understood it, although he received reports from two Nevada correspondents.

One was a rather questionable source, Abner C. Cleveland of White Pine County, who had changed from friend to enemy and back again. Cleveland now sought to convince Stewart that he had never really supported Newlands in 1898, "I never have been for Newlands for anything on earth. . . . I am against Newlands to the end, he is not my style of man." More important to Stewart was Cleveland's remark that reports in Nevada confirmed the fact that the Southern Pacific people were for Newlands.[89] A more reliable report of the new position of the railroad officials came from George T. Mills, chairman of the Republican State Central Committee, who indicated in letters to Stewart that the Southern Pacific would not oppose Newlands.[90]

With DeLamar refusing to run and railroad support moving to New-lands, Stewart was in a quandary. A new and apparently significant mining strike in May, 1900, in Nye County, brought a possible answer to his problem. Jim Butler, discoverer of the silver deposits at Tonopah, had become a very popular figure by the end of 1901, since the mining revival marked an end to a twenty-year depression in the state. In a letter to George Mills, Stewart asked, "Tell me confidentially how much of a man he is, what is his [Butler's] fitness and what are his prospects for the place [U.S. Senate]." He told Mills that he had heard Butler had political ambitions "and is very popular."[91] Apparently Mills did not reply favorably, for the Butler candidacy was not mentioned again by Stewart.

While searching for a suitable candidate to run against Newlands, Stewart also sought an issue to convince Nevada voters of the superiority of the Republican Party. He found it in the protective tariff, which he was convinced could be publicized in Nevada to win Republican support from wool growers, borax and lead interests, and the cattle industry.[92] It was a feeble substitute, however, and could not overcome the real advantage of the pro-silver Democrats in Nevada.

What Stewart needed was a strong candidate to run against Newlands. In July, 1902, shortly after he had agreed to attend The Hague Tribunal hearings, he thought he had found his man, in the person of Judge Thomas P. Hawley. In the middle of that month Stewart made a hurried trip to Nevada to obtain a definite commitment from Hawley. Stewart had known the judge for nearly fifty years, having been a member of the committee which examined Hawley for licensing as an attorney, in January, 1857, at Nevada City, California.[93] Hawley had come to Nevada in 1868, during the rush to Hamilton in White Pine County. He was elected to the Nevada Supreme Court in 1872, reelected in 1878 and 1884. In September of 1890, he resigned from the Nevada Supreme Court to accept an appointment to the federal district court.

There he ruled in favor of the Central Pacific Railroad when it brought suit to enjoin Nevada's county assessors from assessing railroad property in conformity with a state law passed March 16, 1901. That act was an attempt to impose some uniformity in assessment procedures by providing that the state's county assessors were to meet as a board and "establish throughout the state a uniform valuation of all classes of property." One of the board's first actions increased the value of the Central Pacific's real estate by $5,000,000. Railroad officials termed it an illegal assessment. Hawley's ruling in the case, on August 12, 1901, granted the injunction to the railroad, noting that the assessors had no power to value any railroad at so much per mile without first selecting the classes of property to which it belonged.[94] Obviously, Hawley's decision ingratiated him with Central Pacific officials, a fact which no doubt figured prominently in Stewart's decision to try to convince him to run against Newlands for the Senate.

Stewart's brief trip to Nevada in late July evoked strong responses from opposition newspapers. One writer attributed the brevity of the visit to Stewart's unpopularity: "It needs not the saying that Mr. Stewart is at this time the most unpopular man in the State of Nevada, and justly so. . . . By popular vote he couldn't be elected to the smallest township office. . . . Just as certain is it that no man can be elected United States Senator who bears the Stewart label."[95] The article reported that Stewart brought along with him "the money bags of the National Republican Committee and the shekels of Mark Hanna. . . . When he last departed for Washington, elected by the Silver party and the Democrats he was followed by curses, brick-bats and old shoes and he comes back hailed with loud acclaim and falls into the arms of H. M. Yerington, Sam Platt, the *News* editor and the Carson Brass Band."[96] Unmindful of the outcry against him, Stewart went ahead with his plans to convince Nevada Republicans to support Hawley, and was rewarded for his efforts when Hawley announced his candidacy for the United States Senate in the last week of July. Stewart was delighted, and predicted to numerous friends a Republican victory in Nevada in November. To his former secretary, Isaac Frohman, Stewart outlined the program he had helped work out— Hawley would run for the Senate, A. C. Cleveland for governor, and when Hawley left the bench, "E. S. Farrington of Elko would be appointed in his place."[97]

Returning east, Stewart made another hurried trip, to New York, to convince Southern Pacific officials to support his candidate. The senator thought his talks successful and so informed Hawley and William Herrin. He told Herrin that "our friends" in New York were pleased with Hawley as a candidate, and warned that a Newlands victory "would place in power the gang of blackmailers who have been pursuing the railroad for more than thirty years and make you a great deal of trouble. The election of Hawley would bury the opposition and secure exemption from annoyance for many years to come." Stewart tried to impress Herrin with the importance of George Nixon in the 1902 campaign, noting that "he can do more than any other man in the State to turn the tide at the proper time. I know he is a Republican and I am confident that his ambitions politically can only be gratified in that party."[98] Either Stewart did not recognize at the time how close Newlands was to Nixon, or else he thought he might break the alliance.

Stewart's letter to Hawley was also filled with optimism about a victory in the fall. The senator offered to help Hawley, and suggested that he use the irrigation issue as part of his attack on Newlands. Stewart reported that a number of persons present at a luncheon with President Roosevelt "all expressed the opinion that we would have had a better bill with less opposition if Mr. Newlands had not been in Congress, especially as far as Nevada is concerned. . . . It looks like Newlands is like a drowning man catching at a straw for him to attempt to boom himself as the originator of irrigation."[99] Stewart was convinced that credit for the irrigation act belonged to the Republican Party, and that Nevada voters should be made aware of that fact. Stewart wanted Republican leaders in Nevada to emphasize President Roosevelt's part in the events leading to a national irrigation act. In a letter to George T. Mills, chairman of the Republican Party in Nevada, the senator belittled as laughable the claim that Roosevelt "was first the pupil and then the ally of Mr. Newlands."[100]

Hawley's candidacy, while receiving enthusiastic endorsements from Stewart and a few others, met with strong opposition from many more, including the rank and file of the Republican Party.[101] A number of the critics concentrated on Hawley's age; he was then 72 years old. Stewart tried to combat that issue with a letter to the editor of the *Carson News:*

> No man is old while he is in full vigor of both body and mind. If measured with Mr. Newlands in these respects Judge Hawley is at least thirty years his junior. . . . I never heard of Mr. Newlands being well a week at a time; it is either rheumatism, gout from English high living, bladder trouble, headache, indigestion, or all these combined, that not only requires a syndicate of puffers to navigate his political balloon but a syndicate of doctors to keep his feeble heart in motion. . . . and any person who will examine the Congressional record of Mr. Newlands will be unable to determine from anything they find there whether he has been dead or alive any time since the 4th of March, 1893.[102]

Stewart continued his letter-writing campaign on behalf of Hawley to the day he sailed for The Hague. He asked George T. Mills to write to Senator John P. Jones for help in having Hawley nominated at the Republican State Convention, due to meet in August. He suggested that Mills ask for financial help from banker Thomas Rickey, "the rich men of Tonopah and the sheep and cattlemen. . . . Get the Republican party started throughout the State."[103] In a letter to Hawley on the morning of his departure for Europe, Stewart reported that the President and the Republican Congressional Committee were interested in his senatorial fight. What was now needed, wrote Stewart, was a man with more political experience than Mills to run the campaign in Nevada.[104]

With that letter Stewart reluctantly ceased direct participation in the 1902 election until his return from The Hague; but even though absent, his influence continued to be felt. When Hawley's name was presented to the Republican State Convention, it was done so as to make "it appear that he was Stewart's man," wrote H. M. Yerington, adding, "Confidentially, Stewart is not very popular in Nevada and Jones far worse, so you can readily see this has been bad business."[105]

Stewart's unpopularity was trumpeted by opposition newspapers in Nevada. "Do Not Be Fooled," admonished one. "Since the days of Benedict Arnold, there probably was never a man so detested as William M. Stewart is by the people of Nevada."[106] Those words, with embellishments, were quoted in a Reno newspaper a few days later, in an article entitled, "Political Methods of Wm. M. Stewart, the Traitor." A number of incidents were cited to prove Stewart's "treason" to the Silver Party. The writer insisted that Stewart was using Hawley as a front, and that a "vote for a Republican candidate for State Senator unquestionably means a boost to Stewart in 1904. . . . And he expects in spite of this record, to be elected. Why? Because he believes that one half of the voters of Nevada are knaves and the other half, fools. In other words those that he cannot hoodwink he will buy."[107]

The newspaper campaign against Stewart continued even as he arrived in Nevada on the way to San Francisco to bury his wife. A Winnemucca paper greeted him as he passed through that town with the headline, "Wm. Mountebank Stewart, who helped Dutch take Holland." The article which followed claimed, "His coming will in no wise disturb the present indicator of the political weathercock, and he will hurt the cause of the fusion ticket in Nevada no more than he will help that of his own party."[108] No doubt much of the vituperation against Stewart stemmed from the conviction that he would be the Republican senatorial candidate in 1904. Labeling him a "traitor" in 1902 appeared an effective way of helping to defeat Hawley and at the same time eliminate Stewart from the 1904 campaign.[109]

When he returned to the political contest in Nevada after his wife's funeral in San Francisco, Stewart had only a little over two weeks to halt Newlands. It was an impossible task. Not only had the Newlands camp achieved fusion of the Democrats and Silverites, but they gained some additional strength by throwing their support behind the popular John Sparks, a gold-standard man, for governor. It was rumored that Sparks was promised the United States Senate post in two years by the Newlands-Sharon faction.[110]

An effort was made to discredit Newlands because his name would not appear on the November ballot. An 1899 Nevada statute provided for a popular referendum for the post of U. S. Senator, but the Silver-Democrats neglected to endorse Newlands as required under the law.[111] Since the Republicans had certified the nomination of Hawley, Stewart's group hoped that popular support could be aroused in favor of their candidate. The Newlands camp probably could have placed his name on the ballot, but the candidate declined to force the issue, arguing, correctly, that the voters might be confused. To ensure his election it would be necessary to inform the voters that they not only had to vote for him, but, more important, to choose his party's legislative ticket.[112]

In spite of Stewart's efforts, the Newlands-Hawley race was no contest. Fusion candidates for the state legislature made a virtual sweep of the election, insuring Newlands's selection to replace John P. Jones.[113] George T. Mills thought the 1902 election a major defeat for the Republicans, but Stewart, the continuing optimist, felt otherwise. Answering a letter from Mills, the senator wrote, "I note what you say regarding the election. . . . I am glad to see that our people are taking the defeat philosophically. We shall be in fine trim for a fight two years hence."[114]

To be ready for such a contest, Stewart knew that he had to have the support of Central Pacific officials. Throughout the election campaign of 1902, he had tried desperately to demonstrate his loyalty to the new leaders of the company. He was understandably upset, therefore, when word reached him that George Mills had stated that the Central Pacific Railroad had opposed the Republican Party in the Nevada campaign. Stewart immediately wrote William Herrin, legal counsel for the company, apologizing for Mills's action. Stewart explained that many Nevadans believed the railroad had helped the Democrats during the election, since a number of railroad employees had taken leaves of absence and canvassed the state for that party. He asked Herrin to report to him anything from Mills or those connected with him that was "unfriendly to the railroad . . . and I think I can have the matter corrected."[115]

The selection of Newlands by the Nevada legislature, in January, 1903, led one Reno newspaper to declare, "By the election of Honorable Francis G. Newlands the State of Nevada has, for the first time in its history, chosen a United States Senator strictly on merit."[116] Such sentiments, and the obviously distasteful task of escorting the congressman to be sworn in as Nevada's junior senator, may have disturbed Stewart, but he had been in politics too long to become overly upset. He made the necessary accommodations, pushed aside the election of 1902, and looked forward to that of 1904.

Almost as upsetting as the Newlands victory to Stewart were a series of problems which developed with his children and grandchildren after his wife's death. She had died intestate, and it was assumed that all personal property in her name would go to her husband. However, about a year before she was killed, the Stewarts had given their Carson City home to their granddaughter, Bessie Hofer, daughter of Anna Stewart, who had died earlier. Bessie Hofer assumed the house was an outright gift and demanded to share in the division of Mrs. Stewart's possessions, which included a great deal of valuable furniture, silver, and art objects that she had gathered in her foreign travels. The granddaughter, in a letter on November 8, 1902, stated that she had sent a power of attorney to Charles H. Cragin, in order to protect her interests. She indicated that since her grandmother had died intestate, ''you, Aunt Bessie, Aunt Maybelle and myself each have an interest in the estate, my portion divided in three. This house here as you know being an absolute gift before death.''[117]

The letter deeply disturbed Stewart, who immediately wrote to George T. Mills, enclosing a copy of what he termed ''an unkind, ungrateful and wicked letter which I have just received from my granddaughter, Bessie Hofer.'' He insisted that the agreement on the Carson house was that it would go to Bessie Hofer, but that a life estate was reserved for himself. He suggested that Mills check the deed, but that his right to the Carson home ''during my life is unquestionable.''[118] A short time later Stewart received a letter of apology from his granddaughter, indicating that she had rescinded the power of attorney and asking forgiveness for having caused the senator so much trouble.[119] He evidently did, for the two remaining daughters and the granddaughter shared equally in the distribution of Mrs. Stewart's personal belongings. According to Stewart, the settlement was agreed to only reluctantly by his two daughters, who continued to believe that there should have been some deduction from the granddaughter's share because of the home.[120]

A little more than a year after his first wife's death, Stewart remarried. His bride, May Agnes Cone of Madison, Georgia, was the widow of Theodore C. Cone. According to a newspaper announcement, Stewart had met Mrs. Cone previously in Washington, D.C., and had courted her briefly before the marriage. At the time, Stewart was seventy-eight years of age, and his new wife some thirty years his junior.[121]

After the 1902 election, most of Stewart's time in the Senate was spent in caretaking activities. He made a number of attempts in those months, as he had been doing for many years, to have Nevada's Civil War Claims adjusted, but without success.[122] He also supported separate statehood for Arizona, New Mexico, and Oklahoma territories, at the same time defending his own state when Nevada was used as a good example of why these areas should remain territories.[123] One of his longest speeches came during a debate on Chinese exclusion, when he related again how, in July, 1870, he had prevented Charles Sumner from pushing through an amendment that would have made possible the naturalization of Chinese. He warned that the United States could not allow the Chinese to compete with "our labor," but that Americans ought nevertheless to maintain friendly trade relations with China.[124]

Perhaps Senator Stewart's most interesting involvement at this time was his support of the Panama Canal. On January 4, 1904, he made a strong speech favoring the Panama route over the alternate Nicaraguan route, arguing that no one should refuse to cooperate with the majority because "they differ as to the location of the canal."[125] That attitude was in marked contrast to Stewart's earlier position, first enunciated in 1895, favoring a Nicaraguan canal. As late as June, 1902, he opposed a Panama route, stating that the proposed Panama canal was a scheme of the "French swindlers," and, speaking from personal experience, that the climate at Panama was unhealthy, "the most dismal place on earth . . . during the six or eight months when there is no wind blowing."[126]

On this issue, Stewart's role was simply that of an administration supporter. He favored the Nicaraguan route as long as the President and fellow Republicans did, but moved to advocacy of the Panama route after the Panamanian Revolution opened the door to a November, 1903, treaty conveying the so-called Canal Zone to the United States. Stewart justified these events in a speech which mirrored administration rationale to the effect that Panama had a right to secede from the confederacy of New Granada, and the United States had license to intervene to protect transit over the isthmus under an 1846 treaty with Colombia. He insisted that Colombia was to blame for the revolt, not the United States. In February, 1904, Stewart joined other senators favoring acquisition of Santo Domingo as part of the Caribbean defense of the proposed Panama canal, adding that the United States should have taken Santo Domingo during the Grant regime.[127]

Stewart's position favoring a Panama canal was predictable in light of his past expansionist attitudes, his earlier support of an isthmian canal to open additional shipping for the Southern Pacific Company's ocean vessels, and his desire to follow Republican policies. However, his speeches during April and May, 1904, favoring the building of submarines to replace battleships for coastal defense, expressed unusually independent opinions. He suggested that battleships were engines of the past that would be superseded by submarines and other submersible devices. During these months, he sought unsuccessfully to have Congress raise the Navy's quota from three to ten submarines.[128]

Although he was involved in a myriad of congressional issues during 1903 and 1904, Stewart's main interest continued to be the game of politics, particularly the possibility of reelection in 1904. Actually, the first indication that he might be a candidate had come in August, 1902, when he wrote his former partner, William Herrin, "I may or may not want another term. All will depend upon my physical and mental condition at the time."[129] By the fall of 1903, Stewart felt physically and mentally equal to the task, and seriously considered announcing his candidacy. To test Nevada's political waters, Stewart's secretary, Charles Kappler, visited the state. He reported precisely what the senator wanted to hear, that Nevada would support Roosevelt for the presidency and that leading Republicans favored Stewart for the United States Senate.[130] Once publicized, however, the possibility of a Stewart candidacy brought a number of letters from Nevada; some favored the senator, but many more opposed him.

One of the strongest letters in opposition was sent to Kappler from a firm Stewart supporter, Charles A. Norcross, editor of the *Reno Evening Gazette*. Norcross indicated that there was great antagonism within the Republican Party to a Stewart reelection campaign. He suggested that if Stewart were serious about the race, the way to win was to pay each legislator $6,000 to support him, $1,000 when nominated, and another $5,000 after his election. Such a campaign, Norcross wrote, would cost $25,000 before the election, and it would be necessary to keep Stewart's name out of the campaign to avoid attacks against him.[131] In a later letter to Stewart, Norcross was even more pessimistic. He told the senator that the prejudice in Nevada against him could not be eradicated by election day: "Some day the people of this State will awaken to their senses and build a monument to you, but now they are not for you, and I only wish I felt confident of some way of causing them to change their minds. . . . I think every true friend you have in Nevada who is at all cognizant of the facts will plead with you to stay out of this fight."[132]

The most important attempt to keep Stewart out of the 1904 campaign came in February, in a long letter from a number of influential Nevada Republicans. The letter noted, "We believe it is the general consensus of opinion among the party leaders that it would be inadvisable for you to come into the fight this time." They pointed out that there were only two holdover Republican state senators and one had already declared against him. They warned Stewart that he couldn't win without Silver

Party support, which was unlikely to be forthcoming since he had left the Silver Party and declared the silver question to be dead. The writers emphasized that unity was necessary for the Republicans to win, but that harmony could not be achieved with Stewart.[133] Further indication of the anti-Stewart movement in Nevada in 1904 is shown in a letter from George Nixon to Francis G. Newlands in which he states emphatically, "Senator Stewart in no sense will be a factor in the fight (Senatorial) this fall."[134]

Not all the news from Nevada was bad. J. C. Hagerman, a Stewart stalwart from Virginia City, wrote the senator that despite opposition from some Republicans, he still represented the party strength in Nevada.[135] U.S. Attorney Sardis Summerfield encouraged Stewart to run, writing that he was worth more to Nevada than "any twenty men who could be sent to Washington."[136] Another endorsement came from Alfred Chartz, at one time one of Stewart's main enemies. He wrote Kappler that there wasn't any responsible opposition to the reelection of Senator Stewart, and that the attacks against him in a few newspapers were desultory, weak, and not new.[137]

Charles Norcross, however, from his vantage point as editor of the *Reno Evening Gazette,* continued to see only defeat for a Stewart campaign. He wrote Kappler that John Sparks would probably be the nominee of the Democrats and the Silver Party, and "Stewart cannot win against John Sparks." Norcross also noted that Nixon was making a "quiet canvass of Republicans and I am told that he has met with great encouragement." He suggested that Stewart send a letter to the nominating convention recounting his services and then announce that he would not be a candidate for reelection.[138]

By the spring of 1904, actions by Nevada Republicans were closing off Stewart's options. Most important was the return of George S. Nixon to the Republican Party. In his announcement, Nixon said he felt that he could best serve his state by joining the Republicans, since they, and particularly President Roosevelt, were strong supporters of irrigation legislation.[139] By emphasizing the irrigation issue and ignoring the silver question, Nixon was able to avoid much of the adverse publicity that had accompanied Senator Stewart's earlier switch to the Republicans. One embarrassing question did surface, when the Democratic *Nevada State Journal* asked how the strongly Republican *Carson News* could conduct its pledged anti-railroad campaign in view of the fact that Nixon was at the time the political agent of the Central Pacific Railroad.[140] No answer was forthcoming from the Nixon camp.

Nixon's return to the Republican Party was further evidence that the party's plans for the United States Senate did not include William Stewart. It appeared that officials of the Central Pacific Railroad were also involved in the scheme to dump Stewart. The *Nevada State Journal* reported that shortly after Nixon's announcement, he visited Washington, D.C., and New York to solicit support from railroad officials.[141] The newspaper concluded that Nixon would not have been thought of as a candidate except for his railroad connections.[142]

Nixon's move from the Silver Party and his attempt to acquire railroad support appeared to disrupt the political union of Nixon, Newlands, and Sharon. The latter, once again chairman of the Silver Party State Central Committee, publicly criticized Nixon, stating that he could see no reason why Nixon or any other "loyal silver man" should return to the party that killed the silver question. Sharon's remarks were obviously made in his official capacity, for he added, "I am determined that the State shall no longer be misrepresented by an old fraud and humbug like Stewart . . . any man . . . is better than old Stewart."[143] Newlands criticized Nixon's action because the latter tried to involve the Southern Pacific Railroad in his campaign. Newlands believed that any such move on the part of the railroad violated a promise made after the 1898 Nevada campaign, when William Herrin vowed that the Southern Pacific would stay out of Nevada politics. Newlands asked the chairman of the National Democratic Committee to use his good offices to convince Harriman and other leading Southern Pacific officials to keep the railroad out of Nevada politics.[144] Such criticism appeared to be dictated by the fact that Newlands as a Democrat could not publicly favor the Nixon switch to the Republicans.

Nixon's move to the Republicans in 1904, following Newlands's switch to the Democrats two years earlier, may have provided the pattern for Nevada's famous bipartisanship of later years. The Newlands-Nixon attempt to control the Nevada political scene dated at least from Nixon's abortive race against Senator Jones in 1897. These politicians certainly realized, as Wallace and Stewart had earlier, that the Silver Party could not continue to dominate Nevada politics in the face of the acceptance of the gold standard nationally. Thus they used the Silver Party adroitly to further their own political ends. And as the Silver Party began to disintegrate, each was able to move to prominence in the major national parties with a minimum of local criticism.

The potential Stewart candidacy did not fade quietly. As late as the first week in April, 1904, there were indications in Nevada that Stewart would run for the Senate. Some thought Nixon was a "stalking horse" for the senator.[145] But time and forces beyond his control were working against Stewart. When he suggested to the Republican leadership in Nevada that he be named a delegate to the Republican National Convention, the local party members saw an opportunity to force the senator to step down. In a telegram received the day prior to the meeting of the Nevada convention, Stewart read, "Only possible combination we can make to send you to National Convention is to agree to pass resolution at convention endorsing Nixon for Senator. If you approve of same will you authorize some one to announce that you will not be candidate for Senator."[146]

So, finally, it had come to this. His nearly fifty years of service to Nevada was to be brushed aside to satisfy someone else's political ambition, just as he had many times pushed others aside to satisfy his own. It was not the first time he had been pressured to leave the U.S. Senate and, ironically, the railroad had been in the background the other time also. Stewart could read the political winds as well as anyone, and he knew they were not blowing his way. He had been outflanked in New York with the railroad officials and in Nevada within the Republican Party. Yet, thirty years earlier, circumstances had been different. Then he had other things to look forward to, a new career in mining and law, and perhaps other political arenas. As Stewart approached his eightieth year, such prospects seemed very dim indeed. Still, he knew what he had to do. Although Stewart wanted to be senator much more than he wanted to be a delegate to the National Republican Convention, on April 12, he sent a telegram to the Republican State Convention at Virginia City, stating that he would not be a candidate for the U.S. Senate in 1904.[147] Stewart's friends in the convention were so angry at the manner in which the senator was treated that they refused to support Nixon, who then withheld his endorsement of Stewart as a delegate.[148] Thus, the senator was deprived of enjoying even the minor sop that had been offered in return for his agreement not to be a candidate.

The Democratic and Silver Party newspapers in Nevada did little more than acknowledge Stewart's withdrawal from the 1904 Senate race. Republican ones, however, treated him more kindly. An old friend, Charles A. Norcross, editor of the *Reno Evening Gazette,* noted that, had time permitted, "the convention would have paid some proper tribute to the aged statesman and political warrior who has for so long been the most powerful factor in Nevada politics." The writer went on to cite Stewart's many achievements, noting, "These are honors great indeed. They mark the calibre of no ordinary man, but on the contrary of one of the giants of our age. . . . In this state he fought his enemies to a standstill and gloried in the combat. The bark of the cur at his heels he treated with contempt. He battled only with the strong and never knew defeat."[149] The *Carson News,* in an editorial, also summarized Stewart's accomplishments and concluded:

> In personal characteristics he stood and stands unique. His vigorous constitution and aggressive mind defies the years and mocks the demands of time. . . . He would have made the world's greatest general had he seen fit to enter the military life. He absolutely refused to recognize the possibility of defeat—no matter what the odds against him, and opposition and enemies melted before the vigor of his campaigns. Senator Stewart stands today as at least one of America's most wonderful men.[150]

The game was over. All that was left was for the Republican State Convention to endorse Nixon for the U.S. Senate, as it did at Winnemucca on August 8, 1904. A few days later, the fusion conventions (Democrat and Silver) named Governor Sparks as their candidate.[151] For the first time in eighteen years, William Morris Stewart was not a candidate for the United States Senate from Nevada.

But Stewart's name simply would not stay out of the 1904 campaign picture. Rumors persisted that the senator was the real Republican candidate and would replace Nixon at the proper time. Charles Norcross labeled such notions lies and wrote that he knew, "absolutely and unequivocally," that Stewart was not a candidate for United States senator, "or for any other office." In a later edition of his newspaper, Norcross charged that such speculation about Stewart was the work of the Sharon press and that Stewart, one of the founders of the state of Nevada, did not deserve to be maligned.[152] Finally, the aged senator had to write his own denial, in words which left little room for rebuttal:

> The suggestion that I, who have been so often honored by the people of Nevada by election to the United States Senate, will run for that office in the name of another is too disgraceful to remain without an emphatic denial. I would be sorry if the people of Nevada could have so mean an opinion of me as to suppose that I would play on Mr. Nixon the game that was played on me six years ago. . . . When I notified the Republican Convention that I should not be a candidate for the United States Senate I meant exactly what I said.[153]

However, when the editor of the *Nevada State Journal* accepted the Stewart denial, he received a letter from a reader who called Stewart "a Sly Old Fox," who would jump in the race if he thought he had a chance of winning.[154]

The Real Republican Candidate
in the Foreground

Cartoon poster indicative of the fear that George Nixon, the Republican choice for U.S.
Senate in 1904, was a "stalking horse" and the real candidate, Stewart, would emerge
at the right moment. *(Nevada Historical Society Photo)*

Nixon was no "stalking-horse" for Stewart. When the election was over it appeared that he had beaten Sparks in a very close race. A few days after the balloting, a Reno newspaper credited Nixon with 29 legislative votes and Sparks with 27. On November 17, the *Nevada State Journal* conceded the defeat of Sparks, implying that he had been overcome by treachery within his own party, an oblique reference, no doubt, to Newlands.[155]

Under the system of election by the state legislature, winning a favorable slate at the November election did not guarantee selection by the lawmakers at their January meeting. About a month after the election it became apparent that another attempt might be made to bypass the voters' choice. Stewart was approached by Sam Davis and asked if he would be available for the Senate if the legislature could be deadlocked against Nixon. Davis hinted to Stewart that the suggestion had come from "some of the boys," who were planning to block Nixon and had asked him to find out where Stewart stood, if they could do so.[156] Nixon found out about the planned strategy and wrote to Stewart, no doubt to inform the senator that he knew what was going on:

> In reference to the possible hitch in my election, will say I don't think there is any danger as the legislature stands 31 Republicans and 25 Democrats, and while such men as Sam Davis may try to stir up a little opposition, I do not think it will amount to anything; at the same time I am keeping a close watch on the situation and will be ready to meet the enemy on common ground should it become necessary.[157]

A couple of weeks later, Davis became more specific, indicating that a number of Republican leaders had decided to shelve Nixon and thought Stewart was the only man who could fill the breech. He told Stewart, "You have but to remain an idle spectator of the row in your own party until they call on you to break the dead-lock and you have but to allow your name to be used at the last moment to have all of John Sparks strength turned over to you."[158] Stewart made no move, and George Nixon later wrote to thank Stewart for his help in obtaining the Senate seat and for his congratulations after Nixon's victory. Nixon stated in the letter that no opposition had developed in the legislature, and that the whole idea was simply "one of Sam Davis' dreams."[159]

While these machinations took place in Nevada, Stewart was in Washington, completing his senatorial duties. The habits of a life-time were not broken, and he proceeded in the third session of the Fifty-eighth Congress, his last, to attack issues with the same vigor he had shown in the past. A picturesque view of Stewart as he completed his last years in the Senate was drawn in a San Francisco paper by his contemporary and sometime opponent, Tom Fitch, who proclaimed:

Never was there a Berserker in all the realm of Odin who loved to fight for the fight's sake, for the joy of combat, better than United States Senator William M. Stewart. Glorious, incomparable, indomitable, undismayed, tireless "Old Bill." Though fortune forsake him, though death snatch from him his nearest, though the favored of Plutus intrigue for his toga, though the wand of age has changed his tawny hair and beard to silver, his steel blue eyes have not lost their glitter, nor his port its erectness, and he springs to the front in the tournament of Senatorial debate as vigorous and alert as when he engaged in the contest of the court-room forty years ago.[160]

In that last session no major issue drew Stewart's attention, but he accommodated his Nevada constituents as he had always done, and maintained better than average attendance and voting records. Again he supported statehood for New Mexico, Arizona, and Oklahoma, and again found that when he did so, some senator would chide him about his own state's entrance into the Union. During debate on the statehood issue, when a number of senators pointed out that Arizona and New Mexico territories should be combined as one state, just as Utah and Nevada should have been earlier, Stewart objected, conveniently forgetting that just such a solution was his goal when Utah Territory sought statehood in the 1880's. Instead he spoke strongly about the need to remove people from territorial status, for "territorial government is not satisfactory to a growing people and an ambitious people." Stewart advocated admitting the two territories separately, arguing that both had the necessary resources.[161] Stewart spoke against civil service reform, repeating earlier assertions that Congress would make better appointments to government positions than would the civil service system. And he continued his fight for better control of food and drink, not necessarily by imposing government standards, but by publishing analyses of edible items sent across state borders.[162]

Stewart's last speech in the United States Senate was delivered on March 2, 1905. He spoke in favor of an appropriation for geological surveys in mining regions, asking that $25,000 be added to the $175,000 requested by the Geological Survey. He noted, "I know something about the investigations which are being made and their importance and the importance of this appropriation to carry them out. I do not care about going into details, but I hope the chairman will allow the amendment to go on the bill. I think it is useful. I am not generally for extravagance in appropriation, but this is an important item."[163] It seems particularly fitting that Stewart's senatorial career began and ended with mining legislation.

CHAPTER 13

A DREAM THAT FAILED:
THE BULLFROG-RHYOLITE YEARS

SOMETIME before the end of his last Senate term, Stewart decided to move his new family to southern Nevada. The state was in the midst of a second great mining boom which, by 1905, rivaled the earlier Comstock Lode that catapulted Stewart into a substantial fortune and political prominence. The chance to make a new start must have seemed particularly attractive because Stewart's personal financial condition had deteriorated to the point that he was almost bankrupt.[1]

If Stewart had many financial obligations, he also had a few assets. The most important was the Ashburn Farm, which he had purchased some years earlier. Although the farm had not been profitable to Stewart, it is clear that it represented a major resource. The property consisted of nearly 2,500 acres of land, two good dwelling houses and other buildings which could be used by tenants, a fine bar, a shed for 200 head of cattle, and accommodations for 20 dairy cows. It was stocked with 16 heavy work mares, about 60 cows and heifers, and about 200 steers.[2] Stewart wanted $80,000 for it, with personal items to be sold separately.[3]

Stewart had not found a buyer for the Ashburn property when he moved to Nevada in 1905, but his finances had improved somewhat by that time. The sale of his Washington home, at 1800 F Street, enabled him to clear his current debts and put some money in the bank for the move to Nevada.[4] He received additional money in May, 1904, from an auction of the remaining mahogany and teakwood furniture that the first Mrs. Stewart had purchased during her travels. His daughters protested the sale, but Stewart reminded them that he had allowed them to choose what they wanted on two occasions and would not do so again.[5]

Stewart did not appear to be particularly worried about his future in Nevada. Although approaching eighty years of age, his faith in his own ability never wavered. He faced this new challenge, as he had done so many times in the past, with optimism and a firm conviction that he could take advantage of the new boom as he had the earlier one on the Comstock.

The senator had visited the new discoveries during political trips in 1902 and 1904, and had marked the town of Tonopah as his first choice for law offices and a home. In January, 1905, he was given an annual pass over the Tonopah Railroad by John W. Brock, president of that line, and the next month he negotiated for the purchase of a house in Tonopah.[6] However, his attempts to locate there were not successful, probably because of the strong, active bar there, so he decided to tour the entire southern Nevada area before making a commitment.[7] Thousands of people had swarmed into southern Nevada by the time Stewart was exploring the region in the spring of 1905. Three new mining districts—Tonopah, Goldfield, and Bullfrog—were booming; two railroads had been completed into the area and two others were projected. The future of Nevada again seemed secure.

To view the whole region before choosing a location, Stewart had a wagon specially built for desert travel. Purchased in Salt Lake City, Utah, it was covered with canvas and had a thirty-five-gallon water tank in the interior. Stewart was accompanied by one of his secretaries, James D. Finch, and a mining expert.[8] Ultimately, he decided to locate in the newest of the three major areas, the Bullfrog Mining District.

Located by Ernest Cross and Frank "Shorty" Harris, in August, 1904, Bullfrog was the most isolated of the new boom camps, 80 miles south of the railroad connection at Goldfield, and over 100 miles north of the new town of Las Vegas. At the time, the decision to locate at Bullfrog seemed wise. Most of the good mining property at Tonopah and Goldfield had been taken, and both towns had numerous young, capable, ambitious lawyers. The Bullfrog District, on the other hand, was just opening when Stewart and his entourage arrived in April, 1905. Unfortunately, Bullfrog never lived up to the expectations of its promoters. It produced less than $2,000,000 through 1910, when it became obvious to just about everyone that the Bullfrog excitement was over.

But between 1905, when he arrived, and 1908, when he left, the district boomed, and Stewart tried to take advantage of the situation. He organized a law firm of Stewart, Martinson and Finch. George Martinson was a graduate of Stanford Law School. James D. Finch, a young attorney and former Stewart secretary, was first associated with the senator in the publication of the *Silver Knight-Watchman* when he was only seventeen years of age. With Stewart's encouragement, Finch had received his law degree from the National Law School in Washington, the last in the line of young lawyers helped through law school by Stewart.[9] Finch soon left the firm, evidently at the instigation of Stewart, who suggested that he would be better off in Washington.[10] It was not a happy parting. Finch later wrote Stewart that on returning to Washington he had taken a job as secretary to Senator Newlands, but decided after a few days not to remain "with your bitter opponent. . . . Although I think you treated me a little shabby, Senator, in leaving me to browse on the desert and find my way home the best I could, yet I certainly hope for your financial, political and physical success."[11]

Stewart's presence in the Bullfrog district at first occasioned a great deal of interest. The local newspapers made the most of the situation, since not every boom town could boast a distinguished-looking former U.S. senator as a permanent resident. He was called upon to be the principal speaker on July 4 at Rhyolite, the leading town of the district, and according to the paper was given a rousing reception by the crowd. The article noted that his "silvery locks and flowing gray whiskers are the only evidence of the Senator's Age."[12] The following month, the newspaper reported extensively on the home and office that Stewart was completing in Bullfrog, on a large plot of ground at the corner where the main street of Bullfrog intersected the main street of Rhyolite. Writers noted that Stewart had invested about $20,000 in the buildings and improvements, and that the residence property occupied a town block. The modern, one-story house had ten rooms, "all plastered and finished in fine woods." Included in the house were a number of modern items—a tub, showerbaths, toilet, hot and cold water, a cooking range, and other improvements. In addition to the home there was a chicken coop with 200 or more birds, and a stable housing the "best pair of mules between Tonopah and Las Vegas." The reporter added that Stewart wanted to add a "fine cow."

Stewart's office was located near the house and was itself a rather substantial building, containing four rooms, one of which housed the senator's 1,200-volume law library.[13] Stewart's home and office were described by a visitor in October, 1908:

> The architecture, both of the law office and the dwelling-house, was adapted to the desert—long, low buildings surrounded on all sides by wide porches. His love of the beautiful was in evidence here. Plastered concrete was selected for the material, probably because of its coolness in summer, but to relieve the color he had ornamentation, plaster of an old-rose color on the corners. The interior was decorated in a manner very

Former Senator Stewart's home in Rhyolite, Nevada. Not as opulent as those he had built in Nevada City and in Washington, D.C.; it was an unusual building for that boom town. (*Nevada Historical Society Photo*) unusual for the rough mining camps. In the large yard surrounding the building, he planted trees, roses, and other shrubs.[14]

Although not as pretentious as some of his previous homes, the Bullfrog dwelling was, like the others, somewhat of a showcase because of its location in the middle of the southern Nevada desert.

The house and furnishings no doubt were attempts by Stewart to make living in Nevada more acceptable to his second wife and her daughter, Vera. One can only guess at the cultural shock that they must have felt as they moved from the nation's capital to a small, isolated, desert mining camp. A few months after moving into the new home, Stewart wrote, "We are comfortably housed in Bullfrog, a mining camp now supposed to be beyond the limits of civilization; but when several contemplated railroads reach us we expect to be the center of the United States as least."[15] A short time later, Stewart closed his autobiography with a glowing account of the Bullfrog district and his new life there. He indicated that his wife had adapted well to the area and "makes my home more delightful than it would be in any other part of the world." He was particularly pleased with the climate and noted that "the cool breezes at night make it a comfortable place to sleep in the hottest weather." Stewart wrote that he was engaged in the profession of law, "and acquiring interests in mines and assisting in their development. The fascinating business of mining is a perennial source of hope. It inspires both mental and physical vigor, and promotes health and contentment."[16]

Stewart's efforts to establish a law practice, however, floundered from the beginning. By the end of 1905, his partnership with Martinson had dissolved, partly because the firm was unable to establish a branch office in Tonopah.[17] In the early part of 1906, Stewart arranged access to the Tonopah area through William Forman, later prominent in Reno legal circles.[18] Stewart suggested that Forman take care of his own office expenses in return for the use of Stewart's name in advertising, and indicated that he would interest himself only as desired by clients, and that when he was employed with Forman, fees would be divided equally.[19] Stewart's legal cases in Tonopah were of a minor nature, and his overall lack of legal activity demonstrated the difficulty of operating a law office isolated by distance and poor transportation from the county seat. He made two efforts to correct that situation, in 1906 and 1907.

The first attempt involved a scheme to create a new county in southern Nevada, with the town of Rhyolite as county seat. Stewart's interest in such a move predated his decision to locate there. In an exchange of

Stewart's main law office in Rhyolite, Nevada. He also had offices at Tonopah and Goldfield. (*Nevada Historical Society Photo*)

letters with George Nixon in December, 1904, the senator indicated support for a move to redraw the boundaries of Nye and Esmeralda counties in order to form a new county from the southern parts of both.[20] After a year of frustration while trying to establish a legal practice, Stewart revived his interest in county division in the spring of 1906, outlining his plans to Frank Mannix, publisher of the *Bullfrog Miner*.[21]

Stewart's idea received enthusiastic support when he presented it to the Rhyolite Board of Trade, on November 19, 1906. The latter had been waging a continuing, but unsuccessful attempt to have the Nye County Commissioners establish a town government for Rhyolite under the Town Board Act of 1881. The members of the Board of Trade supported Stewart's plan as an alternate way to assure local government for their community. They agreed to draft a memorial petition to the next legislature, seeking the proposed county division. The plan included the establishment of two new counties in southern Nevada, one would be carved from Nye County and named Bullfrog, with its county seat at Rhyolite, the other would be taken from Lincoln County, with Las Vegas as its county seat. In addition to the formation of the new counties, the boundaries of Esmeralda, Eureka, Lander, and White Pine counties would be adjusted. The proposal, including a detailed map of the changes, appeared in the *Rhyolite Herald* for December 14, 1906.[22]

The plan's chance of success was enhanced when one of the members of the Rhyolite Board of Trade, L. O. Ray, was elected to the state assembly from Nye County. However, the county division plan encountered immediate opposition from representatives of Lincoln, Nye, and Esmeralda counties. Ray reported to his constituents that the plan as outlined by Stewart was too complex and had no chance of succeeding.[23] Although the question of establishing new counties continued until the 1909 legislature created the new Clark County from Lincoln, Stewart took no part in the county division question after his own plan failed in 1907.

That disappointment, and a serious illness in the early months of 1907, brought a sad admission in April of that year that his legal inactivity was due to his distance from a county seat.[24] After recovering from his illness, Stewart made a last effort to establish a law practice in a county seat. His opportunity came in February, 1907, when the state legislature passed a measure locating the county seat of Esmeralda County at Goldfield, effective May 1 of that year. Stewart began attempts to locate at Goldfield in April, and formed a partnership with James K. Reddington of that city in late summer. It was reported that henceforth he would divide his time between his Goldfield and Rhyolite law offices.

However, Stewart's name was no longer magic and it was soon apparent that Goldfield offered little hope for the development of a lucrative law practice for Stewart.[25] As a result, he shifted his emphasis to mining development and promotion.

Stewart's interest in mining was sparked within a few months of his settlement in southern Nevada. By the end of 1906, he was president of the Gold Crest Mining Company of Rhyolite, the Diamond-Bullfrog Mining Company, and the Diamond Bullfrog Extension Company, and was interested in many other mines, including the Hazel Mines Company, the Shoshone Bullfrog Gold Mining Company, and the Gold Summit Mining Company.[26] Of all these mining promotions, the Diamond-Bullfrog was the most important. Stewart held some 300,000 shares, but the majority of the stock was owned by investors in Pittsburgh, Pennsylvania.[27] Although seriously involved in promoting the mine, Stewart maintained a certain distance in a letter to a prospective client, "I am residing at Bullfrog, Nevada, practicing my profession, not dealing in stocks. . . . I have no stock of my own for sale, but the Company has Treasury stock set apart for the development of the mine."[28]

Letters to Stewart from a number of shareholders indicate that the Diamond-Bullfrog Company was in stock difficulty from the beginning. Stewart was accused by one investor of using proxies to set up a "dummy" corporation and disregarding the expressed wishes of the Pittsburgh stockholders.[29] Another wrote that his family had lost $25,000 on the company and, in his opinion, "it was a fine stock jobbing proposition."[30] Stewart admitted that the company was in trouble, owing the bank over $8,000, and indicated a willingness to sell 250,000 shares of his stock at twenty-five cents per share.[31]

None of Stewart's southern Nevada mining properties were productive. Some, if not all, were paper developments, and were no more successful as mining promotions than they were in producing ore. Yet Stewart remained optimistic, as evidenced from a chance meeting with George Springmeyer, a young attorney at Goldfield. The former senator was resting at a stage stop near that town, traveling, as he often did, by mule. Springmeyer was asked if he would like to meet the legendary Stewart, and during the visit, as Springmeyer later recalled, Stewart talked not about politics or his senatorial career, but about mining, about the fortunes he had lost and those that could still be made. He assured the young man that as soon as he finished resting he would "get on my mule and ride out and make another fortune."[32] Unfortunately that did not happen. It is clear that Stewart spent more on these pro-

Former Senator Stewart on muleback, his favorite mode of travel in the desert and the way he and his family reached Nevada from California during the Comstock rush. The caption on the picture indicates that it was the last photo of Stewart. *(Nevada Historical Society Photo)*

motions than he made, and was probably assisted in financing these schemes by the sale of Ashburn Farm, which was completed in January, 1907.[33]

Neither law nor mining took much of Stewart's time or energy during these years and he was soon involved in a number of local matters. He was appointed a trustee of the public schools for the Bullfrog-Rhyolite School District in the fall of 1905, and acted as chairman of a Republican rally at Rhyolite in the fall of 1906.[34] Stewart was also frequently called upon to speak before local groups. Most of these talks were really lectures by Stewart on his role in mining legislation on the national level. At other times he related his experiences in mining, from his Comstock days to the present, generally repeating the story of how he had prevented thievery from Panamint by casting the silver bullion into huge balls of 700 pounds each.[35]

Stewart also found time to establish a private school for his eleven-year-old stepdaughter, Vera, and several other girls her age. This school, taught by Mrs. Helen B. Hawley of Connecticut, opened early in October, 1906. Stewart paid $25 for his stepdaughter, evidently the amount charged each student. The schoolroom was one of the rooms in his office building, for which he received $15 per month in rent.[36] The school lasted less than two years.

Although far removed from the national political arena, Stewart continued to be interested in certain national issues, particularly the question of railroad reform. Although such concern was seemingly at odds with the role he had played during much of his political career, he was really concerned not so much about railroad reform as about the Progressive movement. Once more accommodating himself to the prevailing winds, he joined the Republican bandwagon of Theodore Roosevelt. The first evidence of his new mood came in 1905, as he was finishing his autobiography. At that time he wrote, ''While I commend the foresight, energy, and courage of such builders as C. P. Huntington and his associates, I realize that the railroads are subverting the Government and destroying the freedom and independence of the people.'' He indicated that government ownership of the railroads was preferable to control by private corporations, since ''irresponsible corporations are blind to the wrongs of the masses, and treat with contempt the reasonable complaints of the people.''[37]

Stewart congratulated Senator Robert M. LaFollette on his Senate speech against railroad usurpation of government, which Stewart agreed would bring an unscrupulous group of schemers, stimulated by greed and wealth, to replace ''the government of the fathers.''[38] In another letter, to President Roosevelt, Stewart again expressed his newfound antagonism to railroads and trusts: "If the people can be made to see before it is too late that they must grapple directly with railroads and trusts or lose their liberty, free institutions may be rescued from impending danger." He congratulated the President for exposing the railroads, and hoped he would also expose the elevator trusts, "which the railroads have created to rob the farmers."[39] In spite of his statements against the railroads, Stewart was not averse to accepting annual passes from the Southern Pacific in 1906, for himself and his family.[40]

Only occasionally while at Bullfrog did Stewart correspond with friends of another era. On one such occasion, acknowledging a Christmas gift from his former secretary, Isaac Frohman, he tellingly wrote: "You can hardly appreciate the gratification it gives me to have at least one of the young men who I have tried to benefit, remain my fast friend. . . . Mrs. Stewart and Vera are with me here. We are keeping house and are very comfortable in our new home."[41] Frohman seems to have been the only one of Stewart's protégés to keep in touch with him, writing again after the San Francisco earthquake and fire to describe that disaster.[42]

Most of Stewart's correspondence during this period had a distinct domestic flavor. In an attempt to beautify his home at Bullfrog, he ordered eucalyptus trees and rosebushes from a California nursery, and wrote to the Secretary of Agriculture to inquire about the best grass seed for the desert.[43] In another letter he reported that four mules "is too many," and asked his correspondent to look for a horse for him.[44] Later, in the fall of 1906, Stewart gave an old friend in Virginia City a rare glimpse of his personal life in Bullfrog, "We had a delicious water melon out of the garden yesterday, and there are still three small ones left. . . . Today is very windy — Oh, if these horrid winds would only pass us by, there wouldn't be anything to wish for — but money, and of course we are all going to get that."[45]

The unaccustomed luxury of free time, which was ample in a mining district in decline, gave Stewart the opportunity to complete a project he had first explored in 1895, when he sought someone to write his biography. His first choice at that time was James A. Lynch. After some prodding, Lynch provided Stewart with an outline, but Stewart thought it unsatisfactory and broke off further negotiations.[46] The project then lay dormant until his retirement from the Senate in 1905, when he revived the idea in a different format. Stewart now decided to dictate his memoirs and then employ someone to revise the rough draft and put the material in readable form. His first choice was an old friend, Nannie

Lancaster. When she refused to consider the job, he employed George Rothwell Brown to rewrite the rough draft in such a manner "as to popularize it and make it readable."[47] Stewart spent many hours in dictation at his Bullfrog offices, as described by Roy Hardy, at the time a young mining engineer in the Bullfrog district:

> I met him in Rhyolite when he had a little office there. . . . I had a cabin near his. In his little stone office building in Rhyolite he used to write his memoirs. With that foghorn voice, I could hear him write a sentence and repeat it to himself. That was his autobiography, and if you haven't read it you should. He was a dynamic person. He took charge when he was around; everybody knew he was there.[48]

By the time his autobiography was ready to be published, in 1908, the Stewarts were preparing to leave the Bullfrog area to return to Washington, D.C. The dream of gaining another fortune from the new mining boom had long since evaporated, for neither law nor mining brought the success Stewart had envisioned. The rapid decline of the district after 1907, his own failing health, and his wife's obvious desire to return east all played a part in the decision. The *San Francisco Call* noted in its issue of May 18, 1908, that Stewart would "leave the desert forever," and blamed the decline of the Bullfrog and Rhyolite stocks for the decision.[49] A Nevada newspaper noted that "Senator Stewart was down again," and that although he had been a millionaire several times, he was unable to repeat the process in the Bullfrog district.[50]

Before Stewart's ties to Nevada were completely broken, he made arrangements with Dr. Jeanne E. Wier, founder and executive secretary of the Nevada Historical Society, to donate his extensive library of books and manuscripts to the Society. For both of them, it was one of the most important actions in long and busy careers. In her diary of August 16, 1908, Wier recorded her delight in the collection: "The greatest event of the morning was the inspection of Senator Stewart's office and deserted home. If the Society can acquire the papers and manuscripts left here by him, this treasure will alone repay me for the hardships of this summer trip to the South."[51] Evidently successful in her quest, she arrived back in Rhyolite two months later, on October 18. The next day, she recorded in her diary, "Saw Stewart custodian and got permission to pack books. Spent the remainder of the day in Sen. Stewart's office. What a treasure we have obtained here! I can scarcely believe it is really ours."[52] Thus through the generosity of Senator Stewart and the tireless efforts of one of Nevada's most important historians, the papers were saved for the use of future generations.

Little is known about Stewart's activities after leaving Nevada in the spring of 1908, but one of the last official actions of the senator's long career occurred when he appeared before the House Committee on Mines and Mining in the spring of 1909. His testimony was largely a reminiscence of early mining in California and Nevada.[53] Shortly thereafter, on March 20, he entered Georgetown Hospital in Washington, where doctors performed a prostate operation on March 31. Stewart failed to recover from the operation and died at 7:05 A.M. on April 23, 1909.[54]

Nevada's Acting Governor Denver Dickerson proclaimed that flags in the state were to fly at half staff until after the funeral, which was variously reported to be planned for Carson City, Washington, D.C., or San Francisco. Newspapers in Nevada and elsewhere noted Stewart's passing, usually in laudatory tones. Most of the obituaries credited him with writing the National Mining Law of 1866, composing the Fifteenth Amendment, and waging a strong fight to remonetize silver. Some emphasized the role he had played in Nevada statehood, and one writer placed him on "the stage of public life" as "one of the strongest and best known characters in our country's history during the last half-century."[55] A few covered his career in detail, using as their main source Stewart's *Reminiscences*. He was described extravagantly in one obituary as a large man, six feet, four inches in height, who wore a wide-brimmed soft hat and with his white hair and beard, "was the living incarnation of Santa Claus and on this account as well as on account of his kindly disposition, he appealed strongly to the imagination of the children." A more perceptive note came from the same paper the following day, when the editor wrote, "He lacked the saving grace of humor to have made him a tremendous figure in public affairs through a greater role he could have had upon those with whom he came in contact. . . . He was respected and feared more than loved."[56]

Stewart had outlived most of his contemporaries, and his death drew little attention from prominent politicians at the time. Newlands, as might have been expected, said little. However, Senator Nixon did introduce a joint resolution proposing the erection of a statue in honor of Stewart in the nation's capital. The resolution was sent to the Committee on Library and there remained.[57] There was no other formal notice of Stewart's death taken in the Senate where he had served so long and faithfully those interests he thought were important.

Stewart's remains were cremated and the ashes placed in an urn to be buried next to his first wife in Laurel Hill Cemetery in San Francisco. When that graveyard was destroyed in 1940, by order of city officials, the Stewarts and many others were reburied in the Laurel Hill Mound of Cypress Lawn Cemetery, in San Mateo County, California. Stewart's remains were marked by stone number 351.[58]

Although Stewart left a will, drawn by his friend Isaac Frohman, there was little of a material nature to distribute. The document named Mrs. Stewart as the executrix, and made no provision for any of his children or grandchildren, since he had distributed his first wife's estate among them. Even had they been named, they would have received nothing from Stewart's estate, for the senator left debts totaling $25,000 and insufficient assets to cover them. His widow received a few shares of Chevy Chase stock and several hundred shares of worthless Nevada mining stocks.[59] Evidently, he left no real estate except his Bullfrog home and office, which he had been unable to sell before leaving that area. His earlier homes had been sold or given away, and the various plots of land acquired from the Central Pacific Railroad had been disposed of long before his death, to help pay constant debts.

Stewart's dream of gold, so vivid as he set out for the Mother Lode in 1850, ended in failure, like that of thousands of others. Yet few of those who shared with him the quest left a legacy of so many solid achievements.

By 1920 Rhyolite had a population of 14, a sizable drop from the estimated boom figure of 8,000. The Stewart home there could not be sold, and a few years of neglect and vandalism in the desert environment brought the results shown in this picture. *(Nevada Historical Society Photo)*

CHAPTER 14

POSTSCRIPT

WILLIAM MORRIS STEWART was a dominating figure in Nevada history for more than half of a century. From the time he settled on the Comstock in 1860 until his death, his story was the story of Nevada. He was a doer, an action-oriented, legend-making product of the nineteenth-century western mining frontier. A resourceful, opportunistic, ambitious, aggressive, and sometimes ruthless politician and lawyer, Stewart's methods often led him to extremes of behavior which encouraged others to portray him in pure black or white. Was Stewart the genius lauded by George Rothwell Brown when he wrote, "Some of the greatest men the Republic has produced were his play-fellows in the Senate, play-fellows in a great game with Destiny, and when he coped with them he found himself the peer of all, the superior of many"?[1] Or was he, on the other hand, the unprincipled lawyer who "bribed and browbeat witnesses, threatened and physically attacked juries and judges"?[2] Was he a hero,[3] or one of a "Damn set of villains"?[4] Was he the "best friend any man ever had," deserving all "the good things we constantly hear of him," as his loyal secretary Kappler wrote,[5] or was he a "vile man—perfectly unreliable, everywhere—with no feeling of loyalty in his heart," as Mrs. John North insisted?[6] Stewart was all of these things and more to different people, for he was a complex individual whose long life spanned a variety of careers and brought him into contact with a variety of people.

If there was a genius in Stewart's makeup, it was associated with his role as politician. He loved the game and science of politics, and except for the twelve-year interim, from 1875 to 1887, most of his adult life was spent in some kind of political activity. Stewart's career from 1861 to 1905, mirrored the political history of Nevada; no other figure was as important as he to that history during those years. That was the aspect of his life that he enjoyed most. It is generally conceded, by contemporaries and writers since his death, that Stewart was an exceptional politician.[7] The description of Stewart by Sam Davis, a political contemporary who was sometimes a friend and often an enemy, was probably closest to reality:

> Of the big politicians who fought in the arena for the honors of the game Stewart was regarded as the best all round campaigner of the lot. He was a man of tireless energy and resourceful brain and knew every trick and turn in the art of political warfare. Once embarked in a fight it was to the finish and to win. His physical energy was that of a Roman gladiator, and when on the wing week after week with frequently not more than two hours sleep a night, he seemed as fresh as a lark at the end of the fight. His store of reserve vitality seemed practically inexhaustible and his staying qualities the wonder of all observers. With Stewart in a fight it was a case of "Night on the Numidian desert and all the lions up."[8]

As a politician, Stewart readily accepted the dictum that politics was the art of compromise. He knew when to fight and when to concede, and, except for the last years in the Senate, he made very few mistakes of judgment. He seemed to know instinctively what his opponents were planning, probably because he paid particular attention to what his own moves would have been were he on the other side. He seemed to have had built-in antennas which signaled the changes in the political winds. The advantages he gained from being one of the first to follow each new trend outweighed the concomitant charge that he was a political chameleon with no basic principles. His frequent party changes—from Whig, to Know-Nothing, to Democrat, to Republican, to Silver Party and Populist, and back to Republican—brought him high political office and years of recognition as one of the most powerful figures in Nevada politics. His one major miscalculation came when he left the Silver Party too quickly, and rejoined the gold-standard Republicans in 1900. In so doing, he lost any chance he might have had for reelection to the U.S. Senate in 1904.

Without sufficient money of his own, Stewart early understood and accepted the necessity of making whatever financial arrangements were necessary to insure his election. As C. C. Goodwin noted at the time of Stewart's death, a financial "host was always ready to back him." The first such hosts were the powerful mining companies of the Comstock, particularly the "Bank Crowd," who, with the Central Pacific officials, were his primary supporters during his early years in Nevada politics. After 1885, Stewart's role in Nevada cannot be separated from his close association with Collis P. Huntington, head of the Central and Southern Pacific companies, and Charles C. Wallace, the political agent for those interests in Nevada. Stewart and Wallace, with financial support from Huntington and a few other sources, such as the Bank Crowd and John Mackay, worked as an unbeatable team from 1886 to 1900. The 1898 election was the beginning of the end for the two campaigners, for although they won the immediate battle, they lost the war when the Newlands forces gained control of the Silver-Democrats in 1900. The death of Wallace in 1901 was simply tangible evidence that the Stewart-Wallace era in Nevada politics was over.

There were two high points of achievement in Stewart's long political career. The first came in the period from 1860 through 1864, and involved his activities in the first session of the Nevada Territorial Legislature and the Constitutional Convention of 1863. No one can read the contemporary accounts of these meetings and fail to be impressed by Stewart's positive achievements in each. In one instance he aided the transition to a stable territorial government, and in the other, he played a central role in the transition from territory to state.

A second high point came during the first ten years of his senatorial career, when he authored the 1866 mining law and composed the final draft of the resolution which became the Fifteenth Amendment. In both instances, his ability to compromise and his practical knowledge of politics helped to bring the issues to successful conclusions. Not so well known, since it was unsuccessful, was the moderate reconstruction program he offered. This program was considered by many contemporaries and a few modern scholars, to have been a statesmanlike approach to post-Civil War problems. Had it been adopted, there is little doubt that Stewart's name would have taken on added national significance.

Unfortunately, a short time after he returned to the Senate in 1887, Stewart became involved in the hopeless contest to remonetize silver, and his talents and energy were spent almost exclusively on that issue. Although he gained no tangible legislative achievements from these activities, he did receive national recognition as one of the great silver leaders of the day and was called upon many times to make speeches on behalf of the white metal. His reputation in this respect extended to the point of possible nomination for the presidency as a silver candidate, and the mention, more than once, that he should receive a cabinet appointment in case a silver candidate was elected.

Although Stewart's legislative achievements after his return to the Senate, in 1887, cannot be equated with those during his first term, his stature as a political figure, both nationally and in Nevada, was perhaps even greater during his later senatorial career. Before he became a prisoner of the silver question, Stewart was responsible for introducing the subject of irrigation in the 1887 Congress. Although he received no credit for the legislation which was passed, it was Stewart who achieved the establishment of a subcommittee on irrigation in the Senate and who took that subcommittee on a tour of the arid west, bringing a great deal of publicity to the issue of reclamation. It was Stewart, also, who acted as the friend and tutor of Francis G. Newlands on that subject, and by encouraging the latter to become a permanent resident of Nevada, introduced a new force into Nevada politics. These achievements, plus his role as a leading figure in the fight to remonetize silver, qualify Stewart as one of the major architects of Nevada's political life in the late 1880's and the decade of the 1890's.

Stewart loved the United States Senate and took his senatorial commitment seriously. He performed his committee work conscientiously and was well aware of the need to work hard on routine as well as important assignments, remarking once to a friend that he found it "a great advantage to do the work because it places so many Senators and members under obligation to me."[9] He enjoyed debate and was a remarkable antagonist when engaged in a contest on the Senate floor. His education and experience had trained him as an advocate and he became that for every political issue he adopted. His energy and determination to win dictated that he throw himself completely into each new cause. And "tireless Old Bill," as one of his contemporaries noted, was still enjoying Senate debate, "as vigorous and alert as when he engaged in the contests of the court-room forty years ago."[10]

Although Stewart often seemed to be the tool of mining or railroad interests, or both, he did make a conscientious effort to take care of other constituents—state and county officials, newspaper editors, and just about anyone else who wrote him asking for a political favor. Long before the direct election of senators, Stewart was acutely aware of the necessity of keeping the proper profile before the people. In light of his actions favoring capitalists, his letters to some of his other constituents appear rather hypocritical. To one supporter, who had sent him $100 for doing a favor, Stewart replied self-righteously in returning the money, "I am surprised that you should send the money to me and regret that you supposed I would accept it. I have always done all I possibly could in your behalf and shall continue to do so."[11] To a friend in Carson City, who had informed Stewart of the discovery of oil in Nevada and hinted at possible investment, he noted that if the find was on an Indian reservation he could not be personally interested, for, "I have made it a rule under no circumstances to have any personal interest in any measure or question that can possibly come before Congress or any of the Departments. There is so much personal legislation here that it is a menace to the country." He went on to write that he was disgusted "with the corruption of the times. It is an outrage for a man by his own vote to double his fortune by doubling the value of the bonds he holds."[12]

In legislative achievement, Stewart stands high above Nevada's other U.S. senators before 1900, and truly deserves the designation as "the ablest of the Comstock Senators."[13] In itself, of course, that does not place Stewart in the higher echelons of ability among all United States senators, since those from Nevada were a mixed lot, to say the least.[14] The record indicates, however, that despite strong criticism,[15] Stewart was a better than average senator during his twenty-eight years of service. Stewart might rank today as a great national statesman had not indiscretions such as the Emma Mine scandal and his alliance with the railroad interests obscured his many notable achievements.

Stewart's first love, of course, was the law, and it was the unique circumstances on the Comstock which made possible the flowering of a legal career that had its origins in the California gold fields. Stewart saw the opportunities in a place where there were few legal precedents or laws governing the opening, operation, and disposal of mines, and he proceeded to take advantage of each situation. Through a combination of ability, aggressiveness, ruthlessness, and luck, he soon became the Comstock's most successful lawyer, although never recognized as its best legal mind.

Stewart's preeminence among Comstock lawyers was readily acknowledged by his contemporaries. One called him "dynamic, majestic, ruthless, cunning, resourceful. . . .There were many against him and many for him, but on the whole I think Stewart led the legal procession."[16] Others agreed, admiring his success while recognizing both his shortcomings as a lawyer and the manner in which he overcame these by his aggressive tactics. Thus his old friend, C. C. Goodwin, noted that Stewart was often faced by better lawyers, "who ripped his arguments," but his appeals to juries and judges usually won the day. In writing about Stewart's legal and political careers, Goodwin stated, "He was one of the most extraordinary men who ever lifted his head above the level in California and Nevada; one of the most forceful personalities in the nation."[17] That forcefulness was described less flatteringly by another author, who compared Stewart to a "tornado," gesturing violently and speaking in loud and often angry tones: "His manner was anything but gentle, his expression anything but studied, his counte-

nance anything but inviting. He never appealed. He always demanded.
. . . Success greatly gratified, defeat deeply disturbed him.''[18] Another
contemporary thought that Stewart's great success as a Comstock lawyer
was due to his determination to win at any cost and his supreme confidence in his own ability to match his adversary with any weapons that
might be employed against him. A client's case became a personal challenge to Stewart to overcome his opposition by whatever means possible.[19] His methods often brought strong criticism, with terms such as
scoundrel and villain. He was accused of bribing witnesses and threatening juries and judges in order to bring his cases to successful conclusions. Stewart's own autobiography has been cited as proof of many of
these charges.[20]

From the standpoint of ethics, Stewart's legal career reached its
lowest points in his feud with John North during the early years of the
Comstock Lode, and in his involvement in the 1870's in the Emma Mine
scandal. His greatest achievement as a lawyer came when he acted as
senior U.S. counsel in the Pious Fund case, before The Hague Tribunal.
Although he continued to practice law until the time of his death, his
legal career in Nevada was essentially over when he left the Comstock
in 1864. He was involved in a few Nevada cases from time to time after
that date, particularly during his twelve-year absence from the U.S.
Senate. However, his most important legal work during that period
concerned California cases. Stewart's involvement in a number of water
right cases in Kern County, California, is regarded generally as of high
quality, and it was Stewart who showed how the Sharon-Hill case could
be taken out of the California courts, which had held against Sharon,
into the federal courts, which ruled in favor of the Sharon estate. In final
analysis, however, Stewart did as much for the practice and acceptance
of mining law through his legislative and political efforts in county,
state, and national arenas as he did through his activities as a lawyer.

Some of Stewart's least praiseworthy moments came in the promotion of mining stock. Mining finance held for him a fascination that
started in his early career in the camps in California and followed him to
the closing years of his life in the Bullfrog Mining District of Nevada.
It climaxed, of course, with his involvement in the Emma Mine affair.
He wrote once, in opposing a lottery for the state of Nevada, that he had
never gambled in his life, yet that is exactly what he did with his own
and other people's money when he became involved in such promotions
as the Emma Mine, the Panamints, Mexican silver mines, and a number
of worthless properties in the Bullfrog area. The record shows that in
many of these instances, Stewart's activities included unethical and
dishonest behavior unbecoming a leader of his political stature.

If his actions concerning mining promotions were not particularly admirable, the same certainly cannot be said about his long and consistent efforts on behalf of education. The difficulties he experienced in obtaining his own education may have been the source of his interest; but whatever the cause, Senator Stewart sought throughout his career to strengthen the educational system, both on the national level and in the state of Nevada. His first attempt to support education nationally came during his first term in the Senate, when he introduced a bill to grant 1,000,000 acres of land for the benefit of a federal mining college to be located in Nevada. This bill died in committee,[21] but his failure did not dampen his enthusiasm for a national university. The next time he tried along somewhat different lines. In 1888, he introduced a bill to establish a national university to educate teachers, remarking as he did so that the teaching profession was more important to national defense than "the shedding of blood."[22] He continued to support the idea of a national normal university for the next few years, both in and out of Congress, but without success. Although his attempts to get congressional approval for either a national mining school or a national normal school failed, Stewart did succeed in obtaining approval for an Indian school near Carson City, Nevada. He also played a major role in the passage of the so-called Second Morrill Act, in 1890.[23]

On the state level, Stewart's strongest efforts on behalf of education centered on the University of Nevada. Besides the Second Morrill Act, Stewart was instrumental in obtaining a reserve officers training program for the school and in seeing that the university obtained books, maps, documents, publications, and miscellaneous items distributed by the federal government. He consistently prodded state legislators to provide additional funds for the university, noting in one letter, "It seems to me that more good can be accomplished by providing for the University than any other expenditure of money."[24]

Stewart's interest in education extended directly to members of his own family. His daughters were educated in private schools in the United States and Europe, and he provided funds to educate his grandchildren in private schools, and for his eldest grandson to complete his education at Yale University. Stewart's concern for education was also evidenced by his appointment to head a committee on the condition of the public schools of the District of Columbia. The report of the committee was well received and apparently in some demand.[25] Recognition for his interest in higher education also came to Stewart when he was appointed one of the original trustees of Stanford University, a post he held until 1905.[26]

Above all else, in his various careers Stewart was a practical individual who took life as it was, fought it on its own terms, enjoyed much, and regretted little. In 1903, in writing to a classmate from his days at Yale, Stewart noted that his life had been a busy one but that he had never "indulged myself in a vacation. I never have been able to accomplish all I aimed at."[27] He seemed to sum up his basic philosophy in a letter to Senator Nye's daughter, when he wrote, "My family have all grown up, I am now looking after grandchildren. I can hardly realize the great change in a time which seems so short to me. But it is a part of life — we come and go. If we did not go there would be no room for others to come. All we can do is to make the best of it, do what good we can, and enjoy all we can of life."[28]

NOTES

Chapter 1

1. There is some question as to Stewart's year of birth. In his memoirs he gives the year as 1825. See William Morris Stewart, *Reminiscences of Senator William M. Stewart of Nevada,* ed. George Rothwell Brown (New York: The Neale Publishing Company, 1908). Ruth Hermann, in her biography of Stewart, also chooses the year 1825, after an excellent review of available sources. See Ruth Hermann, *Gold and Silver Colossus: William Morris Stewart and His Southern Bride* (Sparks, Nevada: Dave's Printing and Publishing, 1975), pp. 1–2. However, in the William Morris Stewart Papers, located at the Nevada Historical Society, Reno, Nevada, there are a number of citations indicating that the year of his birth was 1827. See particularly the biographical sketch of Stewart in Box 11, Vol. 4 (May 10 to Nov. 4, 1893), and a letter from Stewart to L. C. Taft, Feb. 3, 1896. The *Congressional Directory* also lists the year of birth as 1827, as does Effie Mona Mack, "William Morris Stewart, 1827–1909," *Nevada Historical Society Quarterly,* 7 (1964), 11. The confusion continued in Stewart's obituaries, some choosing the year 1825, others the year 1827.

2. Lionel D. Wyld, *Low Bridge: Folklore and the Erie Canal* (Syracuse, New York: The Syracuse University Press, 1962), pp. 10–12.

3. Stewart, *Reminiscences,* p. 29.

4. *Ibid.,* p. 30.

5. The Academy at West Farmington, Ohio, had been founded in 1828. In 1854, the name was changed to the Western Reserve Seminary and it became the property of the Methodist Episcopal Church. Stewart later wrote to a friend that he considered "the time spent in Farmington as not only the most profitable but the most delightful days of my life." Stewart to Ezekiel F. Curtis, Jan. 31, 1891, Stewart Papers.

6. Stewart, *Reminiscences,* p. 36.

7. Mack, "Stewart," 12.

8. Stewart, *Reminiscences,* pp. 43–44.

9. *Ibid.,* p. 48.

10. *Ibid.,* pp. 48–55.

11. Dale L. Morgan, ed., *In Pursuit of the Golden Dream* (Stoughton, Massachusetts: Western Hemisphere, 1970). In the introduction to this work, Morgan cites a number of diaries of persons who followed the Panama route.

12. Hermann, *Gold and Silver Colossus,* p. 24, cites this arrival date as taken from a Stewart family history to which she had access.

13. Stewart *Reminiscences,* pp. 55–57; Mack, "Stewart," 14–15.

14. Rodman W. Paul, *Mining Frontiers of the Far West, 1848–1880* (New York: Holt, Rinehart and Winston, 1963), p. 16. Paul notes that California's mining population had skyrocketed from an estimated 5,000 persons at the end of 1848, to 50,000 at the close of the year 1850.

15. Stewart, *Reminiscences*, pp. 72–75. See also Mack, "Stewart," 15–16, and Harry L. Wells, comp., *History of Nevada County, California* (Oakland, California: Thompson and West, 1880), p. 171.

16. Stewart, *Reminiscences*, p. 76.

17. Mack, "Stewart," 18, 92–93.

18. Winfield J. Davis, *History of Political Conventions in California, 1849–1892* (Sacramento, California: State Library, 1893), p. 16.

19. *Ibid.*, pp. 19–20.

20. Stewart, *Reminiscences*, p. 89.

21. Oscar T. Shuck, ed., *Representative and Leading Men of the Pacific* (San Francisco: Bacon and Company, 1870), pp. 634–645.

22. *Ibid.*, p. 634; Stewart, *Reminiscences*, p. 76; Oscar T. Shuck, ed., *History of the Bench and Bar of California* (Los Angeles: Commercial Printing House, 1901), pp. 505–507.

23. Stewart, *Reminiscences*, p. 89. It is obvious from these activities that Stewart's pro-Southern sympathies predated his marriage to Annie Foote.

24. *Ibid.*; Wells, *History of Nevada County*, p. 148.

25. W. B. Lardner and M. J. Brook, *History of Placer and Nevada Counties, California, With Biographical Sketches* (Los Angeles: Historic Record Company, 1924), p. 348. Lardner, although giving details of the meeting, does not mention that Stewart was chairman. The latter fact comes from Stewart's *Reminiscences*, p. 127. See also Paul, *Mining Frontiers of the Far West*, p. 172.

26. Rodman W. Paul, *California Gold: The Beginning of Mining in the Far West* (Cambridge: Harvard University Press, 1947), pp. 213–214. Stephen J. Field is credited with being the author of the 1851 California statute. See also, Chauncey F. Black and Samuel B. Smith, eds., *Some Account of the Work of Stephen J. Field*...(N. p.: S. B. Smith, 1882), pp. 3–8.

27. Paul, *Mining Frontiers of the Far West*, pp. 172–173.

28. Wells, *History of Nevada County*, pp. 138–139; Lardner, *History of Placer and Nevada Counties*, p. 400. Stewart claimed that his appointment by Governor Bigler was in return for a favor he had done earlier for Bigler. See his *Reminiscences*, p. 117.

29. *Sacramento Daily Union*, Nov. 3, 1854, p. 2, col. 1; Nov. 13, 1854, p. 2, col. 1.

30. Stewart, *Reminiscences*, p. 103; Mack, "Stewart," 20; Hermann, *Gold and Silver Colossus*, p. 67.

31. Peyton Hurt, "Rise and Fall of the 'Know Nothings' in California," *California Historical Society Quarterly*, 9 (March and June, 1930), 9.

32. *Ibid.*, 43.

33. *Ibid.*, 37–43; Davis, *History of Political Conventions*, p. 44; William G. Copren, "The Political History of Sierra County, California, 1849–1861, Local Elections and Non-Local Issues" (Unpublished M.A. Thesis, University of Nevada, Reno, 1975), p. 138.

34. The house in Nevada City is still standing. It was purchased and restored by Mr. and Mrs. Victor Hermann in the 1960's. See Mack, "Stewart," 20–21. Mrs. Hermann is the author of the Stewart biography previously cited.

35. Stewart, *Reminiscences*, pp. 107–108; Hermann, *Gold and Silver Colossus*, pp. 99–100.

36. Copren, "Political History of Sierra County," pp. 138, 156; Hermann, *Gold and Silver Colossus*, p. 99.

37. Copren, "Political History of Sierra County," p. 156; Hermann, *Gold and Silver Colossus*, p. 126.

38. Copren, "Political History of Sierra County," pp. 188, 200. Copren has a detailed and well-researched summary of Stewart's activities in Sierra County. The term Chivalry Democrat was commonly used to designate Democrats with pro-Southern sympathies. It should be noted that Stewart's pro-Southern leanings, first evidenced in the early 1850's in Nevada City, had been strengthened by his marriage to Annie Foote.

39. *Ibid.,* pp. 225–228.

40. Shuck, *Representative and Leading Men of the Pacific,* pp. 634–645; Wells, *History of Nevada County,* pp. 94–104.

41. Copren, "Political History of Sierra County," pp. 152–153; Russell R. Elliott, *History of Nevada* (Lincoln: University of Nebraska Press, 1973), p. 60.

42. The biographies of Stewart by Ruth Hermann and Effie Mona Mack have a great deal of detail about his family life. This is particularly true of the biography by Hermann, which has material on the Stewarts not available elsewhere in print.

43. Stewart, *Reminiscences,* p. 123; Mack, "Stewart," 23.

44. Mack, "Stewart," 23; Elliott, *History of Nevada,* p. 64.

45. Paul, *Mining Frontiers of the Far West,* p. 63.

46. Stewart indicated that he made his first trip to the Comstock in the fall of 1859, then returned to Downieville with the idea of another trip eastward in the spring of 1860. See his *Reminiscences,* p. 123. This autobiography is also the basis for an earlier and rather remarkable mule-back trip over the Sierra Nevada, early in November, 1850 (p. 69). According to Stewart, while he was prospecting along the north fork of the American River he moved eastward over the Sierra Nevada "and down the eastern slope to Lake Tahoe, a magnificent body of mountain water, at that time, so far as I know, without a name." Stewart noted that he circled the lake to the Truckee River and followed the stream to where Reno is now located. He then retraced his way out of the valley "and followed Donner's trail, which was then known as the Truckee route. When I came to where the Donner party perished I found the log cabins which they had constructed a year and a half previous still in a state of remarkable preservation. . . . I passed over the Truckee route and went down the ridge between Bear River and South Yuba."

47. *Territorial Enterprise* (Carson City, Utah Territory), Dec. 17, 1859, p. 1.

48. Elliott, *History of Nevada,* pp. 59–60.

49. Copren, "Political History of Sierra County," p. 250; Stewart, *Reminiscences,* p. 123; Mack, "Stewart," 29.

50. Elliott, *History of Nevada,* pp. 92–93.

51. Stewart, *Reminiscences,* p. 125. Stewart noted his contribution of $1,000.00, p. 24.

52. Mack, "Stewart," 25.

53. J. Ross Browne, *A Peep at Washoe, and, Washoe Revisited* (Balboa Island, California: Paisano Press, 1959), pp. 64–66.

54. Elliott, *History of Nevada,* pp. 49–68.

55. Mack, "Stewart," 23. The Reese building at Genoa was built by John Reese in the summer of 1851, and is considered to have been the first permanent building erected in the area that later became part of the state of Nevada.

56. Mack, "Stewart," 27; Hermann, *Gold and Silver Colossus,* pp. 171–172. See also, J. Wells Kelly, comp., *First Directory of Nevada Territory* (Los Gatos, California: Talisman Press, 1962), p. 163.

57. Eliot Lord, *Comstock Mining and Miners,* a reprint of 1883 edition (Berkeley: Howell-North, 1959), pp. 131–181.

58. *Ibid.,* p. 97.

59. *Ibid.,* p. 101.

60. *Ibid.,* pp. 102–103.

61. Nevada Secretary of State, *Political History of Nevada, 1973* (Carson City, Nevada: State Printing Office, 1973), p. 59. The appointment of Judge Flenniken was approved December 18, 1860. Robert Flenniken was born in western Pennsylvania in March, 1802, and admitted to practice law in that state in October, 1831. He supported Buchanan for political office of one sort or another from the 1840's. See Phillip G. Auchampaugh, "The Early Career of Robert P. Flenniken, Diplomat and Western Judge," *The Historian,* 10 (Autumn, 1947), 27–43.

62. Lord, *Comstock Mining and Miners,* pp. 104–105.

63. *Sacramento Union,* January 17, 1861, p. 2, col. 5.

64. *Ibid.,* February 21, 1861, p. 2, col. 4.

65. *Ibid.,* March 6, 1861, p. 1, col. 7.

66. Richard Carey Sieber, "Nevada Politics During the Comstock Era" (Unpublished M.A. Thesis, University of Nevada, Reno, 1950), pp. 31–33; Lord, *Comstock Mining and Miners,* pp. 105–109. Stewart, in his *Reminiscences,* pp. 135–139, claimed that he forced Flenniken's resignation at gunpoint, a questionable assertion, to say the least. Flenniken received a salary for the position through March, 1861, and was reported in the Comstock area as late as June, 1861.

67. Myron Angel, ed., *History of Nevada,* reprint of 1881 edition (Berkeley: Howell-North, 1958), p. 73.

68. *Ibid.*

69. Stewart, *Reminiscences,* pp. 141–145.

Chapter 2

1. Stewart is supposed to have received between $100,000 and $200,000 annually in legal fees. In his autobiography he stated that he received $500,000 in fees in four years, *Reminiscences,* p. 151. Mack, in her biography, "Stewart," 28, indicates that he received $165,000 from the Belcher and $50,000 from the Yellow Jacket mines, in single fees. Lord, *Comstock Mining and Miners,* p. 146, sets Stewart's annual income at $200,000.

2. Elliott, *History of Nevada,* p. 68.

3. *Ibid.*

4. *Political History of Nevada, 1973,* pp. 65–68; Elliott, *History of Nevada,* pp. 69–70.

5. Elliott, *History of Nevada,* pp. 70–71; Eleanore Bushnell, *The Nevada Constitution: Origin and Growth,* 4th ed. (Reno, Nevada: University of Nevada Press, 1977), pp. 46–47.

6. Andrew J. Marsh, *Letters from Nevada Territory, 1861–1862,* William C. Miller, Russell W. McDonald, and Ann Rollins, eds. (Carson City, Nevada: Legislative Counsel Bureau, State of Nevada, 1972), pp. 15, 229.

7. *Ibid.,* p. 229.

8. Stewart, *Reminiscences,* pp. 140–141.

9. *Political History of Nevada, 1973,* pp. 60, 69.

10. Lord, *Comstock Mining and Miners,* p. 132.

11. *Ibid.,* pp. 24–32, 133. The Grosh brothers, Ethan Allen and Hosea B., generally are credited with being the first people in Gold Canyon to prospect intelligently for a ledge. They did discover an ore-bearing ledge near the present Silver City in 1857, but both met tragic deaths that year. Persistent rumors credited them with a major discovery, but no survey records were ever found. Lord is positive that "they developed no ledge" (p. 133). The Grosche Company tried to take advantage of the situation by contesting the claims to the Comstock Lode.

12. Charles C. Goodwin, *As I Remember Them*...(Salt Lake City: n.p., 1913), pp. 140–145. For a more detailed biographical sketch of Goodwin, see Angel, *History of Nevada,* p. 321.

13. *Ibid.*

14. Lord, *Comstock Mining and Miners,* p. 146. Lord, a graduate of Harvard University, was working with the U.S. Geological Survey while preparing his work on the Comstock. He lived in Virginia City for a time and interviewed Stewart on a number of occasions. Obviously, he considered Stewart an exceptional person.

15. Merlin Stonehouse, *John Wesley North and the Reform Frontier* (Minneapolis: University of Minnesota Press, 1965), pp. 169–170. Stonehouse uses Stewart's autobiography very effectively to condemn Stewart's actions.

16. Lord, *Comstock Mining and Miners,* pp. 151–173.

17. *Ibid.,* pp. 151–154.

18. *Ibid.,* p. 155; Hubert Howe Bancroft, *History of Nevada, Colorado, and Wyoming, 1540–1888, History of the Pacific States of North America,* Vol. 25 (San Francisco: The History Co., 1890), p. 173; Effie Mona Mack, *Nevada: A History of the State From the Earliest Times Through the Civil War* (Glendale, California: Arthur H. Clark, 1936), p. 415, n. 792.

19. *Gold Hill Daily News,* July 26, 1864, p. 2; *Virginia Daily Union,* July 26, 1864, p. 2, col. 2. The *Union* repeats a story taken from the *Territorial Enterprise.*

20. Stonehouse, *John Wesley North, passim;* See also the North Papers at the Huntington Library, San Marino, California.

21. John Wesley North to Ann L. North, July 18, 1861, North Papers.

22. Ann L. North to George and Mary Loomis, Aug. 31, 1862. Mrs. North indicated that the partnership of her husband and Lewis earned $1500 in fees in a period of six or seven weeks.

23. John W. North to George Loomis, November 2, 1862.

24. Stonehouse, *John Wesley North,* pp. 150–156.

25. Ann L. North to George S. and Mary Loomis, September 13, 1863. According to Mrs. North, her husband received a telegram September 12, from Washington, D.C., informing him that his commission for the judgeship had been sent August 25. The commission was dated August 20. North assumed the duties of office on Monday, September 14, 1864. See also Nevada Territory, *Territorial Supreme Court Transcripts,* #44, p. 1., located in the Nevada State Archives, Carson City, Nevada.

26. John W. North to George S. Loomis, April 20, 1863, May 24, 1863, North Papers.

27. Elliott, *History of Nevada,* p. 77.

28. Bushnell, *Nevada Constitution,* p. 48.

29. Andrew J. Marsh *et al., Reports of the 1863 Constitutional Convention of the Territory of Nevada...,* William C. Miller and Eleanore Bushnell, eds. (Carson City, Nevada: Legislative Counsel Bureau, State of Nevada, 1972), pp. 9–10; *Washoe Times,* Nov. 7, 1863, p. 1.

30. Marsh *et al., Reports of the 1863 Constitutional Convention, passim.*

31. *Ibid.,* pp. 225–228, 241–252, 265–281.

32. *Ibid.,* p. 299. Newspapers on the Comstock followed the tax debate closely. See particularly the *Virginia Evening Bulletin* of Nov. 24, 1863, Dec. 1, 1863, Dec. 2, 1863, Dec. 3, 1863, and the *Gold Hill Daily News* of Nov. 30, 1863, and Dec. 2, 1863.

33. Marsh *et al., Reports of the 1863 Constitutional Convention,* p. 81.

34. *Ibid.,* pp. 95, 98, 99–100, 318–319.

35. *Ibid.,* pp. 333–334, 345, 347.

36. Stonehouse, *John Wesley North,* p. 156.

37. Marsh *et al., Reports of the 1863 Constitutional Convention,* pp. 56, 60, 116–118, 184–187.

38. *Ibid.,* pp. 48–53.

39. *Ibid.,* pp. 44–47.

40. *Ibid.*

41. *Ibid.,* pp. 154–155, 159, 160, 175, 218–221.

42. *Ibid.,* p. 169.

43. *Ibid.,* pp. 363, 394–395.

44. *Ibid.,* p. 394; *Gold Hill Daily News,* Dec. 10, 1863, p. 2. The paper noted that Stewart and former California Governor J. Neely Johnson declared positively they would not be candidates for any office whatever.

45. Marsh *et al., Reports of the 1863 Constitutional Convention,* pp. 413–414.

46. *Ibid.,* p. 394.

47. *Virginia Evening Bulletin,* Dec. 12, 1863, p. 2. The *Sacramento Daily Union,* which had taken a keen interest in the convention's proceedings, published the full text of the constitution, indicating that in general it was superior to that of California, December 14, 1863, p. 2.

48. David A. Johnson, "A Case of Mistaken Identity: William M. Stewart and the Rejection of Nevada's First Constitution," *Nevada Historical Society Quarterly,* 22 (Fall, 1979), 186–198. In this excellent article, Johnson sets the record straight on Stewart's position in the ratification contest. Listing every published account of the first statehood campaign in Nevada, the author leaves no doubt of the widespread misinterpretation of Stewart's role by historians and others.

49. *Ibid.,* p. 191; Angel, *History of Nevada,* p. 85, lists the papers in the territory which opposed the constitution. The *Virginia Daily Union,* which was an early supporter of the constitution,

turned against the document after the Union Party conventions chose the Stewart ticket over the *Daily Union* ticket led by Thomas Fitch.

50. A petition bearing over two hundred signatures of miners, mine superintendents, and independent mine owners was circulated on the Comstock Lode during the ratification fight, opposing the constitution because of the taxation article. See the *Virginia Evening Bulletin,* Dec. 14, 1863, p. 2, col. 3, Dec. 16, 1863, p. 2, col. 1, and p. 2, col. 5. The editor of the *Bulletin* wasn't much impressed with the number signing the petition, noting that anyone on the Comstock could get that many signatures on anything.

51. Ann North to George and Mary Loomis, November 25, 1863; John W. North to George Loomis, Nov. 29, 1863, North Papers. North boasted to his father-in-law that he was "at present on top of the wave politically... Many have told me I could have anything I wanted."

52. Lord, *Comstock Mining and Miners,* pp. 139–140, 174.

53. *Virginia Daily Union,* Jan. 24, 1864, p. 3, cols. 3–4. The card was originally published in the *Territorial Enterprise* on December 22, 1863, but that issue is unavailable. The card was also copied verbatim in a typescript by Mary North Shepard, North's daughter, titled, "A Maligned Judge," to be found in the North Papers.

54. *Gold Hill Daily News,* Dec. 28, 1863, p. 2, col. 3; Dec. 29, 1863, p. 2, col. 2. See also Johnson, "A Case of Mistaken Identity," 193.

55. *Gold Hill Daily News,* Dec. 29, 1863, p. 2, col. 2; Dec. 30, 1863, p. 2, col. 2.

56. Lord, *Comstock Mining and Miners,* p. 144.

57. *Virginia Daily Union,* Jan. 1, 1864, p. 3, cols. 3–4; *Gold Hill Daily News,* Jan. 2, 1864, p. 2, col. 3.

58. *Virginia Daily Union,* Jan. 3, 1864, p. 2, col. 5.

59. Johnson, "A Case of Mistaken Identity," 193.

60. *Gold Hill Daily News,* Jan. 14, 1864, p. 2, col. 3.

61. *Virginia Daily Union,* Jan. 3, 1864, p. 2, col. 1.

62. *Virginia Daily Union,* Jan. 6, 1864, p. 2, col. 3; Jan. 9, 1864, p. 2, col. 6.

63. *Ibid.,* Jan. 10, 1864, p. 2, col. 3.

64. *Ibid.,* Jan. 11, 1864, p. 1, col. 6.

65. *Virginia Evening Bulletin,* Jan. 12, 1864, p. 2, col. 2.

66. *Virginia Daily Union,* Jan. 15, 1864, p. 2, col. 2.

67. John W. North to George S. Loomis, Feb. 7, 1864, North Papers; *Gold Hill Daily News,* Jan. 16, 1864, p. 2, col. 3; Stonehouse, *John Wesley North,* pp. 165–168.

68. *Virginia Daily Union,* Jan. 17, 1864, p. 2, col. 2; *Gold Hill Daily News,* Jan. 18, 1864, p. 3, col. 1; Lord, *Comstock Mining and Miners,* p. 161.

69. *Virginia Evening Bulletin,* Jan. 18, 1864, p. 3, cols. 2–5. Although the other Comstock papers noted the debate, the *Bulletin* reported it in detail.

70. John W. North to George Loomis, Feb. 7, 1864, North Papers.

71. Bushnell, *Nevada Constitution,* p. 50. The preference vote for statehood in September, 1863, showed 6,660 votes in favor of statehood and 1,502 against.

72. John W. North to George Loomis, Feb. 7, 1864, North Papers.

73. Angel, *History of Nevada,* p. 85, cites the taxation clause as the key to the defeat of the 1863 document. During the debates at the second constitutional convention in July, 1864, William Wetherill of Esmeralda County noted that "no Constitution will be adopted by the people of this Territory with a clause in it making it imperative upon the Legislature to tax the mines....That was the very point upon which was based the condemnation of the old Constitution, in Esmeralda County, last fall." Andrew Marsh, *Official Report of the Debates and Proceedings in the Constitutional Convention of the State of Nevada...* (San Francisco: F. Eastman, 1866), pp. 325, 411. In reporting to Washington, D.C., Governor Nye listed the taxation clause as one of three reasons for defeat of the constitution. Bushnell, *Nevada Constitution,* p. 50. Generally, modern scholars have continued to emphasize the mining taxation provision as a major reason for defeat of the 1863 constitution. See Mack, *History of Nevada,* p. 252; Gilman Ostrander, *Nevada, the Great Rotten Borough, 1859–1864* (New York: Alfred A. Knopf, 1966), pp. 38–39; James Hulse, *The Nevada*

Adventure, 3rd ed. (Reno: University of Nevada Press, 1972), p. 103; Elliott, *History of Nevada,* pp. 82–83; Bushnell, *Nevada Constitution,* p. 48.

74. *Virginia Evening Bulletin,* Jan. 20, 1864, p. 2, col. 2. In reporting the defeat of the constitution, the editor wrote: "We say we regret this fact—regret it the more when we consider the causes that led to its defeat, for there is no disguising the fact that the sole cause of the defeat of the Constitution was the nominations for officers to have been elected on its adoption." The editor of the *Gold Hill Daily News,* Jan. 22, 1864, p. 2, col. 1, took a similar approach when he wrote, "The soreheaded political clique who failed to connect in the Nominating Conventions succeeded in raising an outcry against the Constitution sufficient to defeat it." Both Angel, *History of Nevada,* p. 84, and Bancroft, *Nevada . . . ,* pp. 178–179, cite the dual election procedure as a major reason for the defeat of the constitution. In the 1864 constitutional debates, delegate John A. Collins from Storey County, insisted that once the people had decided to defeat the constitution they used every pretext to bring about this end. He noted that there would not have been much opposition to the constitution except "for certain political transaction—and I refer especially to the efforts made to introduce a certain set of delegates into the State Convention." Marsh, *Debates 1864,* pp. 325, 411. Nye wrote that either the taxation clause or the strong suffrage provisions would have been enough to defeat the constitution, "but it was submitted at the same time that the election for State officers was held, and the dissatisfaction with some of the State ticket, and the proceedings of some of the county conventions caused its opponents to act in concert, and all combined they were strong enough to defeat it." Bushnell, *Nevada Constitution,* p. 50.

75. Bushnell, *Nevada Constitution,* p. 50. Governor Nye indicated that the suffrage provisions contributed to the defeat of the document since it "arrayed all the disloyal or secession element against it." The editor of the *Gold Hill Daily News,* Jan. 26, 1864, p. 2, col. 1, wrote that the Copperheads were responsible for the defeat of the constitution.

76. *Virginia Daily Union,* Jan. 20, 1864, p. 2, col. 2.

77. Johnson, "A Case of Mistaken Identity," p. 191.

78. *Gold Hill Daily News,* Jan. 20, 1864, p. 2, col. 2.

79. *Ibid.,* Jan. 21, 1864, p. 2, col. 2.

Chapter 3

1. *Virginia Daily Union,* Jan. 17, 1864, p. 1, col. 7.

2. *Laws of the Territory of Nevada,* 3rd Session, Jan. 12–Feb. 20, 1864, p. 46.

3. John W. North to George S. Loomis, Feb. 7, 1864, North Papers.

4. Lord, *Comstock Mining and Miners,* pp. 155–158; Gary Don Libecap, "The Evolution of Private Mineral Rights: Nevada's Comstock Lode" (Unpublished Ph.D. Dissertation, University of Pennsylvania, 1976), pp. 82–83.

5. *Transcripts, Territorial Supreme Court,* Nevada State Archives, Carson City, Nevada. Transcript 66 is the *Chollar* v. *Potosi* case and 67 is the *Potosi* v. *Chollar* case.

6. John W. North to Ann L. North, April 6, 1864, North Papers.

7. *Opinions of the Supreme Court, Nevada Territory,* Nevada State Archives, Carson City, Nevada, May 5, 1864.

8. *Ibid.; Territorial Supreme Court Appeals,* 66 and 67, May, 1864; Lord, *Comstock Mining and Miners,* pp. 156–160.

9. Lord, *Comstock Mining and Miners,* p. 160.

10. *Political History of Nevada, 1973,* pp. 81–83.

11. David A. Johnson, "Industry and the Individual on the Far Western Frontier: A Case Study of Politics and Social Change in Early Nevada," *Pacific Historical Review,* 51 (August, 1982), 243–263. This excellent article demonstrates clearly the importance of the economic depression on the Comstock in the summer of 1864 in bringing a favorable vote on ratification of the 1864 constitution. See also Elliott, *History of Nevada,* p. 86.

12. *Gold Hill Daily News,* July 19, 1864, p. 1.

13. *Ibid.* See issues for July 21, 22, 25, 26 and 28.

14. *Virginia Daily Union,* July 23, 1864, p. 2, col. 1.

15. *Ibid.,* p. 2, col. 6. See also issue for July 24, 1864, p. 2, col. 1.

16. *Virginia Daily Union,* July 26, 1864, p. 2, col. 2; *Gold Hill Daily News,* July 26, 1864, p. 2. Both of these papers quoted extensively from the article published by the *Enterprise,* July 24, 1864.

17. *Virginia Daily Union,* July 27, 1864, p. 2, col. 1.

18. *Abraham Lincoln Papers,* Series 1:1864, #34785, Reel 78, July 26, 1864. The telegram was sent from Virginia City on July 23, and received in Washington, D.C., on July 26.

19. *Gold Hill Daily News,* Aug. 2, 1864, p. 2, col. 2; Lord, *Comstock Mining and Miners,* pp. 161–162. Lord bases his story about the Tilford speech on the Aug. 2, 1864, issue of the *Territorial Enterprise.*

20. *Gold Hill Daily News,* Aug. 11, 1864, p. 2; *Virginia Daily Union,* Aug. 11, 1864, p. 2, col. 1.

21. *Virginia Daily Union,* Aug. 11, 1864, p. 2, col. 2.

22. Ann North to George and Mary Loomis, August 4, 1864, North Papers.

23. *Washoe Star* (Washoe City, Nevada Territory), Aug. 27, 1864, p. 2; *Virginia Daily Union,* Aug. 25, 1864, p. 2, col. 1; Mary Shepard, "A Maligned Judge..." p. 13, North Papers.

24. *Virginia Daily Union,* Aug. 25, 1864, p. 2, col. 1.

25. *Abraham Lincoln Papers,* Series 1:1864, #35720, Reel 80, Aug. 30, 1864. The telegram was sent from Carson City, Aug. 22, and arrived Aug. 26.

26. Mary Shepard, "A Maligned Judge..." p. 8, North Papers; *Virginia Daily Union,* Aug. 25, 1864, p. 2, col. 1.

27. Smith, *History of the Comstock Lode,* p. 74; Lord, *Comstock Mining and Miners,* pp. 165–171.

28. Johnson, "Industry and the Individual on the Far Western Frontier," 243–264.

29. Stewart, *Reminiscences,* p. 160. The same story is repeated by Stonehouse, *John W. North,* p. 170.

30. Stewart, *Reminiscences,* p. 161. Stewart indicated in his memoirs that he had evidence of Justice Turner's acceptance of a bribe in the Hale and Norcross suit. He made no public effort to repeat the fact at that time.

31. *Ibid.,* pp. 160–161.

32. *Washoe Weekly Star* (Washoe City, Nevada Territory), Aug. 27, 1864, p. 2, col. 1.

33. *Virginia Daily Union,* Aug. 24, 1864, p. 2, col. 1.

34. Bancroft, *History of Nevada...,* p. 175.

35. Angel, *History of Nevada,* p. 335.

36. Bancroft, *History of Nevada...,* p. 175.

37. Angel, *History of Nevada,* pp. 335–336; *Gold Hill Daily News,* Aug. 26, 1864, p. 2; *Washoe Weekly Star,* Aug. 27, 1864, p. 2, col. 1.

38. Stewart, *Reminiscences,* p. 162.

39. *Washoe Weekly Star,* Aug. 27, 1864, p. 2, col. 1.

40. John Franklin Swift, *Robert Greathouse: A Story of the Nevada Silver Mines* (New York: Carleton, 1878), pp. 153–164.

41. Stewart, *Reminiscences,* p. 163.

42. John W. North to Ann L. North, Dec. 7, 1864, North Papers; Angel, *History of Nevada,* p. 335.

43. That position was cited from time to time in the press during the ratification contest. Romanzo Adams in his work, *Taxation in Nevada, A History,* Nevada Applied Series, Vol. 1 (Reno, Nevada: Nevada Historical Society, 1918) pp. 22–23, accepts the idea that the depression in mining in 1864 "was due in considerable measure to the large amount of litigation and to the delay in such litigation on account of the congestion of the court dockets."

44. Johnson, "A Case of Mistaken Identity," 198. Johnson indicates that the economic depression was the fundamental cause in bringing ratification of the constitution.

45. Libecap, "The Evolution of Private Mineral Rights," p. 113.

46. *Nevada Reports* (1868), Vol. III, p. 17. The statement came from Robert M. Clarke, Nevada's second attorney general, May 13, 1867.

47. John W. North to Ann North, Oct. 9, 1864, North Papers.

48. *Ibid.*, Oct. 20, 1864.

49. *Ibid.*, Oct. 22, 1864.

50. Stewart, *Reminiscences,* pp. 165–166.

51. *Virginia Daily Union,* Dec. 10, 1864, p. 2.

52. John W. North to Ann L. North, Dec. 11, 1864, North Papers.

53. Nevada State Legislature, *Journal of the Assembly,* 1st Session (1864-65), pp. 33–40; Angel, *History of Nevada,* p. 88.

54. John W. North to Ann North, Dec. 17, 1864, North Papers.

55. *Ibid.*, Dec. 7, 1864.

56. Stonehouse, *John W. North,* pp. 174–177.

57. John W. North to Ann L. North, Oct. 28, 1864, North Papers.

58. *Gold Hill Daily News,* Aug. 1, 1865, p. 2. In a later issue, Aug. 25, 1864, p. 2, the newspaper advised North "to keep his head shut and his signature out of the newspapers . . . a war with the newspapers . . . will prove but a losing game. We have dropped the hatchet—he had better follow suit."

59. John W. North to Ann L. North, Aug. 24, 1865, North Papers.

60. *Gold Hill Daily News,* Aug. 28, 1865, p. 2.

61. The decision of the referees appears in the *Washoe Times* of Sept. 21, 1865, a copy of which is in the North Papers as #80. There is also a true copy of the proceedings of the referees' award of Sept. 16, 1865, signed by Tod Robinson, William H. Rhodes, and George F. Jones, dated March 20, 1940, and attested to by E. H. Beemer, Washoe County Clerk. The two cases, one against Stewart and the other against the owners of the *Territorial Enterprise,* are on file in the Clerk's Office, Washoe County Court House, Reno, Nevada, as cases #211 and #212, respectively.

62. *Ibid.* The extenuating circumstances listed were: the secrecy about Mott's resignation, Judge North's loans, and the interest of North's confidential friends in the litigation pending in his court.

63. See particularly, Grant Smith, "The Mackay Story," Vol. 1a, pp. 245–246, Grant Smith Papers, Bancroft Library; and Lord, *Comstock Mining and Miners,* pp. 163–164.

64. It wasn't until 1965, with the publication of Merlin Stonehouse's biography, that North's part in the feud with Stewart was properly evaluated. Previous to that, North's daughter, Mary Shepard, had attempted without success to have various Nevada historians and officials right the "wrong" which had been done to her father. These attempts were recorded by Shepard in "A Maligned Judge," a typescript copy of which is located in the North Papers at the Huntington Library.

65. Stewart, *Reminiscences,* p. 166.

Chapter 4

1. *Congressional Globe,* 38th Cong., 2d Sess., Part 1 (1865), pp. 553–554; Jeanne E. Wier, "In Memoriam. William Morris Stewart," *Nevada Historical Society, Biennial Report,* Vol. 2, 1909–1910, p. 46. In this obituary, Wier gives another interpretation of how Stewart gained the four-year term, implying that Nye accepted the two-year term after "a certain house in Carson City, now the home of Justice G. F. Talbot was transferred to Senator Nye in the course of the transaction." There seems to be no justification for this story, since Stewart sold the house to Nye long before the two were elected to the Senate. Also the choice by lot, detailed in the Senate record, makes it unlikely that any such deal was made. The swearing-in ceremony was temporarily delayed when Senator Garrett Davis of Kentucky questioned the right of Congress to delegate power to declare the admission of a new state to the President, as had been done with Nevada. Davis argued that Nevada was not a state unless Congress admitted it, and until such action, the two senators-elect from Nevada could not be seated. His motion to postpone the ceremonies was defeated. Nye and Stewart were conducted to the vice-president's chair by Senator John Conness of California and the oaths were administered.

2. Mack, *History of Nevada*, p. 266; Mack, "Stewart," 35; *New York Times*, Feb. 20, 1865, p. 1, col. 5. The paper noted that Nevada ratified the amendment on February 16, with only two votes against, both Democrats.

3. *Cleveland Leader* (Ohio), quoted in Beulah Hershiser, "The Influence of Nevada on the National Mining Legislation of 1866," *Third Biennial Report of the Nevada Historical Society, 1911–1912* (Carson City, Nevada: State Printing Office, 1913), p. 156.

4. Bushnell, *Nevada Constitution*, p. 312. The citation is from Article XIV (Boundary).

5. *Congressional Globe*, 38th Cong., 2d Sess., Part 1 (1865), p. 663.

6. *Ibid.*, Feb. 10, 1865, p. 712.

7. *Ibid.*, 2d Sess., Part 2 (1865), p. 1429. John A. J. Creswell of Maryland replaced Fessenden on the committee on December 6, 1865. See also Robert W. Swenson, "Legal Aspects of Mineral Resources Exploitation," in Paul W. Gates, *History of Public Land Law Development* (Washington, D.C.: U.S. Government Printing Office, 1968), pp. 716–719; Mack, *History of Nevada*, p. 429. Mack states that Fessenden was one of the original members of the committee.

8. Hershiser, "The Influence of Nevada on National Mining Legislation," pp. 127–167. The Hershiser article has an excellent historical background on mining law, from which I have drawn most of the above material.

9. John F. Davis, "Historical Sketch of the Mining Law in California," Pamphlets on California Mines III, No. 1 (Los Angeles: N.p., 1902), p. 12.

10. Hershiser, "The Influence of Nevada on National Mining Legislation," pp. 135–136.

11. *Ibid.*, p. 128. The idea of "free mining" derives from Germanic practices during the Middle Ages. Local custom gave the individual the right, as discoverer, to mine any metalliferous deposits, so long as he did not encroach upon mineral rights previously acquired by others.

12. Gregory Yale, *Legal Titles to Mining Claims and Water Rights in California Under the Mining Law of Congress, of July, 1866* (San Francisco: A. Roman & Company, 1867), pp. 58–59.

13. Paul, *California Gold*, p. 221. Stephen J. Field, later associate justice of the United States Supreme Court, but then a young assemblyman from Yuba County, is credited with pushing this statute through the California legislature.

14. *Ibid.*, pp. 217–220.

15. Stewart, *Reminiscences*, p. 127. Stewart's report appears to be the only available source for the fact of his chairmanship or his continued claim that he was responsible for the "dips, angles and variations of the vein" rule adopted at this meeting. At the time of the miners' meeting Stewart was in his middle twenties and had been admitted to the California bar only a few weeks earlier.

16. Quoted in Hershiser, "The Influence of Nevada on National Mining Legislation," p. 145.

17. Lord, *Comstock Mining and Miners*, pp. 39–44. An earlier district, the Columbia Quartz District, was organized on the Comstock in January of 1858, but it was not successful. See Lord, pp. 33–35.

18. Hershiser, "The Influence of Nevada on National Mining Legislation," p. 146.

19. *Ibid.*, p. 148.

20. *Ibid.*, p. 152.

21. *Ibid.*, pp. 153–154. The Conness-Johnson amendment was a compromise substituted for an earlier proposal by Stewart that the customs and regulations of the miners in respect to mining claims should be regarded as law and enforceable by the courts of the United States. Conness argued that local rules and regulations were not uniform and that recognition of the possessory rights of the miner would suffice.

22. *Sparrow* v. *Strong*, 3 Wallace (U.S.), 97–106 (1865). The Ramsay letter is included in Appendix 1, pp. 777–780. It is also printed in its entirety in Mack, "Stewart," 43–47.

23. *Ibid.*

24. Hershiser, "The Influence of Nevada on National Mining Legislation," pp. 159–161. Included in these proposals was a bill introduced by Stewart on January 31, 1866, calling for a grant of one million acres of public lands for the benefit of a mining college in Nevada. It died in the Committee on Public Lands.

25. *Ibid.*, p. 160; Paul, *California Gold*, p. 230. Julian's previous support of the idea of sale of the western mining lands is well documented in the bills he introduced in the House.

26. Hershiser, "The Influence of Nevada on National Mining Legislation," p. 162; Yale, *Legal Titles*, p. 11; Mack, "Stewart," 47–50. Justice Stephen Field, a friend of Stewart's from the early gold rush days in California, specifically noted that Stewart was responsible for the 1866 Mining Act, in the case of *Jennison* v. *Kirk*, 98 U.S. 453–462 (1878). It should be remembered, however, that Conness was chairman of the Mines and Mining Committee at the time and presented the written argument in support of the bill when it was presented in the Senate. Paul, in his *California Gold*, pp. 230–233, repeatedly refers to the bill as the Stewart-Conness Bill.

27. *Congressional Globe*, 39th Cong., 1st Sess., Part 4 (1866), pp. 3225–3236.

28. *Ibid.*, pp. 3451–3455.

29. Hershiser, "The Influence of Nevada on National Mining Legislation," p. 163; Yale, *Legal Titles*, p. 11; Mack, "Stewart," 48.

30. *U.S. Statutes at Large*, XIV, pp. 251–253. The saga of the 1866 mining act is well covered in Mack, *History of Nevada*, pp. 432–436, and by Hershiser, pp. 156–164. The debate on the amended canal bill is covered in the *Congressional Globe*, 39th Cong., 1st Sess., Part V (1866), pp. 4022, 4048, 4049, and 4054.

31. Gates, *History of Public Land Law*, pp. 719–720.

32. Paul, *California Gold*, pp. 231–232.

33. Gates, *History of Public Land Law*, pp. 719–720. It should be noted that, a few months before passage of the national mining law, the Nevada legislature approved "An Act concerning the Location and Possession of Mining Claims," which included many of the same guarantees as the national law. Nevada went further, however, by approving at the same time "An Act to provide for the Condemnation of Real Estate and other Property required for Mining Purposes." See *Nevada Statutes* (1866), pp. 141–152 and pp. 196–198. The latter act, particularly, left little doubt as to the priority of mining in the state of Nevada.

34. *Carson News*, Oct. 24, 1911, p. 2, col. 1; *Reno Evening Gazette*, Oct. 25, 1911, p. 2, col. 2.

35. Hershiser, "The Influence of Nevada on National Mining Legislation," pp. 163–164; *U.S. Statutes at Large*, XIV, pp. 242–243. See the *Washoe Weekly Times*, July 29, 1865, p. 2, col. 3, for Stewart's role as president of the Sutro Tunnel Company. Adolph Sutro, a successful San Francisco tobacco merchant, arrived on the Comstock shortly after the June discovery, originally intending to extend his merchandising business to the area. Instead, he built a mill on the Carson River and then began to explore the possibilities of a tunnel to drain the Comstock mines. See Robert E., Jr., and Mary Frances Stewart, *Adolph Sutro* (Berkeley, California: Howell-North, 1962), for an excellent account of Sutro's career.

36. Stewart, *Reminiscences*, pp. 168–187.

37. *Ibid.*, pp. 189–191.

38. *Ibid.*, p. 194.

39. *Ibid.*, p. 195.

40. Willam M. Stewart to John Conness, February 29, 1888, Stewart Papers. In a later interview in the *New York Times*, Feb. 14, 1897, p. 11, col. 4, Stewart said nothing about Johnson's being drunk, but did note that he did not "make a very presentable appearance."

41. Salmon P. Chase, *Inside Lincoln's Cabinet: The Civil War Diaries of Salmon P. Chase*, ed. David Donald (New York: Longmans, Green & Co., 1954), pp. 262–266, 267–269; Hugh McCulloch, *Men and Measures of Half a Century* (New York: Charles Scribner's Sons, 1888), pp. 375–376. McCulloch noted that the swearing-in ceremony took place in Johnson's hotel, conducted by Chief Justice Chase in the presence of the entire Cabinet, except for Seward, and "two or three senators who happened to be in the city. The ceremony was simple. The conduct of Mr. Johnson favorably impressed those who were present when the oath was administered to him. He was grief-stricken like the rest . . . But he was nevertheless, calm and self-possessed."

42. See Howard Beale, *The Critical Year: A Study of Andrew Johnson and Reconstruction* (New York: Frederick Ungar Publishing Co., 1958), pp. 12–15; Lloyd Paul Stryker, *Andrew Johnson: A Study in Courage* (New York: MacMillan Co., 1936), pp. 194–195.

43. *Congressional Globe*, 39th Cong., 1st Sess., Part 1 (1866), pp. 109–111.

44. *Ibid.*, pp. 297–298.

45. *Gold Hill Daily News,* Sept. 26, 1865, p. 2, col. 2.

46. *Congressional Globe,* 39th Cong., 1st Sess., Part 1 (1866), pp. 444–446.

47. Ellis P. Oberholtzer, *A History of the United States Since the Civil War* (New York: Mac-Millan Co., 1936–1937), Vol. 1, p. 166.

48. *Congressional Globe,* 39th Cong., 1st Sess., Part 2 (1866), pp. 1079–1082, 1103–1106.

49. Eric L. McKitrick, *Andrew Johnson and Reconstruction* (Chicago: University of Chicago Press, 1960), pp. 341–343.

50. *Ibid.*

51. *Ibid.,* p. 341.

52. Beale, *The Critical Year,* p. 90.

53. Avery Craven, *Reconstruction: The Ending of the Civil War* (New York: Holt, Rinehart and Winston, 1969), pp. 167–168.

54. *Congressional Globe,* 39th Cong., 1st Sess., Part 2 (1866), pp. 1754–1755; McKitrick, *Andrew Johnson,* p. 343.

55. McKitrick, *Andrew Johnson,* p. 343.

56. *Ibid.,* p. 342. Stewart later wrote an "I told-you-so" letter to General Longstreet, January 3, 1891, indicating that Reconstruction would have been different if his proposals had been followed by Congress and that "the great mistake in reconstruction was the meddling of northern men in southern politics," Stewart Papers.

57. Rembert W. Patrick, *The Reconstruction of the Nation* (New York: Oxford University Press, 1967), p. 74.

58. Lately Thomas, *The First President Johnson: The Three Lives of the Seventeenth President of the United States of America* (New York: William Morrow & Co., 1968), p. 436; Beale, *The Critical Year,* p. 88.

59. Gideon Welles, *Diary of Gideon Welles* (Boston & New York: Houghton, Mifflin, 1911), Vol. 2, p. 475; George F. Milton, *The Age of Hate: Andrew Johnson and the Radicals* (Hamden, Connecticut: Archon Books, 1965), pp. 163–164.

60. *Congressional Globe,* 39th Cong., 1st Sess., Part 2 (1866), p. 1890. The bill passed on April 9, 1866, after the House overrode the veto. See also Claude G. Bowers, *The Tragic Era: The Revolution After Lincoln* (Cambridge, Massachusetts: Houghton Mifflin, 1929), p. 111.

61. Stewart, *Reminiscences,* pp. 199–200. However, Robert W. Winston, *Andrew Johnson: Plebian and Patriot* (New York: Barnes & Noble, 1928), pp. 348–349, insists that Johnson did not make such a promise.

62. *Congressional Globe,* 39th Cong., 1st Sess., Part 3 (1886), pp. 2422–2429.

63. *Ibid.,* pp. 2798–2803.

64. *Ibid.*

65. *Ibid.,* Part 4 (1866), p. 2964.

66. *Congressional Globe,* 40th Cong., 2d Sess., Supplement (1868), "The Proceedings of the Senate Sitting for the Trial of Andrew Johnson, President of the United States," p. 433. See also James G. Blaine, *Twenty Years of Congress: From Lincoln to Garfield* (Norwich, Connecticut, Henry Bill Publishing Company, 1884–1886), Vol. 2, pp. 374–375.

67. Stewart, *Reminiscences,* p. 201.

68. Stewart was called one of the ablest U.S. senators, in an article from the *Washington Chronicle,* July 14, 1868, which was quoted in the *Carson Daily Appeal,* August 2, 1868, p. 2.

69. *Carson Daily Appeal,* August 25, 1868, p. 2.

70. *Ibid.,* Angel, *History of Nevada,* p. 90.

71. *Gold Hill Daily News,* January 6, 1869, p. 2.

72. Nevada State Legislature, *Journal of the Assembly,* 4th Session (1869), p. 28; *Journal of the Senate,* 4th Session (1869), pp. 22, 31. The Nevada legislature had met jointly for its senatorial selections in 1865 and 1867, but met separately and then jointly in 1869, and thereafter. See also *Carson Daily Appeal,* Jan. 13, Jan. 14, 1869, p. 3; and *Gold Hill Daily News,* Jan. 13, 1869, p. 2.

73. John Mabry Mathews, *Legislative and Judicial History of the Fifteenth Amendment* (Baltimore, Maryland: Johns Hopkins Press, 1909), pp. 20–25; William Gillette, *The Right to Vote:*

Politics and the Passage of the Fifteenth Amendment (Baltimore, Maryland: Johns Hopkins Press, 1965), pp. 31, 39–43.

74. Stewart biographers Mack ("Stewart," 57–59) and Hermann *(Gold and Silver Colossus,* p. 232) have credited him with sole responsibility for drafting the Fifteenth Amendment.

75. James Ford Rhodes, *History of the United States from the Compromise of 1850 . . .* (New York: MacMillan Co., 1912), Vol. 6, pp. 201–205. Rhodes maintains that Henderson, "more than any other man in Congress," was responsible for the Fifteenth Amendment.

76. Mathews, *Fifteenth Amendment,* pp. 17–19; Gillette, *Right to Vote,* pp. 39–43.

77. *Congressional Globe,* 40th Cong., 3d Sess., Part 1 (1868), pp. 378–379; *The American Annual Cyclopaedia and Register of Important Events of the Year, 1869* (New York: D. Appleton & Co., 1871), pp. 120–171.

78. Gillette, *Right to Vote,* pp. 54–57, 59–75.

79. *Ibid.,* pp. 59–75; William E. B. DuBois, *Black Reconstruction in America* (New York: Russell & Russell, 1935), pp. 377–379; Appleton's *Cyclopaedia, 1869,* pp. 120–171. The text of the amendment as ratified was: "Section 1. The right of citizens of the United States to vote shall not be denied or abridged by the United States or by any State on account of race, color, or previous condition of servitude. Section 2. The Congress shall have power to enforce this article by appropriate legislation."

80. Gillette, *Right to Vote,* p. 74; Michael L. Benedict, *A Compromise of Principle: Congressional Republicans and Reconstruction, 1863–1869* (New York: W. W. Norton & Co., 1974), pp. 333–334.

81. Gillette, *Right to Vote,* pp. 49, 53–57; Stewart, *Reminiscences,* p. 238. Stewart's autobiography has a good summary of the congressional debates over the Fifteenth Amendment proposal and his part in them. It is obvious that in this instance the senator followed the *Congressional Globe* with a minimum of personal glorification.

82. Benedict, *Compromise,* pp. 324–336; Gillette, *Right to Vote,* pp. 74–77.

83. Gillette, *Right to Vote,* pp. 157–158.

84. *Ibid.*

85. Nevada State Legislature, *Journal of the Senate,* 4th Session (1869), March 1, 1869, pp. 249–251.

86. Mack, "Stewart," 60; Howard Hickson, *Mint Mark "CC": The Story of the United States Mint at Carson City* (Carson City, Nevada: Nevada State Museum, 1972), p. 5.

87. Huntington to Crocker, May 30, 1870, Microfilm Series IV, Reel 3, Letter 521, Huntington Papers. Microfilm from Stanford University, original manuscripts at Syracuse University.

88. Stewart, *Reminiscences,* pp. 334–336; Mack, *History of Nevada,* p. 373; *Congressional Globe,* 39th Cong., 1st Sess., Part 4 (1866), pp. 3256–3267.

89. Collis P. Huntington to Charles Crocker, May 17, 1869, Series IV, Reel 2, Letter 339, Huntington Papers. See also David Lavender, *The Great Persuader* (New York: Doubleday, 1970), pp. 241–242.

90. Huntington to Stanford, August 2, 1870, Series IV, Reel 3, Huntington Papers. The lands in Alameda County, California, were conveyed to Stewart's wife, Annie.

91. Huntington to Hopkins, April 28, 1869, Series IV, Reel 2, Letter 333.

92. Stewart, *Reminiscences,* p. 222.

93. William Hedges Robinson, Jr., "Mark Twain: Senatorial Secretary," *American West,* 10 (January, 1973), pp. 16–17.

94. Stewart, *Reminiscences,* p. 224; Mack, "Stewart," 54–56.

95. Robinson, "Mark Twain," p. 16.

Chapter 5

1. *Congressional Globe,* 41st Cong., 1st Sess., Part 1 (1869), pp. 476, 501, 504, 533–536, 539, 545–547, 675.

2. *Ibid.,* 2d Sess., Part 1 (1870), p. 301; Mack, "Stewart," 59.

3. *Ibid.,* Part 4 (1870), pp. 3027–3028, 3052.

4. *Ibid.,* pp. 3051–3054.

5. *Ibid.,* Part 5 (1870), p. 4467.

6. *Ibid.,* Part 6 (1870), p. 5043.

7. *Ibid.,* Appendix, p. 688.

8. Gates, *History of Public Land Law Development,* pp. 721–723.

9. Stewart, in speaking on behalf of the bill in the Senate, was reluctant to give all the credit to Sargent, "It is no one man's work, but it is the work of a great many men interested in this business." The bill was introduced in the House on January 15, 1872, by Sargent, and signed by the President on May 10, 1872. *Congressional Globe,* 42d Cong., 2d Sess., Part 1 (1871), p. 345; Part 2 (1872), pp. 2454, 2462; Part 4 (1872), pp. 2909, 2992; and Appendix, pp. 715–717.

10. Paul, *California Gold,* pp. 237–238; Paul, *Mining Frontiers,* p. 173.

11. Paul, *Mining Frontiers,* p. 173.

12. *Congressional Globe,* 41st Cong., 2d Sess., Part 4 (1870), p. 3051.

13. J. Laurence Laughlin, *The History of Bimetallism in the United States* (New York: D. Appleton & Co., 1900, pp. 95–98. Laughlin includes a table, p. 98, which shows the slow progress of the bill through Congress.

14. Allen Weinstein, *Prelude to Populism: Origins of the Silver Issue, 1867–1878* (New Haven, Connecticut: Yale University Press, 1970), p. 14; Walter T. K. Nugent, *Money and American Society, 1865–1880* (New York: The Free Press, 1968), pp. 167–172.

15. Neil Carothers, *Fractional Money...* (New York: John Wiley & Sons, 1930), pp. 232–233.

16. Weinstein, *Prelude,* pp. 28–29.

17. *Congressional Globe,* 42d cong., 3d Sess., Part 1 (1873), pp. 661, 668; Part 2 (1873), p. 677.

18. Weinstein, *Prelude,* p. 29.

19. *Ibid.,* p. 28.

20. *Congressional Globe,* 43d Cong., 1st Sess., Part 2 (1874), Feb. 11, 1874, p. 1392, Feb. 20, 1874, p. 1678; George S. Boutwell, *Reminiscences of Sixty Years in Public Affairs* (New York: Greenwood Press, 1968), Vol. 1, pp. 155–156.

21. *Congressional Globe,* 43d Cong., 1st Sess., Part 5 (1874), p. 4865.

22. Stewart, *Reminiscences,* p. 317.

23. William M. Stewart to A. G. Forney, April 11, 1892, Stewart Papers.

24. *Congressional Globe,* 41st Cong., 3d Sess., Part 1 (1871), p. 399, for the vote of January 10, 1871. That vote should not be overemphasized, since the bill spent two more years moving between the two houses. Much more important, it would appear, is the fact that Stewart mounted no opposition to the bill at any stage in the process.

25. *Territorial Enterprise,* Dec. 17, 1872, p. 2; Mary Ellen Glass, *Silver and Politics in Nevada: 1892–1902* (Reno, Nevada: University of Nevada Press, 1969), pp. 8–9.

26. *Territorial Enterprise,* Feb. 4, 1873, p. 2.

27. John M. Townley, "Management of Nevada's State Lands, 1864–1900," *Journal of the West,* 17 (January, 1978), 64–65.

28. *Ibid.,* 66; *Nevada Statutes* (1869), pp. 190–195.

29. *Congressional Globe,* 41st Cong., 3d Sess., Part 5 (1870), p. 4075. The first Congressional Swamp Land Act was passed March 2, 1849, to apply only to swamp lands in Louisiana. On September 23, 1850, Congress passed a law enabling Arkansas and other states to reclaim swamp and overflowed land with the proceeds of sale or direct appropriation in kind, to be applied exclusively to reclaiming such lands by levees and drains. It was this 1850 act referred to in Nye's bill as well as in a similar bill introduced by Charles Kendall in the House of Representatives. See Gates, *History of Public Land Law,* pp. 321–324.

30. Townley, "Management of Nevada's State Lands," 66–67.

31. *Congressional Globe*, 41st Cong., 3d Sess., Part 3 (1871), p. 2004.

32. *Ibid.*, 42d Cong., 2d Sess., Part 5 (1872), pp. 3772, 3807, 3891.

33. Townley, "Management of Nevada's State Lands," 67. Stewart was quoted in the *Pioche Daily Record*, Feb. 7, 1873, p. 2, col. 1, to the effect that he was opposed to a congressional grant of swamp lands to Nevada, but if the people of Nevada wanted such a grant he would either support it or resign from the Senate. The threat was meaningless since he had killed the issue in the Senate before he made the remark.

34. *Nevada State Journal*, Dec. 10, 1873, p. 2, col. 1.

35. *Congressional Record*, 43d Cong., 1st Sess., Part 3 (1874), pp. 2185–2189.

36. *Gold Hill Daily News*, March 25, 1874, p. 2.

37. Stewart, *Reminiscences*, p. 251.

38. *Ibid.*, p. 250; Mack, "Stewart," 63. If such an offer was made it must have been oral. No record of such appointment exists in official sources.

39. Clark C. Spence, *British Investments and the American Frontier, 1860–1901* (Ithaca, New York: Cornell University Press, 1958), pp. 139–190. In his autobiography Stewart is strangely silent on the Emma Mine scandal, and the Mack and Hermann biographies of Stewart pay little attention to his involvement in the affair. Spence, on the other hand, in his excellent summary of British investments in the American mining frontier, gives the Emma Mine scandal a full chapter.

40. *House Report No. 579*, 44th Cong., 1st Sess., (1875–76), p. 46.

41. Spence, *British Investments*, pp. 139–142.

42. *House Report No. 579*, pp. ii, 52 (the letter is quoted therein); Spence, *British Investments*, p. 141.

43. *Ibid.* Professor Spence is cautious in evaluating the publicity campaign. However, the chronology of events, and particularly Stewart's August 5 letter to Lyon, appear to justify the conclusion that the campaign, including the sending of rich ore during this period, was part of a well-orchestrated program.

44. *House Report No. 579*, pp. ii, iii.

45. Spence, *British Investments*, pp. 143–144. Albert Grant was born Albert Gottheimer in Dublin in 1830. He assumed the name of Grant in 1863. He was granted the title of Baron by King Victor Emmanuel, elected to Parliament in 1865, and reelected in 1874. Before his death in 1899, he promoted dozens of mining companies, many of which ended in bankruptcy courts.

46. *Ibid.*, pp. 144–147.

47. *Ibid.*

48. Mrs. Stewart and their two daughters had been in Europe since 1866. Following the custom of many Southern families, Mrs. Stewart wished their children to have the benefit of European travel and schools. Consequently, a program for a stay of two years in Italy, two years in France, and two years in the Germanic states had been devised. There were rumors, when the Stewart family left for Europe, that one of the reasons for leaving at that time was to make certain Mrs. Stewart, with her strong Southern ties and sympathies, was away from Washington during the debates on the Reconstruction policy. During these years abroad Mrs. Stewart purchased a great deal of furniture that ultimately went into the "Castle," her home on Dupont Circle in Washington.

49. *House Report No. 579*, pp. 159–160.

50. *Ibid.*, p. vi.

51. *Ibid.*, pp. 154–155.

52. *Ibid.*, p. 52.

53. Spence, *British Investments*, pp. 153–154. Stewart left to return to the United States on November 25, 1871.

54. See Spence, pp. 151–181, for a detailed story of the Emma Mine and the tortuous machinations of its stock.

55. *House Report No. 579*, p. 50.

56. *Ibid.*, pp. 107–108, 198–199.

57. *Ibid.*, pp. 57, 84, 198–199.

58. *Ibid.,* pp. 262–263.

59. *Ibid.,* pp. 155–158, 189–190.

60. *Ibid.,* pp. 221–224.

61. *Ibid.,* pp. 272–273.

62. *Ibid.,* pp. 751–764. Stewart had earlier (p. 211) testified that he had been paid between $225,000 and $230,000. The discrepancy, obviously, was the $50,000 paid to Lyon because of the threat.

63. *Ibid.,* pp. 569–572.

64. *Ibid.,* pp. 230–231.

65. *Ibid.,* pp. 221–222.

66. *Ibid.,* p. 210.

67. Spence, *British Investments,* p. 159; *House Report No. 579,* pp. 198–200.

68. The letter, dated February 28, 1875, is reprinted in *House Report No. 579,* pp. 212–214. The house referred to was the famous Stewart "Castle," erected in Washington, D.C., in 1873.

69. *Ibid.,* pp. 571–572.

70. Stewart to Frederick B. Jennings, Feb. 14, 1889; Stewart to Thomas H. Bates, May 11, 1892; Stewart to E. F. B. Harston, Feb. 15, 1892; Stewart to F. B. Jennings, Sept. 30, 1893, Jan. 27, 1893.

71. *Washington Evening Star,* August 28, 1970, p. D–1. Stewart, Curtis J. Hillyer, and William Sharon had purchased a large tract of land in the area sometime earlier.

72. *Gold Hill Daily News,* March 21, 1874, p. 2. The description published in the Comstock paper originally came from the Washington correspondent of the *Buffalo Express.*

73. Neill C. Wilson, *Silver Stampede: The Career of Death Valley's Hell Camp, Old Panamint* (New York: MacMillan, 1937), p. 12.

74. Mack, "Stewart," 62–63.

75. *Nevada State Journal,* July 26, 1874, p. 3, col. 2.

76. Ostrander, *Nevada,* p. 70. Ostrander intimates that Stewart withdrew on direct orders from William Sharon, but the Central Pacific obviously did not wish to finance a campaign that might bring it into direct conflict with the manager and guiding genius of the Bank of California.

77. *Nevada State Journal,* July 28, 1874, p. 2, col. 4, quoted an article from the *Sacramento Union,* which indicated that Stewart's "railroad record precludes almost the possibility of any one having the audacity to nominate him."

78. Stewart, *Reminiscences,* p. 261.

Chapter 6

1. This period of Stewart's career presents some difficulties in documentation, since the bulk of the correspondence in the Stewart Papers at the Nevada Historical Society dates from after June, 1886, and congressional sources obviously do not document his private life. Stewart's *Reminiscences,* of course, are available; but they are unreliable in many respects, despite the fact that several writers have accepted them practically unchallenged. Therefore, periodicals, and particularly newspapers, are increasingly important in chronicling these years.

2. *Mining and Scientific Press,* 28 (May 30, 1874), 338. See also Willie Arthur Chalfant, *The Story of Inyo,* rev. ed. (Los Angeles: Citizens Print Shop, 1933), pp. 285–293. Chalfant says the discovery was in April, 1873.

3. *Mining and Scientific Press,* 27 (Aug. 2, 1873), 72.

4. *Ibid.,* 27 (Nov. 29, 1873), 348.

5. *Ibid.,* 28 (Jan. 3, 1874), p. 11.

6. Harry M. Gorham, *My Memories of the Comstock* (Los Angeles: Sutton House, 1939), pp. 108–110.

7. Stanley W. Paher, *Death Valley Ghost Towns* (Las Vegas, Nevada: Nevada Publications, 1973), pp. 40–42; Chalfant, *Inyo,* pp. 285–293; Lee Bourke, *Death Valley* (New York: MacMillan, 1930), pp. 127–130; Wilson, *Silver Stampede,* p. 113.

8. *Mining and Scientific Press,* 29 (Sept. 5, 1874), 149.

9. *Inyo* (California) *Independent,* June 24, 1882, p. 3, cols. 2–5.

10. Quoted in Wilson, *Silver Stampede,* p. 151.

11. Spence, *British Investments,* p. 171.

12. Wilson, *Silver Stampede,* pp. 152–153.

13. *Minerals Yearbook—Mineral Resources West of the Rocky Mountains—1874* (Washington, D.C.: Government Printing Office, 1875), pp. 33–39.

14. *Mining and Scientific Press,* 29 (Aug. 1, 1874), 74.

15. *Reno Evening Gazette,* Feb. 21, 1891, p. 3, col. 2. For a good description of the milling works, see *Inyo Independent,* June 24, 1882, p. 3, cols. 2–5.

16. *Nevada State Journal,* Dec. 2, 1874, p. 2, col. 2, quoting from the *Panamint News* of Nov. 27; Paher, *Death Valley Ghost Towns,* pp. 40–42; Glenn Chesney Quiett, *Pay Dirt...* (New York: Appleton-Century, 1936), pp. 416–418.

17. Wilson, *Silver Stampede,* p. 289. For a brief biographical sketch of Neagle, see the article by Gary L. Roberts in *The Readers' Encyclopedia of the American West,* Howard Lamar, ed. (New York: Thomas Y. Crowell Company, 1977), pp. 807–808.

18. Paher, *Death Valley Ghost Towns,* pp. 40–42; Wilson, *Silver Stampede,* p. 282; Chalfant, *Story of Inyo,* pp. 285–293.

19. *Inyo Independent,* June 24, 1882, p. 3, cols. 2–5. The paper reported that the mine yielded a total in silver and gold of $366,717.83. This sum included $25,180.57 from an earlier shipment of ore to Swansea, Wales, and $341,537.26 produced by the Stewart-Jones company. A total of $107,427.29 was added in 1881.

20. Stewart, *Reminiscences,* pp. 262–263.

21. *Ibid.,* pp. 262–264. The same story about the huge balls of silver is told by numerous writers, but the only basic source is apparently the Stewart autobiography.

22. Paher, *Death Valley Ghost Camps,* p. 4.

23. Stewart, *Reminiscences,* p. 265.

24. *Ibid.* See also Hermann, *Gold and Silver Colossus,* pp. 253–257; Mack, "Stewart," 65–67; William M. Stewart to Lawyers' Cooperative Publishing Company, June 29, 1886; William M. Stewart to Messrs. Britton and Gray, Feb. 25, 1890, Stewart Papers.

25. Grant H. Smith, *The History of the Comstock Lode, 1850–1920* (Reno, Nevada: Nevada Bureau of Mines, 1943), p. 53. Stewart's involvement at Bodie may have come earlier. See the *Morning Appeal,* Aug. 11, 1878, p. 3, col. 2.

26. Stewart, *Reminiscences,* pp. 266–267.

27. Paul, *Mining Frontiers of the Far West,* pp. 103–105.

28. *Albion Consolidated Mining Company* v. *The Richmond Mining Co.,* 19 Nevada Reports 225 (1885).

29. Stewart, *Reminiscences,* p. 265.

30. *Ibid.* Two in particular were Thomas Wren and C. C. "Black" Wallace.

31. *Daily Silver State* (Winnemucca), Dec. 28, 1877, p. 2, col. 1.

32. William M. Stewart to Britton and Gray, Feb. 25, 1890, Stewart Papers; Mack, "Stewart," 190. See Gates, *Public Land Law,* pp. 181, 327, 333, for additional material on these land grants.

33. Edward F. Treadwell, *The Cattle King...* (Fresno, California: Valley Publishers, 1931), pp. 87, 94; *Lux et al.* v. *Haggin et al.,* 69 Cal 255 (1886); 10 Pacific 674 (1886).

34. The story of Sarah Althea Hill and William Sharon is told in some detail in Brooks W. MacCracken, "Althea and the Judges," *American Heritage,* 18 (June, 1967), 61–63, 75–79; and Robert H. Kroninger, *Sarah and the Senator* (Berkeley, California: Howell-North, 1964).

35. MacCracken, "Althea and the Judges," 62.

36. *Ibid.,* 63, 75; Kroninger, *Sarah and the Senator,* pp. 12–13.

37. Kroninger, *Sarah and the Senator,* p. 156; Stewart, *Reminiscences,* pp. 275–277. Stewart blamed Sharon's initial legal defeat on the ineffectiveness of his counsel, General Barnes.

38. *Sharon* v. *Hill,* 24 Fed. 726 (1885). The examiner for the federal court was S. G. Houghton, *Daily Alta California,* Aug. 4, 1885, p. 1, col. 5.

39. *Sharon* v. *Hill,* 24 Fed. 726 (1885).

40. *Ibid.;* Kroninger, *Sarah and the Senator,* pp. 166–171; *Daily Alta California,* Aug. 6, 1886, p. 1, col. 1; MacCracken, "Althea and the Judges," 76–77; 26 Fed. 337 (1885).

41. MacCracken, "Althea and the Judges," 77.

42. Stewart, *Reminiscences,* pp. 275–277.

43. William M. Stewart to W.F. Herrin, March 11, 1888, Stewart Papers.

44. *Sharon* v. *Hill,* 36 Fed. 337 (1888); MacCracken, "Althea and the Judges," 77.

45. Charles Fairman, *American Constitutional Decisions,* rev. ed. (New York: Henry Holt & Co., 1952), p. 137.

46. *Ibid.,* pp. 126–138. Neagle was arrested in California on a charge of murder. He applied to the federal court to be released from state custody, on the basis that federal courts were authorized to release, on writ of habeas corpus, a person held in custody "for an act done or omitted in pursuance of a law of the United States." The circuit court granted the petition, and the Supreme Court of the United States affirmed the judgment releasing Neagle. The federal case, *In re Neagle,* has become a landmark case in intergovernmental relations.

47. *Nevada State Journal,* Jan. 14, 1875, p. 2, col. 1.

48. Elliott, *History of Nevada,* pp. 164–165. "Sackbearers" had been used effectively in earlier Nevada elections. The name derives from the fact that candidates' representatives literally dispensed money from canvas sacks to buy votes and insure the election of their partisans to the state legislature.

49. *Morning Appeal,* May 2, 1885, p. 2.

50. *Ibid.;* Oscar Lewis, *Silver Kings: The Lives and Times of Mackay, Fair, Flood, and O'Brien, Lords of the Nevada Comstock Lode* (New York: Alfred A. Knopf, 1947), pp. 170–172; Ostrander, *Rotten Borough,* p. 106.

51. *Morning Appeal,* May 30, 1885, p. 3, col. 1.

52. *Ibid.,* Sept. 16, 1885, p. 2, col. 3; Sept. 17, 1885, p. 3. The editor's obvious pleasure in Stewart's speech didn't overcome his belief that John Mackay was the best senatorial candidate. It was some months before the paper switched to support of Stewart.

53. Glass, *Silver and Politics,* pp. 31–32.

54. Stewart, *Reminiscences,* p. 277.

55. *Morning Appeal,* Oct. 30, 1885, p. 2, col. 2.

56. *Ibid.,* Nov. 19, 1885, p. 2.

57. *Carson Free Lance,* Nov. 30, 1885, p. 3. See also, Hermann, *Gold and Silver Colossus,* pp. 260–261.

58. *Morning Appeal,* Dec. 1, 1885, p. 2.

59. *Ibid.,* Jan. 28, 1886, p. 2, quoting an article from the *San Francisco Chronicle.*

60. Mack, "Stewart," 95; Ostrander, *Rotten Borough,* p. 105.

61. *Morning Appeal,* Jan. 3, 1886, p. 3; March 16, 1886, p. 2. Other individuals present at the meetings represented C. C. Powning and Senator Fair.

62. Glass, *Silver and Politics,* pp. 48–49.

63. *Morning Appeal,* March 16, 1886, p. 2.

64. *Ibid.,* March 25, 1886, p. 3.

65. John E. Baur, "The Senator's Happy Thought," *American West,* 10 (Jan., 1973), 34–39, 62, 63.

66. *Morning Appeal,* April 24, 1886, p. 2, quoting the *San Francisco Post.*

67. *Political History of Nevada, 1973,* p. 180.

68. William M. Stewart, "The Chinese Question" (Reno, Nevada: Reno Evening Gazette Print, 1886), pp. 1–34. The pamphlet repeated many of the same arguments Stewart had made in Congress during the debates on the Fifteenth Amendment.

69. *Morning Appeal,* May 6, 1886, p. 3. Stewart was criticized for not participating in the city election, which was held on May 3, 1886, in Carson City, and which included a referendum on Chinese exclusion. Stewart was not on the list of registered voters published in the *Appeal* on April 29, 1886.

70. Stewart to D. P. McCargar, July 16, 1886, Stewart Papers.

71. *Morning Appeal,* July 31, 1886, p. 3, col. 3.

72. Stewart to Andrew Maute, July 9, 1886, Stewart Papers. Similar letters were sent to individuals in Lander, Lincoln, Elko, Humboldt, Eureka, White Pine, Churchill, Esmeralda, Washoe, Lyon and Douglas counties.

73. William M. Stewart to Hon. W. Woodburn, July 16, 1886. Woodburn was the incumbent Republican congressman from Nevada and expected to be a candidate for reelection.

74. *Morning Appeal,* July 18, 1886, p. 2, col. 3.

75. Stewart to R. L. Fulton, Aug. 11, 1886; to George W. Rutherford, Aug. 16, 1886, Sept. 6, 1886, and Jan. (?), 1887, Stewart Papers.

76. Stewart to Thomas Ewing, Sept. 2, 1886. Harmon and Requa had been involved as officers in important mines on the Comstock and had made fortunes from their activities there.

77. Stewart to M. S. Thompson, Sept. 6, 1886.

78. *Morning Appeal,* Sept. 19, 1886, p. 2.

79. Townley, "Reclamation in Nevada," pp. 154–156.

80. *Morning Appeal,* Sept. 25, p. 3; Sept. 26, p. 3; Sept. 28, 1886, pp. 2, 3. The Ormsby County Republican Convention was held after the state convention and Stewart gained support from that body. See the *Appeal* for Sept. 29, 1886.

81. *Ibid.,* Oct. 17, 1886, p. 2.

82. *Ibid.,* Oct. 8, 1886, p. 2.

83. Stewart to J. H. Whited, Oct. 28, 1886, Stewart Papers.

84. *Morning Appeal,* Oct. 24, 1886, p. 3.

85. A. C. Cleveland to H. M. Yerington, Oct. 6, 1886, Virginia & Truckee Railroad Collection, Nevada State Museum, Carson City, Nevada. See also H. M. Yerington to A. C. Cleveland, Oct. 12, 1886, Yerington Papers, Bancroft Library.

86. *Morning Appeal,* Oct. 26, 1886, p. 3; Oct. 27, 1886, p. 3.

87. *Ibid.,* Aug. 18, 1886, p. 2.

88. *Ibid.,* Nov. 5, 1886, p. 2.

89. Yerington to F. G. Newlands, Oct. 18, 1886, Yerington Papers.

90. *Morning Appeal,* Oct. 22, 1886, p. 3.

91. *Ibid.,* Nov. 3, 1886, p. 3; Nov. 4, 1886, p. 2.

92. Yerington to D. O. Mills, Nov. 5, 1886, Yerington Papers.

93. *Morning Appeal,* Nov. 7, 1886, p. 2, quoting from the *San Francisco Real Estate Circular.*

94. *Ibid.,* Dec. 23, 1886, p. 2.

95. Stewart to J. W. Haines, Nov. 13, 1886; to "Friend" (W. J.) Hanks, Nov. 24, 1886, Stewart Papers.

96. Stewart to John W. Mackay, Dec. 24, 1886.

97. *Morning Appeal,* Jan 1, 1887, p. 2.

98. *Ibid.,* Jan. 5, 1887, p. 3; Jan. 7, 1887, p. 3.

99. The various California newspapers cited were quoted in the *Morning Appeal,* Jan. 8, 1887, p. 3; Jan. 9, 1887, p. 3.

100. *Journal of the Assembly,* 1887, p. 35. The *Appeal* for January 12, 1887, p. 3, reported that Stewart received 44 rather than 43 votes.

101. *Journal of the Senate,* 1887, pp. 51–57.

102. *The Journals of Alfred Doten,* 3 vols. Edited by Walter Van Tilburg Clark (Reno, Nevada: University of Nevada Press, 1973), III, p. 1654.

Chapter 7

1. Stewart to C. C. Goodwin, Nov. 24, 1886, Stewart Papers. Charles C. Goodwin and the *Salt Lake Tribune,* which he edited during this period, maintained a strong anti-Mormon bias. A story persists in Nevada that John W. Mackay subsidized Goodwin as editor of the *Tribune* in order that the latter might wage a fight against polygamy. See the *Nevada State Journal,* Nov. 16, 1975, which repeats a story told in October, 1939, to the Carson City Club by Alfred Chartz.

2. Stewart to Hon. A. P. Williams, Dec. 8, 1886.

3. Nevada State Legislature, *Journal of the Senate* (1887), pp. 54–57. For an excellent summary of Stewart's plan to annex southern Idaho see Eric N. Moody, "Nevada's Anti-Mormon Legislation of 1887 and Southern Idaho Annexation," *Nevada Historical Society Quarterly,* 22 (Spring, 1979), 21–33. Moody is the first Nevada historian to place the anti-Mormon legislation of 1887 and the annexation of southern Idaho in proper perspective. For a detailed study of the anti-Mormonism in Idaho, see Merle W. Wells, *Anti-Mormonism in Idaho, 1872–92* (Provo, Utah: Brigham Young University Press, 1978).

4. Moody, "Nevada's Anti-Mormon Legislation," 26.

5. *Journal of the Senate* (1887), pp. 114, 128, 129. The actual wording of the oath as it was introduced in the Senate differed from amended versions and from the oath required in the statute which was passed later. See *Statutes of Nevada* (1887), p. 156.

6. *Journal of the Senate* (1887), p. 162; Moody, "Nevada's Anti-Mormon Legislation," 27–28.

7. *Journal of the Senate* (1887), p. 162.

8. Stewart to C. C. Goodwin, Feb. 6, 1887, Stewart Papers.

9. Moody, "Nevada's Anti-Mormon Legislation," 31.

10. *Statutes of Nevada* (1887), pp. 106–108; Moody, "Nevada's Anti-Mormon Legislation," 31.

11. *Statutes of Nevada* (1887), pp. 106–108.

12. *Morning Appeal,* Feb. 9, 1887, p. 2; Feb. 10, 1887, p. 2.

13. Stewart to Hon. Fred T. Dubois, July 6, 1887, Stewart Papers.

14. Stewart to E. J. Curtis, July 6, 1887.

15. Stewart to E. C. Hardy, Jan. 15, 1888.

16. *Congressional Record,* 50th Cong., 1st Sess., Part 7 (1888), pp. 6459–6462. At the same time, Stewart suggested that the Senate allow the people of northern Idaho to hold a plebiscite on the question of joining Washington. The effort failed. See Moody, "Nevada's Anti-Mormon Legislation," 31, n. 45.

17. Washington became a state in 1889, and Idaho in July, 1890. Stewart finally took himself out of the fight for Idaho annexation early in 1889, when he told a correspondent that although he still favored the annexation move, "strong forces were active in preventing the dismemberment of Idaho Territory." See Stewart to Norman Buck, Jan. 29, 1889, Stewart Papers.

18. *Congressional Record,* 50th cong., 1st Sess., Part 1 (1887), p. 120.

19. Stewart to Gilbert Pierce, Dec. 20, 1887, Stewart Papers.

20. Stewart to E. R. Clute, Feb. 29, 1888.

21. *Ibid.,* March 22, 1888.

22. Stewart to C. C. Goodwin, May 8, 1888.

23. Stewart to H. P. Flannery, July 10, 1888.

24. Stewart to T. H. Wells, Sept. 17, 1888.

25. *State of Nevada, Ex Rel. George B. Whitney, Relator* v. *A. M. Findlay, Respondent,* Bicknell, Nevada Reports, 198. Attorneys for Whitney were Trenmor Coffin and George S. Sawyer, and for Findlay, J. D. Torreyson and Thomas H. Wells.

26. Stewart to James S. Wing, April 15, 1890, Stewart Papers.

27. *Nevada State Journal,* April 2, 1893, p. 3, col. 2. See also Stewart to C. A. V. Putnam, March 23, 1893; to David B. Stover, March 24, 1893; and to E. A. Littlefield, editor of the Ogden *Standard,* June 3, 1893, in the Stewart Papers.

28. Stewart to Hon. Geo. Q. Cannon, Feb. 7, 1894, Stewart Papers. He reiterated these views in a letter to Effie G. Snow, Feb. 17, 1894.

29. Stewart to Isaac Trumbo, July 21, 1894.

30. *Ibid.*

31. Geo. Q. Cannon to Stewart, Feb. 1, 1899.

32. Stewart to F. C. Lord, March 29, 1888.

33. Stewart to Sam Wright, March 29, 1888.

34. Stewart to F. C. Lord, March 29, 1888.

35. See various letters in the Stewart Papers for April, 1888.

36. Stewart to F. C. Lord, April 21, 1888.

37. Stewart to S. C. Wright, June 30, 1888.

38. Stewart to J. R. Williamson, June 30, 1888.

39. Stewart, *Reminiscences,* pp. 295–296.

40. *Ibid.,* pp. 292–293; Mack, "Stewart," 71.

41. Stewart to Leland Stanford, June 28, 1888, Stewart Papers.

42. Townley, "Reclamation in Nevada," pp. 158–159. See also A. Hunter Dupree, *Science in the Federal Government: A History of Policies and Activities to 1940* (Cambridge, Massachusetts: Harvard University Press, 1957), pp. 233–236.

43. Townley, "Reclamation in Nevada," p. 161.

44. "Inaugural Address of Governor C. C. Stevenson," *Appendices to the Journals of Senate and Assembly* (1887), pp. 5–8.

45. Townley, "Reclamation in Nevada," pp. 66–68.

46. *Congressional Globe,* 42d Cong., 3d Sess., Part 2 (1873), p. 1365; Part 3 (1873), p. 1930; Townley, "Reclamation in Nevada," p. 150. For additional coverage of Stewart's early activities in Congress regarding irrigation, see Mary C. Rabbitt, *Minerals, Lands, and Geology for the Common Defence and General Welfare, 1879–1904* (Washington, D.C.: U.S. Government Printing Office, 1980), pp. 140–152, 168.

47. Townley, "Reclamation in Nevada," p. 150.

48. Rabbitt, *Minerals, Lands and Geology,* pp. 140–142, 152; *Congressional Record,* 50th Cong., 2d Sess., Part 2 (1889), p. 1641.

49. Stewart to Ed. Kirby, Feb. 15, 1889, Stewart Papers; Stewart, *Reminiscences,* p. 349.

50. Mack, "Stewart," 78–80.

51. Stewart to Wm. F. Herrin, May 14, 1888, Stewart Papers. Stewart rented his home in Carson City, Nevada, to Newlands. See Stewart to H. M. Yerington, Dec. 27, 1888; P. B. Ellis to William M. Stewart, Dec. 26, 1888.

52. Throughout his career Stewart was drawn to "financial hosts," such as C. P. Huntington, William Sharon, and John P. Jones. Newlands may well have joined this list, since Stewart later borrowed some $200,000 from him. See Charles C. Goodwin, *As I Remember Them,* pp. 140–145, for a revealing analysis of Stewart and his relation to money. Goodwin notes that "a host was always ready to back him."

53. Stewart to F. G. Newlands, July 17, 1889, Stewart Papers.

54. Townley, "Reclamation in Nevada," pp. 69–75; James G. Scrugham, ed., *Nevada . . .* (Chicago: American Historical Society, 1935), Vol. 1, p. 342; "Biennial Report of the Board of Reclamation and Internal Improvements," in *Appendices to the Journals of the Senate and Assembly* (1891), pp. 16–35.

55. "Biennial Report of the Board of Reclamation," pp. 16–35.

56. This problem plagued Nevadans until circumstances during and after World War II brought legalized gambling to the forefront of Nevada's economy.

57. Townley, "Reclamation in Nevada," pp. 163–165.

58. *Ibid.,* pp. 165–167.

59. *Ibid.;* Everett W. Sterling, "The Powell Irrigation Survey, 1888–1893," *Mississippi Valley Historical Review,* 27 (December, 1940), 430.

60. Thomas G. Alexander, "The Powell Irrigation Survey and the People of the Mountain West," *Journal of the West,* 7 (January, 1968), 51–53.

61. Wallace Stegner, *Beyond the Hundredth Meridian: John Wesley Powell and the Second Opening of the West* (Boston: Houghton Mifflin, 1953), p. 319.

62. Quoted in Sterling, "The Powell Irrigation Survey," 430.

63. Stegner, *Beyond the Hundredth Meridian,* p. 338; William C. Darrah, *Powell of the Colorado* (Princeton, New Jersey: Princeton University Press, 1951), p. 336.

64. Alexander, "The Powell Irrigation Survey," 51–53.

65. Stegner, *Beyond the Hundredth Meridian,* p. 319.

66. Stewart to Clarence E. Dutton, March 28, 1890, quoted in Townley, "Reclamation in Nevada," p. 167. The letter indicates that Stewart tried to entrap Powell by using other members of the Geological Survey to furnish him with information about Powell.

67. Stewart to Wm. H. Barnes, July 5, 1890, Stewart Papers.

68. Stewart sent similar letters to W. K. Patrick in St. Louis, Missouri; to Theo. Wagner, Orinda Park, California; to D. P. Frazer, Philadelphia, Pennsylvania; to Thomas S. Sedgwick, San Diego, California; to W. H. Halls, San Francisco, California; to W. H. Pratt, Davenport, Iowa; and to Governor R. C. Powers, Phoenix, Arizona Territory.

69. Stewart to John Conness, Aug. 29, 1890.

70. Sterling, "The Powell Irrigation Survey," pp. 431–433.

71. Townley, "Reclamation in Nevada," pp. 168–170.

72. Stewart to T. C. Friedlands, Sept. 6, 1890, Stewart Papers.

73. William Lilley III and Lewis L. Gould, "The Western Irrigation Movement, 1878–1902: A Reappraisal," in *The American West: A Reorientation,* ed. Gene Gressley, University of Wyoming Publications, 22 (1966), pp. 57–74.

74. Stewart, *Reminiscences,* pp. 287–288. See also various Stewart letters for January, 1888, which point out, "The decline in silver is the result of statute law, not of natural causes. Statute law can restore the equilibrium and restore prosperity."

75. Stewart, *Reminiscences,* p. 287.

76. *Congressional Record,* 50th Cong., 1st Sess., Part 2 (1888), pp. 1848–1853.

77. Quoted in Walter T. K. Nugent, *Money and American Society, 1865–1880* (New York: The Free Press, 1968), p. 165.

78. See pp. 69–71, above.

79. Nugent, in *Money and American Society* (pp. 168–172), states categorically, "The demonetization of silver in the Coinage Act of 1873 was known, planned, and brought off by Sherman, Boutwell, Linderman, Knox, Hooper and others in order to secure what they believed, and believed mistakenly, to be the public interest." Allen Weinstein, in *Prelude to Populism: Origins of the Silver Issue, 1867–1878* (New Haven, Connecticut: Yale University Press, 1970), holds the same general view, that "Sherman and his associates acted to demonetize silver not for corrupt private gain but in order to secure a domestic gold standard before the anticipated flood of depreciated silver bullion began arriving at government mints for coinage into legal-tender silver dollars" (p. 14). Still another scholar, Irwin Unger, in *The Greenback Era: A Social and Political History of American Finance, 1865–1879* (Princeton, New Jersey: Princeton University Press, 1964), supports these views, maintaining that the movement for a gold standard came from "the rational needs of a developing international economy, rather than the demands of scheming creditors" (p. 331).

80. Weinstein, *Prelude to Populism,* pp. 95–97. Weinstein states that "Weston . . . first raised publicly the notion of the 'Crime of 1873' when he charged that elimination of silver as a monetary standard in the mint bill of 1873 'was as selfish in its origin as it was surreptitious in the manner of its introduction.' "

81. *Ibid.* See also the *Nevada State Journal,* April 26, 1876, p. 2, cols. 1–3.

82. Stewart to Pete J. Otey, May 16, 1888, Stewart Papers. The idea of a "conspiracy" arose in 1876, according to Weinstein *(Prelude,* pp. 82–85), because the Resumption Act of 1875 stimulated a debate over the issuance of silver coins.

83. Weinstein, *Prelude,* pp. 95–97. Weinstein suggests that the efforts or Jones to restore silver led Nevada to develop its own political style and identity since, for three decades after 1876, no Nevada politician could gain importance in the state until he had demonstrated his soundness on the silver question (pp. 77–78). .

84. Emphasizng the fact that remonetization of silver was a political, rather than an economic issue in Nevada, was the position of the so-called Bonanza Kings, who made fortunes in the second Comstock boom. It was assumed at the time, and for nearly a hundred years thereafter, that Mackay, Fair, Flood, and O'Brien were leaders in the drive to remonetize silver. Weinstein's analysis in his *Prelude to Populism,* pp. 150–175, dispels what the author calls the "Bonanza King Myth." He points out that when Jones first raised the silver issue in Congress in 1876, the Bonanza Kings were already detaching themselves from the economic and political concerns of "less affluent Comstock mineowners"; and they did not support the Bland Act, as is generally believed. Weinstein notes that the Bonanza firm didn't need to seek government support of silver because they already had a secure government market for their bullion through the subsidiary coinage provision of the 1875 Resumption Act:

> The Bonanza firm sold more silver to the United States mints in the four years following passage of the Resumption Act in 1875 than any other single producer of bullion, either domestic or foreign. Far from needing or seeking a new government market for their silver during the struggle over remonetization, the Bonanza Kings already possessed a reliable customer in the Treasury Department, to which it sold whenever more profitable sales in Indian and Chinese trade did not absorb their valuable stock of silver bullion (p. 171).

85. Stewart to S. C. Wright, March 29, 1888, Stewart Papers.

86. *Congressional Record,* 50th Cong., 2d Sess., Part 1 (1889), pp. 460–465.

87. *Ibid.,* 1st Sess., Part 9 (1888), pp. 8243–8244.

88. Stewart to William Windom, March 12, 1889, Stewart Papers.

89. Stewart to President Harrison, April 20, 1889.

90. Stewart to Josephus Mesher, March 27, 1889.

91. *Congressional Record,* 51st Cong., 1st Sess., Parts 1–11 (1889), Index, p. 303.

92. *Ibid.,* Part 6 (1890), p. 5882.

93. Glass, *Silver and Politics in Nevada,* pp. 34–35.

94. *Congressional Record,* 51st Cong., 1st Sess., Part 7 (1890), p. 6183.

95. *Ibid.,* Part 6 (1890), pp. 6029–6033.

96. *Ibid.,* Part 8 (1890), pp. 6982, 7088, 7109, 7218, 7264.

97. Stewart to R. E. Bledsoe, July 24, 1890, Stewart Papers.

Chapter 8

1. *Morning Appeal,* Jan. 4, 1888, p. 2.

2. *Ibid.,* Jan. 11, 1888, p. 2.

3. Quoted in the *Morning Appeal,* Jan. 15, 1888, p. 2. See also Mack, "Stewart," 79, n. 102.

4. *New York Times,* Jan. 9, 1888, p. 1, col. 2 and p. 4, col. 2.

5. *Congressional Record,* 50th Cong., 1st Sess., Part 1 (1888), p. 475; *Journal of Executive Proceedings of the Senate* (1887–1888), Vol. 26, pp. 15, 132, 139–140.

6. Stewart to S. C. Wright, Jan. 21, 1888, Stewart Papers.

7. Stewart to J. W. Woltz, Jan. 21, 1888.

8. Stewart to L. L. Robinson, Jan. 21, 1888.

9. Stewart to R. L. Fulton, Feb. 19, 1888.

10. Allan Nevins, *Grover Cleveland: A Study in Courage* (New York: Dodd, Mead & Co., 1933), p. 339.

11. Stewart, *Reminiscences,* pp. 308–309.

12. *San Francisco Chronicle,* Jan. 10, 1888, p. 4, col. 2.

13. *Congressional Record,* 51st Cong., 1st Sess., Part 7 (1890), pp. 6114–6286.

14. Stewart, *Reminiscences,* p. 297.

15. H. Wayne Morgan, *From Hayes to McKinley: National Party Politics, 1877–1896* (Syracuse, New York: Syracuse University Press, 1969), p. 340.

16. Stewart, *Reminiscences,* p. 297.

17. *Congressional Record,* 51st Cong., 1st Sess., Part 7 (1890), pp. 6940–6941.

18. Stewart, *Reminiscences,* p. 298.

19. *Congressional Record,* 51st Cong., 2d Sess., Part 1 (1890), pp. 678–682.

20. Morgan, *From Hayes to McKinley,* p. 342. See also Stewart, *Reminiscences,* p. 299.

21. *Congressional Record,* 51st Cong., 2d Sess., Part 2 (1891), pp. 1706–1713.

22. *Ibid.,* pp. 1739–1741. Stewart wrote in his *Reminiscences,* p. 305, that "Before Senator Stanford left [for New York] in anticipation of the necessity of his vote, I called at his house and he told me I might pair him in favor of taking up the Apportionment Bill at any time." That statement is in direct conflict with Stewart's public admission to Aldrich that he had no authority to pair Stanford, but knew the California senator wanted to debate the Apportionment Bill.

23. *Ibid.*

24. Stewart, *Reminiscences,* pp. 306–307.

25. Stewart to William A. Meloy, March 9, 1891, Stewart Papers.

26. Stewart to E. A. Angier, Feb. 2, 1891.

27. H. M. Yerington to Stewart, Jan. 28, 1891.

28. Stewart to Governor R. K. Colcord, March 26, 1891.

29. *Congressional Globe,* 39th Cong., 1st Sess., Part 3 (1866), p. 2014.

30. *Walker Lake Bulletin* (Hawthorne), March 28, 1883, p. 2, col. 2.

31. *Ibid.,* May 16, 1883, p. 2, col. 1. See Edward C. Johnson, *Walker River Paiutes: A Tribal History* (Salt Lake City, Utah: University of Utah Printing Service, 1974), pp. 73–80, for a good summary of the attempts to force the abandonment of the Walker Lake Reservation.

32. *Walker Lake Bulletin,* Jan. 14, 1885, p. 2, col. 1.

33. *Statutes of Nevada* (1885), pp. 167–168.

34. *Ibid.,* pp. 143–145.

35. Stewart to J. W. Ross, July 6, 1887, Stewart Papers.

36. Stewart to W. F. Vilas, March 3, 1888.

37. Stewart to J. M. Campbell, March 29, 1888.

38. Stewart to C. H. Barrett, Feb. 1, 1889.

39. See the copies of the letters to the three commissioners appointed, Asa French of Massachusetts, Ebenezer Ormsbee of Vermont, and W. A. Morgan of Kansas, from the Office of Indian Affairs, Dept. of Interior, July 27, 1891, Stewart Papers.

40. *Ibid.*

41. Johnson, *Walker River Paiutes,* p. 76.

42. Copy of agreement between the Walker Lake Indians and the Carson and Colorado Railroad officials, September 8, 1882, signed before the Commissioner of the U.S. Circuit Court, Nineteenth District, H. M. Yerington Papers.

43. C. C. Warner to H. M. Yerington, Sept. 28, 1891.

44. *Walker Lake Bulletin,* Oct. 21, 1891, p. 3, col. 4.

45. *Ibid.*

46. Johnson, *Walker River Paiutes,* p. 76; *Walker Lake Bulletin,* Oct. 21, Oct. 28, 1891. The formal report of the commission was not made public until 1892.

47. Stewart to Commissioner of Indian Affairs, Nov. 27, 1891, Stewart Papers.

48. Stewart to William Webster, Feb. 16, 1892.

49. Stewart to H. M. Yerington, April 7, 1892.

50. Yerington to Stewart, April 8, 1892.

51. Yerington to Stewart, April 17, 1892.

52. Yerington to Stewart, May 4, 1892.

53. Stewart to C. C. Warner, April 26, 1892.

54. *Ibid.*

55. *Walker Lake Bulletin,* August 3, 1892, p. 3, col. 4.

56. Stewart to Henry L. Dawes, March 1, 1888, Stewart Papers.

57. Stewart to Commissioner of Indian Affairs, April 25, 1892.

58. Stewart to Cornelius N. Bliss, Feb. 16, 1898.

59. *Gold Hill Daily News,* May 29, 1874.

60. Stewart to William Thompson and H. R. Beck, Feb. 18, 1889, Stewart Papers.

61. Stewart to Virginia W. Middleton, Feb. 25, 1889. One can't help but wonder what influence, if any, his very good friend, Hannah K. Clapp, had in directing his support of women's suffrage. Clapp was not only a strong suffragette, but an extremely capable and independent woman, who once indicated she would not pay any taxes until she was granted the right to vote. For the latter incident, see "100 Years Ago," *Nevada State Journal,* September 25, 1973.

62. Stewart to Mrs. James Bennett, Dec. 12, 1889, Stewart Papers.

63. Susan B. Anthony to Stewart, April 17, 1900.

64. Stewart to Samuel Gompers, Aug. 28, 1889.

65. Stewart to F. C. Lord, April 12, 1892. It is interesting to note, in reference to Stewart's remarks, that federal troops were, in fact, ordered to Goldfield, Nevada, from San Francisco, in December, 1906, to help quell a strike by miners.

66. Stewart to C. C. Powning, April 22, 1892.

67. *Congressional Record,* 50th Cong., 1st Sess., Part 1, pp. 421–422.

68. Stewart to George Barrington, May 22, 1889, Stewart Papers.

69. Stewart to C. P. Huntington, Feb. 6, 1892.

70. Stewart to H. M. Yerington, Feb. 2, 1888.

71. *Congressional Record,* 50th Cong., 2d Sess., Part 1 (1888), pp. 155–156.

72. Stewart to Chester Griswold, Feb. 27, 1893, Stewart Papers.

73. The University of Nevada was established at Elko, in eastern Nevada, in 1874, just as Stewart was leaving the Senate. He played no part in that development.

74. Stewart to C. S. Young, Dec. 5, 1887, Stewart Papers. As Stewart predicted, growth of the university to the north forced removal of the cemeteries. In the 1960's, the university purchased the land and built a dormitory and parking lot, after the bodies interred there were removed.

75. Stewart to J. F. Hallock, Feb. 2, 1889. Similar letters were sent to John Forbes, C. N. Noteware, J. Poujade, W. E. Sharon, Evan Williams, and H. L. Fish.

76. Stewart to M. D. Foley, Jan. 31, 1891.

77. Samuel B. Doten, *An Illustrated History of the University of Nevada* (Reno, Nevada: University of Nevada, 1941), pp. 74–75. Stewart's activities on behalf of the University of Nevada led the Board of Regents to name a building on the Reno campus Stewart Hall. The structure was razed in the 1950's, after an earthquake damaged it.

78. Stewart to C. C. Goodwin, Jan. 21, 1888, Stewart Papers.

79. Stewart to C. S. Young, Feb. 4, 1889.

80. Stewart to the editor of *Munson's Illustrated Weekly,* Feb. 17, 1890.

81. *Congressional Record,* 50th Cong., 1st Sess., Part 1 (1888), p. 184; Part 2 (1888), pp. 1148, 1181–1183.

82. *Annual Report of the Secretary of the Interior* (Washington, D.C.: Government Printing Office, 1892), pp. 569–571; Scrugham, *History of Nevada,* Vol. I, p. 349. Stewart described his work on behalf of Indian education in Nevada in his autobiography, "I took measures to establish an Indian school at Carson, Nevada, and have done all in my power to secure the education of the Indians of Nevada in such matters as will make them self-sustaining" (pp. 282–283). The school was closed as an educational institution in 1980.

83. Stewart to S. F. Gage, Jan. 5, 1889; Feb. 6, Feb. 11, and Feb. 12, 1890, Stewart Papers.

84. Stewart to C. P. Huntington, Feb. 1, March 1, 1890.

85. *Ibid.,* March 24, June 30, Dec. 29, 1890.

86. *Ibid.,* Feb. 13, 1889.

87. Stewart to Francis G. Newlands, Sept. 13, 1890.

88. Stewart to C. P. Huntington, May 10, 1892.

89. *Ibid.,* Dec. 29, 1880; May 16, 1892.

90. *Ibid.,* Jan. 26, 1893.

91. *Ibid.,* April 22, 1891.

92. Stewart to John P. Jones, May 18, 1891.

93. Stewart to H. M. Yerington, Sept. 16, 1888.

94. Stewart to I. E. Gates, April 11, 1900.

95. Sam Platt to Stewart, Dec. 8, 1897.

96. Stewart to A. J. Cassett, March 11, 1905; Stewart to Maxwell Evarts, March 16, 1905. An earlier request by Stewart for free transportation, although not by railroad, went even further. In 1902, while preparing to attend the Hague Conference, he wrote the president of the International Navigation Company as follows: "Can I presume on your generosity enough to ask you to furnish me with passage to Rotterdam or by the Red Star Line to Antwerp. However, the line will make no difference. If you can arrange this matter for me I shall consider it a personal favor" (Stewart to Clement A. Grisscom, July 12, 1902). Evidently the favor was granted.

97. Stewart to S. F. Gage, Aug. 6, 1892.

98. Stewart to C. H. Sproule, Aug. 13, 1892.

Chapter 9

1. Stewart to Francis G. Newlands, Feb. 9, 1889, Stewart Papers.

2. *Ibid.,* Nov. 8, Dec. 21, 1889.

3. Stewart to Thomas Fitch, May 24, 1890.

4. Stewart to S. C. Wright, May 28, 1890.

5. Stewart to Francis G. Newlands, July 18, 1890.

6. H. M. Yerington to Stewart, June 21, Aug. 17, 1890.

7. Stewart to Francis G. Newlands, Sept. 10, 1890.

8. *Reno Evening Gazette,* Aug. 6, 1890, p. 2, col. 1.

9. *Ibid.,* Aug. 9, 1890, p. 2, col. 1.

10. *Ibid.,* Sept. 4, 1890, p. 1, col. 2; Sept. 6, 1890, p. 2, col. 1.

11. *Ibid.,* Sept. 5, 1890, p. 1, col. 2.

12. *Ibid.,* Sept. 6, 1890, p. 3, col. 2.

13. Francis G. Newlands to F. W. Sharon, Sept. 24, 1890, Sharon Family Papers, Bancroft Library.

14. *Reno Evening Gazette,* Sept. 6, 1890, p. 2, col. 3.

15. *Ibid.,* Aug. 7, 1890, p. 3, col. 3; Aug. 13, 1890, p. 4, col. 3. Stewart had been in Reno on Aug. 6, and in Carson City on Aug. 13, and no doubt understood the political situation.

16. Stewart to Francis G. Newlands, Sept. 13, 1890, Stewart Papers; H. M. Yerington to A. C. Cleveland, Sept. 17, 1890, Yerington Papers, Bancroft Library.

17. Stewart to S. C. Wright, Oct. 3, 1890.

18. *Nevada State Journal,* Oct. 27, 1970, p. 4, col. 5.

19. Stewart to C. C. Goodwin, Jan. 31, 1891, Stewart Papers.

20. Stewart to Thomas Wren, March 7, 1891. Stewart was correct on two counts, the selection of a gold nominee by each of the major parties, and the formation of a third party (People's Party).

21. Stewart to Olney Newell, May 15, 1891.

22. Stewart to Andrew Carnegie, June 10, 1891.

23. Stewart to M. Gadd, July 2, 1891.

24. Stewart to S. D. R. Stewart, Jan. 29, 1889. For the Mexican venture, see particularly a letter from Stewart to Henry Winninghoff, Sept. 12, 1891.

25. Stewart to W. J. Plumb, July 27, 1891; Stewart to John S. Mayhugh, Feb. 18, 1892.

26. Stewart to C. C. Wallace, March 3, 1892.

27. Stewart to S. F. Gage, March 3, 1892.

28. Stewart to J. T. Goodman, March 7, 1892. In another letter, to S. C. Wright, April 11, 1888, Stewart made some unflattering remarks about Woodburn's alleged drinking habits.

29. Stewart to S. C. Wright, March 3, 1892.

30. Stewart to C. C. Wallace, March 3, 1892.

31. Glass, *Silver and Politics in Nevada*, p. 35.

32. *Ibid.*, p. 42. George Nixon came to Nevada as a telegraph operator and station agent for the Carson and Colorado Railroad at Belleville and Candelaria, but soon entered the banking business, first at Reno and then at Winnemucca. His purchase of the *Silver State* newspaper at Winnemucca launched not only his journalistic career, but also his political one.

33. Stewart to George S. Nixon, April 19, 1892, Stewart Papers.

34. Stewart to C. C. Wallace, April 18, 1892.

35. Stewart to S. C. Wright, March 29, 1892.

36. Yerington to Stewart, April 17, 1892, Yerington Papers.

37. Stewart to S. C. Wright, April 19, 1892, Stewart Papers.

38. Stewart to P. B. Ellis, April 25, 1892. Evidently he changed his mind about such standards for fitness when he returned to the Republican Party and the gold standard in 1900.

39. Stewart to C. C. Wallace, March 29, 1892.

40. Stewart to F. C. Lord, March 30, 1892. A similar letter was sent to J. T. Goodman on the same date.

41. Stewart to F. C. Lord, April 14, 1892.

42. Stewart to H. M. Yerington, April 15, 1892.

43. Stewart to S. C. Wright, April 19, 1892.

44. Glass, *Silver and Politics in Nevada*, p. 44.

45. *Morning Appeal*, June 4, 1892, p. 2; Glass, *Silver and Politics*, p. 22.

46. Stewart to C. C. Goodwin, May 3, 1892, Stewart Papers.

47. Glass, *Silver and Politics*, pp. 54–55.

48. *Ibid.*, pp. 63–65. Glass takes a firm position that Wallace's manipulations on behalf of silver in Nevada were made to maintain control of state politics by the Central Pacific. It is interesting to compare the role played by that railroad in trying to control the political destinies of California and Nevada in face of the Populist threat. In California, the silver issue was not as strong as in Nevada, and no major attempt was made there to organize a silver party. However, the California People's Party gave the railroad officials an opportunity to weaken the Democrats and insure victory for the Republicans. The procedure used to accomplish this was detailed in a letter to C. P. Huntington from one of the railroad's officials, who suggested that the company further the organization of the Populists in California and have that party put up a full slate of candidates so as to split the Democratic votes. (William H. Mills to C. P. Huntington, July 9, 1892, Series I Reel 51, Huntington Papers.)

49. Glass, *Silver and Politics*, pp. 48–53.

50. *Ibid.*, p. 53.

51. Stewart to F. G. Newlands, July 7, 1892, Stewart Papers.

52. Stewart to F. C. Lord, July 7, 1892. Stewart's optimism was strengthened by indications from H. M. Yerington that he had "a long conversation with Mr. Huntington. Among other things I brought up your name and he told me most emphatically he proposed to stand by you throughout the fight" (H. M. Yerington to Stewart, May 4, 1892).

53. Stewart to A. J. Streeter, June 28, 1892.

54. Stewart to F. G. Newlands, July 7, 1892.

55. John D. Hicks, *The American Nation* (Boston: Houghton Mifflin, 1946), p. 248.

56. *Nevada State Journal*, Aug. 12, 1892, p. 2; Glass, *Silver and Politics*, p. 56.

57. Glass, *Silver and Politics*, p. 56.

58. Stewart, *Reminiscences*, pp. 310, 318–319.

59. *Silver State* (Winnemucca), Sept. 16, 1892, p. 2; Glass, *Silver and Politics*, pp. 57–60, has an excellent summary of the Winnemucca convention.

60. Stewart to Andrew Maute, Sept. 19, 1892, Stewart Papers.

61. Stewart to C. H. Hinckcliffe, Oct. 2, 1892. The letter was a reflection of one of the continuing problems in "buying" candidates, that is, how to keep them "bought."

62. Stewart to John P. Jones, Sept. 12, 1892.

63. Stewart to C. P. Huntington, Sept. 12, 1892.

64. Stewart to Senator A. P. Gorman, Sept. 12, 1892.

65. Wm. M. Stewart to C. P. Huntington, Sept. 26, 1892, Series I, Reel 51, Huntington Papers.

66. *Ibid.,* Stewart to George S. Nixon, Oct. 4, 1892, Stewart Papers.

67. Wm. M. Stewart to C. P. Huntington, Sept. 28, 1892, Series I, Reel 51, Huntington Papers.

68. Stewart to George Q. Cannon, Oct. 4, 1892, Stewart Papers. In the letter to Cannon, Stewart bemoaned the fact that the *Salt Lake Tribune,* which generally had supported him, was supporting Harrison and sending free papers throughout Nevada to defeat Stewart and the silver question.

69. Kappler's speech, Oct. 29, 1892, is in the Stewart Papers.

70. Stewart to C. P. Huntington, Oct. 28, 1892, Series I, Reel 51, Huntington Papers.

71. Stewart to Huntington, Dec. 7, 1892, *ibid.*

72. H. M. Yerington to D. O. Mills, Dec. 14, 1892, Yerington Papers. Italic words were underlined in the original letter.

73. H. M. Yerington to Stewart, Jan. 1, 1893, Stewart Papers.

74. Stewart to Edward Reynolds, Jan. 3, 1893. Stewart sent similar letters to W. E. Sharon, E. D. Kelley, George S. Nixon, and Hirsch Harris.

75. *Journal of the Assembly,* Jan. 24, 1893, p. 29; *Journal of the Senate,* Jan. 24, 1893, p. 24, Jan. 25, 1893, p. 29.

76. *Nevada State Journal,* March 21, 1937, p. 11, cols. 2–3.

77. George A. Armes to Capt. John F. Rogers, Jan. 25, 1890; Stewart to Francis G. Newlands, March 26, 1890, Stewart Papers.

78. Stewart to Francis G. Newlands, July 4, 1895. This letter is an attempt by Stewart to recapitulate the history of the Chevy Chase Land Company from 1890 to 1895. It appears that Stewart did not receive any cash, but did receive stock for his part in the transaction. The idea that money from Newlands was used to elect Stewart in 1892 appears to be based on hearsay evidence.

79. Stewart to T. R. Hofer, Feb. 6, 1889. This letter indicates that Stewart held some stock in the Consolidated-Virginia mine on the Comstock. Other letters connect him to mines in Amador County, which were supervised by his brother. A letter to Henry Winninghoff, Sept. 12, 1891, indicates that Stewart was then president of the International Mining Company in San Miguel del Mesquital, Mexico, and had promoted stock of the company among his family and friends.

80. Stewart to Henry Winninghoff, Dec. 1, 1891; C. P. Huntington to Stewart, July 13, 1893.

81. *Weekly Nevada State Journal,* Oct. 26, p. 6, col. 6; *Elko Daily Independent,* Oct. 24, 1889, p. 3, col. 2; Oct. 26, 1889, p. 3, col. 2.

82. Stewart to Miss H. K. Clapp, March 29, 1889, Stewart Papers.

83. Stewart to Dr. J. R. Baker, Dec. 20, 1889. See also letters to his grandsons, Harry Hooker, Dec. 9, 1889; to Richard Hooker, Dec. 12, 1889; and to Willie and Tommy Fox, Dec. 9, 1889.

84. There is some confusion over the actual dates of this two-year world cruise. Mack ("Stewart," 77) states that the tour began in 1889, and lasted two years. Hermann *(Gold and Silver Colossus,* pp. 283–285) states that the trip began in 1891, and lasted until 1893. Letters in the Stewart Papers indicate that Mrs. Stewart and her daughter were in various parts of the globe from 1891 to 1893. Thus in a letter to R. Wildman, Jan. 4, 1892, Stewart indicates that he had just received a letter from Mrs. Stewart from Auckland, New Zealand. In another letter, to Henry Winninghoff, March 29, 1892, Stewart says his wife was in Yokohama, Japan. And in a letter to his grandson, Harry Hooker, March 24, 1893, Stewart wrote that his wife was in Paris and would be in New York the early part of April, 1893. Adding confusion is a letter dated Dec. 26, 1888, which indicated that Mrs. Stewart was traveling up the Nile River and through the Holy Land. If the date of that letter is correct, then the two-year tour was really a four-year tour, or she took two trips. More likely is the

fact that the Nile River trip was part of the world cruise and the letter is simply incorrectly dated.

85. Stewart to the Secretary of the Treasury, Dec. 21, 1893, Stewart Papers.

86. Hermann, *Gold and Silver Colossus*, pp. 283–285.

Chapter 10

1. Stewart to C. C. Wallace, Dec. 26, 1892, Stewart Papers.

2. Stewart to George Nixon, April 5, 1893.

3. *Congressional Record,* 53d Cong., Special Sess. (1893), p. 197.

4. Mack, "Stewart," 75–76.

5. See the Stewart Papers, March 13, 1893, for an article titled "Senator Stewart on Silver—Senator Stewart Contraverts the Arguments of Mr. Horr on all important points." The letters to Horr begin Feb. 22, 1893, and end May 25, 1893.

6. *Congressional Record,* 53d Cong., Special Sess. (1893), p. 216.

7. John Sherman, *Recollections of Forty Years in the House, Senate and Cabinet* (Chicago: Werner Company, 1895), pp. 828–829.

8. Stewart to Lawrence J. McParlin, Aug. 10, 1893, Stewart Papers.

9. Stewart to Dr. M. Reeves, Aug. 14, 1893. In the letter, Stewart states that in all the years he had been contending for the restoration of silver, "I had no interest whatever in any silver mine."

10. Stewart to the Board of Directors of the International Mining Company of Washington, D.C., Aug. 5, 1893.

11. *Congressional Record,* 53d Cong., Special Sess. (1893), p. 497.

12. *Ibid.,* p. 499.

13. *Ibid.,* pp. 873, 877.

14. *Ibid.,* pp. 1211–1236, 1247–1258.

15. Sherman, *Recollections,* pp. 391, 395.

16. *Congressional Record,* 53d Cong., Special Sess. (1893), pp. 1232–1233.

17. *Ibid.,* p. 1236.

18. *New York Times,* Sept. 7, 1893, p. 5, col. 1.

19. *Congressional Record,* 53d Cong., Special Sess. (1893), p. 1338.

20. *Ibid.,* pp. 606–705. E. P. Oberholtzer, in his *History of the United States,* Vol. 5, pp. 269–270, describes Jones's speech and the continuing filibuster, "When his voice failed, or he could stand on his feet no longer, a colleague took up the burden and the spate of words continued. The volume of utterance of Stewart, Peffer and Teller could be computed only by application of the yardstick to the *Congressional Record.*"

21. *Congressional Record,* 53d Cong., Special Sess. (1893), p. 2958.

22. *Ibid.,* pp. 2958, 3067, 3100.

23. *New York Times,* Nov. 12, 1893, p. 20, col. 6.

24. Stewart to Dr. C. Q. Nelson, Sept. 13, 1893, Stewart Papers.

25. Stewart to Huntington, Sept. 16, 1893, Series I, Reel 52, Huntington Papers. The same letter is also found in the letterpress books in the Stewart Papers.

26. Stewart to Huntington, Dec. 1, 1893, Stewart Papers. Stewart had many chances in the next few years to demonstrate his appreciation, particularly in regard to the attempt of the railroads to get a federal extension of their debts.

27. Stewart to George S. Nixon, Nov. 4, 1893.

28. *Congressional Record,* 53d Cong., 2d Sess., Part 3 (1894), pp. 2872–2877, 3458.

29. *Ibid.,* Part 1 (1894), pp. 164–165.

30. *Ibid.,* Part 5 (1894), pp. 4222–4224.

31. *Ibid.,* Part 7 (1894), p. 6224.

32. *Ibid.,* Part 5 (1894), p. 4584–4585.

33. *Ibid.,* Part 7 (1894), p. 6224.

34. *Ibid.,* pp. 7090–7093.

35. *Ibid.*, p. 7136. The bill became law later without the President's signature.

36. See particularly the letter from Stewart to W. R. Gorman, April 6, 1894, Stewart Papers.

37. Stewart to W. T. Cheyney, Feb. 5, 1894.

38. Stewart to W. E. Sharon, Dec. 11, 1894.

39. Stewart to Mrs. W. Davis, May 10, 1894.

40. Stewart to A. Jackson, Dec. 27, 1894.

41. Elliott, *History of Nevada*, pp. 189–190. Coxey's idea, modified somewhat, appeared later as one of the early New Deal measures.

42. Stewart to General J. S. Coxey, March 24, 1894, Stewart Papers.

43. *Reno Evening Gazette*, March 31, 1894, p. 1, col. 3.

44. Stewart to J. W. Reid, Nov. 4, 1893, Stewart Papers. In the letter he described himself as "proud of being a Populist." See also Stewart to W. F. Rightmire, Nov. 18, 1893.

45. Stewart to Thomas Wren, Aug. 7, 1894.

46. Stewart to the Editor of the *(Nevada State) Journal*, Oct. 20, 1894.

47. *Congressional Record*, 53d Cong., 3d Sess., Part 1 (1895), pp. 904–907, 927–930.

48. *Ibid.*, p. 2280.

49. *Ibid.*, Part 4, pp. 2885–2889.

50. *Ibid.*, pp. 3114–3116.

51. *Statutes of Nevada* (1895), p. 116.

52. Stewart to Huntington, March 6, 1895, Series I, Reel 53, Huntington Papers.

53. Huntington to Stewart, March 7, 1895, *ibid.*

54. Stewart to "My dear Julien," March 29, 1895, Stewart Papers. Stewart saw difficulties in belonging to a multi-issue party nationally (the Populists) and a single-issue party locally (the Silver Party).

55. Stewart to George Nixon, March 13, 1895.

56. Stewart to George C. Merrick, March 13, 1895.

57. Stewart to William E. Sharon, March 14, 1895.

58. Stewart to Marion Butler, March 15, 1895.

59. Stewart to President Grover Cleveland, April 15, 1895, Microfilm Series 2, Reel 89, Grover Cleveland Papers, Library of Congress. A copy of the letter is also in the Stewart Papers.

60. *Ibid.*, April 30, 1895.

61. Stewart to Cleveland, May 7, 1895, Stewart Papers. Each of the two earlier letters had contained liberal amounts of Stewart's bimetallism philosophy along with the more specific references to policies.

62. Stewart to Marion Butler, July 13, 1895. In the *Silver Knight*, Aug. 22, 1895, p. 3, col. 1, Stewart indicated that there were already 60 lodges or temples in existence at that time. The membership fee was $1.00, and the organization was open to women as well as men. Its objective was the restoration of silver to its rightful place in the monetary system. Stewart was the national president of the organization.

63. *Silver Knight*, Aug. 15, 1895, p. 1, cols. 1–4. Stewart to John P. Young, Aug. 22, 1895. Stewart told Young, the editor of the *San Francisco Chronicle*, that the paper would give him an opportunity to print the silver side of the question and expose the hypocrisy and double-dealing of pretenders.

64. Stewart, *Reminiscences*, pp. 321–322.

65. Thomas A. Bailey, *A Diplomatic History of the American People* (New York: Appleton-Century Crofts, 1955), p. 486.

66. *Silver Knight-National Watchman*, Dec. 26, 1895, p. 1, cols. 4–5.

67. *Ibid.*, Jan. 2, 1896, p. 4, col. 1.

68. *Congressional Record*, 54th Cong., 1st Sess., Part 7 (1896), p. 1118.

69. Stewart to Hon. H. E. Taubenck, Dec. 12, 1895 and Dec. 16, 1895, Stewart Papers. Taubenck was chairman of the National Committee of the Populists.

70. Stewart to Joseph Sibley, Dec. 19, 1895; to Ignatius Donnelly, Dec. 20, 1895; and to M. C. Rankin, Dec. 26, 1895.

71. Stewart to E. T. Winston, Jan. 28, 1896.

72. Stewart to R. C. Chambers, Feb. 4, 1896. See also the *Silver Knight-Watchman,* Jan. 23, 1896, p. 5, col. 4.

73. Stewart to A. Brisbane, March 24, 1896.

74. Stewart to McKinley, April 28, 1896, Microfilm Series I, Reel 1, William McKinley Papers, Library of Congress.

75. Joseph R. Dunlop to Stewart, May 20, 1896; A. J. Utley to Stewart, June 9, 1896; Marion Butler to Stewart, June 29, 1896, Stewart Papers.

76. Stewart to A. J. Utley, July 2, 1896; to William H. Porter, July 2, 1896.

77. Stewart to George Nixon, March 13, 1895.

78. Marion Butler to Stewart, July 6, 1896.

79. L. J. Page to Stewart, July 1, 1896.

80. *Morning Appeal,* July 9, 1896, p. 2, col. 1. A correspondent charged Stewart with making a complete somersault, "hats, pants, and boots, into the democratic [sic] Party" (J. W. Baker to William M. Stewart, Sept. 15, 1896, Stewart Papers).

81. Stewart to Marion Butler, July 14, 1896. Stewart was one of the first to recognize that the Populists should have held an early convention, although earlier he had advised them to hold their convention last.

82. Charles A. Norcross to Stewart, July 20, 1896.

83. *Silver Knight-Watchman,* July 30, 1896, p. 5, cols. 3–6.

84. An interesting poll of the delegates at the National Silver Convention showed 526 to be former Republicans, 147 to be former Democrats, and 78 to be former Populists. The makeup of the National Silver Party and the People's Party probably accounted for some of the difficulty in compromising.

85. Stewart to Charles A. Norcross, July 28, 1896, Stewart Papers.

86. Glass, *Silver and Politics,* pp. 110–112. Newlands's representatives were George Nixon and W. E. Sharon, Stewart's were C. C. Wallace and W. A. Massey.

87. *Ibid.,* pp. 113–114. See also the *Morning Appeal,* Sept. 10, 1896, p. 3, col. 2, and Sept. 11, 1896, p. 2, col. 1.

88. *Morning Appeal,* Aug. 13, 1893, p. 3, col. 3.

89. Bishop Newman to Stewart, Aug. 15, 1896, Stewart Papers.

90. *Morning Appeal,* Sept. 1, 1896, p. 3, col. 3. The letter-writing campaign against Stewart appears to have been part of a plan by gold-standard supporters to embarrass former gold-standard people who had joined the silver ranks. See F. G. Schultz to Stewart, Sept. 1, 1896, Stewart Papers.

91. M. W. Harmish to Stewart, Sept. 4, 1896.

92. These are under date of September 8, 1896, in the Stewart Papers.

93. Senator James H. Kyle to Stewart, Aug. 25, 1896; N. Taylor Phillips to Stewart, Aug. 27, 1896; J. A. Edgerten to Stewart, Sept. 1, 1896.

94. Yerington to D. O. Mills, Dec. 2, 1896, Yerington Papers.

95. Hirsch Harris to Stewart, Jan. 12, 1897, Stewart Papers.

96. C. C. Wallace to Stewart, Jan. 28, 1897; Glass, *Silver and Politics,* p. 111. Glass maintains that the struggle for power between the two groups had started much earlier and simply broke into the open during the campaign to bring about fusion of the silver groups in Nevada.

97. *Morning Appeal,* Jan. 6, 1897, p. 3, col. 2. Nixon should have understood that Nevadans then equated loyalty to silver with loyalty to the state.

98. *Ibid.,* Jan. 14. 1897, p. 2, col. 1 and p. 3.

99. *Ibid.,* Jan. 19, 1897, p. 3, cols. 1–2.

100. *Ibid.,* Jan. 28, 1897, p. 3, col. 2.

101. *Ibid.,* Jan. 21, 1897, p. 3, col. 1. Nixon's prophecy was borne out after the turn of the century as Nevadans struggled to free themselves of the economic and political domination of California. See the chapter, "The Rise of Nevadaism" in Ostrander, *Nevada,* pp. 132–158.

102. C. C. Wallace to Stewart, Jan. 28, 1897, Stewart Papers.

103. Glass, *Silver and Politics,* p. 116.

104. *Congressional Record,* 54th Cong., 2d Sess., Part 2 (1897), pp. 1421, 1876. The charge insofar as it referred to Stewart appears to be unfair, since he had never supported silver to the exclusion of gold. However, Stewart and other bimetallists often wrote and spoke with such emphasis on the restoration of silver that it gave the appearance they were supporting a single standard— silver.

105. *Ibid.,* pp. 2606, 2725; *Silver Knight-Watchman,* Feb. 4, 1897, p. 4, cols. 1–2.

106. *Congressional Record,* 55th Cong., 1st Sess., Part 2 (1897), pp. 1858–1859.

107. *Ibid.,* 54th Cong., 2d Sess., Part 3 (1897), p. 2725.

108. P. J. Quigley to Stewart, Aug. 12, 1897, enclosing a clipping of Aug. 12, 1897, titled "Interview with Stewart," Stewart Papers.

109. *Silver Knight-Watchman,* Aug. 19, 1897, p. 1, col. 2.

110. Alex C. Lassen to Stewart, Aug. 12, 1897, Stewart Papers.

111. *New York Times,* Aug. 24, 1897, p. 4, col. 3.

112. Charles Kappler to Isaac Frohman, June 19, 1897; Stewart to Joseph C. Sibley, April 30, 1898, Stewart Papers.

113. Stewart to Senator James K. Jones, July 19, 1898.

114. In January, 1899, the paper was sold to a group of Democrats who promised to continue the fight for silver. Charles Rodgers to Alex. Del Mar, Jan. 9, 1899, Stewart Papers.

115. Yerington to Stewart, March 19, 1897; Yerington to J. P. Jones, May 7, 1897, Yerington Papers.

116. *Congressional Record,* 55th Cong., 1st Sess., Part 3 (1897), pp. 2259–2264.

117. H. M. Yerington to Stewart, Dec. 18, 1893, Stewart Papers.

118. *Congressional Record,* 54th Cong., 1st Sess., Part 1 (1895), p. 18.

119. *Ibid.,* p. 45.

120. *Ibid.,* 55th Cong., 2d Sess., Part 1 (1897), p. 247.

121. Stewart to William McPherson, Jan. 14, 1898, Stewart Papers.

122. Although Stewart later wrote a friend that the issue of quieting Indian titles in Wadsworth had been settled, it continued to create controversy well into the 1930's. For the later story, see Abbott Joseph Liebling, "The Lake of the Cui-ui Eaters," *New Yorker,* 30 (Jan. 1, 1955), pp. 25– 30; (Jan. 8, 1955), pp. 33–36; (Jan. 15, 1955), pp. 32–36; (Jan. 22, 1955), p. 37.

123. E. H. Belden to Stewart, Jan. 6, 1897, enclosing two articles of Dec. 30, 1896, from the *Missouri World,* Stewart Papers.

124. *Congressional Record,* 54th Cong., 1st Sess., Part 6 (1896), pp. 5102–5106.

125. *Ibid.,* 55th Cong., 1st Sess., Part 3 (1897), pp. 2605–2608. In a letter of Aug. 8, 1898, to Stewart, A. A. Proctor evidenced surprise that Stewart, one of the attorneys for Southern Pacific Company, should be "assisting C. P. Huntington to keep people of Los Angeles out of San Pedro and favoring Santa Monica."

126. Stewart to William Herrin, Aug. 26, 1894, Stewart Papers.

127. William H. Mills to Stewart, Dec. 28, 1897.

128. C. P. Huntington to Stewart, March 2, 1898.

129. *Congressional Record,* 55th Cong., 1st Sess., Part 3 (1897), p. 2688; Stewart, *Reminiscences,* p. 338.

130. C. P. Huntington to Stewart, Feb. 15, 1897; June 4, 1898, Stewart Papers.

131. *Morning Appeal,* Jan. 30, 1897, p. 3, col. 1. The law was passed Jan. 29, 1897.

132. Stewart to Alexander McCone, March 25, 1897, Stewart Papers.

133. *Silver Knight-Watchman,* March 25, 1897, p. 4, col. 2; Stewart's answer to the easterners was published in the *Morning Appeal,* March 29, 1897, p. 3, col. 2.

134. C. C. Wallace to Stewart, March 11, 1898, Stewart Papers.

135. Quoted in Mary Ellen Glass, "The Silver Governors: Immigrants in Nevada Politics, Part II," *Nevada Historical Society Quarterly,* 21 (Winter, 1978), 269. The telegram was dated March 10, 1898.

136. E. D. Kelley to Stewart, March 14, 1898; John Sparks to Stewart, March 14, 1898; George Nixon to Stewart, March 23, 1898, Stewart Papers.

137. Letter to Stewart, March 13, 1898, signed by members of the Elko County Cattle Association, including George W. Russell and others.

138. W. H. Patterson to Stewart, March 13, 1898.

139. Stewart to W. H. Patterson, March 28, 1898.

140. Glass, "The Silver Governors," 269–270; *Morning Appeal,* March 24, 1898, p. 3, col. 2.

141. Quoted in Glass, "The Silver Governors," 270.

142. *Congressional Record,* 54th Cong., 1st Sess., Part 3 (1896), pp. 2122–2123, 2961–2963.

143. *Ibid.,* 2d Sess., Part 3 (1897), pp. 2256–2257.

144. *Silver Knight-Watchman,* March 3, 1898, p. 1, col. 1.

145. Stewart to Stephen T. Gage, March 28, 1898, Stewart Papers.

146. *Silver Knight-Watchman,* March 3, 1898, p. 9.

147. *Ibid.,* March 17, 1898, p. 8.

148. *Ibid.,* April 21, 1898, pp. 8–9.

149. *Congressional Record,* 55th Cong., 2d Sess., Part 4 (1898), pp. 3702–3703.

150. *Silver Knight-Watchman,* April 14, 1898, p. 8.

151. *Congressional Record,* 55th Cong., 2d Sess., Part 4 (1898), pp. 3901–3906.

152. *Ibid.,* p. 4029.

153. *Ibid.,* pp. 4040–4041; *Silver Knight-Watchman,* April 21, 1898, p. 1. Newlands voted for the resolution.

154. *Silver Knight-Watchman,* March 10, 1898, p. 8.

155. *Ibid.,* March 24, 1898, p. 8.

156. Joseph A. Fray, "Silver and Sentiment: The Nevada Press and the Coming of the Spanish-American War," *Nevada Historical Society Quarterly,* 20 (Winter, 1977), 223–239.

157. *Silver Knight-Watchman,* April 28, 1898, p. 8.

158. *Congressional Record,* 55th Cong., 2d Sess., Part 7 (1898), pp. 5170–5178.

159. *Ibid.,* pp. 5471–5472.

160. W. L. Deveroux to Stewart, June 2, 1898, Stewart Papers.

161. *Silver Knight-Watchman,* May 12, 1898, p. 6, cols. 3–4.

162. *Ibid.,* May 19, 1898, p. 6, col. 1.

163. *Congressional Record,* 55th Cong., 2d Sess., Part 7 (1898), pp. 6366–6371.

164. *Ibid.,* p. 6712.

165. See the series of newspaper clippings from the *Lexington Kentucky Leader,* in the file for July 30, 1898, Stewart Papers.

Chapter 11

1. Hirsch Harris to Stewart, Jan. 7, 1897, Stewart Papers.

2. Kappler to Isaac Frohman, June 19, 1897, Stewart Papers.

3. C. C. Wallace to Stewart, Nov. 19, 1897.

4. *Chicago Journal,* Aug. 13, 1897; *Dubuque Telegraph,* Aug. 12, 1897; *Cincinnati Commercial Tribune,* Aug. 12, 1897.

5. L. A. Blakeslee to Stewart, Aug. 13, 1897, enclosing a clipping from the *New York Times,* reporting the purported interview, Stewart Papers.

6. *Silver Knight-Watchman,* Nov. 18, 1897, p. 2, col. 4.

7. S. J. Osborne to C. C. Wallace, Dec. 3, 1897, Stewart Papers.

8. Andrew Maute to C. C. Wallace, Nov. 28, 1897, Stewart Papers.

9. C. C. Wallace to Stewart, Dec. 16, 1897.

10. Stewart to George Ernst, Jan. 11, 1898.

11. Stewart to Wm. F. Herrin, Dec. 24, 1897.

12. George Nixon to Francis Newlands, Feb. 19, 1898, Newlands Papers, Yale University.

13. C. C. Wallace to Stewart, April 24, 1898, Stewart Papers.

14. C. C. Wallace to Stewart, Feb. 21, 1899, March 1, 1899.

15. P. S. Corbett to Stewart, May 15, 1898.

16. C. M. Sain to Stewart, June 19, 1898.

17. *Ibid.*, June 21, 1898.

18. C. C. Wallace to Stewart, June 20, 1898.

19. Nixon to Newlands, March 23, 1898, Newlands Papers.

20. Sharon to Newlands, June 6, 1898, quoted in Glass, *Silver and Politics,* p. 142.

21. *Ibid.*

22. Newlands to Sharon, June 26, 1898, Newlands Papers.

23. *Silver Knight-Watchman,* March 24, 1898, p. 8, col. 3; William M. Stewart, "Analysis of the Functions of Money" (Washington, D.C.: Wm. Ballantyne & Sons, 1898).

24. *New York Times,* July 10, 1898, p. 16, col. 4.

25. *Worcester Spy,* July 12, 1898. The Massachusetts paper had a point, for not only did Stewart use his franking privileges extensively for his own material, but, on occasion, he loaned it to others. In a letter to Joseph C. Sibley, Dec. 5, 1895, Stewart wrote, "I have sent you my frank, which I hope will enable you to circulate your speeches throughout the country. You can keep the frank until you are through with it. Your speeches are the kind of reading matter that the people want at this time."

26. *Silver Knight-Watchman,* May 26, 1898, p. 7, col. 4.

27. Hirsch Harris to Stewart, June 15, 1898; E. D. Kelley to Wm. Stewart, July 9, 1898, Stewart Papers.

28. Stewart to Henry M. Teller, July 30, 1898.

29. Stewart to J. K. Jones, July 31, 1898; to Marion Butler, Aug. 1, 1898. The letter-writing campaign began to pay off in August, as a number of senators and others sent the letters Stewart requested to Nevada newspapers or important Nevada politicians.

30. Mackay had helped Stewart in the election of 1886 and, to a lesser degree, in 1892. There seems to have been no antagonism towards Stewart in 1898, just a lack of interest in Nevada.

31. Isaac Frohman to Stewart, Aug. 1, 1898, Stewart Papers.

32. Wm. Herrin to Stewart, Aug. 13, 1898.

33. Glass, *Silver and Politics,* pp. 135–137; *Morning Appeal,* Sept. 9, 1898, p. 3, col. 2. The Democrats began their convention at Reno on Sept. 7 and the Silver Party delegates met in Reno the following day.

34. Glass, *Silver and Politics,* p. 136; *Morning Appeal,* Sept. 10, 1898, p. 3, col. 3; Jack Millinger, "Political History of Nevada, 1891–1900" (Unpublished M.A. Thesis, University of Nevada, Reno, 1959), pp. 78–82.

35. *Political History of Nevada, 1973;* p. 186.

36. *Morning Appeal,* Sept. 17, 1898, p. 3, col. 1.

37. Stewart to C. C. Wallace, Sept. 14, 1898, Stewart Papers.

38. Telegram from Matt Riehm to Stewart, Sept. 18, 1898.

39. Glass, *Silver and Politics,* pp. 144–145.

40. *Morning Appeal,* Oct. 1, 1898, p. 4, col. 1.

41. *Ibid.*, Nov. 4, 1898, p. 3, col. 2.

42. Charles Norcross to Charles Kappler, Oct. 24, 1898, Stewart Papers. Norcross also suggested that Stewart make an announcement that Newlands was responsible for Nixon's abortive senatorial attempt in 1896, in order to prevent a similar announcement from Newlands in 1898. Obviously, Stewart could make no such charge while Newlands was publicly supporting him.

43. Daniel Holland to Stewart, Oct. 11, 1898.

44. *Morning Appeal,* Nov. 5, 1898, p. 3, cols. 2–3.

45. *Ibid.*, Oct. 19, 1898, p. 2, col. 1.

46. Yerington to Ogden Mills, Oct. 24, 1898, Yerington Papers.

47. *Morning Appeal,* Oct. 18, 1898, p. 3, col. 3.

48. *Ibid.* Among the many charges Cleveland leveled at Stewart was that he had an affair with a Mrs. Glasscock and was named as corespondent in a divorce suit brought by her husband in Washington, D.C. Stewart filed affidavits indicating the case was a blackmail conspiracy, and

denied having any relations with the woman. The charge leveled by Cleveland did not become an issue in the campaign. See the *New York Times,* Sept. 23, 1894, p. 7, col. 1, for the original story of the alleged affair.

49. *Carson News,* Nov. 7, 1898, p. 1, col. 3.

50. *Ibid.,* Nov. 10, 1898, p. 3, col. 3.

51. *Territorial Enterprise,* Nov. 27, 1898, p. 2, col. 1.

52. The almost immediate conclusion of anti-Stewart newspapers that Stewart had been defeated when, in fact, the Silver Party had elected a majority of the legislative candidates, appears to verify the belief that the Newlands forces had been working against Stewart during the campaign.

53. *Morning Appeal,* Nov. 12, 1898, p. 3, col. 2.

54. *Silver State,* Nov. 11, 1898, p. 2, col. 1.

55. In an earlier issue of that newspaper, on Nov. 7, 1898, Nixon had supported both Newlands and Stewart for reelection.

56. *New York World,* Nov. 12, 1898.

57. John L. Garber to Stewart, Nov. 15, 1898, enclosing a clipping from the *Chicago Evening Post,* Stewart Papers.

58. *Carson News,* Nov. 14, 1898, p. 3, col. 3.

59. E. D. Boyle to Stewart, Nov. 17, 1898, Stewart Papers.

60. *Morning Appeal,* Nov. 22, 1898, p. 3, col. 3.

61. *Ibid.,* Nov. 16, 1898, p. 2, col. 1.

62. William H. Mills to Stewart, Nov. 17, 1898, Stewart Papers.

63. *Carson News,* Nov. 30, 1898, p. 3, col. 4; *Silver State,* Nov. 30, 1898, p. 3, col. 2; *Territorial Enterprise,* Dec. 1, 1898, p. 1.

64. *Silver State,* Dec. 3, 1898, p. 2, col. 1 and p. 3, col. 2; *Reno Evening Gazette,* Dec. 3, 1898, p. 1.

65. *Morning Appeal,* Dec. 4, 1898, p. 2, col. 1. The paper noted that this was the first time such a situation had occurred in Nevada, but, in 1880, James G. Fair had to face Adolph Sutro in a similar battle for delegates after an apparent victory at the polls.

66. J. C. Hagerman to Stewart, Dec. 8, 1898, Stewart Papers.

67. *Silver State,* Dec. 3, 1898, p. 2, col. 1 and p. 3, col. 2.

68. C. C. Wallace to Stewart, Dec. 4, 1898, Stewart Papers.

69. *Ibid.,* Dec. 6, 1898.

70. Stewart to W. W. Williams, Dec. 7, 1898.

71. Stewart to J. C. Hagerman, Dec. 8, 1898.

72. Sardis Summerfield to Stewart, Dec. 4, 1898. The Summerfield maneuver demonstrated the importance of controlling the office of U.S. Attorney.

73. Stewart to J. C. Hagerman, Dec. 9, 1898.

74. Stewart admitted in his letter to Hagerman that Wren did write several letters to Newlands, but insisted that he did not give Wren any information. Although Wren could have obtained the material used against Newlands from other sources, it is quite likely that it came from Stewart's office. See particularly the unsigned letter to Francis Newlands, from Reno, Nevada, Dec. 10, 1898, in the Stewart Papers. The letter was obviously written by Wren with material furnished by Stewart or Wallace.

75. Mack, "Stewart," 99.

76. Glass, *Silver and Politics,* pp. 149–150.

77. Roberts, "David Neagle," pp. 807–808.

78. *Morning Appeal,* Jan. 4, 1899, p. 2, col. 1, quoting from the *Carson News;* Glass, *Silver and Politics,* pp. 149–151. H. M. Yerington, in a letter to D. O. Mills, mentioned the "Vigilance Committee" action and worried that if such a committee was formed "there is likely to be trouble." (Yerington to D. O. Mills, Jan. 9, 1899, Yerington Papers.)

79. Glass, *Silver and Politics,* pp. 147–152, has an excellent summary of the newspaper campaigns by the two sides. For details of the Newlands side, see the *Carson News* and the *Nevada State Journal;* for Stewart see the *Morning Appeal,* particularly its Supplement.

80. *Morning Appeal,* Dec. 29, 1898, p. 3, col. 2.

81. *Ibid.,* Dec. 30, 1898, p. 3, col. 3.

82. *Ibid.,* Jan. 13, 1899, p. 3, cols. 2–3; Glass, *Silver and Politics,* pp. 152–153.

83. M. Scheeline to Stewart, Jan. 13, 1899, Stewart Papers.

84. *Morning Appeal,* Jan. 17, 1899, p. 3, col. 2.

85. *Reno Evening Gazette,* Jan. 16, 1899, p. 1, col. 3.

86. Alfred Doten, *The Journals of Alfred Doten,* ed. Walter Van Tilburg Clark (Reno, Nevada: University of Nevada Press, 1973), Vol. 3, p. 2017.

87. Quoted in Glass, *Silver and Politics,* p. 153.

88. *Morning Appeal,* Jan. 20, 1899, p. 3, col. 2. See the Stewart Papers for newspaper clippings on this event, under date of Jan. 20, 1899.

89. Quoted in Glass, *Silver and Politics,* p. 154.

90. *Morning Appeal,* Jan. 23, 1899, p. 3, col. 2.

91. Doten, *Journals,* Vol. 3, p. 2018 (Jan. 23, 1899).

92. *Morning Appeal,* Jan. 25, 1899, p. 3, col. 1.

93. *Journal of the Senate,* 19th Session, pp. 25–26; *Journal of the Assembly,* 19th Session, pp. 25–40; *Morning Appeal,* Jan. 25, 1899, p. 3, col. 1; Glass, *Silver and Politics,* pp. 155–157.

94. *Nevada State Journal,* Jan. 25, 1899, p. 2, col. 1. The editorial was reprinted in the *Carson News* and the *Territorial Enterprise.*

95. *Nevada State Journal,* Jan. 26, 1899, p. 2, col. 2.

96. *Journal of the Assembly,* 19th Session, pp. 25–26.

97. *Ibid.,* p. 40.

98. *Ibid.,* pp. 37–39.

99. *Nevada State Journal,* Jan. 27, 1899, p. 2, col. 3.

100. *Carson News,* Jan. 27, 1899, p. 3, col. 3.

101. *Journal of the Assembly,* 19th Session, p. 44.

102. *Ibid.*

103. *Morning Appeal,* Jan. 27, 1899, p. 2, col. 3.

104. *Ibid.,* p. 2, col. 2.

105. Doten, *Journals,* Vol. 3, p. 2018. Doten sent the story to the *San Francisco Chronicle.*

106. *Territorial Enterprise,* Feb. 4, 1899, p. 2, col. 1. A copy of the *Enterprise* for that date is among the newspaper clippings in the Stewart Papers.

107. Samuel P. Davis, ed., *The History of Nevada* (Reno, Nevada: Elms Publishing Co., 1913), Vol. 1, p. 432. There is a discrepancy in the Davis story, since Gillespie absented himself from both the important vote in the assembly and the later vote in the joint session.

108. *Tonopah Sun,* Dec. 14, 1907, p. 2, col. 2. Mack, in her biography of Stewart, wrote that Gillespie later was "seen as the Southern Pacific ticket agent at the Oakland Mole." (Mack, "Stewart," 100, n. 53.)

109. Stewart to E. D. Stahlman, Feb. 9, 1899, Stewart Papers. He sent a similar letter to a Mrs. Gibson on Feb. 22, 1899.

110. Alex. McCone to Stewart, June 21, 1899. Memory of the 1898 election died slowly. When the Nevada legislature adjourned in March, 1899, the editor of a Reno newspaper noted in summarizing its activities, "They began by electing an alien and a corporation lawyer, not to say a thief and a black-guard, to the United States Senate." (*Reno Evening Gazette,* March 8, 1899, p. 2.)

111. *Nevada State Journal,* Jan. 26, 1899, p. 2, col. 1. For the contests in other states, see the following: *San Francisco Chronicle,* Jan. 18, 1899, p. 1, col. 3 and p. 6, col. 2; *New York Times,* March 20, 1899, p. 1, col. 3; Glass, *Silver and Politics,* p. 160.

112. *Congressional Record,* 55th Cong., 3d Sess., Part 3 (1899), pp. 1735–1736.

113. *Ibid.,* pp. 1830–1834, 1847, 1848.

114. Telegram from DeLamar to Stewart, Feb. 10, 1899, and letter from DeLamar to Stewart, March 11, 1899, Stewart Papers. Stewart had earlier portrayed himself as a friend of the eight-hour-day law, in correspondence with Samuel Gompers.

115. *Congressional Record,* 55th Cong., 3d Sess., Part 3 (1899), pp. 1880–1881.

116. Glass, *Silver and Politics*, pp. 167–168.

117. *Congressional Record*, 57th Cong., 1st Sess., Part 1 (1902), pp. 2617–2618.

118. Stewart to Editor, *Carson News*, March 25, 1902, Stewart Papers.

119. *Congressional Record*, 55th Cong., 3d Sess., Part 3 (1899), pp. 1644–1645.

120. Charles Kappler to P. B. Ellis, June 12, 1899; to Captain Frank Payson, Nov. 11, 1899, Stewart Papers.

121. Stewart to E. C. Baumgras, Dec. 17, 1897.

122. Charles Kappler to Bessie Stewart, April 11, 1897, Stewart Papers.

123. Hermann, *Gold and Silver Colossus*, p. 289.

124. Stewart to H. K. McJunkin, March 23, 1893, Stewart Papers.

125. The catalogue was printed in 1896, by Gibson Brothers in Washington, D.C.

126. Charles Kappler to Isaac Frohman, July 6, 1899, Stewart Papers.

127. Stewart to I. L. Johnson, July 28, 1894, Stewart Papers.

128. Stewart to Allen T. Nye, June 9, 1894, Stewart Papers.

129. As noted earlier, Mrs. Stewart and their youngest daughter had gone on a world tour in the early 1890's. In addition to sums spent on his wife and daughters, the senator had assumed custody of three grandchildren, and paid most of the expenses for sending Bessie Stewart Hooker's two sons to college. The total amount of all of these obligations must have been substantial.

130. Charles J. Kappler to E. C. Platt, Aug. 2, 1895; William F. Herrin to Stewart, Feb. 14, 1899; W. J. Robinson to Stewart, Feb. 10, 1896; Sadie C. Wright to Stewart, June 26, 1896, Stewart Papers.

131. Chas. T. Crane, Farmers & Merchants National Bank of Baltimore, to Stewart, July 14, 1899; Thomas R. Jones, National Safe Deposit, Savings & Trust Co., to Stewart, March 11, 1899; William J. Flather, Riggs National Bank of Washington, D.C., to Stewart, Nov. 2, 1899.

132. Charles Kappler to Isaac Frohman, June 19, 1897, Stewart Papers.

Chapter 12

1. *Elko Daily Independent*, Dec. 29, 1899, p. 2, col. 1.

2. W. Hampton Smith to Stewart, Dec. 18, 1899, Stewart Papers.

3. *Congressional Record*, 56th Cong., 1st Sess., Part 1 (1900), pp. 771–773, 1394, 1535, 1774, 1835, 2378.

4. *Ibid.*, pp. 1866–1869.

5. *Ibid.*, p. 1866.

6. Walter L. Williams, "United States Indian Policy and the Debate over Philippine Annexation: Implications for the Origin of American Imperialism," *Journal of American History*, 66 (March, 1980), 810–831.

7. *Congressional Record*, 56th Cong., 1st Sess., Part 2 (1900), p. 1932.

8. *Ibid.*, Part 4 (1900), pp. 3355–3357.

9. *Ibid.*, Part 6 (1900), pp. 6468–6472.

10. Sam Davis to Stewart, Nov. 26, 1899, Stewart Papers.

11. *Congressional Record*, 56th Cong., 1st Sess., Part 1 (1900), pp. 762, 1026.

12. Mary Ellen Glass, "Hot Summer in the Sierra: An Early Contest for Resource Rights at Lake Tahoe," *California Historical Quarterly*, 51 (Winter, 1972), 307; Douglas H. Strong, "Preservation Efforts at Lake Tahoe, 1880–1980," *Journal of Forest History*, 25 (April, 1981), 84–85.

13. Strong, "Preservation Efforts at Lake Tahoe," 85–88.

14. D. L. Bliss to Stewart, Jan. 24, 1900; Charles Kappler to D. L. Bliss, Feb. 6, 1900, Feb. 22, 1900, Feb. 27, 1900, March 8, 1900, April 4, 1900, Stewart Papers; Strong, "Preservation Efforts at Lake Tahoe," 86–87. The Stewart and Kappler letter files for the spring of 1900 demonstrate quite clearly the close connection between Bliss and Stewart during the fight to have Lake Tahoe declared a national park or reservation.

15. *Congressional Record*, 56th Cong., 1st Sess., Part 4 (1900), pp. 3350–3353, 3420–3422,

3926–3933; Part 5 (1900), pp. 4168–4172, 4211–4225, 4310–4312, 4361–4372, 4416–4420, 4474, 4665–4666, 4763–4765, 4836–4850; Mack, "Stewart," 86–89.

16. *Daily Evening Report* (Virginia City, Nevada), May 19, 1900.

17. C. C. Wallace to Stewart, July 21, 1899, Stewart Papers.

18. Wallace to Stewart, March 10, 1900.

19. *Ibid.*, Dec. 2, 1899.

20. *Ibid.*, May 26, 1900.

21. C. M. Sain to Stewart, April 21, 1900.

22. Wallace to Stewart, June 7, 1900; telegram from Wallace to Stewart, June 27, 1900.

23. Stewart to Wallace, June 22, 1900.

24. Wallace to Stewart, July 8, 1900.

25. Frank Norcross to Stewart, July 10, 1900.

26. E. S. Farrington to Stewart, Aug. 5, 1900, Aug. 10, 1900. There is a telegram from McMillan to Stewart, Aug. 22, 1900, thanking Stewart for his interest in helping "to secure my appointment." A later letter from Farrington, Aug. 24, 1900, acknowledges McMillan's appointment as examiner in the United States Land Office and thanks Stewart for doing this for him.

27. Stewart, *Reminiscences*, pp. 318–319.

28. *Silver State*, Aug. 21, 1900, p. 1, col. 3.

29. *Ibid.*, Aug. 22, 1900, p. 2, col. 1; *Nevada State Journal*, Aug. 24, 1900, p. 3, col. 2.

30. *Nevada State Journal*, Aug. 25, 1900, p. 2, col. 1.

31. *Tuscarora Times Review*, Aug. 25, 1900, p. 3, col. 3.

32. *Morning Appeal*, Aug. 29, 1900. Earlier (Aug. 27, 1900, p. 2, col. 1), the *Appeal* had printed a satirical article about Stewart's return to the Republicans, suggesting that the senator was demonstrating common sense in returning to his old friends, the trusts and corporations.

33. *Nevada State Journal*, Aug. 22, 1900, p. 3, col. 3.

34. *Reno Evening Gazette*, Aug. 22, 1900, p. 1, col. 4.

35. *Ibid.*, Sept. 5, 1900, p. 3, col. 2.

36. *Denver News*, Aug. 24, 1900.

37. *Territorial Enterprise*, Sept. 8, 1900, p. 1, col. 1; Glass, *Silver and Politics*, p. 181.

38. Stewart to Charles H. Tweed, Sept. 19, 1900, Stewart Papers.

39. Glass, *Silver and Politics*, p. 183. According to Glass, "the newspapers of the state refused to print either the speeches or accounts of the rallies where they were delivered."

40. *Political History of Nevada, 1973*, p. 187. Stewart did, however, accomplish one thing by his return to Nevada. He ended the bitter feud with H. M. Yerington which had developed in the 1898 election. See Yerington to D. O. Mills, Oct. 16, 1900, Yerington Papers.

41. Stewart to Captain J. R. DeLamar, Nov. 17, 1900, Stewart Papers.

42. Wallace to Stewart, Jan. 21, 1901.

43. *Ibid.*

44. Glass, *Silver and Politics*, p. 194.

45. Stewart to Wm. Herrin, Feb. 14, 1901, Stewart Papers.

46. Herrin to Stewart, Feb. 20, 1901.

47. Ostrander, *Rotten Borough*, p. 125. Ostrander quotes a letter from Newlands to W. F. Sheehan, Sept. 17, 1904, in which Newlands wrote, "Nixon is State Agent for the Southern Pacific Co. and represents them in all matters of taxation and in a quiet way in matters of legislation."

48. *Congressional Record*, 56th Cong., 2d Sess., Part 3 (1901), pp. 3398–3400, 3405.

49. Charles H. Tweed to Stewart, April 15, 1901, Stewart Papers.

50. *Congressional Record*, 56th Cong., 2d Sess., Part 1 (1901), pp. 541–544.

51. *Ibid.*, 57th Cong., 1st Sess., Part 5 (1902), pp. 5347–5354.

52. *Ibid.*, 2d Sess., Part 1 (1903), pp. 484–485.

53. *Ibid.*, 3d Sess., Part 1 (1904), pp. 298, 356.

54. *Ibid.*, 56th Cong., 2d Sess., Part 3 (1901), pp. 2511–2512.

55. *Ibid.*, 57th Cong., 1st Sess., Part 4 (1902), pp. 3271–3272, 3318, 3562–3563.

56. *Ibid.*, 56th Cong., 2d Sess., Part 3 (1901), pp. 2443, 2409–2410.

57. Stewart to R. McDonald, May 10, 1900, Stewart Papers. Stewart sold the dairy farm in 1907, because it was not making money. See also Mack, "Stewart," 100–101.

58. Rabbitt, *Minerals, Lands and Geology, 1879–1904*, pp. 202–203.

59. *Congressional Record*, 57th Cong., 1st Sess., Part 3 (1902), pp. 2277–2279.

60. *Ibid.*, p. 2977.

61. Stewart, *Reminiscences*, pp. 351–352; Townley, "Reclamation in Nevada," pp. 148–174.

62. Stewart to Wm. Booth, Aug. 10, 1903, Stewart Papers.

63. Stewart had left the Senate by 1906. However, in 1902, Stewart introduced an amendment to an Indian Appropriation Bill that provided for the allotment of Walker River Reservation to individual tribe members, in twenty-acre parcels. After the allotment of agricultural lands, Stewart's amendment provided that the remainder of the land would be thrown open to the public for settlement and mining exploration. See Johnson, *Walker River Paiutes*, pp. 101–102, for a good summary of these events.

64. *Congressional Record*, 58th Cong., 3d Sess., Part 1 (1905), pp. 640, 632–640, 646.

65. Francis J. Weber, *The United States Versus Mexico: The Final Settlement of the Pious Fund* (Los Angeles: The Historical Society of Southern California, 1969), pp. 9–15.

66. *Ibid.*, pp. 15–17.

67. *Ibid.*, pp. 18–20.

68. *Ibid.*, pp. 28–32; Kenneth Johnson, *The Pious Fund* (Los Angeles: Dawson's Book Shop, 1963), pp. 33, 38–40.

69. Weber, *Pious Fund*, pp. 28–32; James P. Gaffey, *Citizen of No Mean City: Archbishop Patrick Riordan of San Francisco, 1841–1914* (Wilmington, North Carolina: Consortium Books, 1976), pp. 213–243.

70. Gaffey, *Riordan*, pp. 214–215; Weber, *Pious Fund*, pp. 28–32.

71. Stewart to John T. Doyle, Jan. 2, 1891, Stewart Papers.

72. Weber, *Pious Fund*, pp. 28–32.

73. Gaffey, *Riordan*, pp. 217–218; Johnson, *Pious Fund*, pp. 58–71.

74. Gaffey, *Riordan*, pp. 219–220. Both Doyle and Riordan objected to the entrance of Ralston, but Riordan finally agreed to add him when Stewart indicated that Ralston would be paid from his own fees.

75. *Ibid.*, pp. 223–226.

76. Johnson, *Pious Fund*, pp. 47–57.

77. Gaffey, *Riordan*, pp. 227–229.

78. Stewart to Clement A. Grisscom, July 12, 1902, Stewart Papers.

79. James D. Finch, Jr., to C. A. Norcross, Aug. 16, 1902, Stewart Papers. Finch, another of Stewart's secretaries, wrote that the party "left this morning."

80. Weber, *Pious Fund*, pp. 32–35.

81. Gaffey, *Riordan*, pp. 230–231.

82. Weber, *Pious Fund*, pp. 32–35. Stewart did not participate to any extent in the oral arguments after his initial statement. J. H. Ralston and Garrett W. McEnerney, the latter hired by Bishop Riordan, to the surprise and resentment of the others, presented the bulk of the U.S. arguments.

83. Johnson, *Pious Fund*, p. 56.

84. Weber, *Pious Fund*, pp. 35–39. The award consisted of a lump sum of $1,420,682.67, to make up the payments since 1869, and an annual sum of $43,050.99 in perpetuity from 1903. Mexico stopped payment of the latter in 1913, and the matter again became an issue between the two countries. It was finally settled on Aug. 1, 1967, when Mexico paid the U.S. a final sum of $719,546.00. The initial award was denounced by some of the counsel for the California bishops, particularly Doyle and Stewart. One of the complaints was that the award was made in Mexican, rather than U.S. dollars, which cut the fees about in half. Stewart carried on a war of letters with Bishop Riordan and refused to accept his share, even going so far as to begin a civil suit to retain his original share, arguing that Riordan had hired additional attorneys without his and Doyle's consent. Stewart's need for money overcame his objections to Riordan's methods, though, and in May, 1904, he worked out a compromise which brought him $62,853.62 in U.S. dollars. This sum

was divided between Charles Kappler, Jackson H. Ralston, and Stewart, each receiving $20,951.20. See Gaffey, *Riordan,* pp. 238–243.

85. *San Francisco Chronicle,* Sept. 13, 1902, p. 1, col. 1. Coverage by the Nevada press generally followed the stories from the San Francisco papers.

86. Stewart to W. W. Foote, Oct. 10, 1902, Stewart Papers.

87. Captain J. R. DeLamar to Stewart, Dec. 16, 1900; Stewart to DeLamar, Dec. 18, 1900.

88. Yerington to D. O. Mills, Feb. 12, 1901, Yerington Papers.

89. A. C. Cleveland to Stewart, Dec. 28, 1901, Stewart Papers.

90. George T. Mills to Stewart, Feb. 20, 1902, June 9, 1902.

91. Stewart to George T. Mills, May 29, 1902.

92. Stewart to Jessie Overstreet, June 12, 1902.

93. *Morning Appeal,* Oct. 17, 1907, p. 1, cols. 3–4.

94. 111 Fed. Reporter 1902, pp. 71–81; Glass, *Silver and Politics,* pp. 197–199.

95. *Morning Appeal,* Aug. 16, 1902, p. 2, col. 1.

96. *Ibid.,* July 27, 1902, p. 2, col. 1.

97. Stewart to Isaac Frohman, Aug. 4, 1902, Stewart Papers.

98. Stewart to Wm. Herrin, Aug. 8, 1902.

99. Stewart to Judge Thomas P. Hawley, Aug. 8, 1902.

100. Stewart to George T. Mills, Aug. 8, 1902.

101. Glass, *Silver and Politics,* pp. 205–206.

102. Stewart to "My Dear Lemmon," Aug. 8, 1902, Stewart Papers. The *News* became a supporter of Stewart when he returned to the Republican Party.

103. Stewart to George Mills, Aug. 15, 1902.

104. Stewart to Judge Hawley, Aug. 16, 1902.

105. Yerington to D. O. Mills, Sept. 3, 1902, Yerington Papers.

106. *Virginia Evening Chronicle,* Oct. 8, 1902, p. 2, col. 1.

107. *Nevada State Journal,* Oct. 11, 1902, p. 2, col. 2.

108. *Ibid.,* Oct. 15, 1902, p. 6, col. 2, quoting the *Silver State.*

109. *Morning Appeal,* Aug. 16, 1902, p. 2, col. 1; *Nevada State Journal,* Oct. 11, 1902, p. 2, col. 2. The same thought appeared in papers at Elko and Gardnerville.

110. Stewart to George T. Mills, Oct. 2, 1902, Stewart Papers.

111. *Reno Evening Gazette,* Oct. 4, 1902, p. 2, col. 1; *Statutes of Nevada* (1899), pp. 86–87.

112. Glass, *Silver and Politics,* p. 209.

113. *Ibid.,* pp. 209–210.

114. Stewart to George T. Mills, Nov. 17, 1902, Stewart Papers.

115. Stewart to Wm. Herrin, Dec. 19, 1902.

116. *Nevada State Journal,* Jan. 28, 1903, p. 1, cols. 1–2.

117. Bessie Hofer to Stewart, Nov. 8, 1902, Stewart Papers.

118. Stewart to George T. Mills, Nov. 12, 1902.

119. Bessie Hofer to Stewart, Dec. 6, 1902.

120. Charles Kappler to I. Frohman, Nov. 15, 1902; Stewart to Isaac Frohman, March 9, 1903; Stewart to Bessie Hofer, March 9, 1903. Stewart placed some of the furniture in storage and sold the only piece of property remaining in Mrs. Stewart's name, the home at 1800 F Street in Washington, D. C. Evidently the estate was not settled until mid-October, 1903. (Thomas Fox to Charles Kappler, Oct. 14, 1903, Stewart Papers.)

121. *San Francisco Chronicle,* Oct. 27, 1903, p. 1, col. 1; *Nevada State Journal,* Oct. 27, 1903, p. 1, col. 3.

122. Stewart to Gov. John Sparks, Dec. 7, 1903; Sparks to Stewart, Feb. 1, 1904, Newlands Papers.

123. *Congressional Record,* 57th Cong., 2d Sess., Part 1 (1902), pp. 310–311; *Appendix* (1903), pp. 31–35.

124. *Ibid.,* 58th Cong., 2d Sess., Part 6 (1904), pp. 5418–5419.

125. *Ibid.,* Part 1 (1904), pp. 432–434.

126. *Ibid.,* 57th Cong., 1st Sess., Part 7 (1902), pp. 6910–6915. His support of a Nicaraguan route had extended to the introduction of a measure providing for a right of way for such a canal. *(Ibid.,* 55th Cong., 2d Sess., Part 6 (1898), p. 5168.)

127. *Ibid.,* 58th Cong., 2d Sess., Part 2 (1904), pp. 1175–1176, 1669–1670.

128. *Ibid.,* Part 6 (1904), p. 5505. The idea may well have come from his grandson, Richard C. Hooker, who was an officer in the U.S. Marine Corps.

129. Stewart to Wm. Herrin, Aug. 8, 1902, Stewart Papers.

130. Stewart to C. M. Sain, Nov. 13, 1903.

131. C. A. Norcross to Charles Kappler, Nov. 21, 1903.

132. C. A. Norcross to Stewart, Dec. 27, 1903.

133. P. L. Flanigan and others to Stewart, Feb. 1, 1904. The tone of this letter, and the individuals involved in writing it, made it appear that the Republican Party in Washoe County, if not in the entire state, had decided at this early date to dump Stewart.

134. George Nixon to Francis G. Newlands, Feb. 3, 1904. Nixon Letters, Nevada Historical Society, Reno, Nevada.

135. J. C. Hagerman to Stewart, Jan. 6, 1904.

136. Sardis Summerfield to Stewart, Feb. 8, 1904.

137. Alfred Chartz to Charles J. Kappler, Feb. 9, 1904.

138. C. A. Norcross to Charles J. Kappler, Feb. 14, 1904.

139. *Reno Evening Gazette,* March 12, 1904, p. 2, col. 1. The announcement was made through a letter to A. S. Thompson of Pioche, who had offered Nixon his proxy for the next meeting of the Silver Party Central Committee.

140. *Nevada State Journal,* March 16, 1904, p. 2, cols. 1–2. Evidently, railroad officials had decided not to back Stewart again after the bitter 1898–99 campaign. That decision first emerged when C. C. Wallace met with Nixon in Winnemucca, shortly after the 1899 legislative choice. Apparently it was solidified when Nixon was made the Southern Pacific agent in Nevada.

141. *Nevada State Journal,* March 24, 1904, p. 1, col. 1. The same article, from Washington, D.C., was printed in the *Morning Appeal,* March 25, 1904, p. 3, col. 4.

142. *Nevada State Journal,* March 30, 1904, p. 2, col. 1.

143. *Morning Appeal,* March 29, 1904, p. 3, col. 4.

144. F. G. Newlands to Wm. F. Sheehan, Sept. 17, 1904, Newlands Papers.

145. *Nevada State Journal,* April 2, 1904, p. 2, col. 2.

146. Telegram from Matthew Kyle to Stewart, April 11, 1904, Stewart Papers.

147. *Territorial Enterprise,* April 13, 1904, p. 3, col. 2. The same day, Nixon sent Stewart a telegram thanking him for the "courtesy of your action." (George Nixon to Stewart, April 12, 1904, Stewart Papers.)

148. George Mills to Stewart, April 18, 1904.

149. *Reno Evening Gazette,* April 13, 1904, p. 2, col. 1.

150. *Carson News,* April 15, 1904, p. 2, col. 1.

151. *Nevada State Journal,* Aug. 9, 1904, p. 1, cols. 3–4; Aug. 23, 1904, p. 1, cols. 3–4; Aug. 24, 1904, p. 1, cols. 1–2.

152. *Reno Evening Gazette,* Oct. 10, 1904, p. 2, col. 1; Oct. 11, p. 2, col. 1.

153. *Ibid.,* Oct. 11, p. 2, cols. 1–2.

154. *Nevada State Journal,* Oct. 14, 1904, p. 5, col. 1.

155. *Ibid.,* Nov. 11, 1904, p. 1, col. 3; Nov. 17, 1904, p. 2, col. 1; *Morning Appeal,* Nov. 13, 1904, p. 2, col. 1. Publicly, Newlands had continued to condemn Nixon for rejoining the Republicans and for becoming the state agent of the Central Pacific Railroad. See the *Morning Appeal,* Oct. 23, 1904, p. 3, cols. 1–4, for the report of the Newlands speech in favor of John Sparks.

156. Sam Davis to Stewart, Dec. 15, 1904, Stewart Papers.

157. George Nixon to Stewart, Dec. 17, 1904.

158. Sam Davis to Stewart, Jan. 1, 1905; Davis, *History of Nevada,* Vol. 1, p. 433.

159. George Nixon to Stewart, Jan. 23, 1905, Stewart Papers. Stewart received a telegram from George Mills, Jan. 25, 1905, informing him that Nixon had been chosen by the legislature without opposition.

160. *Lyon County Times,* Oct. 17, 1903, reprinting an article from the *San Francisco Call.*

161. *Congressional Record,* 58th Cong., 3d Sess., Part 1 (1905), pp. 448–449, 969, 1190.

162. *Ibid.,* Part 3 (1905), pp. 2167–2169; Part 1 (1905), 745–746.

163. *Ibid.,* Part 4 (1905), p. 3836.

Chapter 13

1. His obligations ranged from $5 to $2500, and creditors were a constant source of worry. For details, see the following correspondence in the Stewart Papers: C. E. Mack to N. Soderbert, Oct. 13, 1900; Williams and Edwards, attorneys, to Stewart, Sept. 13, 1902; M. M. Fadely to Stewart, Jan. 20, 1902; John B. Brooke Co. to Stewart, July 22, 1902; William Herrin to Stewart, Aug. 20, 1902, and Oct. 10, 1902. Besides such debts he was still paying various sums to relatives. For example, his daughter, Bessie Stewart, was given $100 per month allowance in May of 1901 (Charles Kappler to Mrs. Stewart, May 10, 1901). Later, in a letter to his granddaughter, Bessie Hofer, Stewart regretted not being able to send money as she had requested, since he had sent $500 to Mrs. Stewart, who "is now East and her expenses are large." (Stewart to Bessie Hofer, May 4, 1906.)

2. Stewart to H. W. Hilleary, Feb. 11, 1904.

3. H. W. Hilleary to Stewart, May 20, 1904.

4. See miscellaneous canceled checks in the Stewart Papers.

5. *San Francisco Call,* May 31, 1904, p. 7, col. 1.

6. John W. Brock to Stewart, Jan 12, 1905; Stewart to H. H. Clark, Feb. 14, 1905, Stewart Papers.

7. Stewart took advantage of his railroad connections to obtain the use of an entire railroad car to transport his furniture, books, and household goods, to Nevada. He and his family moved westward on railroad passes.

8. *Tonopah Daily Sun,* April 13, 1905, p. 1, col. 4; *Beatty-Bullfrog Miner,* May 13, 1905, p. 1.

9. Stewart initiated a practice, followed by many later Nevada senators, of giving help to young, ambitious men who wished to become lawyers. Besides Finch, two others, Isaac Frohman and Charles Kappler, became quite well known in legal circles in the west and in Washington, D.C.

10. Stewart to "My Dear Jimmie" (Finch), July 7, 1905, Stewart Papers.

11. James D. Finch to Stewart, Jan. 10, 1906. Finch returned to Nevada in March, 1907, to become the official reporter of the Supreme Court of Nevada, an office he held until March, 1908. Later he became Secretary to Acting Governor Denver Dickerson. In 1910, he returned to the practice of law in Carson City after Dickerson's defeat in the gubernatorial race. He later became an important figure in Democratic Party politics in Nevada.

12. *Rhyolite Herald,* July 7, 1905, p. 1, col. 3.

13. *Ibid.,* Aug. 11, 1905, p. 1, col. 2. See also Ed. Coonfield, "Bullfrog," *Nevada Magazine,* 36:2 (1976), pp. 20–22.

14. Jeanne E. Wier, "In Memoriam," p. 47.

15. Stewart to Miss Nannie Lancaster, Dec. 13, 1905, Stewart Papers.

16. Stewart, *Reminiscences,* p. 358.

17. Stewart to the West Publishing Co., Dec. 26, 1905, Stewart Papers.

18. Wm. Forman to Stewart, Jan. 12, 1906.

19. Stewart to Wm. Forman, Jan. 15, 1906.

20. Phillip I. Earl, "Tomorrow Comes the Song: The Attempt to Create Bullfrog County, 1906–1909," (Unpublished typescript, Feb. 26, 1982, in possession of Mr. Earl), p. 10; George Nixon to Stewart, Dec. 17, 1904, Stewart Papers.

21. Earl, "Tomorrow," p. 11; *Bullfrog Miner,* March 9, 1906, p. 3, col. 4.

22. *Rhyolite Herald,* Dec. 14, 1906, p. 4, cols. 1–4; Earl, "Tomorrow," pp. 16–17.

23. *Rhyolite Herald,* March 29, 1907, p. 6, col. 4; Earl, "Tomorrow," pp. 19–20; Dan V. Noland to Stewart, Jan. 28, 1907, Stewart Papers. The legislature never voted on the issue in 1907.

24. Stewart to George W. Baker, April 10, 1907.

25. *Bullfrog Miner,* Aug. 31, 1907, p. 10, col. 4; the *Beatty-Bullfrog Miner,* Aug. 31, 1907, p. 2, col. 3, indicated that Stewart's law office had been moved to Goldfield. However, it is apparent that the law office and his law books remained in Rhyolite after the establishment of the Goldfield partnership with Reddington.

26. Stewart to Geo. B. Boswell, Jan. 4, 1906, Stewart Papers.

27. Stewart to A. J. Diebold, Jan. 9, 1906.

28. Stewart to A. L. Thrall, Oct. 26, 1906. Stewart indicated that the company was offering 10,000 shares at seven cents per share.

29. George B. Boswell to Stewart, Jan. 21, 1907; Stewart to George Boswell, March 26, 1907.

30. W. N. Epping to Stewart, March 19, 1907.

31. Stewart to A. J. Diebold, Feb. 6, 1907; Stewart to W. N. Epping, March 4, 1907. Stewart told Epping that he "preferred sacrifice to disaster."

32. Sally Springmeyer Zanjani, *The Unspiked Rail: Memoir of a Nevada Rebel* (Reno, Nevada: University of Nevada Press, 1981), p. 109. Zanjani details the account of that meeting given to her by her father, pp. 109–111.

33. J. H. Ralston to Stewart, Jan. 24, 1907, Stewart Papers.

34. Letter of appointment of William Stewart as Trustee of the Public Schools of Bullfrog-Rhyolite School District, Oct. 26, 1905. He failed to qualify the first time appointed, but was reappointed on Jan. 27, 1906. See the *Rhyolite Herald,* Oct. 12, 1906, p. 1, col. 3, for an account of the rally.

35. *Rhyolite Herald,* Dec. 14, 1906, p. 10; July 12, 1907, p. 10.

36. Stewart to Mrs. Billups, Oct. 1, 1906, Stewart Papers.

37. Stewart, *Reminiscences,* pp. 342–346.

38. Stewart to Robert M. LaFollette, May 5, 1906, Stewart Papers.

39. Stewart to the President of the United States, June 13, 1906.

40. W. F. Herrin to Stewart, Jan. 3, 1906; Stewart to Herrin, Jan. 8, 1906.

41. Stewart to Isaac Frohman, Dec. 27, 1905.

42. Isaac Frohman to Stewart, April 24, 1906.

43. Stewart to Golden State Nursery, April 30, 1906; Stewart to the Secretary of Agriculture, various dates, 1906.

44. Stewart to James Morgan, May 9, 1906.

45. Stewart to "Dear General" (J. C. Hagerman), Oct. 12, 1906.

46. Stewart to Capt. James A. Lynch, Sept. 3, 1895, Sept. 5, 1895.

47. Stewart to Miss Nannie Lancaster, Dec. 13, 1905.

48. Roy A. Hardy, *Reminiscence and a Short Autobiography* (Oral History Project, University of Nevada-Reno, 1965), p. 4. The Stewart autobiography was reviewed in the *New York Times,* June 20, 1908, pp. 352, 354, by Adolphe Flauber, who accepted without question everything that Stewart had written and noted that "no work of fiction could be more absorbing than these reminiscences."

49. *San Francisco Call,* May 18, 1908, p. 1, col. 6.

50. *Gardnerville Record-Courier,* May 29, 1908, p. 3, col. 1.

51. Jeanne Elizabeth Wier, "Diary (1908)," *Nevada Historical Society Quarterly,* 4 (Jan.–Mar., 1961), 14.

52. *Ibid.,* 16–18; *Rhyolite Herald,* Oct. 28, 1908, p. 1, col. 1.

53. *Rhyolite Herald,* April 22, 1909, p. 7, col. 1.

54. *Reno Evening Gazette,* April 23, 1909, p. 1, col. 1.

55. *Rhyolite Herald,* April 28, 1909, p. 1, col. 3.

56. *Reno Evening Gazette,* April 23, 1909, p. 1, col. 1; April 24, 1909, p. 4, col. 1.

57. *Congressional Record,* 61st Cong., 1st Sess., Part 2 (1909), p. 1770.

58. Mack, "Stewart," 105, 108. Mack compiled a detailed account of Stewart's death from notices in Washington and New York newspapers.

59. *New York Times,* May 7, 1909, p. 1, col. 4. Mrs. Stewart also received a horse and carriage and books worth $300. The article reported that $6,000 to $8,000 was loaned to Stewart by Washington sources before he went to the hospital, and the remainder of the debt, $17,000 to $19,000, was owed to various Nevada banking institutions.

Chapter 14

1. Stewart, *Reminiscences,* Introduction, p. 19.

2. Stonehouse, *John Wesley North,* pp. 161, 169–170.

3. See the biographies of Stewart by Effie Mona Mack and Ruth Hermann.

4. *House Report #579,* 44th Cong., 1st Sess. (1875–76), pp. 198–199, letter from James E. Lyon to Friend (Tom) Almy, May 31, 1873.

5. Charles Kappler to H. S. Foote, July 1, 1902, Stewart Papers.

6. Alice L. North to George and Mary Loomis, Dec. 18, 1864, North Papers.

7. Glass, *Silver and Politics,* pp. 16, 119. Glass called Stewart "a true political animal," and "the completely professional politician."

8. Davis, *History of Nevada,* Vol. I, p. 440.

9. Stewart to Herrin, quoted in Rothman, *Politics,* p. 54. The idea was mirrored in an article in the *Morning Appeal,* March 28, 1888, p. 2, where it was noted that "Senator Stewart is the active Senator from that State. He has half a dozen measures pending of importance to Nevada and the Coast. Stewart is an old hand in Washington and knows how to push things in committee and out of it. . . . Stewart is indefatigable in his attendance in the Senate, and is an active and alert committeeman."

10. *Lyon County Times,* Oct. 17, 1903, p. 1.

11. Stewart to P. S. Corbett, May 21, 1902, Stewart Papers.

12. Stewart to S. P. Davis, April 18, 1888.

13. Lewis, *Silver Kings,* pp. 34–35.

14. They included James W. Nye, an able administrator and excellent orator, but unfortunately deteriorating mentally during his second Senate term; William Sharon and James Fair, both elected by money and accomplishing nothing during their terms in the U.S. Senate; and John P. Jones, intelligent and considered by most the intellectual superior of Stewart, but with very little legislation to show for a thirty-year senatorial career.

15. Stegner, *Beyond the Hundredth Meridian,* p. 304.

16. Gorham, *My Memories of the Comstock,* p. 31.

17. Goodwin, *As I Remember Them,* pp. 14–45.

18. (San Francisco) *Daily Evening Post,* July 29, 1882, p. 2, col. 1.

19. Lord, *Comstock Mining and Miners,* p. 146. Lord interviewed Stewart in 1880, and much of what he wrote about the senator came from Stewart himself.

20. Stonehouse, *John Wesley North,* pp. 161, 168–170.

21. *Congressional Globe,* 39th Cong., 1st Sess., Part 1 (1865), p. 520.

22. Stewart to C. C. Goodwin, Jan. 21, 1888, Stewart Papers.

23. Wier, "In Memoriam," p. 45; Mack, "Stewart," 82, 84.

24. Stewart to Hon. J. F. Hallock, Feb. 2, 1889, Stewart Papers. Similar letters were sent to John Forbes, C. N. Noteware, J. Poujade, W. E. Sharon, Evan Williams and H. L. Fish. Included with the letters, in the file for August and September of 1892, is a nine-page letter detailing the many ways Stewart had helped the University of Nevada.

25. J. G. Gurley to Stewart, April 19, 1900; A. J. Lyle to Stewart, April 19, 1900. There are a number of other letters in the Stewart file requesting copies of the report.

26. Mack, "Stewart," 81–83.

27. Stewart to A. N. Lewis, Jan. 21, 1903, Stewart Papers.

28. Stewart to Mrs. Bingham, May 4, 1892.

BIBLIOGRAPHY

Manuscript Collections

Cleveland, Grover. Papers. Microfilm Series 2, Library of Congress, Washington, D.C.

Grant, Ulysses S. Papers. Microfilm series, Library of Congress, Washington, D.C.

Huntington, Collis P. Papers, 1856–1901. Microfilm series, New York Times, New York City.

Lincoln, Abraham. Papers. Microfilm series, Library of Congress, Washington, D.C.

McKinley, William. Papers. Microfilm Series 1, Library of Congress, Washington, D.C.

Newlands, Francis G. Papers. Yale University, New Haven, Connecticut.

Nixon, George. Letters. Nevada Historical Society, Reno, Nevada.

North, John Wesley. Papers. Huntington Library, San Marino, California.

Smith, Grant. Papers. Bancroft Library, Berkeley, California.

Stewart, William M. Papers. Nevada Historical Society, Reno, Nevada.

Virginia and Truckee Railroad Collection. Nevada State Museum, Carson City, Nevada.

Yerington, Henry J. Papers. Bancroft Library, Berkeley, California.

Unpublished Works

Copren, William G. "The Political History of Sierra County, California, 1849–1861, Local Elections and Non-Local Issues." Unpublished M.A. Thesis, University of Nevada, Reno, 1975.

Earl, Phillip I. "Tomorrow Comes the Song: The Attempt to Create Bullfrog County, 1906–1909." Typescript, Feb. 26, 1982. In possession of author. Reno, Nevada.

Libecap, Gary Don. "The Evolution of Private Mineral Rights: Nevada's Comstock Lode." Unpublished Ph.D. Dissertation, University of Pennsylvania, 1976.

Mack, Effie Mona. "Life and Letters of William Morris Stewart, 1827–1909. A History of His Influence on State and National Legislation." Unpublished Ph.D. Dissertation, University of California, Berkeley, 1930.

Merrifield, Robert Brent. "Nevada, 1859–1881; The Impact of an Advanced Technological Society upon a Frontier Area." Unpublished Ph.D. Dissertation, University of Chicago, 1957.

Millinger, Jack. "Political History of Nevada, 1891–1900." Unpublished M.A. Thesis, University of Nevada, Reno, 1959.

Sieber, Richard C. "Nevada Politics During the Comstock Era." Unpublished M.A. Thesis, University of Nevada, Reno, 1950.

Townley, John M. "Reclamation in Nevada, 1850–1904." Unpublished Ph.D. Dissertation, University of Nevada, Reno, 1976.

Public Documents

Nevada Constitutional Convention. *Official Report of the Debates and Proceedings in the Constitutional Convention of the State of Nevada.* San Francisco: F. Eastman, 1866.

Nevada State Legislature. *Appendices to the Journals of the Senate and Assembly*.

————. *Journals of the Assembly*.

————. *Journals of the Senate*.

————. *Statutes of Nevada*.

Nevada Supreme Court. *Nevada Reports*.

Nevada Secretary of State. *Political History of Nevada, 1973*. Carson City, Nevada: State Printing Office, 1973.

Nevada Territory. *Territorial Supreme Court Appeals*. Nevada State Archives, Carson City, Nevada.

————. *Laws of the Territory of Nevada*. First Regular Session, 1861. San Francisco: Valentine and Company, 1862.

————. *Laws of the Territory of Nevada*. Third Regular Session, 1864. San Francisco: Valentine and Company, 1862.

————. *Territorial Supreme Court Opinions*. Nevada State Archives, Carson City, Nevada.

————. *Territorial Supreme Court Transcripts*. Nevada State Archives, Carson City, Nevada.

United States Congress. *Official Congressional Directory*.

————. *Congressional Globe*. Washington, D.C., 1834–1873.

————. *Supplement to the Congressional Globe*. "Trial of the President," 40th Cong., 2d Sess., 1868.

————. *Congressional Record*. Washington, D.C., 1873–

————. *Statutes at Large*.Vol. 14 (1866), 251–253.

United States House of Representatives. "The Emma Mine Investigation," House Report 579, 44th Cong., 1st Sess., 1875–76.

United States Senate. *Journal of the Executive Proceedings of the Senate of the United States of America*. Vol. 26, Dec. 12, 1887, p. 3; Jan. 10, 1888, p. 132; Jan. 16, 1888, p. 140.

United States Secretary of the Interior. *Annual Report, 1892*. Washington, D.C.: Government Printing Office, 1892.

United States Courts. *U. S. Reports, Jennison* v. *Kirk,* 98 U.S. 453–462 (1878); *Sparrow* v. *Strong,* 3 Wallace, 97–106 (1865).

————. *Federal Reports*. Blatchford, *Reports . . . Circuit Court, Second Circuit*, 24 vols., 1845–1887.

Utah Territory. *Carson County Court Record Book,* Oct. 2, 1855–July 30, 1861; Sept. 13, 1860–May 13, 1861.

Washoe County Clerk's Office, Reno, Nevada. *John W. North* v. *William M. Stewart,* File 211.

————. *John W. North* v. *J. T. Goodman and D. McCarthy,* File 212.

Books

Angel, Myron, ed. *History of Nevada*. Reprint of 1881 ed. Berkeley, California: Howell-North, 1958.

The American Annual Cyclopaedia and Register of Important Events of the Year, 1869. New York: D. Appleton & Co., 1871.

Bailey, Thomas A. *A Diplomatic History of the American People*. New York: Appleton-Century Crofts, 1955.

Bancroft, Hubert Howe. *The Works of Hubert Howe Bancroft*, Vol. 25, *History of Nevada, Colorado, and Wyoming, 1540–1888*. San Francisco: The History Co., 1890.

Beale, Howard K. *The Critical Year: A Study of Andrew Johnson and Reconstruction*. Reprint of 1930, Harcourt-Brace ed. New York: Frederick Ungar Publishing Co., 1958.

Benedict, Michael Les. *A Compromise of Principle: Congressional Republicans and Reconstruc-'tion, 1863–1869*. New York: W. W. Norton & Co., 1974.

Black, Chauncey F. and Samuel B. Smith, eds. *Some Account of the Work of Stephen J. Field as a Legislator, State Judge, and Justice of the Supreme Court with an Introductory Sketch by J. Norton Pomeroy*. N.p.: S. B. Smith, 1882.

Blaine, James G. *Twenty Years of Congress: From Lincoln to Garfield*. 2 vols. Norwich, Connecticut: Henry Bill Publishing Co., 1884–86.

Bourke, Lee. *Death Valley*. New York: MacMillan Co., 1930.

Boutwell, George S. *Reminiscences of Sixty Years in Public Affairs*. 2 vols. New York: Greenwood Press, 1968.

Bowers, Claude G. *The Tragic Era: The Revolution After Lincoln*. Cambridge, Massachusetts: Houghton Mifflin Co., 1929.

Browne, J. Ross. *A Peep at Washoe, and, Washoe Revisited*. Balboa Island, California: Paisano Press, 1959.

Bushnell, Eleanore. *The Nevada Constitution: Origin and Growth*. Fourth edition. Reno: University of Nevada Press, 1977.

Carothers, Neil. *Fractional Money*. New York: John Wiley and Sons, 1930.

Chalfant, Willie Arthur. *The Story of Inyo*. Revised edition. Los Angeles: Citizens Print Shop, 1933.

Chase, Salmon P. *Inside Lincoln's Cabinet: The Civil War Diaries of Salmon P. Chase*, ed. David Donald. New York: Longmans, Green & Co., 1954.

Craven, Avery. *Reconstruction: The Ending of the Civil War*. New York: Holt, Rinehart & Winston, 1969.

Darrah, William Culp. *Powell of the Colorado*. Princeton, New Jersey: Princeton University Press, 1951.

Davis, John F. *Historical Sketch of the Mining Law in California*. Los Angeles: n.p., 1902.

Davis, Winfield J. *History of Political Conventions in California, 1849–1892*. Sacramento, California: State Library, 1893.

Doten, Alfred. *The Journals of Alfred Doten*, ed. Walter Van Tilburg Clark. 3 vols. Reno: University of Nevada Press, 1973.

Doten, Samuel B. *An Illustrated History of the University of Nevada*. Reno: University of Nevada, 1924.

DuBois, William E. B. *Black Reconstruction in America*. New York: Russell & Russell, 1935.

Dunn, Arthur Wallace. *From Harrison to Harding: A Personal Narrative Covering a Third of a Century, 1888–1921*. 2 vols. New York: G. P. Putnam's Sons, 1922.

Dupree, A. Hunter. *Science in the Federal Government: A History of Policies and Activities to 1940*. Cambridge, Massachusetts: Harvard University Press, 1957.

Elliott, Russell R. *History of Nevada*. Lincoln: University of Nebraska Press, 1973.

Fairman, Charles. *American Constitutional Decisions*. Revised edition. New York: Henry Holt & Co., 1952.

Foner, Philip S. *The Spanish-Cuban-American War and the Birth of American Imperialism*. 2 vols. New York: Monthly Review Press, 1972.

Gaffey, James P. *Citizen of No Mean City: Archbishop Patrick Riordan of San Francisco, 1841–1914*. Wilmington, North Carolina: Consortium Books, 1976.

Gates, Paul W. *History of Public Land Law Development*. Washington, D.C.: U.S. Government Printing Office, 1968.

Gillette, William. *The Right to Vote: Politics and the Passage of the Fifteenth Amendment*. Baltimore: Johns Hopkins Press, 1965.

Glass, Mary Ellen. *Silver and Politics in Nevada, 1892–1902*. Reno: University of Nevada Press, 1969.

Goodwin, Charles C. *As I Remember Them . . . .* Salt Lake City, Utah: n.p., 1913.

Gorham, Harry M. *My Memories of the Comstock*. Los Angeles: Sutton House, 1939.

Grant, Ulysses S. *Personal Memoirs*. 2 vols. New York: Charles L. Webster & Co., 1885–86.

Hardy, Roy Alger. *Reminiscence and a Short Autobiography*. Oral History Project, Getchell Library, University of Nevada, Reno, 1965.

Harpending, Asbury. *The Great Diamond Hoax and Other Stirring Incidents in the Life of Asbury Harpending*, ed. James A. Wilkins. Norman: University of Oklahoma Press, 1958.

Harvey, William H. *Coin's Financial School*. Cambridge, Massachusetts: Harvard University Press, 1963.

Hermann, Ruth. *Gold and Silver Colossus: William Morris Stewart and His Southern Bride*. Sparks, Nevada: Dave's Printing & Publishing, 1975.

Hicks, John D. *The American Nation*. Boston: Houghton Mifflin Co., 1946.

Hickson, Howard. *Mint Mark "CC.": The Story of the United States Mint at Carson City*. Carson

City, Nevada: Nevada State Museum, 1972.

Johnson, Edward C. *Walker River Paiutes: A Tribal History.* Salt Lake City: University of Utah Printing Service, 1974.

Johnson, Kenneth. *The Pious Fund.* Los Angeles: Dawson's Book Shop, 1963.

Kappler, Charles J. *The Record and Services of Hon. Wm. M. Stewart in the Senate of the United States Since His Election in 1887.* N.p. [1892].

Kelly, J. Wells, comp. *First Directory of Nevada Territory.* Los Gatos, California: Talisman Press, [c. 1962].

Kroninger, Robert H. *Sarah and the Senator.* Berkeley, California: Howell-North, 1964.

Laughlin, J. Laurence. *The History of Bimetallism in the United States.* New York: D. Appleton & Co., 1900.

Lavender, David. *The Great Persuader.* New York: Doubleday & Co., 1970.

Lewis, Oscar. *Silver Kings: The Lives and Times of Mackay, Fair, Flood and O'Brien, Lords of the Nevada Comstock Lode.* New York: Alfred A. Knopf, 1947.

Lord, Eliot. *Comstock Mining and Miners.* Reprint of the 1883 ed. Berkeley, California: Howell-North, 1959.

Lyman, George D. *The Saga of the Comstock Lode: Boom Days in Virginia City.* New York: Charles Scribner's Sons, 1934.

Mack, Effie Mona. *Nevada: A History of the State From the Earliest Times Through the Civil War.* Glendale, California: Arthur H. Clark, 1936.

Marsh, Andrew J. *Letters From Nevada Territory, 1861–1862.* Ed. William C. Miller, Russell W. McDonald, and Ann Rollins. Carson City: Legislative Counsel Bureau, State of Nevada, 1972.

Marsh, Andrew J. et al. *Reports of the 1863 Constitutional Convention of the Territory of Nevada as Written for the Territorial Enterprise.* Carson City: Legislative Counsel Bureau, State of Nevada, 1972.

Mathews, John Mabry. *Legislative and Judicial History of the Fifteenth Amendment.* Baltimore: Johns Hopkins Press, 1909.

McCulloch, Hugh. *Men and Measures of Half a Century.* New York: Charles Scribner's Sons, 1887.

McKitrick, Eric L. *Andrew Johnson and Reconstruction.* Chicago: University of Chicago Press, 1960.

Milton, George F. *The Age of Hate: Andrew Johnson and the Radicals.* Hamden, Connecticut: Archon Books, 1965.

Morgan, Dale L., ed. *In Pursuit of the Golden Dream.* Stoughton, Massachusetts: Western Hemisphere, 1970.

Morgan, H. Wayne. *From Hayes to McKinley: National Party Politics, 1887–1896.* Syracuse, New York: Syracuse University Press, 1969.

Nevins, Allan. *Grover Cleveland: A Study in Courage.* New York: Dodd, Mead & Co., 1933.

Nugent, Walter T. K. *Money and American Society, 1865–1880.* New York: Free Press, 1968.

———. *The Money Question During Reconstruction.* New York: W. W. Norton & Co., 1967.

Oberholtzer, Ellis Paxson. *History of the United States.* 5 vols. New York: MacMillan Co., 1917–39.

Ostrander, Gilman M. *Nevada: The Great Rotten Borough, 1859–1964.* New York: Alfred Knopf, 1966.

Paher, Stanley W. *Death Valley Ghost Towns.* Las Vegas: Nevada Publications, 1973.

Patrick, Rembert W. *The Reconstruction of the Nation.* New York: Oxford University Press, 1967.

Paul, Rodman. *California Gold: The Beginning of Mining in the Far West.* Cambridge, Massachusetts: Harvard University Press, 1947.

———. *Mining Frontiers of the Far West, 1848–1880.* New York: Holt, Rinehart & Winston, 1963.

Rabbitt, March C. *Minerals, Land and Geology for the Common Defence and General Welfare.* 2 vols. Washington, D.C.: U.S. Government Printing Office, 1979–80.

Rhodes, James Ford. *History of the United States From the Compromise of 1850 to the Final Restoration of Home Rule in the South in 1877.* New York: MacMillan Co., 1912.

Rothman, David. *Politics and Power: The United States Senate, 1869–1901.* Cambridge, Massachusetts: Harvard University Press, 1966.

Scrugham, James G., ed. *Nevada: A Narrative of the Conquest of a Frontier Land.* 3 vols. Chicago: American Historical Society, 1935.

Sherman, John. *Recollections of Forty Years in the House, Senate and Cabinet.* Chicago: Werner Co., 1895.

Shuck, Oscar T., ed. *History of the Bench and Bar of California.* Los Angeles: Commercial Printing House, 1901.

————. *Representative and Leading Men of the Pacific.* San Francisco: Bacon & Co., 1870.

Spence, Clark C. *British Investments and the American Frontier, 1860–1901.* Ithaca, New York: Cornell University Press, 1958.

Stewart, Robert E., Jr. and Mary Frances. *Adolph Sutro.* Berkeley, California: Howell-North, 1962.

Stewart, William M. *Analysis of the Functions of Money.* Washington, D.C.: Wm. Ballantyne & Sons, 1898.

————. *The Chinese Question.* Reno, Nevada: Reno Evening Gazette Print, 1886.

————. *The Free Coinage of Silver: Honest Money for the People of the United States.* New York: Tribune Association, 1893.

————. *Reminiscences of Senator William M. Stewart of Nevada,* ed. George Rothwell Brown. New York: Neal Publishing Co., 1908.

————. *Silver and the Science of Money.* Washington, D.C.: n.p., 1894.

————. *The Silver Question: Bondholders' Conspiracy to Demonetize Silver Legislation Affecting National Debt and Gold and Silver.* San Francisco: Geo. Spaulding & Co., 1885.

Stegner, Wallace. *Beyond the Hundredth Meridian: John Wesley Powell and the Second Opening of the West.* Boston: Houghton Mifflin Co., 1953.

Stonehouse, Merlin. *John Wesley North and the Reform Frontier.* Minneapolis: University of Minnesota Press, 1965.

Stryker, Lloyd Paul. *Andrew Johnson: A Study in Courage.* New York: MacMillan Co., 1936.

Swift, John Franklin. *Robert Greathouse: A Story of the Nevada Silver Mines.* New York: [Carleton, Publisher, 1878].

Thomas, Lately. *The First President Johnson: The Three Lives of the Seventeenth President of the United States of America.* New York: William Morrow & Co., 1968.

Townley, John M. *Alfalfa Country: Nevada Land, Water and Politics in the Nineteenth Century.* Reno: College of Agriculture, University of Nevada, Reno, [c. 1981].

Treadwell, Edward F. *The Cattle King: A Dramatized Biography.* Fresno, California: Valley Publishers, 1931.

Unger, Irwin. *The Greenback Era: A Social and Political History of American Finance, 1865–1879.* Princeton, New Jersey: Princeton University Press, 1964.

Weber, Francis J. *The United States Versus Mexico: The Final Settlement of the Pious Fund.* Los Angeles: Historical Society of Southern California, 1969.

Weinstein, Allen. *Prelude to Populism: Origins of the Silver Issue, 1867–1878.* New Haven, Connecticut: Yale University Press, 1970.

Welles, Gideon. *Diary of Gideon Welles.* 3 vols. Boston: Houghton Mifflin Co., 1911.

[Wells, Harry L.] *History of Nevada County, California.* Oakland, California: Thompson & West, 1880.

Wells, Merle W. *Anti-Mormonism in Idaho, 1872–1892.* Provo, Utah: Brigham Young University Press, 1978.

Wilson, Neill C. *Silver Stampede: The Career of Death Valley's Hell Camp, Old Panamint.* New York: MacMillan Company, 1937.

Winston, Robert W. *Andrew Johnson: Plebian and Patriot.* New York: Barnes & Noble, 1928.

Wyld, Lionel D. *Low Bridge: Folklore and the Erie Canal.* Syracuse, New York: Syracuse University Press, 1962.

Yale, Gregory. *Legal Titles to Mining Claims and Water Rights in California Under the Mining Law of Congress, of July, 1866.* San Francisco: A. Roman & Company, 1867.

Zanjani, Sally Springmeyer. *The Unspiked Rail: Memoir of a Nevada Rebel.* Reno: University of Nevada Press, 1981.

Articles and Periodicals

Alexander, Thomas G. "The Powell Irrigation Survey and the People of the Mountain West." *Journal of the West,* 7 (January, 1968), 48.

Auchampaugh, Phillip G. "The Early Career of Robert P. Flenniken, Diplomat and Western Judge." *The Historian,* 10 (Autumn, 1947), 27–43.

Baur, John E. "The Senator's Happy Thought." *The American West,* 10 (January, 1973), 35–39.

Beebe, Lucius. "Panamint: Suburb of Hell." *American Heritage,* 6 (December, 1954), 64–69.

Brodhead, Michael J. "Accepting the Verdict: National Supremacy as Expressed in State Constitutions, 1861–1912." *Nevada Historical Society Quarterly,* 13 (Summer, 1970), 3–19.

Bullard, F. Lauriston. "Abraham Lincoln and the Statehood of Nevada," *American Bar Journal* (March and April, 1940), pp. 1–9.

Considine, H. L. "Reminiscence of Nevada Early-Day Legislatures," *Nevada State Journal,* Feb. 21, 1937.

Fry, Joseph A. "Silver and Sentiment: The Nevada Press and the Coming of the Spanish-American War." *Nevada Historical Society Quarterly,* 20 (Winter, 1977), 223–240.

Glass, Mary Ellen. "Hot Summer in the Sierra: An Early Contest for Resource Rights at Lake Tahoe." *California Historical Quarterly,* 51 (Winter, 1972), 306–314.

————. "The Silver Governors: Immigrants in Nevada Politics, Part II." *Nevada Historical Society Quarterly,* 21 (Winter, 1978), 263–278.

Hershiser, Beulah. "The Influence of Nevada on the National Mining Legislation of 1866." *Nevada Historical Society Third Biennial Report, 1911–1912,* pp. 127–167.

Hurt, Peyton C. "Rise and Fall of the 'Know Nothings' in California." *California Historical Society Quarterly,* 9 (March, 1930), 16–50; (June, 1930), 99–128.

Hutchinson, William H. "The Law Comes to Panamint." *Westways,* 42 (July 7, 1950), 10–11.

Johnson, David A. "A Case of Mistaken Identity: William M. Stewart and the Rejection of Nevada's First Constitution." *Nevada Historical Society Quarterly,* 22 (Fall, 1979), 186–198.

Lilley, William III and Gould, Lewis L. "The Western Irrigation Movement, 1878–1902: A Reappraisal." *The American West: A Reorientation,* ed. Gene M. Gressley. Laramie: University of Wyoming Publications, Vol. 33, 1966, pp. 57–74.

Mack, Effie Mona. "William Morris Stewart, 1827–1909." *Nevada Historical Society Quarterly,* 7 (Centennial issue, 1964).

MacCracken, Brooks W. "Althea and the Judges." *American Heritage,* 18 (June, 1967), 61–63.

Mining and Scientific Press. August, 1873–September, 1874.

Moody, Eric N. "Nevada's Anti-Mormon Legislation of 1887 and Southern Idaho Annexation." *Nevada Historical Society Quarterly,* 22 (Spring, 1979), 21–33.

O'Leary, Paul M. "The Scene of the Crime of 1873 Revisited: A Note." *Journal of Political Economy,* 68 (1960), 388–392.

Roberts, Gary L. "David Neagle (1847?–1926)." *The Reader's Encyclopedia of the American West,* ed. Howard Lamar. New York: Thomas Crowell Company, 1977, pp. 807–808.

Roberts, Gary L. "In Pursuit of Duty." *American West,* 7 (September, 1970), 27–33.

Robinson, William Hedges, Jr. "Mark Twain: Senatorial Secretary." *American West,* 10 (January, 1973), 16–17.

Sterling, Everett W. "The Powell Irrigation Survey, 1888–1893." *Mississippi Valley Historical Review,* 27 (December, 1940), 421–434.

Strong, Douglas H. "Preservation Efforts at Lake Tahoe, 1880–1980." *Journal of Forest History,* 25 (April, 1981), 78–97.

Townley, John M. "Management of Nevada's State Lands, 1864–1900." *Journal of the West,* 17 (January, 1978), 63–74.

Wier, Jeanne E. "In Memoriam. William Morris Stewart." *Nevada Historical Society Biennial Report,* Vol. 2 (1909–1910), pp. 45–47.

Williams, Walter L. "United States Indian Policy and the Debate over Philippine Annexation: Implications for the Origin of American Imperialism." *Journal of American History,* 66 (March, 1980), 810–831.

Newspapers

Beatty-Bullfrog Miner (Beatty, Nevada).
Carson Free Lance (Carson City, Nevada).
Carson Independent (Carson City, Nevada).
Carson News (Carson City, Nevada).
Daily Alta California (San Francisco).
Daily Silver State (Winnemucca, Nevada).
Elko Daily Independent (Elko, Nevada).
Gardnerville Record-Courier (Gardnerville, Nevada).
Gold Hill Daily News (Gold Hill, Nevada).
Inyo Independent (Inyo, California).
Lyon County Times (Yerington, Nevada).
Morning Appeal (Carson City, Nevada).
Nevada State Journal (Reno, Nevada).
New York Times.
Reno Evening Gazette (Reno, Nevada).
Rhyolite Herald (Rhyolite, Nevada).
Sacramento Union.
San Francisco Chronicle.
The Silver Knight-Watchman (Washington, D.C.).
Territorial Enterprise (Virginia City, Nevada).
Tonopah Sun (Tonopah, Nevada).
Tuscarora Times Review (Tuscarora, Nevada).
Virginia Daily Union (Virginia City, Nevada).
Virginia Evening Bulletin (Virginia City, Nevada).
Virginia Evening Chronicle (Virginia City, Nevada).
Walker Lake Bulletin (Hawthorne, Nevada).
Washoe Times (Washoe City, Nevada).
Washoe Weekly Star (Washoe City, Nevada).

INDEX

Aguinaldo, Emilio, 228; Philippine insurgent, 215; Stewart compares with Tecumseh and others, 222, 230

Alaskan Government Bill, 223, 224

Albion Consolidated v. *The Richmond,* 87

Aldrich, Nelson W.: favors Federal Elections (Force) bill of 1890, 127–129; challenges Stewart's version of 1873 Mint Act passage, 166

Aldrick, Louis, 8

Alemany (Bishop of California), 234

Allison, William B., 74

Amador County, California, 148

American Party, 8. *See also* Know-Nothing Party

Analysis of the Functions of Money, Stewart's pamphlet on silver question, 193–194; summary of main points in newspaper, 199–200; Stewart uses franking privilege to distribute, 200, 310 n. 25

Anderson, George, 76

Anthony, Susan B., 136

Anthony (U.S. Senator from Rhode Island), 47

Apaches, Chiricahua, 94

Apportionment Bill, 128

Arizona statehood, 252

Arlington Hotel, Carson City, 209

Army Appropriation bills, 141, 230, 231

Ashburn farms, Virginia, 182, 231; purchase by Stewart and description of, 217, 218; model dairy operation there, 231; later description, 253; sold, January 1907, 262

Ashtabula, Ohio, 3

Aspirez, Manuel, 235

Asylum for Mental Diseases, suggested home for A. C. Cleveland, 203

Aurora, Esmeralda County, Nevada, 24; suggested as site for Nevada state capital in 1863 Convention, 25

Babcock, Elizabeth C., 159, 160

Baker, Edward D., 10

Baldwin, Alexander W. ("Sandy"): law partner of William M. Stewart, 14, 15; in Chollar suit against Potosi, 21; repeats Judge Hardy bribery charge against John North, 37; supports Union Party candidates in 1864 election, 42; Federal Judge, 64

Baltimore and Ohio Railroad, 141

Bancroft, Hubert Howe, 40

Bank Crowd, 97; opposes Sutro's tunnel scheme, 67; and Nevada Borax deposits, 138; favors high tariff, 186; and Stewart, 269, 270. *See also* Bank of California

Bank of California, x, 39, 67, 82, 93, 203, 226; and Walker River Indian reservation, 133; Yerington, lobbyist for, 138; and Nevada Silver clubs, 151

Bartine, Horace: supports Federal Elections bill in House, 126; and Nevada Indian reservations, 133–134; Stewart suggests for judgeship, 144; in 1890 Congressional campaign, 144–146; in 1892 election, 156

Battle of Standards, 1896 election, 184

Baxter, General H. Henry: reorganizes Emma Mine Company, 75; involved in Emma Mine scandal, 75–79

Bender, D. A., 133

Benton, Thomas Hart, 50, 51

Biddle, Nicholas, 163

"Big Bonanza," Comstock Lode, 72, 83

Bigler, John, 8

Bimetallic League: organized in 1892 at Washington, D.C., 153; in 1896 formation of National Silver Party, 177

Bimetallic Party, 174, 175

Bimetallic Union, 177

Bimetallism, 163, 166, 170, 181, 231. *See also* Free Silver; Remonetization; Silver demonetization

Bingham, Mrs. (Senator Nye's daughter), 275

Bipartisanship in Nevada politics, 247

Blackburn, John, 16

"Blackmailing suits," by Newlands forces in 1898, 207

Blaine, James G.: proposal in House of Representatives to guarantee Negro Suffrage, 62; Stewart accused of slandering, 107; in 1888 Republican National Convention, 111

Bland, Richard, bill of 1894, vetoed by Cleveland, 169

Bland-Allison Silver Act: supported by John P. Jones, 120–122; supported by McKinley in 1878, 178

Bliss, Duane, 158, 223

Bloody Run, California, 5

"Bloody Shirt," possibility of revival in Lamar nomination, 124

Bodie, California, 86

Boise, Idaho Territory, 105

Bonanza Kings, 91; attitude toward remonetization of silver, 299 n. 84

Borax interests: Nevada, 110; want protective tariff, 170

Boston Globe, 119

Boundary expansion of Nevada: debated in 1863 Convention, 25; 1865 bill annexing one degree of territory to Nevada from Utah Territory, 46; Stewart proposal in 1886 campaign, 96; at expense of Idaho Territory, 99, 100–105; at expense of Utah, 100, 105–109

Boutwell, George S., 62, 63

Bowers Company, 15

Boyle, Edward D., 205

Bragg, Allen, 226

Breckenridge, John, 55

Breese, Sidney, 49

Brisbane, Arthur, 177

Brock, John, 254

Brosnan, Cornelius M., 23

Brown, George Rothwell: edits Stewart's autobiography, 264; quoted on Stewart, 268

Browne, J. Ross, 12

Bryan, William J.: Nominated by Democrats in 1896 on silver ticket, 179; campaign of 1896, 182, 184; Stewart refuses to support in 1900, 227, 228

Bryan Club, organized in Reno by Charles Norcross, 180

Brydges-Willyams, Edward, 76

Buchanan, James, 9, 13, 16; signs Nevada Organic Act, March 2, 1861, 18

Buckalew, Charles, 47

Buffalo, New York, 3

Bullfrog, Nevada, 255, 259, 260, 263, 264. *See also* Bullfrog Mining District

Bullfrog "county," proposed by Stewart, 259

Bullfrog Miner, 259

Bullfrog Mining District, 254, 255, 257, 266, 273

Bullfrog-Rhyolite School district, 262

Bullion Tax, 217

Burlingame Treaty, 100

Burning Moscow Company v. *Ophir Mining Company,* 28, 29, 37

Butler, David, 10

Butler, Jim, 238

Butler, Marion: Stewart enlists support for Joseph Sibley, 175; Stewart suggests Populists nominate Bryan in 1896, 179; Stewart wants endorsement in 1898 election, 201

California, Admission to Union forces mineral land policy, 50

Campbell, John M., 132

Cannon, George Q.: Stewart writes he favors Utah statehood, 109; congratulates Stewart on 1899 selection to U.S. Senate, 109; and railroad pass, 142

Caribbean defense, 244

"Carl," opposes 1863 constitution, 31

Carnegie, Andrew, 163; Stewart criticizes his gold stand, 148

"Carolina," 4

Carson and Colorado Railroad, relations with Walker River Indians, 133–135

Carson and Tahoe Lumber and Fluming Company, 223

Carson City: made county seat of Carson County, Utah Territory, 19; becomes territorial capital of Nevada Territory, 19; 1863 Constitutional Convention meets there, 23; supported as site for state capital, 25; Union Party Convention, 29; anti-Chinese movement in, 94, 95; suggested by Stewart as dual capital with Boise, 105

Carson City Mint, 149, 152, 184; Stewart's role in establishment, 64; fight to reopen, 100; federal patronage, 143; Roswell Colcord becomes superintendent, 197

Carson County, Utah Territory, 10, 14, 16, 18; part of Nevada Territory, 13; county seat moved from Genoa to Carson City, 19

Carson Morning Appeal, 61, 92, 93, 95,

96, 98, 124; supports Stewart in 1898 election, 203, 204; charges against Newlands supporters in 1898 election, 205; cartoon supplement against Newlands in 1898 election, 209; in Leidy incident, 211; in Gillespie incident, 214

Carson News: supports Newlands in 1898, 204, 205, 209; accuses George Leidy of bribery, 213; Stewart on Hawley's age, in, 240; anti-railroad campaign, 246; Stewart's achievements summarized, 249

Carson Tribune, 149

Casserly, (U.S. Senator from California), 70

Cassidy, George: announces for U.S. Senate, 98; defeated for Senate, 100; introduces bill to open Walker River Indian Reservation for mining purposes, 131; in Silver League meeting, 153; in organization of Silver Party, 225

"Castle Stewart," 217; built on Dupont Circle, Washington, D.C., description, 80; sold to W. A. Clark, 218

Cattle quarantine in Nevada, 189; Nevada cattlemen support against cattle from California, 190–191; Governor Sadler's actions concerning, 190–191; Stewart's position on 190, 191

Central Pacific Railroad, 153, 204, 205, 208, 209, 210, 229, 269; Stewart's early relations with, 64–66; and Swamp Land issue, 72–74; role in Stewart's decision to retire in 1875, 82; role in Stewart's return to Senate in 1887, 93–100; opposes state-funded reclamation projects, 112; and Chinese immigration, 137, 138; Stewart's efforts on behalf of, 140–142, 174, 187, 188; and Tahoe National Park, 222, 223; Judge Hawley rules in favor of, 238; in 1902 Nevada Senate race, 242; supports Nixon in 1904 race, 247, 317 n. 140; control of Nevada Silver Party, 303 n. 48

Chagres River, Isthmus of Panama, 4

Chandler, William E., 177, 184

Chandler, Zachariah, 47

Chartz, Alfred, 246

Chase, Salmon P.: in Sparrow case, 52; swearing-in of Andrew Johnson as President, 56, 57

Cherokee Creek, 5

Chevy Chase Land Development Company: involvement of Stewart and Newlands, 158, 159, 219; stock in to second Mrs. W. M. Stewart, 266; history of, 304 n. 78

Chicago and Northwestern Railroad, 142

Chicago Journal, opposes Stewart in 1898 election, 196

Child, John, 13

Chinese, 64; naturalization, 66, 98, 244; anti-Chinese movement in Carson City in 1886, 94, 95; referendum on immigration, 94; Stewart on Chinese immigration, 98; exclusion, 110, 244; Stewart and anti-Chinese movement in Congress after 1887, 137, 138

Chinese Embassy, 218

Chinn, Jack, 208–211, 214, 215

Chivalry Democrats, 9, 278 n. 38

Chollar Mining Company v. *Potosi Mining Company:* 1861–1865, 21, 22, 37; Chollar wins suit, 21; loses second suit against Potosi, 34; appeals Potosi decision, 35; in slander suits against Stewart, 45

"Citizen's Vigilante Committee," 209

Civil Rights bill of 1866, 59

Civil Service Law, 217

Civil War, 27, 42, 51, 62, 126

Civil War claims of Nevada, 243

Clapp, Hannah, 159–160, 301 n. 61

Clark, William A.: purchases Stewart "Castle," 218; Stewart supports for U.S. Senate seat, 224

Clark County, Nevada, created, 259

Clayton, Powell, 235

Clemens, Orion, 19; calls 1863 Constitutional Convention to order, 23

Cleveland, Abner C.: works for Stewart's election in 1886, 97; opposes Stewart in 1892 campaign, 149; opposes Stewart in 1898 campaign, 201, 202, 203; "stalking horse" for Newlands, 201–203; Republican candidate for U.S. Senate in 1898, 203, 204, 310 n. 48; nominated for U.S. Senate, 1899, 211, 212; opposed to Newlands in 1902 campaign, 237; runs for governor in 1902, 239

Cleveland, Grover: closes Carson City Mint, 100; pocket vetoes Idaho transfer bill, 105; signs Utah Enabling Act, 109; associated with gold standard, 121; nominates Lamar for U.S. Supreme Court, 124; nominated for President in 1892 on gold standard platform, 153, 155; forces repeal of Sherman Silver Act, 161–167; use of patronage to break silver filibuster, 167; vetoes Bland silver certificate bill, 169; monetary policies challenged by Stewart, 175; and Venezuela affair, 176

Coddington, James, 17
Colcord, Roswell, 143; superintendent of
    Carson City Mint, 197–198
Cole, Cornelius, 70; on irrigation issue, 113
Colombia, 244
Comins, Henry A.: in 1898 election, 211; and
    direct election of U.S. Senators, 217
Compromise of 1850, 8, 13, 49
Comstock. *See* Comstock Lode
Comstock, Henry P., 15
Comstock Company, 31
Comstock Lode, 27, 29, 34, 39, 55, 67;
    discovery, 10, 18, 23, 51; and Pyramid Lake
    Indian War, 12; and early legal battles,
    14–16; geology of, 15; production decline,
    92; Big Bonanza on, 72, 83; Tonopah and
    Goldfield, a second "Comstock," 253;
    Comstock Lode reviewed, 273; Stewart's
    first trip to, 279 n. 46
Comstock senators, Stewart the ablest, 272
Comstock Union League: supports Stewart in
    1864, 43; vindication for criticism against
    Stewart, 45
Cone, May Agnes, 243. *See also* Stewart,
    Agnes
Confederate States of America, 18, 57, 58
Conger, Edwin H.: introduces silver purchase
    bill, 122; Sherman Silver Purchase Act of
    1890, 122
Congressional Record, 165, 166, 169
Conkling, Roscoe, 62, 63
Conness, John, 40; first Chairman, Committee
    on Mines and Mining, 47; adds amendment
    to "Courts" bill, 52; and National Mining
    Act, 53, 54; after Lincoln's assassination,
    56, 57
Consolidated-Virginia mine, 72
Constitutional Convention of 1863, 23–26;
    Stewart's role in, 270, 282 n. 50
Constitutional Convention of 1864, 36
Constitution of 1863, 24; battle over ratification
    of, 26–33; defeat of, 32, 282 n. 73, 283 n. 74
Constitution of 1864: ratified by voters, 41;
    reasons for ratification, 41, 42, 284 n. 43 and
    n. 44
Contention Mine, Tombstone, Arizona
    Territory, 87
Corbett-Fitzsimmons fight, Carson City, 189
Cornish, W. D., 229–230
"Cosmos," opposes 1863 constitution, 30, 31
"Courts Bill," becomes law, 52
Coxey, General Jacob S., 171–172
Cradlebaugh, John, 13, 14; removed by
    President Buchanan, 16; refuses to leave

post, 16; authority recognized by Judge
    Flenniken, 16; defeated in 1864 try for U. S.
    Senate in Nevada, 43
Cragin, Charles H., 243
Credit Mobilier, 66
"Crime of '73": background and provisions,
    69; Stewart's position on, 118; first exposed
    by Stewart, 119; Stewart charged with
    supporting, 203. *See also* Mint Act of 1873
Crocker, Charles, 64, 65
Cross, Ernest, 254
Cuban independence: Stewart favors, 192, 193;
    position after war, 194; favors retention of,
    221
Cuban Insurrection, 184, 195; covered by
    Silver Knight-Watchman, 176; Stewart
    favors recognition of Cuban belligerency in
    1898, 191–192; anti-Spanish articles in his
    newspaper, 193
Cumming, Alfred: appointed territorial
    governor of Utah Territory, 13; appoints
    John Child as probate judge of Carson
    County, 13
Curler, Benjamin, 172
Cypress Lawn Cemetery, San Mateo County,
    California, 266

Daggett, Rollin, 91, 95, 96
Daily Alta California, 124
Daily Financial News, 185
Dairy Regulation, Stewart promotes, 231
Daly, Marcus, 185
Davis, Garrett, 285 n. 1
Davis, Sam: recommended as Minister to
    Sandwich Islands, 149; supports Stewart in
    1898 election, 204, 214; and Lake Tahoe
    National Park, 222; plans to block Nixon in
    1904 campaign, 251; describes Stewart, 269
Dayton, Nevada, 58
Death Valley, California, 83
Deer Creek Diggings, California, 1. *See also*
    Nevada City, California
Deficiency Act, aids Central Pacific Railroad,
    229
Deficiency Bill, defeated, 174
DeLamar, Joseph R.: wants bills defeated,
    216–217; and Stewart Castle, 218; 1900
    Congressional candidate, 224; 1902
    Senatorial candidate, 228; no interest in
    Senate race, 237, 238
DeLong, Charles: defeated in 1864 for U.S.
    Senate, 43; Senate challenge to Stewart in
    1868, 61; named Minister to Japan, 61

Democratic Central Committee, 155
Democratic Party, National: moves toward support of silver, 178; adoption of silver plank revives Nevada Democrats in 1896, 181–184
Democratic Party, Nevada: in Nevada Territory, 42; in election of James Fair in 1880, 91; in 1894 election, 173; fuses with Silverites, 181; 1896 election revitalizes, 182; failure to fuse with Silverites in 1898, 201; in 1898 election campaign, 195–215; fusion with Silverites in 1900, 228; fusion in 1904, 248, 249. *See also* Silver Party of Nevada
Democratic State (California) Convention of 1858, 9
Depression on the Comstock in 1864, part played in ratification of 1864 Constitution, 41, 42
Deseret News, 109
Devil's Gate, Nevada Territory, fort erected there by David Terry, 16
"Devil" theory of history, in passage of 1873 Mint Act ("Crime of '73"), 118
DeYoung, Michel Harry, 188
Diamond-Bullfrog Extension Company, 260
Diamond-Bullfrog Mining Company, 260
Dickerson, Denver, 265
"District Ring": alleged frauds in government of District of Columbia, 74; Stewart appointed to investigating committee, 74
Dodge, Frederick, 132
Doolittle, James R., 36
Doten, Alf., 214
Doughty, James, 172
Downieville, California, 9–12, 86
Doyle, John Thomas, 234–236
Dupont Circle, Washington, D.C., "Castle Stewart," 80

E Clampus Vitus, 92
Edmunds-Tucker Act, and Mormon Church, 108
Education, 3, 4; Stewart's interest in University of Nevada, 138, 139; proposes national Mining College, 139, 286 n. 24; proposes national university to educate teachers, 139; role in establishment of Indian school in Nevada, 139, 140; Stewart establishes private school at Rhyolite, Nevada, 262; appointed to committee to investigate schools in Washington, D.C., 274; Stewart's role in reviewed, 274

Eight-hour day, 217
Elections: of 1864, 32, 42; of 1868, 60, 61; of 1874, 82; of 1886, 94–99; of 1890, 144–147; of 1892, 144–158; of 1894, 172, 173; of 1896, 176–183; of 1898, 191–195, 215; of 1900, 224–228; of 1902, 237–242; of 1904, 245–251
Electro-Magnetic Traction Company, 219
Elko, Nevada, fusion of Democrats and Silverites in 1896, 181
Ellis, Colonel A. C., 98
Emma Mine Company scandal, x, 84; background, 75–76; Stewart's involvement in, 75–80, 291 n. 39; in Stewart's 1886 campaign for U.S. Senate, 97; reviewed, 272, 273
Emmett, George, 197–198
Enabling Act, Nevada: introduced, 36; passed Congress and signed by Lincoln, 36
Erie, Pennsylvania, 3
Erie Canal, 1, 3
Ernst, George, 196
Esmeralda County, 259
Eureka, Nevada, 86, 87, 93, 213, 259
Eureka Consolidated, 87
Evarts, William, 77

Fair, James G., 93; elected U.S. Senator as Democrat, 91; record, 91; scheme to move Apaches to Catalina Island, 94; in 1886 campaign, 98–100
Farrington, Edward S., 239; Republican nominee for Congress, 224–228
Federal Elections Bill of 1890 (Force Bill), 157; battle over in Senate, 128; repeal attempt, 169; and silver issue, 169. *See also* Force Bill
Federalist Party, 6
Fessenden, William P., 47; proposal to guarantee Negro suffrage, 62
Field, Stephen J., 7, 40, 65; in Sharon-Hill case, 89, 90, 91
Fifteenth Amendment to the U.S. Constitution, 47, 66; debate in Congress, 62–63; Stewart's role in final wording, 63; Stewart and Nevada ratification of, 63; Stewart credited with writing, 64, 265, 270
"Fighting Claims," on the Comstock, 20
Filibuster, Silverites on Sherman Act repeal, 165–167
Finch, James D., 142; with *Silver Knight-Watchman,* 254; in Bullfrog district, 254, 255, 318 n. 9; later activities in Nevada,

318 n. 11
Findlay, A. M., 107, 108
Fitch, Thomas: in Storey County Union Party
Convention, 29; editor of *Virginia Daily
Union,* 30; opposes ratification of 1863
constitution, 30–33; supports Judge North,
38; calls for state silver convention, 122; in
1890 Congressional campaign, 144; word
portrait of Stewart, 251–252
Flanigan, Patrick L., 211, 212
Flannery, Harry, 211, 212
Flenniken, Robert P.: appointed Judge, Utah
Territory, 16, 279 n. 61; recognizes Cradle-
baugh's authority in Utah Territory, 16
Foot (United States Senator from Vermont),
56–57
Foote, Henry S.: law partnership with William
M. Stewart, 8; joins California Know-
Nothing (American) Party, 8; defeated in try
for U.S. senatorship from California, 9;
supports Stewart's Reconstruction plan, 58
Foote, Henry S., Jr., 157, 158
Foote, William W., 237
Force Bill of 1890, 126–130. *See also* Federal
Elections Bill of 1890
Ford's Theatre, assassination of Lincoln, 56
Forman, William, 257
Fort Churchill, Nevada, 12
Fox, Andrew W., 159
Fox, Anna ("Annie"), 159, 243
Fox, Bessie, 160. *See also* Hofer, Bessie
Fox children, 159, 160
Freedmen's Bureau Bill, 57; Stewart votes to
sustain Johnson veto, 58, 59
"Free Mining," concept, 286 n. 11; recognized
in Benton bill, 50, 51; in "Courts bill," 52;
in 1866 National Mining Act, 54, 55
Free Silver: issue in Nevada politics in 1880's,
92; importance to Republican Party, 121,
147; in Nevada Silver Convention, 122, 150;
supported by Nevada political parties, 150;
supported by national People's Party, 152;
and Nevada Silver League, 153–155; and
Nevada Silver Party, 155–159; in 1892
campaign, 144–158; in 1896 campaign,
177–185; Stewart ties to War (Spanish-
American) Revenue Bill, 194; eliminated as
national issue after 1896, 194, 227; active in
Nevada politics to 1908, 231, 232
Frémont, John, 50
Frohman, Isaac, 219, 239; former Stewart secretary, in 1898 election, 201; correspondence
with Stewart, 263; draws Stewart's will, 266
Fulton, Robert, 226; Southern Pacific Railroad

land agent in Nevada, 229
Fusion: attempts to fuse Populists, Silverites
and Democrats nationally in 1896, 180–181;
fusion of Democrats and Silverites in 1896
Nevada election, 181; "Fusion Party"
(Silver-Democrats) sweep 1896 election in
Nevada, 182; failure of fusion in 1898
election, 201; fusion succeeds in 1900,
225–228; succeeds in 1902, 241; succeeds
in 1904. *See also* Silver-Democrats

Gage, Stephen, 191; works for Stanford's
nomination for President in 1888, 111;
relations with Stewart, 140; and railroad
patronage, 142–143; in 1892 Nevada
election, 156; in 1898 Nevada election, 208,
209
Gedney, F. S., 213
Genoa, Utah Territory, 11, 14; Stewart's law
office there in 1859, 14; county seat of
Carson County, Utah Territory, 19;
suggested as site for Nevada state capital, 25
Georgetown Hospital, 265
Geronimo, 94
Gillespie, Willard: in 1898 election, 212–214;
Assembly investigation of, 213, 214,
312 n. 108
Gladstone, William 200
"Glove" bill, law passed by Nevada legislature
to allow Corbett-Fitzsimmons fight, 189
Gold clause, and Senator Stewart, 182
Gold Crest Mining Company, 260
Goldfield, Nevada, 254, 259, 260
Gold Hill, Nevada, 67, 95, 145
Gold Hill Daily News: admits defeat in 1863
ratification battle, 33; fight against
"corrupt" territorial judiciary, 36–40;
supports Stewart for U.S. Senate, 43; warns
North to drop slander suits, 44; doesn't favor
Stewart's reelection in 1868, 61; charges
corruption in 1898 election, 214
Gold Hill Mining District, 14, 51
Gold Standard Act, United States, 220
Gold Summit Mining Company, 260
Gompers, Samuel, 136
Goodwin, Charles C.: editor *Salt Lake Tribune,*
101, 296 n. 1; quoted on Stewart's part in
1866 National Mining Law, 55; Stewart
suggests depriving Mormons from political
power to, 103, 104, 107; quoted on Stewart,
269, 272
Gorgona, Isthmus of Panama, 4
Gould and Curry Mining Company v. *The*

North Potosi Mining Company: single versus multiple ledge theory, referee appointed, 34–35; Nugent decision, 39

Grand River, Ohio, 1

Grant [Gottheimer], Albert, 76–79

Grant, Ulysses S.: reviews troops, 56; Stewart asks for advice on 15th amendment proposal, 62; supports ratification of 15th amendment, 64; Stewart's relations with, 74–75; offers Stewart Supreme Court post?, 75; and Mint Act of 1873, 165–166

Grass Valley, California, 5; Comstock ore assays, 10

Great Basin, 11

Greathouse, Clarence, 86

Greeley, Horace, 58

Grizzly Ditch, 5

Grosche Gold and Silver Mining Company, 20

Grosh brothers, 20, 280 n. 11

Guadalupe-Hidalgo, Treaty of, ?, 13, 47

Guam, 215

Guggenheims, 218

Guthrie, James, 47

Hagerman, J. C., 246

Haggin, James B., 87, 88, 113

Hague Tribunal, ix, 233, 235, 236, 238, 273. *See also* Permanent Court of International Arbitration

Haines, James W., 143

Hanna, Mark, 239

Hansborough, Henry C., 232

Hardy, James, 15; accuses Judge North of bribery, 28, 37

Hardy, Roy, 264

Harriman, Edward, 247

Harris, Frank ("Shorty"), 254

Harrison, Benjamin, 155, 156, 157; Stewart tries to enlist in free-silver fight, 121; signs Sherman Silver Act, 122; nominated for President in 1892, 153

Harvey, William H. ("Coin"), 171

Hawaiian Islands, 184, 191, 221; Stewart favors annexation by legislation, 194

Hawley, Helen B., 262

Hawley, Thomas P., 239; contests Newlands in 1902 Senate race, 238–242; nominated by Republicans for U.S. Senate, 240; defeated, 242

Hawthorne, Nevada, 133, 134

Hay, John, 235

Hays, Colonel Jack, 12

Hazel Mines Company, 260

Hearst, George, 99

Henderson, John B., 62

Herrin, William F.: forms a law partnership with Stewart, 86, 87; in Sharon-Hill case, 88–90; in 1898 election, 197, 201; and Captain DeLamar, 216; loans money to Stewart, 219; in 1900 Nevada election, 226; and Southern Pacific Railroad agent in Nevada, 229; in 1902 Senate race in Nevada, 239, 242; and 1904 campaign in Nevada, 245, 247

Hill, Sarah Althea: legal battle with Sharon, 88–90; held in contempt of court, 89, 90; case reviewed, 273

Hillyer, Curtis J., 64; legal fees in Emma Mine case, 77

Hobart, Walter S., 95

Hofer, Bessie (Fox), 158; education, 160; quarrels with Stewart, 243. *See also* Fox, Bessie

Hofer, Theodore, 143

"Home-rule," 96

Homes, Stewart's, 9, 10, 80, 253, 255–257, 263, 278 n. 34, 316 n. 120

Hooker, Elizabeth, 160, 243

Hopkins, Mark, 65

Horr, R. G., 163

House Foreign Affairs Committee, investigation of Emma Mine promotion, 76–79

Huntington, Collis P.: relations with Stewart during first Senatorial term, 64–65; and Chinese immigration, 138; Stewart's efforts on behalf of, 1887–1893, 140–142; and Santa Monica plans of Senator Jones, 141; in 1892 Nevada election, 156–158; involved in Mexican railroad, 159; Stewart disagrees with on Sherman Silver Act repeal, 168, 169; regrets action of Congress on railroad indebtedness bill, 174; and Santa Monica project, 187, 188; asks favor of Stewart, 188; opinion of Stewart, 188, 189, 262; in 1898 Nevada campaign, 197; death, 228; relations with Stewart reviewed, 270. *See also* Central Pacific Railroad; Southern Pacific Railroad

Idaho Territory, Stewart's attempt to add to Nevada, 96, 99 101–105. *See also* Boundary expansion

Imperialism in Cuba, 194; in the Philippines, 194, 215, 216, 220–222, 230

Indian Affairs, Commissioner of, 134, 135, 186; verifies land claims of Pyramid Lake

Indians, 132, 133

Indian Affairs, Senate Committee on, ix, 135, 187, 221, 232

Indians, 11, 12, 130, 222, 233; Senate investigation commission visits Walker River and Pyramid Lake Reservations, 133–135. *See also* Walker River Indian Reservation

"In-lieu lands," 222, 223

International Bimetallic Conference, 173, 184

International Mining Company, Stewart's Mexican interests, 148, 159, 164, 218, 273

International Navigation Company, 236

Interstate Commerce Act, 140, 141, 142

Irrigation: Stewart supports strong program of, 95; proposes survey of arid lands, 111–113; becomes major issue in 1886 Nevada election, 112; Select Senate committee tour of arid West, 114; Powell-Stewart fight over irrigation policies, 115–118; Stewart suggests irrigation project in Pyramid Lake Indian Reservation, 134; Senate debate on issue in the 1890's, 232; Stewart belittles Newlands's role in, 232; President Teddy Roosevelt quote on Newlands Act, 240; issue in 1904 Senate race, 246; Stewart's role in, summarized, 271

Irrigation and Reclamation: Select Committee on, established, 112; Stewart made chairman of, 112; tours arid states, 113–115

Irrigation Clique, 112

Irrigation Congress, first, at Salt Lake City, Utah, 232

Johnson, Andrew: signs mining act of 1866, 54; reconstruction battles, 55–60; Stewart's description of, 56; supports Stewart's reconstruction plan, 58; vetoes Civil Rights bill, 59; impeachment, 60

Johnson, David, 33, 281 n. 48

Johnson, J. Neely: Know-Nothing Governor of California, 7; President of 1864 Nevada constitutional convention, 7; Justice of Nevada Supreme Court, 7, 23

Johnson, Reverdy, 52

Jones, George F., 44

Jones, Horace, 35

Jones, James K.: purchase of *Silver Knight-Watchman*, 186; Stewart asked for endorsement of, 201, 207; does not endorse Stewart in 1898 campaign, 208

Jones, John P., 83, 98, 99, 122, 170, 175, 195, 198, 220; enters 1872 Senate race in Nevada, 82; involved with Stewart in Panamint mining, 84; question of support for Stewart in 1886, 95, 97; and George M. Weston, 119; nation's first bimetallist, 120; member of Silver Commission in Congress, 120; supports Bland-Allison Act, 120; plan to develop Santa Monica, California, 141; and Carson Mint patronage, 143; criticizes Newlands in 1890 Congressional race, 145–146; role in 1892 Nevada election, 147, 156; major silver speech, 166–167; wins 1896 election, 182; defeats Nixon challenge in Nevada legislature, 182, 183; favors International Bimetallic Conference in 1897, 185; votes against Spanish-American War resolution, 193; lack of activity in 1900 election, 225–226; bows out of 1902 Senate race, 237; Stewart asks for his help for Hawley, 240; Newlands replaces in Senate, 242, 247

Jones, Sam, 95, 145

Julian, George W.: Chairman of House Committee on Public Lands, 51; opposes concept of "free mining" and advocates sale of mineral lands, 51, 52, 53, 54

Kappler, Charles: in 1892 Nevada campaign for Stewart, 156, 157; manages *Silver Knight-Watchman*, 185; in 1898 election in Nevada, 198, 209; and Ashburn farms, 218; notes Stewart's financial problems, 219; accompanies Stewart to The Hague, 233, 236; role in 1904 Nevada Senate campaign, 245–251; quoted on Stewart, 268

Kappler, Mrs. Charles, 233, 236

Kearney, General Stephen, 49

Keating, Robert P., 171

Kelley, E. D., 190

Kendall, Charles W.: introduces Swamp Land measure, 73; Kendall's bill opposed by Stewart, 73

Kern River Land and Canal Company: water and land rights in California, 88; reviewed, 273

Kinkead, John M.: appointed territorial treasurer of Nevada Territory, 19; serves in 1863 and 1864 Constitutional Convention, 19, 23

Kirkpatrick, Judge Moses, 14, 52

Know-Nothing Party, 269; organized in California, 8, 9. *See also* American Party

LaFollette, Senator Robert M., 262
Lake Tahoe National Park, 222, 223
Lamar, Lucius, Q. C., 126, 129, 130;
nominated by Cleveland for U.S. Supreme
Court, 124; confirmed by Senate, 125;
Stewart condemned for supporting, 157
Lancaster, Nanny, 263, 264
Lander County, Nevada, 23, 24, 259
Lane, Charles D., 223
Lassen, Alex C., 185
Las Vegas, Nevada, 255; proposed as county
seat of new Clark County, 257
Latin Union, 165
Latter-day Saints, Church of Jesus Christ of,
108, 109. *See also* Mormons
Laurel Cemetery, San Francisco, 237, 265, 266
Lease, Mary, 154
Lecompton Constitution, 9
Lee, Benjamin Watkins, 8
Leidy, George W., 211–213
Lewis, James F.: law partnership at Washoe
City, Nevada, with John W. North, 22;
Chief Justice of Nevada Supreme Court, 22
Lincoln, Abraham, 22, 43, 60; appoints
Nevada territorial officers, 19; relations with
Nevada statehood movement, 36–38; and
Senator Stewart, 55, 56
Locke, Powhatan B., 44, 45; territorial judge,
unusual behavior in Chollar-Potosi cases, 35;
resigns under pressure, 39
Lodge, Henry Cabot, 126
Lord, F. C., 110, 136
Los Angeles and Independence Railroad, 86
Lux, Charles, 88
Lynch, James A., 263
Lyon, James E., discovers Emma Mine in
Utah, 75; employs Stewart as attorney, 75;
involved in Emma Mine Company scandal,
75–79; accusations against Stewart,
79–80, 97
Lyons, New York, 1, 3, 4
Lyons Union School, 4

McAllister, Hall, 88
McConnell, John R.: district attorney, Nevada
County, California, 6; elected California
Attorney-General, 7; leave of absence from
office, 7, 8, 9; relations with Stewart, 7–9
McCulloch, Hugh, 57
McGowan, A. J., 212
Mackay, John, 95, 98, 99; possible U.S.
Senatorial candidate in 1886, 91; favors
Stewart for U.S. Senate, 93; in 1898 election

campaign in Nevada, 198, 201; loans money
to Stewart, 219, 270; and Alaskan Govern-
ment Act, 223
McKinley, William, 227; nominated on gold
standard in 1896 by Republicans, 178;
in 1896 campaign for ''Battle of the
Standards,'' 184, 185, 218, 220; and
Spanish-American War, 191–194; patronage
in Nevada, 197; and annexation of the
Philippines, 215; 1900 election n Nevada,
226; Stewart supports in 1900, 228, 231
McKissick's Opera House, Stewart's speech
on irrigation, 112
McLaughlin, Patrick, 10, 15
McMillan, William, 226
Maguire's Opera House, scene of North-
Stewart debate, 31
Mannix, Frank, 259
Maricopa Railroad Bill, 140, 141
Mariposa, California: speculators, 84; Wallace
dies there, 229
Marsh, Charles, 5
Marshall, James, 46
Martinson, George, 254, 257
Maryland Standard Telephone Company, 219
Mason, N. H. A., 212
Mason, Colonel R. B., 49
Mason Valley ranchers, and Walker River
Indians, 133
Maxson, Colonel H. B., 198
''Memo of Agreement,'' Stewart's role in, 75
Memphis Silver Convention of 1895, 177
Meredith, Henry, 8; law partner of Stewart, 11,
12, 14
Mesick, Richard, supports Judge North on
Comstock cases, 38; suggested as replace-
ment for North, 40
Mexican Company, Comstock mining
company, disputes Ophir claims, 15
Mexican International Railroad, proposed, 159
Military post, Reno, Stewart supports, 136
Miller, Henry: involved in California water and
land suits, 88; in Nevada cattle quarantine
issue, 190
Miller and Lux: want cattle quarantine limited,
190; in Stewart campaign for election in
1898, 201
Mills, Darius O., 98, 158, 182, 237
Mills, George T., 238, 241, 242; Chairman,
Republican State Central Committee, 237;
and 1902 election, 240; in reference to
Bessie Hofer, 243
Mills, William, 188, 205, 222
Mineral lands of United States: system of

reservation, 47; leasing system, 49; sale of, 49; indiscriminate location, 49; "free mining," 50; Nevada legislature and "free mining," 51; possessory rights in "Courts" law, 52; rules of mining district in Sparrow case, 52; possessory rights in 1866 National Mining Law, 55

Miner's Code, adopted in California, 7, 51

Miner's District Meeting, 6, 7; in California gold rush, 50; 1851 California law recognizes Miner's rules, 50; recognized by U.S. Supreme Court in *Sparrow* v. *Strong*, 52, 53; recognized in National Mining Law of 1866, 55

Miner's "Magna Carta," 55. *See also* National Mining Law of 1866

Mines and Mining, Senate Committee on: established, 47, 54; Stewart appears before, 265

Minnesota Constitutional Convention, Judge North's role in, 22, 32

Mint Act of 1873: debate in U.S. Senate, 69–72, 92, 165; opposed by Weigand, 71; in Stewart's Senate campaign of 1886, 97; John Sherman's part in passage, 110, 111; Stewart explains position on, 118–120; the question of conspiracy, 119; in newspaper debates, 163; and Bishop Newman, 181; in election of 1898 in Nevada, 203. *See also* "Crime of '73"

Mitchell, Miles N., 29, 30

Mixed Claims Commission, in the Pious Fund Case, 234, 235, 236

Moffat, David H., 185

Moffatt, Robert, 10

Morgan, T. J., 132–133

Mormons, in western Utah Territory, 13; Test Oath mandated in Nevada, 104, 105, 107; Test Oath unconstitutional in Nevada, 108; irrigation system compared to Powell's plan, 115. *See* Latter-day Saints

Mother Lode, California, 5, 266

Mott, Judge Gordon N., 35, 52; opens territorial court in Carson City, 20; resigns from Territorial Bench, 21; elected to Congress, 22

Multiple-ledge theory of Comstock Lode, 15; in Nevada territorial courts, 20; disavowed by Judge North, 28; upheld by Judge North in 1864, 34; disavowed by referee John Nugent, 39

Musser, John, 10; as "provisional" delegate to Washington, D.C., 11; has bill introduced in Congress to establish Nevada Territory, 18

National Law School, Washington, D.C., 255

National Mining College, 139, 274, 286 n. 24

National Mining Law of 1866 (an Act granting the right of way to ditch and canal owners), ix, 66, 67; background, 47–53; fight in Congress for "free mining," 51; Congressional debate on National Mining bill, 53–55; passed, 54, 55, 287 n. 33; credited to Stewart, 64; applicable to Alaska, 223; Stewart's part in writing reviewed, 265, 270

National Mining Law of 1870, 67, 68

National Mining Law of 1872: authored by Aaron Sargent of California, 68; floor fight led by Stewart, 68

National Silver Committee, wants silver convention for Nevada, 122

National Silver Convention, Stewart urges Newlands to attend, 144

National Silver Party, 174, 175; formed in Washington, D.C., 1896, 177; attempt to merge with Populists, 177; nominates Bryan for President, 180. *See* Bimatallic Party; Bimetallic League; Bimetallic Union

National teacher's college, 139, 274

National Watchman, 176

Neagle, Dave: at Panamint boom, 85; marshall in Sharon-Hill case, 90; kills David Terry, 91, 294 n. 46; Stewart "bodyguard" in 1898 election, 208, 209, 215

Negro suffrage, 22, 32, 57, 126; Stewart supports at Dayton, Nevada, 58; fight in Congress for constitutional protection, 61, 62–63; guaranteed in 15th Amendment, 63–64

Nevada Board of Reclamation and Internal Improvements, 114–115

Nevada boundaries, 46. *See also* Boundary expansion

Nevada City, California, 1, 5, 6, 11, 86, 238; Miner's meeting, 1852, at, 7, 9; Comstock assays, 1859, 10. *See also* Deer Creek Diggings

Nevada County, California, 5, 6, 7, 9, 10, 11, 51; Miner's District meeting, Stewart as Chairman, 51; Nevada County Mining Code of 1852, 69

Nevada Democrat, The, 6

Nevada Historical Society, obtains the Stewart papers, 264

Nevada Journal, Nevada City, California, 6; announces discovery of Comstock Lode, 10

Nevada Mining Law, 287 n. 33

"Nevada" Party, in 1886 election, 93

Nevada Silver Association, 92

Nevada Silver Convention, 122; nonpolitical, 150

Nevada Silver League, 153; alignment with People's Party, 154; becomes Nevada Silver Party in September, 1892, 155

Nevada State Journal, Reno: predicts Stewart victory in 1898, 204, 207; criticizes Stewart's selection by the legislature, 212; in Gillespie incident, 213; in 1904 campaign, 246, 247; concedes defeat of Governor Sparks in 1904 election, 251

Nevada Stock Farm, 218

Nevada Territorial Legislature, 270

Nevada Territory, 11, 19, 23, 27, 33, 36; Organic Act signed by Buchanan, 18, 22

Newlands, Francis G., 90, 140, 175, 182; accompanies tour of arid west, 113, 114; political ambitions, 114; 1890 campaign for Congress, 144–146; at National Silver Convention, 144; criticizes Senator John P. Jones, 145–146; in 1892 Congressional campaign, 149–159; joins Silver League, 155; suggested role in uniting Nevada Populists and Democrats, 179; temporary chairman of National Silver Party Convention, 180; in fusion movement of 1896, 181; position on Nixon challenge of Jones, 182–183; introduces resolution to annex Hawaiian Islands, 194; in 1898 Senate campaign and election, 195–215; elected to Congress as Silver-Democrat in 1898, 201; contests Stewart for U.S. Senate, 206; ousted from Silver Party in 1898, 211; defeated in 1899 legislature, 212, 224; in Congressional election of 1900, 224–228; role in irrigation after 1890, 232; bids for U.S. Senate, 237–242; elected, 242; employs James D. Finch as secretary, 255; on Stewart's death, 265; control of Silver-Democrats, 270; importance of William M. Stewart to, 271

Newlands Reclamation Act, 232

Newman, Bishop John P., 181

New York Herald, 119

New York Sunday World, 177

New York Superior Court, 4

New York Telegram, 163

New York Times, 124, 166, 167; interview with Stewart on decline of silver issue, 185; reports Stewart rejoining Republican Party, 196

New York Tribune, 58

New York Weekly Tribune, 163

Nicaraguan Canal, 184; Stewart favored from 1895 to 1903, 244

Nixon, George: editor of Winnemucca *Silver State,* 150, 248; organizes first Nevada Silver club, 151; calls for state meeting of silver clubs, 153; challenges Jones for U.S. Senate, 182–183, 195, 196; favors maintaining quarantine against California cattle, 190; cautions Newlands about contesting Stewart, 197, 199; predicts Stewart victory in 1898 election, 204; switches to Newlands in 1898 campaign, 206; importance in 1902 Nevada Senate race, 239; says Stewart will not run in 1904, 246; rejoins Republican Party, 246; accused of being political agent of Central Pacific Railroad, 246; supported by Central Pacific in 1904, 247; wins 1904 election, 251; and new southern Nevada county, 259; proposes statue in honor of Stewart, 265

Noonday Mine, Bodie, California, 86

Norcross, Charles A.: wants Stewart to bring Populists and Democrats together in Nevada, 179; organizes Bryan club in Reno, 180; reports to Stewart that Newlands is his enemy in 1898 election, 202; suggested as Southern Pacific Railroad agent for Nevada, 229; suggests Stewart not run in 1904, 245, 246; cites Stewart's achievements, 248

Norcross, Frank, 226

North, John W., appointed surveyor-general of Nevada Territory by Lincoln, 19; appointed Territorial Judge, 21; opened law office in Carson City, 22; helped lay out Washoe City, 22; law partnership with James F. Lewis at Washoe City, 22; president of 1863 Constitutional Convention, 23–26; in 1863 ratification battle, 27–33; popularity after 1863 Constitutional Convention, 28; rules against single-ledge theory, 28; opposed in Storey County nominating convention, 29; defeated for governor in State Union Party Convention, 29; opposes Stewart in ratification fight, 26–33; favors Potosi in case against the Chollar Company, 34; appoints John Nugent as referee in single-ledge case, 34, 35; resigns from Territorial Judiciary, 38; accepts John Nugent's report that Comstock Lode is a single ledge, 39; supports Union Party candidates in 1864 election, 42; initiates slander suits against William M. Stewart and owners of *Territorial Enterprise,* 43; cleared of corruption charges by referees, Stewart held guilty of slander, 44, 45, 285 n. 61, n. 64; leaves

Nevada, 45; difficulties with Stewart reviewed, 273

North, Mrs. John, 268

Northern Pacific Railroad Company, 113, 141

North Star, Stewart accused of belonging to, 9

Noteware, C. N., 23

Nugent, John: referee in Gould and Curry case, 35; reports Comstock Lode is a single ledge, 39

Nye, James Warren, 22, 51, 61; appointed Territorial Governor of Nevada by Lincoln, 19; arrives Carson City, July 7, 1861, 19; calls for elections, 19; designates Carson City as meeting place for territorial legislature, 19; calls for constitution under Enabling Act, 36; chosen to U.S. Senate, 43; introduces Sutro Tunnel right of way bill, 55; votes to override Johnson's veto of Civil Rights Bill, 59; little interest in Mint Act of 1873, 69–71; introduces measure to give swamp lands to Nevada, 72, 73; daughter's letter from Stewart, 275

Nye County, Nevada, 196, 238, 259

O.K. Corral fight, supposedly witnessed by Stewart, 87

Oleomargarine interests, Stewart defends, 231

Ophir Company: organized, 15; employs W. M. Stewart as attorney, 15; legal quarrels on the Comstock, 15; North rules against in Burning Moscow case, 28, 29

Ophir Company v. *McCall et al.*, 15

Ophir Diggings, 10; publicized in San Francisco, 10. *See also* Ophir Company

Ordinance of 1785, establishes reservation of mineral lands for government, 47

Organic Act, Nevada Territory, signed by President Buchanan, 18

O'Riley, Peter, discovery of Conmstock Lode, 10, 15

Ormsby County, 9, 114; anti-Chinese issue in, 137; donates land for Indian school, 139

Ormsby House, Carson City, 93, 183, 209

Pacific Railroad, 133; subsidy opposed in 1863 Convention, 24

Pacific Railroads: Senate Committee on, 140, 188; Stewart as member and Chairman, 74

"Palace Hotel" Party, in 1886 Nevada election, 93

Panama Canal, Stewart favors in 1904, 244

[Panama] Canal Zone, 244

Panama route, taken by Stewart, 1, 4

Panamint Mining Company, organization, 83; Senators Jones and Stewart purchase company, 84; questionable promotion by the two Senators, 84–85; builds mill, 85; boom fizzles, 85–86; thievery from, 262; reviewed, 273

Panamint Mountains, 208; ore body found in Surprise Canyon, 1873, 83; ore strike announced in *Mining and Scientific Press*, 83

Panamint, Nevada, 85; boom fades quickly, 85

Panamint News, 85

Panic of 1893: and repeal of Sherman Silver Act, 164, 166; and Venezuelan affair, 176

"Paramount allegiance," clause debated in 1863 Constitutional Convention, 25

Park, Trenor W.: reorganizes Emma Mine Company, 75; involved in Emma Mine scandal, 75–79; enters Panamint Mining Company promotion, 84

Patterson, Webster H., 190

Paul, Frank, 213, 214

Payson, Colonel Francis L., 222

Payson, Mary Isabelle ("Maybelle"), 160, 222

Penrod, Emanuel, 15

People's Mass Meetings, in 1863 Constitutional ratification battle, 30–32

People's Party, 155, 156, 161, 187; adopts free-silver plank in 1892, 152; alignment with Nevada Silver League, 154; Weaver nominated for President on strong silver plank, 154; Stewart joins during Sherman Silver Act repeal fight, 168; Stewart doesn't want local unit in Nevada, 172; local unit formed in Nevada in 1894, 172–174; attempts to merge with National Silver Party in 1896, 177; nominates Bryan for President in 1896, 180; Nevada unit of People's Party, 181, 202

Permanent Court of International Arbitration, 233. *See also* Hague Tribunal

Perpetual Emigrating Fund Company, of Latter-day Saints, 108

"Philadelphia," 4

Philippine Islands, 184, 191; Stewart advocates capture and retention of, 194, 215, 216; Stewart opposes independence, 216; Filipinos and American Indians compared, 221, 222; favors railroad as a civilizing influence, 230, 231

Pious Fund case, background, 233–235; before Hague Tribunal, 236; reviewed, 273; award to California Bishops, 236, 315 n. 84

Piper's Opera House, Stewart's speech to refute charges against him, 97–98

Platt, Sam, 142, 239

Political Conventions, Nevada: of 1863, 29–32; of 1864, 42; of 1886, 96; of 1888, 107, 110–111; of 1890, 147; of 1892, 152–156, 172–173; of 1894, 172; of 1896, 178–181; of 1898, 201, 202; of 1900, 228; of 1902, 240, 241; of 1904, 249

Populists, 178, 179, 180, 181, 182, 184, 186, 187, 269. *See also* People's Party

Potassium cyanide, Stewart favors low tariff on to benefit mining interests, 186

Potosi Mining company, 37; opposes Chollar Mining Company in single-ledge suit, 21, 22; Territorial Supreme Court upholds Chollar, March, 1863, 21; Potosi gains permanent injunction against Chollar in 1864, 34, 35

Powell, John Wesley, 232; directs irrigation survey, 112; with tour of arid states in 1889, 113; fight with Senator Stewart over policies, 115–118; plan for irrigation of arid west, 115, 116; resigns from U.S. Geological Survey, 117

Powning, Christopher, C.: possible candidate for U.S. Senate in 1886, 95; defeated in Washoe County primary, 96; drops out of Senate race in 1886, 96; tries to defeat Stewart in Republican caucus, 99; opposes Stewart as delegate to National Republican Convention, 110; and Reno military post, 137

Progressive Movement, 262, 263

Protective Tariff, 110, 120, 138, 170, 184, 186, 238

Protective Tariff League, 138

Public Lands, Senate Committee on, 53, 54, 72, 73

Puerto Rico, 194, 215, 221

Pyramid Lake Indian Reservation, 134; resolution from Nevada legislature to reduce size of, 131; Stewart tries to reduce size of, 186–187

Pyramid Lake Indians, 130, 132, 135. *See also* Pyramid Lake Indian Reservation

Pyramid Lake Indian War: causes of, 11; events of, 12

Radical Republicans, 57; pressure on Stewart, 58–60; Stewart joins on Civil Rights Act veto, 59; support Constitutional guarantee of Negro suffrage, 62–63

Ralston, Jackson Harvey, 235–236

Ralston, James H.: opposed to "net proceeds" tax, 23; suggests rotation of state capital in 1863 Convention, 24, 25

Ralston, William, 113

Ramsay, Alexander, 52, 53

Ray, L. O., 259

Reconstruction of South, 55, 57, 60, 62, 125; Stewart's plan of, 58, 59, 288 n. 56

Reddington, James K., 259

Reese building, Genoa, Utah Territory, Stewart establishes law office in 1859, 14, 279 n. 55

Reminiscences, Stewart's autobiography, 4, 263–265

Remonetization of silver, 101; major issue in U.S. Senate, 120, 121; not achieved with 1890 Sherman Silver Act, 122; supported by Nevada political parties, 150; supported by People's Party, 152; becomes national issue, 161; debate on in repeal of Sherman Silver Act, 164–168; kept alive in Congress by Stewart, 169–171; and Coxey's army, 172; Stewart ties to issuance of government bonds, 173; *Silver Knight-Watchman* newspaper to fight for, 175, 176; in 1896 election campaign, 182; Stewart presses for in 1897–1898, 184, 185; and Spanish-American War expenditures, 193–194; in reference to War Revenue bill, 193; Stewart loses place as spokesman for, 231; Stewart's role in reviewed, 265, 270, 271. *See also* Free Silver

Reno, Nevada, 257; Senate irrigation committee holds hearing at, 114

Reno Evening Gazette, 145, 146; on Stewart's return to Republicans in 1900, 228; opposed to Stewart in 1904, 245, 246; Stewart's achievements cited by, 248

Republican National Committee, in 1902 Nevada Senate race, 239

Republican National Convention, 22; Stewart and Jones as delegates in 1888, 110; Stewart on platform committee of, 110–111; adopts modified silver plank in 1888, 111; in 1892, 152; in 1904 election, 248

Republican Party, 22, 55, 57, 62, 125, 127, 129, 147, 151; nomination of McKinley on gold standard platform in 1896, 178; Nevada Republicans and gold standard plank, 181; Stewart reported rejoining, 195, 196; in Nevada state convention of 1898, 202; in 1898 election campaign in Nevada, 195–216; Stewart officially rejoins, 220, 226, 227, 231; Nixon rejoins, 246, 247;

Nevada Republicans support Nixon in 1904, 248, 249
Republican State Convention, 147, 240; attempt to adopt "home rule" regulation in 1886, 96; Stewart bows out of 1904 race, 248; Nixon supported in 1904, 249
Res adjudicata, in Pious Fund case, 235, 236
Rhodes, William H., 44
Rhyolite, Nevada: principal town of Bullfrog district, 255; proposed as county seat of new county of Bullfrog, 257, 259
Rhyolite Board of Trade, 259
Rhyolite Herald, 259
Rich and Lucy Ella Company, 16
Richmond Consolidated, Eureka, Nevada, 87
Riordan (Bishop), and Pious Fund case, 235–236
Rising, Richard, 14, 52
Robertson, J. Barr, 84
Robinson, Tod., 44, 285 n. 61
Roop, Isaac, 13
Roosevelt, Theodore, 232, 240, 245, 246, 262, 263

Sackbearers: Fair's use of in 1880 election, 91; description of, 295 n. 48
Sadler, Reinhold, 189–191
Sain, Charles M., 198
Saint Louis Company, 16
Salt Lake Tribune, 101, 296 n. 1
San Francisco, California, 4, 8, 10, 64, 86, 93, 95, 96; earthquake described by Frohman, 263
San Francisco Call, story about Stewart's departure from Nevada in 1908, 264
Santa Monica, California, 141, 146, 183, 187, 188
Sargent, Aaron, 6, 7; member of Congress and U.S. Senator from California, 7; with Stewart in Sierra County, 10; importance in 1870 mining law, 67; author of 1872 National Mining Law, 68
Savage Mining Company, 15
Sawyer, Judge Lorenzo, 89–90
Schenck, Robert, 76; involved in Emma Mine scandal, 76–79
Searles, Niles, 7; becomes Nevada County district attorney, 1854, 8; meets President Lincoln, 56
Second Judicial District, Utah Territory, Cradlebaugh removed and Flenniken appointed, 16
Second Morrill Act, 139, 274

Sharon, Frederick W., 90, 146
Sharon, William ("Will") E., 145, 171, 201, 210, 225; in 1898 election, 198, 199, 206; ousted from Silver Party, 211; as Southern Pacific agent, 237; importance in 1904 election, 247
Sharon, William P., 93; wants to be U.S. Senator, 82; legal battle with Sarah Althea Hill, 88–90; employs Stewart in Hill case, 89; as U.S. Senator from Nevada, 91; Stewart and settlement of the Sharon estate, 114, 226
Sharon v. Hill, 88–90; hearings before Master of Chancery, 89; holding against Hill, 90; reviewed, 273
Sherman, John, 92, 97, 122, 178; introduces bill to sell public mineral lands, 53, 54; introduces Mint bill in 1870, 69; deceptive actions in passage of Mint Act of 1873, 70–72, 298 n. 79; Stewart accuses of conspiracy in passage of 1873 Mint Act, 118–120; admits deception in passage of Sherman Act, 163, 164; in fight to repeal Sherman Silver Act of 1890, 164–168
Sherman Silver Purchase Act, 122, 153; repeal of, 161–167, 169
Sibley, Joseph C., 174, 175; and purchase of *Silver Knight-Watchman,* 184–185
Sierra County, California, 9, 10, 11
"Silver and Science of Money," Stewart monograph to publicize silver arguments, 171
Silver Clubs, Nevada: first one organized by Nixon in 1892, 151; Stewart supports organization throughout nation, 121. *See also* Silver Party
Silver-Democrats: results from fusion of Democrats and Silverites in Nevada election of 1896, 181–183; failure of fusion in 1898, 201; successful fusion in 1900, 225–228; in 1902, 241, 242; in 1904, 249
Silver demonetization: due to 1873 Mint Act ("Crime of '73"), 118; Sherman's deception in, 118–121; and the economic depression in Nevada, 118; and the Latin Union, 165; Sherman's defense of, 165, 166; Stewart blames nation's money woes on, 176; Stewart accused of voting for, 184, 185, 203. *See also* "Crime of '73"; Mint Act of 1873
Silver Knight newspaper, 175
"Silver Knights of America," 175–176
Silver Knight-Watchman: Stewart's instrument to fight for remonetization of silver, 176; supports Bryan for president in 1896, 180;

Stewart tries to sell, 185–186; on the Cuban insurrection and Cuban independence, 191–193; favors annexation of Hawaiian and Philippine Islands, 194; Stewart uses in 1898 Nevada election campaign, 200; sold, 219; and James D. Finch, 254

Silver Party Central Committee, 210; Newlands and Sharon ousted from, 211; controlled in 1900 by Newlands and Sharon, 225; expunges record of 1900 action, 228

Silver Party of Nevada, 154, 269; formation, 155–156; sweeps 1892 election, 157; in 1894 election, 172–173; fuses with Democrats in 1896, 181; and cattle quarantine issue, 189–191; in 1898 election, 195–215; in 1900 election, 224–226, 228; in 1902 Nevada race for U.S. Senate, 239; Stewart accused of treason by, 241; Nixon leaves it, 246, 247; in 1904 election, 249; and Central Pacific Railroad, 303 n. 48

Silver-Republicans, 196, 225; importance to Stewart, 197, 198

Silver State, Winnemucca, 150; predicts Stewart victory in 1898, 204; switches to Newlands in 1898 election, 206; notes Stewart's return to Republican Party, 227

Single-ledge theory of Comstock Lode, 15; in territorial courts of Nevada, 20, 21; ruled against by Judge North in Burning Moscow case, 28; disavowed by Judge North in Chollar-Potosi case, 34; John Nugent appointed to referee single-ledge case, 34–35; theory upheld by Nugent, 39

Sitting Bull, 222, 230

Slander suits by John North against Stewart, 43, 44, 45, 46, 285 n. 1

Smith, Grant, 86

Southern Pacific Railroad, 65, 86, 111, 140, 141, 158; Stewart's efforts on behalf of, 187, 188; wants Nevada cattle quarantine limited, 190; in 1898 election in Nevada, 197, 204, 210, 211; in 1900 election, 226–228; supports Newlands in 1902 Senate race, 237, 239; Stewart's annual passes, 263. *See also* Central Pacific Railroad

Spanish-American War, 235; covered in Stewart's newspaper, 176; Stewart blames bondholders for, 192; war resolution in Congress, 192–193; Stewart outlines his terms for peace, 194

Spanish in Cuba, 191; Stewart accuses of cruelty, 193; advocates withdrawal of, 194

Sparks, John: wants cattle quarantine on California cattle, 190; candidate for governor as Silver-Democrat in 1902, 241; Democratic candidate for U.S. Senate in 1904, 246, 249

Sparrow v. *Strong,* 52

Spelter, Napoleon B., fictionalized name for William Morris Stewart, 41

Springmeyer, George, 260

Squatter sovereignty: in western Utah Territory, 13; in mining, 50; relative to Nevada Indians, 131

"Stalking-horse," Nixon as, for Stewart in 1904, 247, 251

Stanford, Leland: relations with Stewart during latter's first term, 65; role in Lamar confrontation vote, 126; vote on Federal Elections (Force) Bill of 1890, 128, 129; horse stables, 218

Stanford, Mrs. Leland, 128, 129

Stevens, Alexander, 58

Stevenson, Charles C.: possible U.S. Senatorial candidate in 1886 election, 91; supports irrigation issue, 112

Stewart, Agnes: widow of Theodore C. Cone, marries William Stewart, 243; named executrix of Stewart's will, 266

Stewart, Anna (second Stewart daughter), 243. *See also* Fox, Anna

Stewart, Annie Elizabeth, 160; marries William M. Stewart, 8, 55; travels with daughters, 80, 291 n. 48; ill health, 236; killed in auto accident, 237; distribution of personal belongings, 243

Stewart Indian school, 139, 140, 187, 274

Stewart, Joseph, 12

Stewart, Mary Isabelle ("Maybelle") (youngest Stewart daughter), 160–161, 222

Stewart, Samuel D. R. (brother of William Stewart), 148

Stewart, Vera Cone (Stewart's adopted daughter), 257; school at Rhyolite for, 262, 263

Stewart, William Morris: birth, 1; early family relations, 2–5; education, 3, 4; arrives in California, 4; runs for sheriff of Nevada County, California, 5; selected delegate to Whig Party National Convention of 1852, 5; studies law with John McConnell, 6; joins Democratic Party, 6; admitted to California bar, 1852, 6; appointed District Attorney, Nevada County, 6; Chairman, Nevada County Miner's meeting, 6; appointed acting Attorney-General of California, 8; law partnership with Henry S. Foote in San Francisco in 1854, 8; joins Know-Nothing Party (American Party), 8; marries Annie Elizabeth

Foote, May 31, 1855, 8; moves to Nevada City, California, 9; law partnership with John R. McConnell in Nevada City, 1855, 9; rejoins Democratic Party, 9; builds mansion in Nevada City, 9; establishes law practice at Downieville, California, 9; edits *Sierra Citizen* newspaper, 9; joins Comstock rush in fall of 1859, 10, 279 n. 46; law partnership on Comstock with Henry Meredith in March, 1860, 11; part in Pyramid Lake War, 12; moves family to Virginia City, 12; law partnership with Judge Moses Kirkpatrick and Richard Rising and then with Alexander Baldwin, 14; mine and mill ownership on Comstock, 17; elected to Territorial Council from Ormsby County, 19; resigns from Council in 1862, 19; central figure in Comstock legal wars, 21, 22; achievements in 1863 Constitutional Convention, 23–26; opposes simultaneous vote on Constitution and election of officers, 26; disavows U.S. Senate seat in 1863, 26; supports ratification of 1863 Constitution, 26–33, 281 n. 25; accuses Judge North of accepting bribe, 28; controls Union Party nominating conventions, 29; wages fight against "corrupt" territorial judiciary, 36–42; candidate for U.S. Senate in 1864, 42; becomes first U.S. Senator from Nevada, 43; slander suits filed against him by John W. North, 43; found guilty of slander of North, 46, 285 n. 1; proposes Senate committee on Mines and Mining, 47; explains mining rules to Senator Ramsay, 53; writes new mining bill protecting "free mining," 54; leads successful fight for passage of National Mining Act of 1866, 54, 55; relations with President Lincoln, 55–57; after Lincoln's assassination, 56; purportedly at Johnson's swearing-in ceremony, 56–57; supports Johnson's reconstruction policies, 57–58; Stewart's Reconstruction Plan, 58–59; votes to override Johnson's Civil Rights veto, 59; votes to convict Johnson of impeachment, 60; chosen by Nevada legislature for second term in 1868, 61; role in final draft of 15th Amendment resolution, 63; role in ratification of 15th Amendment by Nevada legislature, 64; relations with Central Pacific Railroad and C. P. Huntington in first Senatorial term, 64, 65; employs Mark Twain as his secretary, 65; opposes Sutro Tunnel in Senate, 67; role in passage of 1872 mining law, 68; shows little interest in passage of Mint Act of 1873, 70;

Stewart endorses Gold Standard in 1874, 70–71; opposes Nye Bill ceding swamp lands to Nevada, 72–73; opposes Kendall Bill to cede swamp lands to Nevada, 73; appointed member of "District Ring" investigation committee, 74; Supreme Court appointment, 75; involved in Emma Mine scandal, 75–79, 291 n. 39; bows out of 1874 Senate race, 82, 292 n. 76; in Panamint Mining Company promotion, 84; law partnerships with Clarence Greathouse, William Herrin, and Peter Van Clief, 86; employed by Haggin and Tevis in water and land suits in California, 87–88; in Sharon-Hill case, 89–90; returns to Nevada to run for U.S. Senate, 91–92; activities in 1886 Senate campaign, 94–100; selected by Nevada legislature, 100; outlines Senatorial policies before Nevada legislature, 103; expansion plans against Idaho and Utah, 101–109; supports Utah statehood, 109; at 1888 Republican National Convention, 110; submits resolution in Senate to conduct irrigation survey of arid west, 111–113; dispute with John W. Powell over irrigation policies, 115–118; explains position in regard to passage of 1873 Mint Act, 118–121; accuses John Sherman of conspiracy in passage of Mint Act, 118–120; role in approval of Lamar, 124–126; opposes Federal Elections (Force) Bill of 1891, 126–129; relations with Pyramid Lake and Walker River Indians after 1887, 130–135; wants Walker River Indian Reservation opened to mining, 132; introduces bill for abandonment of Walker River Indian Reservation, 134–135; on women's suffrage, 136; on eight-hour day, 136; requests military post for Reno, 136, 137; and the University of Nevada, 138, 139; role in establishment of Indian school in Nevada, 139, 140; relations with Collis P. Huntington, 1887–1893, 140–142; use of Carson Mint for patronage, 143; involvement in 1890 Congressional election in Nevada, 144–147; role in 1892 election campaign, 148–158; silver mine interests in Mexico, 148; opposed to separate silver party in Nevada in 1892, 150; hesitates joining silver club movement, 151; hesitates supporting Newlands in 1892, 152; proposes 1892 national silver convention, 153; supports Newlands in Congressional fight in 1892, 154; accompanies Weaver party in Nevada, 154–155; joins Silver League, 155; chosen by state legislature for fourth term in U.S. Senate, 158; "kidnaps" the Fox

grandchildren, awarded custody of the three
Fox children, 159–160; debates silver issue
in *New York Telegram,* 163; debates silver
question with R. G. Horr, 163; plays major
role in opposing repeal of Sherman Silver
Act, 163–168; joins national People's Party,
168; links silver issue to major national
issues, 169, 170; fights in Senate for adjustment or refund of Central Pacific indebtedness, 174; takes lead in forming National
Silver Party, 174; attacks Cleveland's monetary policies, 175; supports Teller as Presidential choice for Democrats, 179; attends
Democratic Convention of 1896, 179; tries to
consolidate Populists and Democrats on
national level, 179; suggests Populists nominate Bryan in 1896, 179; role in Silver and
Populist Conventions of 1896, 180; campaigns in Nevada in 1896 election, 181–182;
and argument with Bishop Newman, 181;
personal finances, 182; 1897 remarks on
decline of silver issue, 185; revives campaign
to abandon Walker River Reservation and
reduce Pyramid Lake Reservation, 186–187;
favors Santa Monica as port of Los Angeles,
188; opinion of Huntington, 189; remarks on
Corbett-Fitzsimmons fight, 189; position on
1898 cattle quarantine issue, 190–191; favors
Cuban insurrection, 192; demands Cuban
independence, 192–193; recommends issuance of silver certificates to finance 1898 War,
193; favors annexation of Hawaiian and Philippine islands, 194; activities in 1898 election, 195–215; wins fifth term in U.S.
Senate, 212; supports retention of Philippine
islands, 216, 220–221; against Philippine
independence, 216; opposes direct election
of U.S. Senators, 217; opposes Civil Service
Law, 217; Mexican mining losses, 218, 219;
attempts to sell the ''Castle,'' 218; purchases
Ashburn farms in Virginia in 1895, 218;
financial problems, 219; returns to Republican Party, 220, 227; votes against Gold
Standard Act, 220; compares American
Indians with Filipinos, 221; and Alaskan
Government bill, 223–224; attempts to block
Newlands in 1900, 224–225; tries to enlist
Wm. Herrin against Newlands, 226; supports
E. S. Farrington for Congress, 226; cam-
paigns in Nevada for Farrington and
McKinley, 228; wants DeLamar against
Newlands in 1902, 228; favors building a
railroad in the Philippines, 230; favors oleo-
margarine interests, 231; wants strong dairy

controls, 231; role in Pious Fund Case,
233–236; first wife killed in automobile
accident, 236–237; supports Thomas P.
Hawley in 1902 Senate race, 238–242; cited
as traitor to Silver Party, 241; Stewart re-
marries, 243; Chinese exclusion again, 244;
position on Isthmian Canal, 244; role in election of 1904, 245–251; opposition to in 1904
election, 245, 246; bows out of 1904 Senate
race, 248; last speech in U.S. Senate, 252;
sells Washington home, 253; financial problems, 253, 318 n. 1; returns to Nevada, 253;
tours southern Nevada, 254; organizes law
firm in Bullfrog district, 254; builds home and
law office at Rhyolite in Bullfrog district,
255, 256; proposes new county in southern
Nevada, 259; illness in 1907, 259; law partnership in Goldfield, 260; mining promotions
at Bullfrog, 260; establishes private school
at Rhyolite, 262; made trustee of Rhyolite
school district, 262; anti-railroad letters to
Senator LaFollette and President Roosevelt,
262, 263; describes life at Rhyolite, 263;
dictates his memoirs, 264; leaves Bullfrog
area and Nevada, 264; gives papers to Nevada
Historical Society, 264; testifies before
House Mining Committee, 265; enters
Georgetown Hospital in March, 1909, 265;
dies after operation, April 23, 1909, 265;
obituaries, 265; burial, 265–266; his will,
266; his achievements, 268–275; Stewart's
party changes, 268; his financial backers,
269, 270, 297 n. 52; political tutor of Francis
G. Newlands, 271; attitudes toward his constituents, 271, 272; rank as U.S. Senator,
272; legal career summarized, 272–273; his
ethics, 273; importance to mining law, 273;
attitude toward education, the University of
Nevada, 274; his philosophy, 275
Stockton, Senator John P., 59
Submarines, Stewart favors in coastal defense,
244–255
Summerfield, Sardis, 183; U.S. District
Attorney, 197–198; blocks Webster suit
against Stewart, 207; encourages Stewart to
run for Senate in 1904, 246
Sumner, Senator Charles, 56, 66, 244
Sutro, Adolph, 55, 67; biographical sketch of,
287 n. 35
Sutro Tunnel, 55, 67, 287 n. 35
Swamp Land Act: passed by Nevada legis-
lature, 72; fight in Congress to have swamp
lands ceded to Nevada, 72–73; National Act
of 1850, 72, 73, 290 n. 29

Swift, John F.: supported by North for Nevada Territorial judiciary, 40; published novel about Washoe bar, spotlights Stewart, 41

Tahoe Forest Reserve, 223
Taxation, Mine: in 1863 Constitutional Convention, 24; "net proceeds" provision in ratification fight, 27, 28, 33; "net proceeds" provision adopted in Second Constitution, 1864, 36, 282 n. 50
Teller, Henry P.: forms Irrigation Clique in Senate, 112; joins remonetization battle, 173; bolts Republican National Convention, 178; potential Democratic candidate in 1896, 179; visits Nevada in 1898 election campaign, 201; attitude toward imperialism, 221
Territorial Enterprise, 28, 91; wages fight against "corrupt" judiciary, 36–40; publishes petition for resignation of territorial judges, 37; owners charged by North with slander, 43; attacks Stewart in 1898 election, 203; predicts Newlands victory, 204; in Gillespie incident, 214
Terry, David, 7; represents defendants in Ophir case, 15, 16; attorney for, then husband of, Althea Hill, 89–90; held in contempt of court, 89–90; killed by Dave Neagle, 9, 208, 294 n. 46
Test Oath, against polygamy, 103; in Nevada legislature, 104, 105; declared unconstitutional by Nevada Supreme Court, 108
Tevis, Lloyd, involved in California water and land contests, 88, 113
The Hague, 233, 235, 236, 237, 240, 241
Thornton, Harry I., law partnership with Stewart at Downieville, 9, 11
Tombstone, Arizona Territory, Stewart visits, 86–87
Tonopah, Nevada, 238, 254; Stewart establishes law office there, 257
Topliffe's Theater, Virginia City, constitutional ratification meeting there, 30
Trumbull, Lyman, 59, 63
Turner, George, 44, 52; territorial judge, 35; resigns, 39
Tuscarora, Nevada, Stewart hanged in effigy there, 227
Twain, Mark (Samuel Clemens), relations with Stewart, 65
Tweed, Charles H.: president of Southern Pacific Railroad, 228; outlines Stewart's relationship with the railroad, 229, 230

Union Pacific Railroad, 64, 66, 142, 229, 230
Union Party: in 1863 Constitution ratification battle, 27–30; ticket defeated in 1864 election, 32, 33, 42
Union Republican Party, 42, 61. *See* Union Party
United States Geological Survey, 84, 117, 252
University of Nevada, Reno, 138, 139, 274
Utah Enabling Act, 109
Utah Territory, 13, 46, 47, 96, 252; Stewart's attempt to annex part of, 99, 101, 105–109; Stewart opposes then favors Statehood, 107, 108; Utah becomes State, 109. *See* Boundary expansion

Van Clief, Peter, 11; law partnership with Stewart at Downieville, 9; law partnership with Stewart at San Francisco, 86
Venezuela question, Stewart ties to silver issue, 176
Virgin, Will, protégé of Stephen Gage, 208–209
Virginia and Truckee Railroad, 97, 141, 203, 222
Virginia City, 14, 25, 29, 40, 67, 71, 97, 110; description by J. Ross Browne, 12; and Carson and Colorado Railroad, 133; General Weaver visits, 155
Virginia City Miner's Union, opposed to military post in Reno, 136
Virginia Daily Union: opposes ratification of 1863 constitution, 30–33; defends North from Stewart attacks in 1864, 37, 38; refuses to support Stewart for U.S. Senate in 1864, 43
Virginia Evening Bulletin, favors ratification of 1863 constitution, 31

Wadsworth, Nevada, 131; squatter claims by whites on Pyramid Lake Indian Reservation, 132, 134, 147; issue revived in 1897, 187
Walker Lake Bulletin, urges abandonment of Walker River Indian Reservation, 130–132
Walker Lake Indians, 130, 133. *See also* Walker River Indian Reservation
Walker River Indian Reservation: pressures to force abandonment, 130–135; rumors of mineral deposits there, 130; Nevada legislative resolution to open for mining purposes, 131; Stewart revives abandonment idea, 186, 187; Stewart wants opened for mining, 232–233; opened to mining, 233, 315 n. 63

Wallace, Charles C. ("Black"), 151, 158; role in Stewart's 1886 campaign for U.S. Senate, 93–100; agent for Central Pacific in Nevada, 93; railroad patronage, 142; in 1890 Congressional race, 146, 150, 151, 152; role in formation of Nevada Silver Party, 153–154; in repeal of Sherman Silver Act, 161; interprets Nixon's challenge of Senator Jones in 1896 election, 183; interprets 1896 election for Stewart, 183, 184; Southern Pacific agent, 190; reports Newlands will not challenge Stewart in 1898, 196; activities in 1898 election campaign, 195–215; activities in Silver Party Central Committee in 1898, 210, 211; opposes DeLamar for House seat from Nevada, 224; opposes fusion of Democrats and Silverites in 1900, 225; loses control of Silver Party Central Committee, 225, 226; dies at Mariposa, California, 229; importance to Stewart summarized, 270

Warner, C. C., Nevada Indian Agent, and Carson and Colorado Railroad officials, 133–135

Washington Territory, 103, 105

Washoe City, Nevada Territory, 22

Washoe Indians, Stewart works in their behalf, 135

Weaver, General James B.: nominated for President by Populists on silver plank, 154, 156; visits Nevada, 154–155

Webster, William, 207

Weigand, Conrad, 71

Welles, Gideon, 59

Wells, Thomas H., 107

Wells, Virginia, 65

Wells Fargo, refuses to haul bullion from Panamint mines, 85

West Farmington Academy, Ohio, 3, 277 n. 5

Westinghouse, George, 219

Weston, George Melville, 119

Whig Party, 62, 69; California State Convention, 5; disintegration in California, 8

Whitman, C. B., 61

Whitney, George B.: challenges Nevada Test Oath, 107–108; wins suit before Nevada Supreme Court, 108

Wier, Jeanne E., 264

Williams, Abram P., 103

Williams, Evan, 114–115

Williams, Thomas, 43

Williams, Thomas H., 43; Democratic opponent of Stewart in 1868 election, 61

Williams, Warren W., 214; nominated for U.S. Senate, 211, 212

Williams Station on Carson River, 11

Wilson Tariff bill, Stewart links to remonetization of silver, 169–170

Windom, William, 121

Women's suffrage, 22, 108; Stewart's position, 135, 136, 301 n. 61

Woodburn, William, 155, 158; opposes Stewart in 1892 campaign, 149; nominated for U.S. Senate, 212

Worthington, Henry C., 52

Wren, Thomas, 96, 147, 151; in Richmond-Albion case, 87; possible Senatorial candidate in 1886, 95, 99, 100; calls for state meeting of silver clubs, 153; Populist nominee for Congress, 1898, 202; and Newlands in 1898 election, 311 n. 74

Wright, Sam: Superintendent of Carson City Mint, relation to Stewart and patronage, 143; in 1890 Congressional election, 144; in 1892 election, 149; debt owed him by Stewart, 219

Yale University, 4, 275

Yerington, Henry M.: lobbyist for Bank Crowd, supports Stewart financially, 97; indicates Stewart victory to his boss, D. O. Mills, 98, 99; and Walker River Indians, 133–135; and tariff for borax, 138, 186; in 1890 Congressional campaign, 145; opposes free-silver movement, 151; his position in 1896 election, 182, 184; supports Newlands against Stewart in 1898, 199, 203; accused of trickery by Stewart, 207; supports Newlands for U.S. Senate in 1902, 237, 239; at 1902 Republican Convention, 241

Young, Brigham: territorial governor of Utah, 13; opposed to mining, 47

Yuba River, Stewart brings water from through Grizzly Ditch, 5